PUSHKIN

PUSHKIN

The Man and His Age

ROBIN EDMONDS

St. Martin's Press
New York

FOR ENID

Library of Congress Cataloging-in-Publication Data
Edmonds, Robin.
Pushkin : the man and his age / Robin Edmonds.
p.   cm.
ISBN 0-312-13593-9
1. Pushkin, Aleksandr Sergeevich, 1799–1837—Biography.
2. Authors, Russian—19th century—Biography.   I. Title.
PG3350.E33   1995
891.71'3—dc20
[b]   95-34753   CIP

First published in Great Britain by Macmillan London

First U.S. Edition: November 1995
10   9   8   7   6   5   4   3   2   1

Contents

Acknowledgements

My first words of thanks go to the late Professor John Fennell. More than anyone else, it was he who persuaded me that this book ought to be written; and after reading successive drafts of my Introduction, shortly before his death he convinced me that I could do it.

The book is dedicated to my wife, who has not only read my typescript, chapter by chapter, but has patiently tolerated my long absorption with the paradoxes of Pushkin's elusive character. The others who have kindly read the typescript in full are Dr John Gooding, Ms Katie Owen, Professor Stephen White, who has read the proofs as well, and Mr Kyril Zinovieff (FitzLyon), who has also helped over some points of translation from Russian. Their benevolent but unsparing criticism has always been stimulating; the defects that remain are my own. At the time when preliminary drafts of the opening chapters of the book were in preparation, a valuable input was made by Mr Roland Philipps and by Dr Michael Shotton. And from start to finish Mr Peter Robinson (at the Curtis Brown Group) has been a tower of strength.

On specific points, I have been helped by the advice that I have received from Sir Richard Bayliss, Lord Beloff, Lord Blake, Mr Richard Bone, Professor Anthony Briggs, Professor Douglas Johnson, Dr Natalya Mikhailova, Mr Geoffrey Murrell and Mrs Kathy Murrell, Dr Sergei Nekrasov, Mr Peter Oldham, Dr Donald Prater, Professor Sir Dimitri Obolensky, Dr Aleksei Sadovsky, Miss Tatiana Wolff and Mrs April Zinovieff (FitzLyon).

Maurice Baring's translation of the poem 'The Prophet' has been quoted in full by permission of A. P. Watt Ltd, acting on behalf of the Trustees of the Maurice Baring Will Trust. The Historical Branch of the Foreign and Commonwealth Office kindly supplied me with a copy of Lord Durham's despatch from St. Petersburg regarding Pushkin's death. Since this document is normally lodged at the Public Record Office, Kew (and is therefore in Crown copyright), my quotation from it appears by permission of the Controller of Her Majesty's Stationery Office.

Once again, my proofs have been read, with an eagle eye, by Sir Edgar Williams. The quality of the Index is due to the skill of Mr Douglas Matthews.

The extent of my indebtedness to Russian Pushkinists will be evident from my Note on Sources (also from the Preface). Moreover, I have been overwhelmed by the generosity of Russian friends, who have insisted on giving me the better part of a hundred books about Pushkin. In this country, the Slavonic Languages section of the Taylor Institution Library at Oxford has been a regular port of call. The assistance given me there by the Librarian, Dr David Howells, and his staff has been unstinting: nothing has ever been too much for them. As well as to them, I also extend my thanks to the London Library, the Library of the Britain–Russia Centre and the Wiltshire County Library.

Mrs Elizabeth Holder took the photographs. The map was drawn by Mr Stephen Ramsay. The early chapters were at first word-processed by Miss Laura Tatham. Mrs Carol Ann Smith then took over, completing the word-processing of the majority of the book.

To everyone I am deeply grateful; and to Mr Kyril Zinovieff (FitzLyon) I must express my very particular gratitude.

List of Illustrations

SECTION ONE

SECTION TWO

List of Illustrations

The author and publishers are grateful to the following for kind permission to use illustrations:

Izobrazitel'noe iskusstvo, Moscow, for numbers 1, 7, 8, 12, 20, 21, 25, 32.

The Taylor Institution Library, Oxford, for numbers 4, 5, 9, 10, 11, 13, 14, 15, 16, 17, 18, 19, 22, 23, 26, 27, 28, 29, 30 and 31.

Tatiana Wolff for number 6.

Note on transliteration, nomenclature, calendar and currency

For the translation of cyrillic, the Glasgow University system, used for many years in *Soviet Studies* (now *Europe–Asia Studies*), is followed in this book, with modifications which are intended – irrespective of consistency – to make Russian names as readily comprehensible as possible for the reader unfamiliar with the Russian language and the Russian system of nomenclature.

Thus, no attempt has been made to alter time-honoured anglicized spellings of place names and the anglicized names of tsars, nor the traditionally gallicized spelling, Tchaikovsky; and Tolstoy has been preferred to Tolstoi, for similar reasons. Russian surnames of foreign origin, of which several occur in the text, present a particular problem. Their foreign spelling is used, although on first appearance the (transliterated) Russian form is also given in brackets: e.g. Benckendorff (Benkendorf). The same practice has been adopted for less well-known place names and personal names. Where personal names have widely accepted and sufficiently similar English equivalents, and if they occur often in the text, the English versions have been used: e.g. Alexander instead of Aleksandr and Natalya instead of Natal'ya.

The customary Russian combination of first name and patronymic is used only where, without it, the reader is liable to become confused – for example, where more than one member of the same family is under discussion. Pushkin is therefore referred to as a general rule simply as Pushkin, but as Alexander Sergeevich in instances such as Chapter 2, dealing with his ancestry and childhood.

Except where otherwise stated, all dates follow the Julian calendar, which remained in use in Russia until after the 1917 Revolution. In order to convert Julian dates to Gregorian, eleven days should be added in the eighteenth century and twelve in the nineteenth century. For distances, miles and kilometres have both been used; and occasionally *versts* (a *verst* was just over one kilometre).

Comparisons with the contemporary value of the rouble are meaningless; and only a rough idea can be given of its value in the early nineteenth century. The most helpful comparison may be between the value of the Russian currency at the beginning and at the end of the nineteenth century. In order to convert an 1800 Russian rouble into a 1900 Russian rouble, a multiplier of approximately four should be applied. However, the depreciated condition of the Russian currency even at the end of the nineteenth century was such that, although one hundred years ago the par value of the British sovereign was six roubles, twenty-eight kopeks, the real value of a British sovereign was as much as ten roubles (*Handbook for Travellers in Russia, Poland and Finland*, John Murray, London, 1893.) It may also be worth recalling that the cost of a first-class ticket from London to St. Petersburg via Berlin was then thirteen pounds sixteen shillings.

Preface

Prefaces that set out to expound to the reader of a book exactly why and in what circumstances it came to be written tend to be tedious. In this case the question, why write a life of Pushkin? has been put to me often enough to warrant a few words of explanation.

I was fortunate to be introduced to Pushkin's writing (in Russian) over half a century ago. It then seemed inconceivable that others might not share my youthful enthusiasm – I was nineteen – not only for his poetry, but for his prose as well. (Roughly half of what Pushkin wrote was in prose.) It took me some time to realize that the problem was not just a matter of taste or of translation, but also of ignorance; and that this (western) ignorance extended as much to Pushkin the man as to Pushkin the writer.

From this low base-line considerable progress has since been made in presenting Pushkin's writing to the West, especially in the last twenty-odd years, even though the problem of translating his poetry remains intractable. The gulf between, at one end of the spectrum, Vladimir Nabokov's 'ideal of literalism' and, at the other, Charles Johnston's 'inveterate rhymestering' – in each case, their own description of their style of translating Pushkin – is as wide as ever. Why is it that the (sometimes complex) verse of major Russian poets of our own century can be appreciated even through the lens of translators whose own poetic talent is not particularly distinguished, whereas the limpid simplicity of Pushkin's poetry has, over the years, attracted the attention of translators into English many of whose efforts have borne out the seventeenth-century couplet: 'Such is our Pride, our Folly or our Fate/That few, but such as cannot write, translate'? The musicality of the sound of Pushkin's poetry in Russian ears and his extraordinary gift for choosing precisely the right Russian word are among the several reasons that make up the answer to this important question, which lies outside the scope of this book. All translations from both Russian verse and Russian prose in the book are mine, with one exception (see Chapter 7). My translations of Pushkin's verse are in plain prose, following the wise example set by John Fennell and Dimitri Obolensky. The effect is flat, but prose at least offers a margin of safety.

The picture of Pushkin presented in the strictly biographical field in the west has not kept pace with the forward strides recently made by western literary analysis of his work. The passage of time – over half a century – has taken its inevitable toll on the first (and the most thorough) life of Pushkin written in English; and it is now nearly thirty years since Leonard Schapiro observed in one of his Yale lectures – with justice – that the influence on Russian thought of Pushkin's spirit and personality was probably greater than that of anyone else in his century. Not only was Pushkin an exceptional man, who lived his turbulent life in one of the most extraordinary periods of Russian history. His influence over all Russians has extended far beyond the nineteenth century. Given what seemed to be a major biographical gap on both sides of the Atlantic, it occurred to me that I might perhaps be able to fill it.

Early soundings in the late 1980s received a mixed bag of responses. A senior member of an American publishing house was willing to bet that many literate Americans would be hard put to distinguish Pushkin from Gogol, Gorky and Pasternak, while a British house was under the impression that the needs of English-speaking readers had been met since the Second World War by two works. Both of these were out of print – the actual, unhappy, state of biographical affairs in English is briefly described at the end of the Note on Sources. Such doubts were brushed aside by the encouragement offered by the *Pushkinovedy* (experts on Pushkin) whom I consulted in Russia. In Britain the enthusiasm shown for my project by the outstanding Russianist of my generation, John Fennell, was backed by the advice of my literary agents. I thus set out to write a life of Pushkin, studied within the parameters of his historical context.

Without Pushkin's historical setting, his life cannot readily be understood. I have therefore sought to examine and, I hope, illuminate the links between Pushkin the man and what Anna Akhmatova over a century later called 'the Age of Pushkin'. This book is in no sense a literary biography. Since the life of a great writer cannot possibly be understood separately from what he or she wrote, references to and quotations from Pushkin's works abound in the pages that follow. But their main purpose is not literary analysis, but to illustrate the development of Pushkin's character and of his ideas. In consequence some of his works are examined in greater detail than others. With two exceptions, however (in Chapter 11), no attempt is made to offer synopses of his major poems or prose works. For this deliberate decision no further explanation will be offered in the text of the book.

Readers feeling the need of synopses are strongly recommended to consult John Bayley's *Pushkin* (see Introduction).

Before embarking on this project, I reflected on the fundamental question: if a great artist stands or falls by his work, how much does it matter, in the final analysis, how he lived? In the case of Pushkin, it does matter, for reasons that will become apparent as the story of his life unfolds. But even if this were not so, the life of every artist forms what is, in a sense, the background to his work. In a painting of the High Renaissance, the background helps to illuminate the foreground. In the superb triptych painted by Giorgione in the cathedral of his native Castelfranco the eye is first caught by the three figures in the foreground and afterwards directed towards the beautiful landscape painted in the background. Together, they form a harmonious whole.

Finally, I have also been conscious of the currents of the modern debate on the nature and purpose of biography in general. A great distance now separates us from Lytton Strachey, 'here and there' lowering his 'little bucket' down into 'that great ocean of material', over which he rowed in order to 'bring up to the light of day some characteristic specimen, from those far depths, to be examined with a careful curiosity', as he put it in his preface to *Eminent Victorians*. Today, a book may well be commended on the ground that it is the 'definitive' biography of a particular man or woman – no source untapped, no gap unfilled, no judgement left open for further debate. My personal preference – as an historian – for the approach of the rifle to that of the scatter-gun notwithstanding, I hope that this book does not overlook any source of major importance. But it also takes account of the significant fact that, in Russia itself, no biography of Pushkin has so far claimed to be definitive.

Following some of the hagiographical distortions of past – particularly Soviet – years, a Russian reappraisal of Pushkin's life will doubtless be forthcoming before long. Meanwhile a foreign biographer of Russia's national poet and national hero does well to approach his subject not only as dispassionately as he can, but also with a certain degree of humility. If this account of Pushkin's life and of the age in which he lived encourages more people to read what he wrote, it will have achieved its purpose.

Ramsbury, Wiltshire, 1994

Pushkin's Family Tree

Petr Petrovich Pushkin,
born 1644, died 1692
married Fedos'ya Yur'evna Esipova

Alexander Petrovich,
born in the 1690s, died 1726–7,
married Evdokiya Ivanovna Golovina
(died 1725)

Fedor Petrovich,
died 1727–8,
married Kseniya Ivanovna Koreneva

Lev Alexandrovich,
born 1723, died 1790,
married
1. Maria Matveevna Voeikova
2. Olga Vasil'evna Chicherina
born 1737, died 1802

Aleksei Fedorovich,
born 1717, died 1777,
married Sarra Yur'evna Rzhevskaya

Maria Alekseevna,
born 1745, died 1818,
married Osip Abramovich Gannibal,*
born 1744, died 1806

Sergei L'vovich,
born 1767, died 1840,
married Nadezhda Osipovna Gannibal,
born 1775, died 1836

Nadezhda Osipovna Gannibal,
born 1775, died 1836,
married Sergei L'vovich Pushkin,
born 1767, died 1840

Alexander Sergeevich Pushkin†
born 1799, died 1837

* Osip Abramovich Gannibal was the third son of Abram (Petr) Petrovich Gannibal, born in the last decade of the seventeenth century in Africa and adopted early in the eighteenth by Peter the Great, whose godson he was. For an account of his extraordinary career, see Chapter 2.

† Alexander was the second of three surviving children. His elder sister, Olga, was born in 1797 and died in 1868; his younger brother, Sergei, was born in 1805 and died in 1852.

Introduction

'I must put my house in order,' said Pushkin when he was dying.

Within two days his house became a shrine for his Motherland, and the world has not seen a fuller, more resplendent victory. The whole epoch (not without a creaky start, of course) began bit by bit to be called Pushkin's. All the beauties, the ladies-in-waiting, the *salon* hostesses, the Dames of the Order of St. Catherine, the members of the imperial court, the ministers, the senior generals and those who were not senior, gradually began to be referred to as 'contemporaries of Pushkin', and thereafter they simply went to their rest in the card indexes and the indexes of names (with inaccurate dates of birth and death) of editions of Pushkin's works.

He conquered both time and space. They say now: the Age of Pushkin, Pushkin's St. Petersburg . . .

— Anna Akhmatova, 26 May 1961

The final decade of the twentieth century has so far disproved most forecasts about the outcome of the tidal wave of change that swept across Russia and the other former Soviet Republics during the 1980s. But one thing can still be predicted with some confidence. As the year 1999 draws near, the millions for whom Russian is their first language will look forward to it, not just as the approach of the new millennium but the two hundredth anniversary of the birth of the man whose house in St. Petersburg has remained a 'shrine for his Motherland'.[1]

Alexander Pushkin was no exception to the rule that poets have long occupied a special position in the Russian political spectrum (not least during the Soviet period of Russian history). In the 1830s most members of the imperial court and the bureaucracy had come to regard Pushkin as – at best – a talented man who was an awkward customer or – at worst – a rogue.[2] The last thing they wanted on the Moika Canal in St. Petersburg (the house, later renumbered 7, in which Pushkin rented the first floor towards the end of his life) to become was a national monument. Once he had died in January 1837, forty-eight hours after being wounded in a duel (fought on snow-covered ground, like Onegin's in Pushkin's poem), they did all they could to play down the whole melancholy affair. Superficially, they at first succeeded. For example, in his *Lettres de Russie*, written after spending two months in Russia two years later, the Marquis de Custine exempted the tsar's behaviour towards Pushkin (and his younger contemporary, Lermontov) from the welter of criticism of Russia for which his book is celebrated.[3] In reality, as usually happens in Russian history, truth could not indefinitely be ignored: in this case the fact that in 1837 Russia lost her greatest poet.

It is as such that all Russians today revere Pushkin. Nevertheless, what has varied from one Russian generation to another has been the assessment of Pushkin's paradoxical character in general and, in particular, of the tortuous chain of bizarre events that led up to his death at the age of thirty-seven. Often triggered by the unearthing of fresh documentary evidence, swelling the massive pile of material already accumulated, these swings of opinion have sometimes been of the order of one hundred and eighty degrees: veering, for example, from Pushkin seen as the victim of conspiracy, to Pushkin over-whelmed by fate, to Pushkin determined to meet death, weapon in hand. And the final word has not yet been spoken.

Quite apart from this Russian controversy, the foreign biographer of Pushkin must be struck from the outset by the stark contrast between his literary reputation (for the most part) abroad and his lonely eminence as a poet in his own country. Pushkin's language is deeply embedded in the consciousness of every Russian speaker from childhood onwards.

In *Exegi Monumentum*, a poem written during the year before he died, Pushkin, then a man under attack, declared that he had '. . . erected a monument to myself, not made by hands; the path to it, trodden by the people, will not be overgrown; it has raised its defiant head higher than Alexander's column'. And he foresaw that he would be 'famous as long as even one poet remains alive in the sublunary world. The rumour of my fame will pass through all great Russia and every race living in her will speak my name.'[4] This much – discussed poem was not published until after Pushkin's death. Before the nineteenth century was over, the poet and polymath, Vladimir Solev'ev, went so far as to say that he would give the whole of the works of Tolstoy for an unpublished poem of Pushkin; Tolstoy himself, sometimes a curmudgeon in his judgement of other writers (he even tried to rubbish Shakespeare), said of *The Tales of Belkin* that 'not only Pushkin but nothing else at all had ever roused my admiration so much';[5] and Turgenev would gladly have burned all his own work in order to have written just four lines of Pushkin's *Conversation between the Bookseller and the Poet*.[6]

Making every allowance for Russian hyperbole, Pushkin's own prophecy was fulfilled – all this at a time when Flaubert was complaining to Turgenev that '*il est plat, votre poète*'. Pushkin himself might have understood Flaubert's comment, since his own view was that 'nothing is more difficult than to translate Russian verse into French, for – given the conciseness of our language – one can never be brief enough'.[7] He would, however, have reacted differently to a remark included by Matthew Arnold in a verbose essay, ironically published in 1887, the year of the fiftieth anniversary of Pushkin's death. Although the subject of the essay was Tolstoy (mainly *Anna Karenina*), Arnold inserted in parenthesis – without a word of explanation – this astounding sentence: 'The crown of literature is poetry, and the Russians have not yet had a great poet.'[8]

In our own century, after a first (unfortunately somewhat misleading) attempt by Maurice Baring to explain the greatness of Pushkin's poetry,[9] the English-speaking world had to wait until 1937, the centenary of Pushkin's death, for a detailed and scholarly study of his life.[10] It was only in 1971 that Pushkin's position in the mainstream of European literature was anchored for English-speaking readers by John Bayley's *Pushkin: A Comparative Commentary*. True, it is a rarity for any translation – not just a translation from Russian – to 'have leaped across the boundaries of time and have rendered in a new language the movement and truth of the original in the same way in which the translated author created both'.[11] Shakespeare, who has been fortunate in most of his translators, had to wait over three hundred years for a major Russian poet (Pasternak) to translate his works. Even today Pushkin's *Evgenii Onegin* is still familiar to many only through the distorting lens of Tchaikovsky's opera, rather as if the text of one of Jane Austen's novels had been revamped by a librettist and set to music by Elgar. Pushkin may have to wait for his translator into English verse as long as Shakespeare did for his translator into Russian.

The main focus of this book is on Pushkin as a man: a study of his turbulent but creative life, lived at a critical period of Russian history, the evolution of his character, the development of his ideas and his relationship to other people and to other writers, both living and dead. As opposed to a '*biographie romancée*',[12] its principal aim is to add an extra dimension to our knowledge of Pushkin's own expression of himself. With the aid of this additional dimension, not only can the appreciation of his work (by which Pushkin – like all great artists – ultimately stands or falls) be deepened and enhanced, but also the understanding of the impact that he exerted on his times. This was of such power that when Akhmatova (in the ironical passage forming the epigraph to this chapter) looked back at that epoch, long after Nicholas I and his collaborators had become yesterday's men, she observed that it had gradually come to be called the 'Age of Pushkin': a posthumous victory which has lost none of its force for Russians, regardless of the nature of the regime under which they have been governed throughout our own century.

This biography may, moreover, throw some light on the extraordinary contrast just described between Pushkin's reputation at home and abroad. In the process it will become evident that Pushkin's literary reputation does not rest solely on the musical beauty of his limpid verse, but also on a few superb short stories, pithy letters, penetrating literary criticism and – last but by no means least – the unfinished notes left behind at his death, which, had he lived longer, might have been enough to confirm his reputation as an historian.

Any objective account of Pushkin's life and analysis of his character must confront a second, equally remarkable, contrast. In this case, however, both poles of the antithesis are represented most forcefully by Russians, one of them Pushkin himself. Writing to an intelligent woman, Pushkin said: 'Would you like me to speak really frankly to you? Perhaps I am elegant and proper in my writings, but I am an absolute vulgarian at heart and my inclinations are all coarse.'[13]

The opposite view of Pushkin was taken by Nabokov over a century later:

A singular case of a man's outer life fusing so organically with his inner one, that the story of his actual existence seems a masterpiece of his own pen, now lyrical, now sarcastic, now tragic, while his writings seem to be in their turn the footnotes to his life ... And as if this were still not enough, life played up to him, involving him in struggles which would disclose in the most vivid way the essential features of his nature and placing at regular intervals along the road of his life sheer cliffs for him to inscribe his name with his pen or his dagger.[14]

Even though in his mature work Pushkin was at pains to distance himself from his heroes and his heroines, it is scarcely surprising that some of the forty thousand lines of poetry and the roughly equal amount of prose that Pushkin wrote should have autobiographical overtones; and there is even some foreshadowing of his death. Pushkin's insight into his own character was far from negligible even as a young man. In contrast to Nabokov, those of his contemporaries who knew Pushkin best and admired him most were aware of the paradoxes inherent in his personality, as was the first of his biographers, Pavel Annenkov, whose work earned even Nabokov's praise.[15] There is no single key to an understanding of Pushkin's elusive personality. There are, however, three threads which may guide the student of Pushkin towards this goal and without which he or she is unlikely to reach it – Pushkin's love of work, his creativity; the historical period in which he was born and lived; and his sexuality.

Of these three threads, the first is by far the most important. It has never been better described than in the words of one of his closest friends:

Deep within him there lay concealed a moral strength, protective and saving ... This strength was love of work, the necessity of work, the insuperable necessity to express himself creatively, to force out from himself sensations, images, feelings ... Work was for him the shrine, the font in which sores were healed, courage and freshness overcame the feebleness of exhaustion, his weakened powers were restored. When he felt the onset of inspiration, when he got down to work, he was calmed, he became courageous, he was reborn.[16]

This inner strength, masked by superficial characteristics which suggested the opposite to other, less perceptive, contemporaries of Pushkin, served him well almost up to the end of his life. Each of the other two threads led him towards the two major caesuras in his life –

the first in 1826, when Pushkin first met the new tsar, Nicholas I; the second in 1831, when he married Natalya Goncharova. And both of these two threads – Pushkin's historical context and his sexuality – were combined in the drama that led to his death.

The biographer cannot ignore the number of women whom Pushkin had loved (by his own reckoning, one hundred and thirteen including his fiancée) up to the time of his engagement to be married.[17] Like Lord Melbourne, Pushkin liked to 'talk broad' in male company and in correspondence with men – a habit which the prudery of his Soviet editors attempted to mask. No useful purpose, however, is served by trying to play Leporello to Pushkin's Don Giovanni.[18] For example, the identity of the girl to whose feet Pushkin devoted so many lines of *Evgenii Onegin* (the so-called pedal digression) is intriguing, but not essential to a study of Pushkin's life.[19] By contrast, the question why he chose (in his own words) a 'shy-cold' wife must be addressed. For Pushkin's decision to marry, at the age of thirty-one, an uncultivated, penniless, eighteen-year-old beauty, nobody but Pushkin was responsible.

On the other hand, the historical context by which he was constrained in one way or another throughout his life is quite another matter.

Pushkin was born in one of the last months of the eighteenth century, just before a turning point in Russian history. The first quarter of the nineteenth century began in Russia with the assassination of the tsar Paul; it rose to a climax with Napoleon's retreat from Moscow in 1812, followed by his defeat and by the Russian army's occupation of Paris; and it ended dramatically with the suppression of the Decembrist Revolt in 1825. The years during which Pushkin grew up were those in which Russia emerged for the first time as the strongest military power on the European continent, under tsar Alexander I, who at first toyed with the idea of giving Russia 'the blessing of a free constitution'[20] and then dreamed of himself as the saviour of a Europe, which – the domination of Napoleon having been destroyed – would be freed from oppression and revolution in equal measure.

For the first six years after the final defeat of Napoleon, the work of directing the concert of Europe established at the Congress of Vienna was – for practical purposes – largely in the hands of three men: Prince Metternich, Viscount Castlereagh and Count Capodistria.

The strikingly different foreign ministers of Austria, England and Russia (respectively a Roman Catholic, an Ulster Protestant and an Orthodox Greek) resembled each other in only one respect: each of them was an aristocrat. For this was the golden afternoon of the ascendancy of the European aristocracy. Pushkin, a direct descendant of an ancient family, was keenly aware of his family's position in Russian history. When a fellow poet, Kondratii Ryleev (a revolutionary soon to die on the gallows) reproached Pushkin, then aged twenty-six, for his pride in his centuries-old nobility, urging him, 'For God's sake, be Pushkin!' the rough draft of Pushkin's reply included this significant parenthesis '(N.B., my nobility is more ancient)' – that is to say, more than six hundred years old.[21] And shortly afterwards he wrote to his closest school-friend: 'Six Pushkins signed the Election Charter! And two made an "X", because they did not know how to write! And I, their literate descendant, who am I, where am I?'[22] (The Act of Election was that of the first Romanov tsar in 1613. By implication, the Romanovs were, compared with the Pushkins, newcomers.) For the greater part of his adult life Pushkin was nominally a member of the Russian foreign ministry, a department of state then considered acceptable – like the army – for a man of his social standing. At the same time he consciously strove to earn his living by his pen and thus became Russia's first strictly professional poet. Yet he tried to combine this with living the life of a Russian nobleman, including the traditional pursuits of wine, women and – until the very end – cards.

A handful of early poems and the surviving fragments of the mysterious Chapter 10 of *Evgenii Onegin* (prudently burned in 1830) notwithstanding, Pushkin was not a political radical. Had his repeated requests for permission to travel abroad been granted, things might have been different. Confined within the boundaries of his own country, he did not apply to the problems of his own day – as opposed to the earlier history of Russia – his formidable intellectual powers with the same degree of rigour as those of his contemporaries who thought deeply about the need for far-reaching constitutional and social reform of the Russian Empire. Despite attempts by Soviet critics to paint him in political colours closer to their own, he was accurately described by a contemporary as 'a liberal conservative'.[23] (If he had been an Englishman, might he perhaps have been a Whig?) True, even that was not a label to be worn lightly in Russia once the erratic political aspirations of Alexander I, originally the pupil and admirer of the Swiss republican, Frédéric César de Laharpe, had settled into their final cast of melancholy mysticism. And the label became even more dangerous for Pushkin after December 1825, when some three thousand troops in St. Petersburg revolted, refusing to take the oath of allegiance to the new tsar, Nicholas I. Led by men who were Pushkin's friends, five of whom were hanged, this was the first real attempt at revolution in Russia. It has gone down to history as the Decembrist Revolt.

Pushkin was barely twenty-one when he first blotted his political copy-book in the eyes of Alexander I, who was, however, persuaded by Pushkin's friends at court not to send him to Siberia, but instead to let him be appointed to a post in southern Russia. Before Pushkin left St. Petersburg, Pushkin's official superior, John Capodistria, wrote these words: 'Monsieur Pushkin . . . removed for some time from St. Petersburg . . . may make . . . an excellent servant of the government or, at least, a writer of the first rank.'[24] After six years' 'removal', the last two spent at his family's country home in formal exile and under police surveillance, Pushkin was summoned by Nicholas I to Moscow where – at four o'clock on 8 September 1826 – their tête-à-tête encounter began in the Kremlin, at the end of which Pushkin walked out, as he believed, a free man. Had the events during the ten months preceding this meeting taken a different course for Pushkin, he might have been walking in chains to Siberia, one of over a hundred Decembrist exiles. As it was, the meeting in the tsar's study in the Chudov Palace marked a turning-point in Pushkin's life, both for better and for worse. For better, because during those years he was able to write (though not always to publish) a series of masterpieces. For worse, because the uneasy relationship that developed over the next ten years between the poet and the sovereign, and between Pushkin and the bureaucrats who served the tsar, would become a major factor in the imbroglio in St. Petersburg that ended with his death.

By the time that Pushkin died Capodistria was himself already dead, assassinated in Greece, whose first president he had become in 1827. His assessment of the young Pushkin has long been forgotten. What is famous is the white-hot verdict on Pushkin's death pronounced in a poem circulated in manuscript in St. Petersburg, which earned its writer his exile to the Caucasus (Mikhail

Lermontov's *The Death of a Poet* was written in January 1837, but not published in his lifetime). The final lines of Lermontov's fierce indictment accused the imperial court of complicity, ending with the warning that they would not 'wash away the honourable blood of the poet with all your black blood'.[25] A century and a half afterwards Pushkin's death has been described as 'perhaps . . . the greatest single tragedy in the history of literature'.[26]

All three of these statements about Pushkin – the first Greek, the second Russian and the third British – leave some room for debate. What would Pushkin's life have been like if he had lived away from St. Petersburg for most of his adult life and not just 'for a time', as Capodistria assumed? Could the tsar and his chief of police have done more than they did to prevent the duel from taking place? And, had Pushkin lived longer, how much more would his protean genius have added to his 'monument, not made by hands'? Nevertheless, these three statements together illustrate the main elements of the contradiction which Pushkin could not resolve. On the one hand stood his passionate dedication to achieving the supreme mastery of Russian words and, on the other, his love of what he himself called the 'stern, harmonious' city of St. Petersburg.[27] From the early eighteenth century onwards, the capital of the Russian emperors provided the setting for the lineal descendant of the 'Third Rome', with its tinsel masquerade and intrigues worthy of the Second Rome (Byzantium).[28] It was in this setting that, for the greater part of his adult life, Pushkin attempted to fulfil what he defined in one of his most famous lyric poems as the dual purpose of living.[29]

It was Pushkin's misfortune to live through the turning point of Russian history early in the nineteenth century, when – to adapt Lewis Namier's epigram about Germany in 1848[30] – Russian history failed to turn. On the contrary, it lapsed into a thirty-year period of stagnation, ending in the disaster of the Crimean War, which exposed to the world the full extent of the internal weaknesses of the Russian colossus and in the process destroyed the Russian claim to continental military hegemony for nearly a hundred years. But what did turn once and for all in Russia was the whole course of Russian literature – a flowering of astounding brilliance, variety and depth. And for this change of course, what Alexander Herzen called 'the vast phenomenon of Pushkin'[31] became, and has remained for his successors, the guiding star.

CHAPTER ONE

Imperial Zenith: The Historical Context

Great empires and little minds go ill together.

—Edmund Burke, 1775

During Pushkin's short lifetime, 1799–1837, the Russian Empire was ruled by three men: first – briefly – by Paul I, followed in turn by two of his sons, Alexander I and Nicholas I. (Nicholas's reign continued for almost another twenty years after Pushkin's death in 1837.) Pushkin 'saw three tsars': according to family tradition, which he himself clearly believed, in 1800, when barely one year old, he met Paul during a walk with his nanny.[1] A stickler for etiquette – an obsession inherited by Nicholas I – Paul is said to have scolded Pushkin's nanny and ordered her to take the baby's cap off. This eccentric encounter was a poor augury for Pushkin's future at the imperial court; and indeed his relationship with each of Paul's successors proved to be far from happy. Even though, in Akhmatova's words, Pushkin posthumously 'conquered both time and space', while he was alive things looked very different, not least to Pushkin himself.

It has been observed about one of Pushkin's French contemporaries, Hector Berlioz (with whom he had more than one characteristic in common), that he 'had the imprudence to be born into a not very musical nation in one of its least truly musical periods'.[2] However wild the swings of the Russian political pendulum in the twentieth century, resistance to change lies close to the sceptical core of the Russian character.[3] A child of the *fin de siècle*, Pushkin was fated to spend his adult years under one of the most obscurantist regimes in the history of his conservative country. The thirty-seven years spanned by Pushkin's life at first blossomed into a sudden spring of hope, but by the end they were sinking into a grim winter of disillusion. Yet these years also saw the Russian Empire at the zenith of its power in Europe, following the Russian defeat of Napoleon. It is impossible to understand this paradox without first glancing backwards at the preceding period of Russian history, which the early Tolstoy could describe as 'the great century'.[4]

It was only in the course of the eighteenth century that Russia became a major actor on the European stage. 'For a long time Russia remained foreign to Europe,' wrote Pushkin. She 'entered Europe like a ship being launched, with the beating of drums and the thunder of guns'.[5] For a large part of the eighteenth century the country was at war. Six wars were fought in the thirty-four years – 1762–96 – of the dazzling reign of Catherine II (referred to as such by Russian historians, never as Catherine the Great). Her reign was 'dazzling' partly because her territorial conquests extended the European frontiers of the Russian Empire almost to those that bounded it right up to the Revolution of 1917. They more than doubled the population of the empire, which at the time of Pushkin's birth numbered about forty million; and they quadrupled the revenues of the Russian state.

Yet Catherine's reign was dazzling also in the sense that her spectacular successes diverted men's eyes from the scale and the range of the weaknesses of the Russian state and of Russian society. The state remained an autocracy, whose absolutism was tempered only by corruption and incompetence. Society was ironically described by a Russian liberal in 1802 as consisting of two classes – 'the slaves of the sovereign and the slaves of the landowners. The first are free only in relation to the second. There are no truly free people in Russia, apart from beggars and philosophers' – and as Pushkin wrote, at least in outward appearance 'nothing so resembled a Russian village of 1662 as a Russian village of 1833'.[6] At the heart of Russia's social weaknesses lay the problem of serfdom. Under Catherine almost the entire peasant population was in effect enserfed; and yet they constituted more than half the tax-paying population of the Russian Empire. In the course of forty years Catherine II and Paul I in turn distributed as gifts to favourites vast tracts of government land that were accompanied by nearly one and a half million peasants, who thus became serfs.[7] (Paul's accession to the throne alone cost a million acres and one hundred thousand serfs given away in this manner.) By contrast, a decree of Catherine's short-lived husband, Peter III, exempted the nobility from the obligation of state service to which they had always been subject. Although in practice virtually all nobles continued to perform some kind of service for another hundred years, with honourable exceptions (such as the great Russian general, Alexander Suvorov) their governmental duties were often largely nominal.

The social consequences of the steadily widening gap between the peasantry at one end of the Russian spectrum and, at the other, what ought to have been the ruling class (the intervening commercial class was still minute), were such that at the end of the eighteenth century the nobility 'was unable to become the active leader of society, so that the greatest benefit that it could confer on society could only consist of determination not to do it any harm'. The verdict was pronounced just over one hundred years later, not by a Marxist theoretician, but by the Professor of History at Moscow University.[8] True, there were exceptions. Princess Ekaterina Dashkova, for example, may have been eccentric – she succeeded in domesticating rats – but she did serve as the first president of the Russian Academy. Not a single doctor of medicine qualified from Moscow University during Catherine's long reign, however.

In the eighteenth century some nobles totally dispossessed their serfs and converted their estates virtually into slave-owning plantations. The crimes then committed against the Russian peasantry pale into insignificance by comparison with the horrors of Soviet agricultural policy in the 1930s, however. Moreover, even in the eighteenth century there were good Russian landowners who lived on their estates (as opposed to paying them the odd visit or neglecting them altogether). Be that as it may, what was significant for the economic development of Russia as a whole was the absence of incentive for agrarian innovation. There was no Russian Coke of Norfolk, nor a 'Turnip' Townshend. It requires an effort of imagination to realize the fact that Russian country houses of this period, teeming with domestic serfs but mostly built of wood, belonged to the same century as the homes of the gentry of Georgian England, quite apart from the country palaces of the English aristocracy such as Blenheim or Holkham. And the growth and scale of Russian industrial development was correspondingly stunted.

The contradictions of Russian society were masked by a resplendent veneer of French culture. Not only did Catherine herself correspond with Voltaire from 1763 until his death fifteen years later.

The French language and the literature of the French Enlightenment captured the minds of the educated class of the Russian Empire. To speak French was obligatory; indeed many of them despised their own language; and it was said of Catherine's eldest grandson, Alexander I, that until the end of his life (1825) he was unable to conduct a reliable conversation in Russian on any complicated matter. Many members of this class (Pushkin's father is an example) amassed libraries of French books. These were not for show – they read them. But what very few of them attempted to do for themselves in the eighteenth century was to apply the ideas of the Enlightenment to the political, economic and social reality by which they were surrounded. One of those who did, a landowner of integrity and the owner of a fine library, committed suicide six years before Pushkin's birth, explaining in his will that disgust at Russian life was 'the motive compelling me to decide my fate of my own volition'.[9]

Pushkin's earliest historical writing – notes on the eighteenth century unpublished in his lifetime – proves that he was under no illusions about the remarkable Lutheran girl, small in stature but with a large sexual appetite, who had arrived in St. Petersburg from a minor German principality as a penniless young bride, learnt Russian, was received into the Orthodox Church, changed her name and – after reaching the throne by a palace coup – went on to rule as an eastern despot, though in western European fancy dress. 'Her splendour blinded,' he wrote, 'her affability was attractive, her munificence bound people to her. The very voluptuousness of this cunning woman confirmed her sway.'[10] Catherine's vast imperial legacy was inherited – at one remove – by Alexander I: 'at one remove', because on 11 March 1801, after a reign of less than five years, Paul I was assassinated, with Alexander's connivance (or – as Alexander Herzen later put it – he hoped that the conspirators would kill his father 'but not to death').[11] The regicides who strangled Paul were all courtiers. In Pushkin's words, describing 'Caligula's last hour', the tsar 'sees clearly before his eyes, he sees – in their ribbons and stars, drunk with wine and hatred' the 'secret murderers' approaching 'with boldness on their faces and fear in their hearts'.[12]

Alexander's accession to the throne, when Pushkin was almost two years old, was greeted with tears of joy in St. Petersburg. People embraced each other in the streets of the capital, whether they were friends or strangers, as though it were Easter Sunday. Seldom has any

Russian reign begun with such widespread public rejoicing and ended on such a dying fall. It has been an historical convention to divide Alexander's reign into two halves. During the first, surrounded by a small informal committee of liberal advisers, the tsar drew up an ambitious programme of wide-ranging reform. This achieved little, partly because the reforms were never put into practice and partly because of the distraction of the Napoleonic Wars. During the second half of Alexander's reign, beginning roughly with his return from the Congress of Vienna, when he 'suddenly felt himself a stranger in his own country',[13] he not only ran out of administrative steam, but made some dangerously retrograde appointments. Of these the outstanding example in Alexander's declining years was Count Aleksei Arakcheev.

Arakcheev, who acted – in effect, though not in name – as prime minister, gave his name to the period as the *Arakcheevshchina* (an attempt, it was said at the time, to make a barracks out of Russia and to station a sergeant at its gates as well). In the end his mistress was murdered by her own serfs: a blow from which, in spite of Alexander's sympathy, he never recovered.[14] In one of his many epigrams, Pushkin described Arakcheev as 'friend and brother' to Alexander, 'full of malice, full of vengeance, without wit, without feelings, without honour'.[15] It was during this period that Alexander gave to M. L. Magnitsky, a renegade liberal turned ultra-reactionary, full powers to reform the recently instituted University of Kazan (Kazan') where Tolstoy studied a quarter of a century later, and Lenin later still. This reform was to be carried out according to the principles of the Holy Alliance. The ludicrous results included teaching philosophy on the basis of the Epistles of St. Paul and political science on that of the Old Testament. The new broom was not confined to Kazan; it spread to the University of St. Petersburg, where D. P. Runich got rid of half of its thirty-four professors between 1821 and 1825. And for four years, from 1824 to 1828, both the Ministry of Education and the Censorship Department were headed by an admiral, Alexander Shishkov, whose conservative political views were matched by his strongly held belief that Church Slavonic was the root and foundation of modern Russian (historically accurate, but not a view likely to encourage a linguistic innovator of Pushkin's calibre).

Alexander's suspicious and secretive nature both fascinated and baffled his contemporaries. For Napoleon, he was a shifty Byzantine, 'the Talma of the North', while for Castlereagh it was 'unfortunately his habit to be his own minister and to select as the instrument for his immediate purpose the person who may happen to fall in most with his views'.[16] Indeed he went further than this, sometimes appointing two men with opposing views to perform one and the same function, thus keeping his own options open to the last possible moment. In this respect there is a strange parallel between Alexander I and Franklin Roosevelt, who did much the same thing just over a century later. The most conspicuous example was Alexander's appointment of two utterly different men as joint foreign secretaries: Count Karl Nesselrode (Nessel'rode) and Count John Capodistria (Kapodistria). The family of the senior of these two ministers, Nesselrode, was of German origin. A run of the mill bureaucrat, who owed his forty years of office to his readiness to agree first with Alexander I and then with Nicholas I, his chief claim to fame is the fact that he is the only Russian foreign minister ever to have been a member of the Church of England. At the time of his birth, in Lisbon in 1780, his father was serving there as Russian ambassador. In deference to his (Protestant) mother's wishes, Karl was christened in the British Embassy chapel.

On the other hand, Capodistria, a Corfiote Greek,[17] was a man of exceptional ability and intelligence. Both his influence on Alexander, while it lasted, and his later career were of historical significance. Moreover, although there is little archival evidence to this effect, it was generally assumed by Pushkin's contemporaries that Capodistria used his influence with Alexander to secure Pushkin's appointment to southern Russia in 1820, as the alternative to Siberian exile. Unfortunately, Capodistria had left St. Petersburg by the time Pushkin was dismissed from the imperial service four years later; and when he was readmitted to the foreign ministry at the end of 1831, Capodistria had just been assassinated.

The character of Alexander has remained an enigma for historians. Nevertheless, there can be little debate about one of his characteristics: he was an extraordinarily impressionable man. The political range – varying from liberal to reactionary – of those who in turn formed the closest circle of this ideological jackdaw is in itself evidence of this. The man who led his army from Russia across Germany to France was greeted by the Parisians as a liberator when he and the King of Prussia entered the city in March 1814. Yet at home he was hesitant, even timorous. Pushkin himself later dismissed Alexander as a harlequin 'in his face and in his life'; and towards the end of the century something of the conflict which underlay the outward appearances of Alexander's character was expressed by a Russian historian in these words:

> It is possible to pretend, not only in front of other people but also to oneself ... when he [Alexander I] encountered ideas that were new to him in conversation with an intelligent interlocutor, he tried to show him, and still more to convince himself, that these had long been his own, sincerely held, ideas, as they were of every decent man ... He tried to illuminate his own mind, which was dark for himself, by means of a light that was strange to him. Under the impact of circumstances he did not grow; he only revealed himself; he did not change, but only became more and more himself.[18]

Although Alexander's conduct of foreign policy benefited from the moderating advice of Capodistria until he resigned the foreign secretaryship in 1822, his zeal for domestic reform had begun to peter out ten years earlier, when he suddenly dismissed his brilliant liberal adviser, Mikhail Speransky, who had drafted his major plan of internal reform. Thus by the time Pushkin left school and entered government service in 1817, the second, obscurantist phase of Alexander's reign had already begun; and it intensified right up to Alexander's death in 1825. When Pushkin dined with Speransky many years later, he remarked to him: 'You and Arakcheev stand at the opposite doors of that reign, like the geniuses of Evil and Good.'[19]

Ethnically speaking, both Alexander I and Nicholas I were more German than Russian. Hence the acerbic comparison between the two tsars drawn half a century after Nicholas's death: whereas 'Alexander related to Russia like a timorous and cunning diplomat, foreign to the country, Nicholas I – also like a foreigner – and also a frightened man – was because of his very fear a more decisive detective.'[20] The way in which these two men, each in turn, sought to steer their barnacled and unwieldy ship of state was very different, however. At first Alexander stood on the bridge, issuing orders which he believed would transform the ship into a modern vessel, but when his orders brought about no visible difference in the ship's performance, he simply gave up, withdrawing to his cabin. Nicholas, on the other hand, a glutton for hard work and with a passion for detail, tried to achieve the same result working from the engine room, with the assistance of a crew of mechanics. His painstaking attempt to work through an enlarged bureaucracy was as much a failure as his elder brother's earlier espousal of grandiose ideas.

It is not easy to be fair to Nicholas. Queen Victoria tried. In a letter to her uncle, the King of the Belgians, written during a state visit paid by Nicholas to London, she wrote on 11 June 1844:

> He is stern and severe – with fixed principles of *duty* which *nothing on earth* will make him change; very *clever I do not* think him, and his mind is an uncivilized one; his education has been neglected; politics and military concerns are the only things he takes great interest in; the arts and all softer occupations he is insensible to, but he is sincere, I am certain, *sincere* even in his most despotic acts, from a sense that that is the *only* way to govern; he is not, I am sure, aware of the dreadful cases of individual misery which he so often causes, for I can see by various instances that he is kept in utter ignorance of *many* things, which his people carry out in most corrupt ways, while he thinks that he is extremely just ... And I am sure *much* never reaches his ears, and (as you observed) how can it?[21]

Queen Victoria was wrong in supposing that Nicholas was kept in ignorance by his own bureaucrats. On the contrary, one of his first acts as tsar was to set up the notorious Third Department within his personal chancery, under one of his closest advisers, General Alexander Benckendorff (Benkendorf). Benckendorff was responsible for all matters of state security; and in addition he was chief of police. During the last decade of Pushkin's life he acted increasingly as intermediary between Nicholas I and Pushkin. It is hard to reconcile some of the letters in their correspondence with the description of him offered by a British historian: 'not only an amiable companion, but a genuinely kind man, and his main characteristic was extreme vagueness. He sometimes could not even remember his own name.'[22] It must also be remembered that Benckendorff was a bureaucrat, loyal to an autocratic ruler, who – so far as Pushkin was concerned, as in everything else – called the shots.

At home, Nicholas seems to have been a straightforward and cheerful man, a good host, witty, even a lover of music, who had quite a good baritone voice.[23] As tsar, he was a notorious martinet, with an especial affection for uniforms and parades. Although he held high military rank from the age of eighteen onwards, he never came under fire in battle, nor did he ever command men in action (during the French campaign he was kept well away from the front line). On the central issue of serfdom, Nicholas's attitude is typified by a speech that he made at the session of the Council of State on 30 March 1842, in the course of which he said: 'There is no doubt that serfdom in its present situation in our country is evil, palpable and obvious for all, but to attack it *now* would be something still more harmful.'[24] Instead, he set up secret commissions to examine the solution of the problem; and although their work did help to serve as the basis for the reforms eventually introduced by his successor, Alexander II, they never came to anything in his lifetime.

This failure notwithstanding, Russia's hard-earned reputation as the strongest military power in continental Europe, and the political influence abroad that went with this position, were unchallenged for nearly forty years from the downfall of Napoleon onwards. At home, however, the atmosphere of Nicholas's rule became increasingly stifling, so much so that the so-called *mrachnoe semiletie* (the sombre last seven years of Nicholas's reign) constituted a period which almost invites comparison with the final years of Leonid Brezhnev's ascendancy in the following century. And what history most remembers Nicholas for is his minute, written in his own hand, about the punishment of running the gauntlet, which remained in use in Russia during his reign. Of two Jews who had tried to escape the plague by running over the Turkish border, Nicholas wrote: 'Send the guilty ones through one thousand men twelve times. God be thanked, there has been no death penalty with us and I shall not introduce it.'[25]

All this said, Nicholas would never have succeeded Alexander if his elder brother, Konstantin, had not married a commoner, a Polish Roman Catholic;[26] it was only after an interregnum of nearly a month that he decided to accept the throne; and when he finally did so, he found himself immediately challenged by the Decembrist Revolt. For the rest of his life Nicholas used to refer to the Decembrists in conversation as *mes amis du quatorze*. The revolt of 14 December 1825 and the reaction to it coloured the whole of his long reign.

THE DECEMBRISTS

It was forty years before the full dimensions of what happened in 1825–6 – described in Chapter 7 – were recognized in Russia.

Although Tolstoy never succeeded in coming to grips with the Decembrists in writing, it is to his credit that he was 'ashamed to write about our triumph in the struggle against Bonapartist France without having described our failures and our shame'.[27] For the first thirty years after the suppression of the Decembrist Revolt, it remained officially a non-subject; and the Decembrists living out their lives in Siberia – at first as prisoners and then as exiles – seven thousand *versts* from St. Petersburg, were officially non-people, so much so that the children born of the courageous wives who joined some of the exiles were declared illegitimate on the instructions of the Russian government. Paradoxically the first attempt (other than the official report of the governmental investigating committee) to describe what had happened in December 1825 was made by the state secretary, Baron Modest Korff (Korf),[28] who wrote his 'Accession to the Throne of Emperor Nicholas I' in eighteen days and presented it to the Grand Duke Alexander at the beginning of 1848. When he had become tsar Alexander II insisted that the book should be published, which – after some revision – it was in 1857. For all its blandness, it was a sell-out.

From the vantage point of his exile in London, Herzen was able to launch an attack on Korff's account of the revolt. On 20 September 1857 he published what he called his first 'antikorfist', in the form of 'A Letter to Emperor Alexander II'. Nor was this Herzen's only response to Korff's attempt to prove that the Decembrist Revolt was 'a masquerade of licence plotting a crime'. In one of his articles published in his periodical, the *Bell* (Kolokol), he wrote:

> It is clear how this servile brochure came to be written during the reign of Nicholas, although one cannot but be amazed that he was able to read such heavy, clerkish, vulgar flattery. It somehow carries the crudely-cut stamp of his time – poverty of thought, conventional forms, a narrow horizon, official coldness, the ruthlessness of a mediocre, repulsive, official sentimentality; not that air in which a man may breathe freely but an oppressive atmosphere of the second order[29]

The amnesty granted by the new tsar in 1856 enabled twenty-nine surviving Decembrists to return from Siberia to Russia. Fortunately some of them retained keen memories, above all Pushkin's close school-friend, Ivan Pushchin. Their memoirs enabled the painful truth gradually to be reconstructed in the second half of the nineteenth century. Moreover, crucial documents slowly came to light; and they have continued to be unearthed even in our own century.[30]

What were the origins of the movement which brought three thousand troops out on to Senate Square in St. Petersburg, without their overcoats, on a freezing cold morning on 14 December 1825 and caused them to refuse to take the oath of allegiance to Nicholas I? Observers then and historians since have offered a variety of answers. At one end of the Russian political spectrum, an elderly arch-reactionary, Count Rostopchin, sarcastically observed at the time that, whereas in the French Revolution shoemakers wanted to become aristocrats, these were Russian aristocrats who wanted to become shoemakers. At the opposite end, the great Polish poet, Adam Mickiewicz, exclaimed: 'A curse on the people which murders its prophets!'[31]

Much weight has been attached to what might be called the French factor, succinctly expressed in the epigram: 'Their fathers were Russians who passionately wanted to be Frenchmen; their sons [Decembrists] were Frenchmen by education, who passionately wanted to become Russians.'[32]

It is true that through most of Russian history great internal changes have usually been the fruit of external events. Thus, the Petrine reforms helped to finance the wars which Peter the Great conducted in order to destroy Swedish hegemony in East Central Europe; the emancipation of the serfs was decreed in the wake of the Crimean War; the parliamentary reforms of 1905 followed the Japanese defeat of Russia; and the success of the Bolshevik Revolution in 1917 was scarcely conceivable except in the aftermath of three terrible years of war and economic privation.

Those who follow this line of thought point to two undeniable facts. Whereas eighteenth-century Russian freethinkers had acquired their ideas through reading the literature of the French Enlightenment, their successors had directly encountered – and in some cases been educated by – French émigrés (including the Jesuits, who entered the Russian Empire by way of Poland). Others were educated in Paris itself. Still more important was the impact of the Russian Patriotic War of 1812–14 and the subsequent Russian participation in the allied occupation of France. The young officers who came home from the extraordinary experience of liberating

Germany and capturing Paris had seen a new world with their own eyes.

It would have been surprising if these men had not returned with a new vision. Not only did they reflect whether the best way of training an army of serfs, recruited for twenty-five years, was to flog them, rather than to teach them to read and write. They were equally concerned about the way in which Russia itself should be governed. The primary cause of the Decembrist movement was that the Russia to which the Decembrists returned from abroad was governed by a tsar, Alexander I, who had given up all hope of introducing internal reforms. In the face of this dismal prospect, whatever their differences among themselves on the kind of constitution now required by Russia, the Decembrists were united in their belief that 'the Sovereign must place himself at the head of the Spirit of the Age ... that Sphinx which devours those who do not understand it'. And for them Russia 'must perforce borrow from Europe, and could never graft anything on her own ancient institutions', although for anyone willing to look back as far as the *veche* democracy of medieval Novgorod, Western Europe (the Decembrists' principal model) did not have the sole prerogative of a tradition of political freedom.[33] Their broad philosophy was never better summed up than in the words of Wilhelm Küchelbecker (Vil'gelm Kyukhelbeker). In his deposition to the investigating committee after the suppression of the revolt, he declared that the principal reason that had compelled him to take part had been his dismay at the moral consequences of oppression for the Russian people: 'Looking at the brilliant qualities with which God has endowed the Russian people ... I was grieved to think that all this might be crushed, wither away and perhaps soon perish altogether, without bringing forth any fruit in the world.'[34]

Of the Decembrists on whom sentence was passed in 1826, only twelve had reached the age of thirty-four and the great majority were under thirty years old. Unlike Küchelbecker – a civilian, whose family had moved to Russia from Germany only in the 1770s – most of them were officers. A large proportion were members of guards regiments – that is to say, not only representatives of the most illustrious families in Russia, but also some of the best educated. In the circumstances then prevailing, it was natural for men such as these, bursting with ideas of reform, to discuss them together. This could be done only within four walls. In spite of the fact that Russia was an autocracy and that by that time Alexander I's principal minister, adviser and friend was Arakcheev, it had not yet become dangerous to belong to a secret society. Many liberal-minded Russian officers were freemasons. So it came about that on 9 February 1816 six guards officers, whose average age was less than twenty-one, met at a flat in St. Petersburg: Sergei and Matvei Murav'ev-Apostol, their cousins, Nikita and Alexander Murav'ev, Ivan Yakushkin and Prince Sergei Trubetskoi. There they formed the Union of Salvation. They were soon joined in this venture by Mikhail Lunin. A cavalry officer, older than most of his fellow Decembrists (he was born in 1787 and in 1816 he spent some time with Saint-Simon in Paris), this remarkable man was the only conspirator to be sentenced to imprisonment in Siberia for a second time, after his first term of imprisonment expired; and the circumstances in which he died there are mysterious.[35]

Later recruits to the movement included General Mikhail Orlov, Mikhail Fonvizin and Colonel Pavel Pestel (Pestel'). Among these the outstanding figure, both for the force of his intellect and the strength of his willpower, was Pestel, a Lutheran, whose family was of Baltic origin. The Union's aims included the establishment of constitutional government and the abolition of serfdom. In the following year, during nearly ten months of which the whole imperial guard accompanied the court to Moscow, the conspirators met several times and reorganized their Union, which was given a new name – the Union of Welfare – and a statute, the Green Book, which set up a Supreme Committee consisting of six members. It was not long before the government got wind of what was afoot. In 1820, therefore, the Union was dissolved. Thereafter it was replaced by two secret societies: the northern society, based on the capital, but with a Moscow membership, and the southern society, based primarily on Tul'chin in the Ukraine, the location of Second Army headquarters. Although the two groups kept in contact and attempted to establish a common programme, they never succeeded in reaching any firm agreement.

Of the two groups, the northern society was the more moderate. The Russian constitution drafted by Nikita Murav'ev abolished serfdom, but retained the office of the emperors as a kind of president on the American model. In general the provisions of the Murav'ev constitution reflected those of the constitution of the United States.

Murav'ev, together with Prince Obolensky and Prince Trubetskoi, formed a triumvirate to run the northern society. Obolensky and Trubetskoi were obliged to leave the capital for a time; and by 1825 the most potent voice in the society in St. Petersburg was that of a former artillery officer, the poet Kondratii Ryleev.

The constitution of the southern society – the *Russkaya pravda*, drafted by Pestel – was radical. It too abolished serfdom, but it provided for a detailed programme of agrarian reform; and it also proposed to convert Russia into a republic. After a temporary dictatorship, legislative power would rest with a unicameral assembly with a life of five years, one-fifth of its membership being elected annually. Executive power was to be held by a state council, consisting of five members elected for five years, one each year.[36] Moreover, Pestel's society established links with two other, quite different, groups which did not have links with the northern society. One of these was a small organization called the Society of United Slavs, whose members, drawn from the minor nobility, aimed to free all Slav races from autocracy and to set up a federation of free Slavs. The other was far more significant: the Polish Patriotic Society, with whom a redrawing of the boundaries between Russia and an independent Poland was discussed. For Pestel, only Poland could claim the right to self-determination; all other ethnic groups within the Russian Empire were to be Russified. Pestel owed these two additional links partly to the energy of a much younger cavalry subaltern, Mikhail Bestuzhev-Ryumin, whose impetuous character was about as far removed from his own as it is possible to imagine. Both of them were to die on the gallows in 1826.

Thanks in part to the disparate nature of the southern Decembrist society and partly to the ability of a repulsive counter-intelligence officer, Count Witte, operating in southern Russia, Alexander I was forewarned. (Witte was half-Polish, half-Greek.) Pestel himself was arrested even before the outbreak of the Decembrist Revolt. Nevertheless, it is not clear why the tsar did not take effective action while he could. At the micro level of explanation, there was acute jealousy between Witte and Arakcheev. Seen against a larger canvas, however, it is not fanciful to suppose that Alexander never reconciled his conscience with his own part in the conspiracy that brought about the assassination of his father Paul. There is even a story that it was Alexander who conveyed a warning to Nikolai Turgenev, 'as the advice of one Christian to another', about the danger he was in. In consequence Turgenev was able to go abroad; and when he was condemned to death, it was *in absentia*.[37]

This then was the state of the two secret societies in the final month of 1825. The names of the conspirators will recur in the chapters that follow. Though not a member of either Decembrist society himself, Pushkin knew almost all the principal conspirators; and two of them who were exiled to Siberia for life were among his closest friends at school. His attitude towards the Decembrists and their attitude towards him is far from simple. There can be no single definitive view of a relationship that changed through the years, above all in 1826. Because it was in that year that Pushkin and the new tsar, Nicholas I, came to terms, 1826 has been described in this book as the first caesura in Pushkin's life.[38] The problems with which Pushkin had to contend during the last years of his life were indeed of a different order from those of his first twenty-seven years; nor did the development of his own political and historical ideas stand still. He could never forget the Decembrists, however. When Eisenstein was thinking of making a film about Pushkin, he envisaged making the first half of the film, dealing with the early years of Pushkin's life, in colour, whereas the second half, covering the last years of the poet's life in St. Petersburg, was to have been mainly in black and white.[39]

CHAPTER TWO

Pushkin's Origins

All happy families resemble each other, every unhappy family
is unhappy in its own way

—Tolstoy, the opening sentence of *Anna Karenina*

On 26 May 1799, the feast of the Ascension, Nadezhda Osipovna
Pushkina gave birth to her first son, in the family's town house,
in what was then known as German Street, in Moscow. He was
christened Alexander in the Church of the Epiphany a fortnight later.
The Gannibals – the family of the boy's mother – had attained noble
rank barely half a century earlier. By contrast, his father, Sergei
L'vovich Pushkin, was descended in a direct line from one of the
oldest families in Russia. Thus, Alexander Sergeevich automatically
entered the world of the *dvoryanstvo* by virtue of his birth. Expressed
in these simple terms, the privileged position in Russian society to
which he had the inherited right to look forward sounds a foregone
conclusion. In reality, the boy's prospects were less clear-cut.

For this reservation there are two reasons: one particular and the
other general. The particular reason derives from the fact that the
families of Alexander Sergeevich's father and mother were glaringly
disparate. By blood, therefore, he was from the outset an unusual
and potentially explosive mixture. The Janus-like[1] exterior of his
character which – in parallel with his literary genius – he swiftly
developed even as a boy, still more as a young man, sometimes baffled
his friends and usually misled his enemies. Pushkin was himself
sometimes morbidly conscious of the special legacy of his lineage. Of
the reaction of others to the contrasts involved in his complex
personality he took little account throughout his life.

The general reason at once becomes apparent when the differences
between the Russian *dvoryanin* (literally, a man of the court, *dvor*)
and an English aristocrat or a French nobleman, as they were at the

end of the eighteenth century, are taken into consideration. Any attempt to compare, let alone to equate, the Russian nobility with the Western European aristocracy falls foul of the fact that a feudal system, in its classic European form, never existed in Russia; there was no territorial aristocracy there of the kind familiar in Western Europe. The Russian social system therefore had neither a feudal nor a bourgeois tradition. The intelligentsia – itself a Russian word – did not yet exist in this period. (The small merchant class was not categorized as belonging to the bourgeoisie, which was a sort of dumping ground for Russians of many different kinds, including even factory workers at this time.) The word which, for want of a better, is generally used to translate *dvoryanstvo* is 'nobility' (the word 'gentry', often used in describing Polish society, is misleading in the Russian context). To English ears 'nobility' does not have the right ring; it is a translation from *noblesse,* the word used for *dvoryanstvo* in the French that was still the language of the Russian imperial court at the turn of the century.

The *dvoryanstvo* constituted the apex of a human pyramid numbering about forty millions when Pushkin was born. It was indeed a highly privileged class. An obvious example is the fact that a Russian noble was exempt from corporal punishment (the *knut* was reserved for the millions below him). But no less important was access to education. The Russian educational system still being in its infancy at the turn of the century, most Russian nobles were educated at home by tutors (and afterwards, if their parents could afford it, sent abroad to foreign universities to complete their studies). Pushkin himself was one of the exceptions to this general rule, being sent to the imperial boarding school which was inaugurated just when he entered it; but the products of Russian universities did not make their mark in Russian life until shortly after his death. For a poor but intelligent boy the option was a seminary school: a route followed by Speransky towards the end of the eighteenth century and by Stalin a hundred years later.

In the eighteenth century there were, strictly speaking, no censuses in Russia. By 1858, however, the total number of both sexes entitled to noble status in the Russian Empire was 604,000.[2] Although the privileges established by law were common to all of them, the divisions of wealth and status within the noble class were immense. At one end of the income scale of the Russian nobility stood

landowners like Count P. B. Shereme'tev, who owned – at the lowest
reckoning – sixty thousand serfs,[3] and those who had already made
vast fortunes from the newly-exploited mineral wealth in the Urals
and further east. At the other, there were villages in which there
lived men bearing names distinguished in Russian history but so
impoverished that their standard of existence was little higher than
that of the surrounding serf population. At best, the 'dispossessed,
homeless, landless, proletarian brothers and sisters of the comfortable
owners of inherited estates' either 'lived as pensioners in the owner's
house' or 'flitted miserably from one house to another'.[4]

The aim of the reforms of Peter the Great at the turn of the
seventeenth and eighteenth centuries was to break the power of the
nobility. His reforms swept away the ancient order of the *boyar*, once
the highest dignity in Russia: a title held by three Pushkins in the
course of the seventeenth century. The main branch of the Pushkin
family was untitled. The only hereditary title in Russia until the
eighteenth century was that of *knyaz'*, prince. (The title of the tsar's
sons, literally 'great prince', is confusingly translated 'grand duke' in
English, although there were never any dukes in Russia.) From then
on the titles of baron and count began to be conferred – among many
importations from the Baltic States and Central Europe. But the
greatest Petrine reform, which remained in force during Pushkin's
lifetime and well beyond it, was the Table of Ranks. Originally there
were fourteen in all, rising from a junior official ('collegial registrar')
at the bottom of the ladder up to chancellor, equivalent to field
marshal, at the top. The Table's social significance lay in the fact
that, from 1721 onwards, a private soldier of humble birth became
eligible for commissioned rank; and the children of holders of the
eight senior ranks in the Petrine Table, roughly down to that of the
civilian equivalent of major, became hereditary nobles. Peter the
Great died in 1725; his Table of Ranks survived until the Russian
Revolution nearly two hundred years later.

This new system was superimposed on a social hierarchy
previously based on birth and genealogy alone. At the same time there
was an influx of foreigners into Russia during the eighteenth
century: some adventurers, some men of substance and some men of
talent (the architect Charles Cameron was a notable Scottish
example). Taken in conjunction with the increasing tendency of
successive tsars to convert into imperial grandees both their own

personal favourites and senior servants of the state (such as Field-Marshal Kutuzov,[5] created Prince of Smolensk), all this combined to bring about a gradual transformation of the Russian noble class by 1800.

As Pushkin put it in his poem, *My Genealogy*, 'We have an aristocracy that is new by birth, and the newer it is, the more aristocratic'. This poem is full of irony, accentuated by the circumstances that provoked Pushkin to write it.[6] But a remark that expresses his mature view of the position of the Pushkin family in Russian society is one which he made in the course of a talk, recorded by himself, with the Grand Duke Mikhail (younger brother of Nicholas I) towards the end of 1834: 'Speaking of the old nobility, I said "We, who are gentlemen, just as well born as the Emperor and yourself...".'[7] The Pushkins were indeed an ancient family. Of the families included in the *gosudarev rodoslovets* (a sort of official stud-book) in the reign of Ivan the Terrible, only thirty odd, including the Pushkins, were still extant three centuries later. By 1800, however, the Pushkins were already a family financially on the way down. Both Alexander Sergeevich's parents had estates, but these had shrunk in size during the eighteenth century.

At the time Alexander Sergeevich was born, the Gannibals had been Russian for less than a hundred years. His mother, Nadezhda Osipovna Pushkina, was known as 'the beautiful creole'. The reason for this was that her grandfather was black; and according to her daughter-in-law the palms of Nadezhda's hands were rather yellow.[8] Alexander Sergeevich was proud of and fascinated by his great-grandfather, who had died eighteen years earlier – so much so that to the line of verse 'beneath the sky of my Africa' (in the first chapter of *Evgenii Onegin*) he added a long explanatory note, which begins with the words: 'The author, on his mother's side, is of African descent. His great-grandfather, Abram Petrovich Annibal [Pushkin used the French spelling here], was kidnapped in his eighth year from the shores of Africa and brought to Constantinople. Having rescued him, the Russian Ambassador sent him as a present to Peter the Great, who had him baptized in Vilno.'[9] Although much of this note is of dubious accuracy, Pushkin's great-grandfather was certainly christened – Petr Petrovich – in Vilno in 1707, his godparents being Peter the Great and the Queen of Poland. Apparently because he had previously been known as Ibrahim, he was allowed to use the Russian form, Abram, as his Christian name; and by 1725 he had adopted the name Gannibal as his surname.

Pushkin had access to his maternal family papers (and in 1817 he met one of Abram's sons, a senior general, who plied him with vodka, at Mikhailovskoe). Nevertheless, he never attempted to identify where in Africa his great-grandfather was born. 'Gannibal' – the Russian form of Hannibal – at first sight suggests North Africa. It has, however, been generally accepted that this was not so, and that Abram was born about 1693 in a region where – as he himself claimed in 1742, in his petition to the Russian Senate applying for a certificate of nobility and a coat of arms – he had been a member of 'the high nobility'. Although this petition gives the name of a town 'in the demesne of my father' it does not add in what country the town was situated.[10] Nevertheless, it is Ethiopia that is assumed to have been Abram's country of origin. The evidence about Abram's boyhood is extremely sketchy. It is far from established how he got to Constantinople or how he made his transition from the Sublime Porte to the Russian capital. What is certain is that, on his arrival, Peter the Great became his personal patron and that in 1716 the tsar sent him to Paris for his military education: the start of a long career which, although the paths both of his public and of his private life did not run smooth, he none the less ended as a full general and the owner of a large estate (including Mikhailovskoe, with one thousand four hundred serfs).

The portrait of Abram Petrovich as a young man in Paris and St. Petersburg which his great-grandson drew in his *Blackamoor of Peter the Great*[11] – the opening chapters of a novel never completed – is charming, but it bears only a tenuous relation to what we know of his early career. Once he had entered the tsar's service within Russia, however, the facts become easier to establish. True, he enrolled in the French school of military engineers (it was his expertise in fortifications that later made his name in Russia) and he took part as an officer in the French army in the War of the Spanish Succession. But, unlike the hero of Pushkin's novel, he never set foot in the fast set of the corrupt and dissolute court of Philippe, Duc d'Orléans, the Regent of France. On the contrary, his years in Paris were spent in extreme poverty. On his return to St. Petersburg in 1724, Peter the Great gave him a commission in his own Preobrazhensky Regiment. During his subsequent military career there was more than one period when he found it prudent to go to ground in the country. It was only after Peter the Great's daughter, Elizabeth, came to the throne that he was granted the Mikhailovskoe estate and promoted major-general. His first marriage, in 1731, was to a Greek, whom he succeeded in persuading the government to imprison for five years for infidelity, although both sides had erred in equal measure. She ended her days in a convent. His second wife, to whom he was bigamously married for nearly twenty years, was German. Abram Petrovich himself died in 1781, a patriarch nearing ninety, who had fathered eleven children, all by his second wife.

The romantic nature of his birth and his early years apart, it seems probable that Abram Petrovich Gannibal differed 'in nothing from a typical career-minded, superficially educated, coarse, wife-flogging Russian of his day, in a brutal and dull world of political intrigue, favouritism',[12] and that the Gannibals were 'a patriarchal, half savage, half literate, family'.[13] (Both these are descriptions written by Russians.) It is hard to imagine two families more different than the Gannibals and the Pushkins in the late eighteenth century. Remarkably, however, Nadezhda Osipovna was not the first Gannibal to marry a Pushkin. Her mother was born Maria Pushkina, marrying Abram Petrovich's third son, Osip Gannibal; thus Sergei L'vovich, the poet's father, was Nadezhda Osipovna's second cousin. Osip Gannibal, like his father, attempted bigamy, deserting Maria after only three years. But he was less successful than his father, because in 1784 his second marriage was declared invalid by Catherine II; and Maria retained the title and prerogative of his legitimate wife, including a quarter of the large properties that Abram had been awarded earlier in the century. Hence the part played by Mikhailovskoe in the life of Alexander Sergeevich Pushkin.

Alexander Sergeevich was proud of his paternal ancestry for quite other reasons. The Pushka or Pushkin family emerges from the mists of early Russian time around 1400. Alexander Sergeevich's line of descent from Konstantin Pushkin, born early in the fifteenth century, was direct. (Because Konstantin's father was called Grigorii, this was the name given by Pushkin to his younger son, who lived into our own century.) The Pushkin family had not, however, been distinguished in any way since the end of the seventeenth century, when a Pushkin was executed by Peter the Great – that is, unless the story of two startling murders is taken into account

(Alexander's paternal great-grandfather strangled his wife in 1725 and his grandfather allegedly hanged his children's French tutor, whom he suspected of being his wife's lover). The social level of Alexander Sergeevich's parents was that of the middle nobility. At the beginning of the nineteenth century a family of this kind, especially if they lived in either St. Petersburg or Moscow, lay open to a permanent temptation to imitate, as best they could, the way of life of the so-called *vysshii svet* – the *haut monde* described in the opening chapters of *War and Peace* – regardless of whether they had anything like the means to do so.

There were some compensations. Sergei L'vovich had a considerable library of French books; both he and his brother were well read in French, therefore; and Vasilii achieved a reputation as a minor poet. There was, however, more to it than that. Both his father Sergei and his uncle Vasilii were social climbers. Their pursuit (especially Sergei's) of the *haut monde* in the end left them broken.[14] It was this curious combination of a snobbish dilettante as a father and, as a mother, the moody, capricious descendant of military boors, which formed the at first sight improbable background to the first twelve years of the life of Russia's greatest poet.

In the marriage of Pushkin's parents the problem was not infidelity – Nadezhda Osipovna was a stronger character than Sergei L'vovich – but fecklessness. In 1798, at the age of thirty-one, two years after his marriage to Nadezhda Osipovna in St. Petersburg, Sergei L'vovich resigned his commission in the Egersky Regiment; the couple, with their baby daughter, Olga, then moved to Moscow. Clearly unsuited for military life, Sergei L'vovich took no part in the campaigns of the opening years of the nineteenth century, although Alexander I gave him some minor employment, for which his salary can only have been minimal. From 1817 onwards he did nothing for the rest of his life, never even visiting his own family estate, Boldino (in Nizhnii Novgorod province, with twelve hundred serfs), whose administration he left to a steward. He took equally little interest in the Mikhailovskoe estate.

Whether either of these properties would have benefited by the presence of Sergei L'vovich is open to question. He was a hot-tempered man, although his rages seldom lasted for long. His chief concern seems to have been to reserve what energies he had for social life, avoiding responsibility for anything else, including the running of his own household; and as he grew older and his financial circumstances worsened, he also grew increasingly mean. The Pushkin household in Moscow was run by Sergei L'vovich's bossy, but erratic, wife, who – spoiled as a child – was given to prolonged sulks as a grown-up. Not only did they move house annually from 1799 to 1807, including one brief return to St. Petersburg (hence the infant poet's meeting with Paul I), but Nadezhda Osipovna had a habit of continually moving furniture from one room to another, changing the functions of each room in the process. The consequent disruption was on such a scale that she was said by one of Alexander Sergeevich's contemporaries to be obliged to send out for crockery whenever more than two people were invited to dinner.[15]

The conditions of disorder in the Pushkins' life in Moscow were relieved by the fact that the summer months were spent in the country on a small estate at Zakharovo, forty-four kilometres from Moscow. Nadezhda Osipovna's mother had bought Zakharovo in exchange for Kobrino, her family property near St. Petersburg, which she sold in 1799. Even Zakharovo was mortgaged ten years later; and in January 1811 it was sold for forty-five thousand roubles.[16] Nevertheless, it was during these summers at Zakharovo that Alexander Sergeevich first got to know the beauty of the Russian countryside; his love for it was reinforced later in life.

The feeling that the Pushkins were camping – not living – in their home can hardly have failed to induce a feeling of instability in the small boy. To make matters worse, his mother's favourite seems to have been his elder sister, Olga. He disliked his tutors, of whom there was a succession. They were mainly French, as was the custom at that time in a Russian family of this social standing, but they included a Miss Bailey, whose efforts to teach the boy English met with little success (he had to study the language all over again in later life). He was also confronted early in his boyhood by the tragedy of death: not only that of the first nanny, Ul'yana, of whom little is known, but also of three of his siblings, one of whom – Nikolai – was five when he died in 1807.

Neither parent seems to have taken much trouble over their remarkable elder son until the time came for him to go to school at the age of twelve. The member of the family who seems to have come closest to understanding the contradictions of his character – now fiery, now withdrawn – was his maternal grandmother, Maria

Alekseevna. More perceptive than either of his parents, she observed of her grandson:

> I do not know what he will become: the boy is intelligent, he loves books, but he works badly, it is rare that he recites his lessons correctly; sometimes one cannot move him nor send him to play with the children, and sometimes he gets agitated and excited and one does not know how to calm him down; he throws himself from one extreme to the other; he does not know the happy medium. God knows how this will finish, if he does not become reasonable[17]

Alexander Sergeevich never did have much truck with the happy medium, nor did he ever become 'reasonable'. No one seems to have realized until he went to boarding school – and even then only gradually – that he was a literary genius. In spite of his excellent memory, he simply did not bother with subjects which did not interest him, like mathematics. On the other hand, when reading the works of authors who did engage his attention, already as a boy he showed the beginnings of the power of discrimination which he developed in his later study of an exceptionally broad range of literature.

It is the biographer's misfortune that Pushkin destroyed most of his autobiographical notes, which might have illuminated these early years more clearly than the fragments of evidence that have been handed down by those who knew him then. What is reasonably certain, however, is that Alexander Sergeevich's nanny, Arina Rodionovna, and his sister, Olga, were much closer to him than either parent. (For example, it was to Olga – not to his parents – that he recited his first play, a comedy written in French, imitated from Molière.[18] This recital took place before he was twelve years old.) From the age of ten he had Nikita Kozlov, a serf from Boldino, twenty-one years older than himself, as his personal servant, who stayed with him for the rest of his life and beyond (he was one of the very few who were present at the poet's burial). Arina was also born a serf – and she was always illiterate – but she was emancipated by Pushkin's maternal grandmother in the year of his birth. She chose to stay on with the Pushkin family and she thus became successively nanny to Olga, to Pushkin himself and to his younger brother, Lev. It seems that she was not the nanny whom the tsar Paul I scolded in 1800 when he met the infant Pushkin out for a walk in St. Petersburg. It may therefore not have been with Arina that Pushkin was later taken for walks in the Yusupov Garden in Moscow, as recorded in his own autobiographical notes. Be that as it may, there is no doubt that between the ages of six and twelve it was Arina to whom he was closest, in a family environment to which, in the same notes, Pushkin applied the adjective 'intolerable'.[19]

Most young children love grown-ups who tell them stories. Arina not only told Pushkin stories but she also poured out peasant traditions and proverbs. An exceptionally imaginative child such as Pushkin had good reason to love Arina. Moreover, her remarkable powers of story-telling were again exercised in later years, this time with tangible poetic results, when she used to spend the evenings talking to Pushkin at Mikhailovskoe during his two-year exile on his mother's estate. When this exile was brought to an end by Nicholas I's summons to Pushkin for an audience in Moscow in September 1826, Arina wept; but she was glad of the opportunity to get rid of Pushkin's smelly Limberg cheese, to which he was addicted. A letter dictated by her in the year before she died described him as constantly in her heart and in her mind. The depth of Pushkin's own feelings towards Arina is evident from more than one of his poems; and during his exile at Mikhailovskoe a letter drafted near the end of 1824 says it all:

> I spend all day on horseback – in the evening I listen to tales told by my nanny, the prototype of Tatyana's nanny [a reference to the nurse in the famous letter-writing scene in Chapter 3 of *Evgenii Onegin*.]; you saw her once, it seems to me, she is my one and only friend – it is only when I am with her that I am not bored.[20]

What should have marked out Alexander Sergeevich to his parents and everyone else who met him – and did indeed impress his schoolmates – was the number of hours that from an early age (often at night) he spent reading. There is a story that, told to leave the room by his uncle Vasilii, who was about to recite some unsuitable verses, he shouted: 'I know everything already!' He probably did. His desire for reading as a boy, which he himself described in his autobiographical notes, gave him at this astonishingly early age a detailed knowledge not only of seventeenth- and eighteenth-century French literature, but also of some of the classics in French translation – Plutarch's *Lives*, the *Iliad* and the *Odyssey*, for example.[21]

Curiously enough, we cannot be wholly confident about Pushkin's physical appearance at this age. The authenticity of the lesser-known portrait (by an unknown artist), which depicts a small boy in conventional style, is extremely doubtful. Geitman's well-known engraving of Pushkin as he was perhaps ten years later was not executed until 1822, by which time Pushkin was in Kishinev. Geitman seems deliberately to emphasize what he presumably regarded as Pushkin's African traits. Here too views differ. (Geitman's engraving may even have been derived from a drawing of Pushkin's younger brother, Lev, at school.) The common factor, as it is to all of the many descriptions of Pushkin as a man, is the flash of his eyes: blue, penetrating and startlingly expressive – something which no one who met Pushkin, even briefly, ever forgot.[22]

The deficiencies of Alexander Sergeevich's parents were counterbalanced by the quality not only of his father's library, but also of some of his friends. Already as a young boy Alexander Sergeevich was introduced at home to leading literary figures, such as Nikolai Karamzin, Petr Vyazemsky and Vasilii Zhukovsky. Karamzin was the first great Russian historian. Pushkin greatly admired his work, although their relationship had its ups and downs. After 1820 they scarcely met, because Karamzin died not long after Pushkin was released from exile; but Vyazemsky and Zhukovsky became Pushkin's close friends for the rest of his life.

Prince Vyazemsky, a liberal member of the high aristocracy, was Irish on his mother's side. A little less than seven years older than Pushkin, he was at the same time a poet, literary critic and journalist. Pushkin and he did not always see eye to eye, whether on politics or on poetry, but the quality of their friendship was such that these disagreements, unlike some of the polemics in which Pushkin indulged with other people, had no lasting effects. Pushkin was also a close friend of Vyazemsky's wife and of his family.

Zhukovsky was almost old enough to be Pushkin's father. Indeed, towards the end of Pushkin's life their relationship became so close that he was a kind of surrogate father, extending to Pushkin the relationship that Sergei L'vovich never offered to his elder son. He was himself the offspring of an unusual union: his mother was a captive taken from the Ottoman Empire during one of the Russo-Turkish wars. Personally he was a sad man, unable to marry the woman whom he loved. A poet distinguished mainly for his translations, Zhukovsky was one of the first to recognize Pushkin's outstanding talent. At court – in his capacity as tutor to Nicholas I's children – he did all he could to soften the edges of Pushkin's abrasive relationship with the tsar and Benckendorff. After Pushkin's death, it was he who arranged for the tsar to make financial provision for his family, and also preserved Pushkin's papers from the depredations of the tsar's Third Department.

Another important friendship that Pushkin owed to his Moscow childhood was with the Turgenev brothers, all three of whom were older than himself. (The novelist, Ivan Turgenev, was – at most – their distant cousin.) It was on the advice of the eldest of these three brothers, Alexander, born in 1784, that in 1811 Pushkin's parents applied for him to be enrolled in the imperial lycée. Here Alexander Turgenev used to visit the boy and encouraged his precocious poetic talent. And it was he who, on the tsar's instructions, accompanied Pushkin's body to its final resting place. The second brother, Nikolai, a distinguished Decembrist, was a political émigré during the last twelve years of Pushkin's life. Some of the politically radical verses of Pushkin's early period were written in the Turgenevs' house in St. Petersburg.

Pushkin did not like the city of his birth, Moscow. Perhaps this was at first because of the recollection of his childhood years, later reinforced by a series of disagreeable altercations with his mother-in-law, who lived in Moscow at the time of his marriage. By contrast, he was fascinated by St. Petersburg. The capital was described by Pushkin's great Polish contemporary, Adam Mickiewicz, as:

> The fancy of the tsar, and he set out to found a city not for men but for himself: a monument to vanity. Into the depths of fluid sands and marshy swamps he bade them sink a hundred thousand piles and trample down the bodies of a hundred thousand men, earth having fallen on the bodies of the serfs[23]

By contrast, Pushkin's introduction to *The Bronze Horseman* speaks for itself:

> Люблю тебя, Петра творенье,
> Люблю твой строгий, стройный вид,
> Невы державное теченье,
> Береговой её гранит,
> Твоих оград узор чугунный,
> Твоих задумчивых ночей

Прозрачный сумрак, блеск безлунный,
Когда я в комнате моей
Пишу, читаю без лампады,
И ясны спяшие громады
Пустынных улиц, и светла
Адмиралтейская игла,
И, не пуская тьму ночную
На золотые небеса,
Одна заря сменить другую
Спешит, дав ночи полчасз.
Люблю зимы твоей жестокой
Недвцжный воздух и мороз,
Вея санок вдоль Невы широкой,

Девичьи лица црче роз,
И блеск, и шум, и говор балов,
А в час пирушки холостой
Шипенбе пенистых бокалов
И пунша пламенб голубой.
Люблю воинственную живостб
Потешных Марсовых полей,
Пехотных ратей и коней
Однообразную красивостб,
В их стройно зыблемом строю
Лоскутья сих знамён побелных,
Сиянье шапок зтих медных,
Насквозь простреленных в бою.
Люблю, военная столица,
Твоей твердыни дым и гром,
Когда полнощная царица
Дарует сына в царский дом,
Или победу над врагом
Россия снова торжествует,
Или, взломав свой синий лёд,
Нева к морям его несет
И, чуя вешни дни, ликует.

I love you, Peter's creation, I love your stern, harmonious look, the mighty flow of the Neva, her granite embankments, the iron pattern of your railings, the transparent twilight and the moonless brilliance of your pensive nights, when I write and read in my room without a lamp, and the sleeping masses of the deserted streets shine and the Admiralty spire gleams, and without admitting night's darkness to the golden heavens, dawn hastens to replace dusk, leaving night a bare half-hour. I love the motionless air and the frost of your brutal winter, the rush of sleighs along the broad Neva, the girls' faces brighter than roses, and the sparkle, the noise and the talk at balls, and at the hour of a bachelor's feast the hiss of sparkling wine-glasses and the blue flame of punch. I love the warlike liveliness of Mars' playing-fields, the uniform beauty of the hosts of infantry and cavalry, the tatters of those victorious colours in their harmoniously swaying order, the gleam of those bronze helmets, raked with shots fired in battle. Martial capital, I love the smoke and thunder of your stronghold, when the northern empress presents a son to the royal house, or when Russia once again celebrates victory over her enemy, or when, having broken its blue ice, the Neva carries it to the seas and, scenting the days of spring, exults . . .[24]

Pushkin observed that Moscow's decline relative to St. Petersburg was the inevitable consequence of the rise of St. Petersburg, where Peter the Great had transferred the capital of his empire eighty-seven years before Pushkin was born. 'Two capitals', wrote Pushkin, 'cannot flourish in the same degree in one and the same state, just as two hearts do not exist in the human body.' After recalling the earlier competition between Moscow and St. Petersburg, Pushkin goes on to ask:

Where has that noisy, festive, carefree life got to? Where have the balls, the banquets, the eccentrics, the bundles of mischief got to? – Everything has disappeared . . . The streets are dead; it is rare that one hears the noise of carriages on the roadway; the women rush to the windows when one of the chiefs of police rides past with his Cossacks.

Pushkin contrasts all this with the good old days of Moscow, when a rich eccentric would build himself a Chinese house on one of the principal streets of the city, complete with green dragons and wooden mandarins under golden sunshades.[25] Moscow's relative decline at this point in the nineteenth century may be ascribed in part to the fact that large tracts of it, being built of wood, were destroyed by the fire that broke out in 1812 during the Napoleonic occupation of the city. Nevertheless, after 1812 the rich rebuilt their Moscow houses in stone; and the atmosphere of Moscow University was in Pushkin's time more liberal than that of the University of St. Petersburg.

In the early nineteenth century Russia's two capital cities were remarkable for two characteristics, one of which Pushkin himself described. First, the hazards of travelling from one to the other. One

of the stanzas of *Evgenii Onegin* lambasts the bridges rotting from
neglect, the bugs and fleas which prevent the traveller from getting a
wink of sleep at post stations, the absence of inns and the high-
sounding but in fact miserable menu which the traveller finds teasing
his appetite in a cold hut.[26] Secondly, their size: they were quite
small. (The same could indeed be said of Paris in the same period.)
When Pushkin and his wife settled in St. Petersburg, the total urban
population of the Russian Empire was fewer than two million, of
whom 445,000 lived in St. Petersburg and 323,000 in Moscow.

Among the few hundred thousand inhabitants of St. Petersburg
and Moscow in Pushkin's day, the members of the upper stratum,
whether or not they held appointments in the service of the state,
followed an intensive social round, limited only by the restrictions of
Orthodox fasts, above all 'Great Lent' (*velikii post*, the fast before
Easter). It so happens that the merry-go-round of this period is the
subject of one of the most brilliantly descriptive passages in Russian
literature: the opening chapters of *War and Peace*. Tolstoy here
portrays different kinds of parties given in St. Petersburg and
Moscow in 1805, which he then contrasts with life in a large country
house at the time. Life in both cities and also in the countryside
changed little in the interval between then and Pushkin's period.

Tolstoy's portrait is of *salon* elegance in the capital; of a name-day
party in the house of a rich family in Moscow; and of the old-
fashioned dignity of a grandee, the elder Prince Bolkonsky, who,
exiled by Paul I, but now free to return to St. Petersburg, prefers to
continue living in the calm of his estate, *Bald Hills*, about one
hundred and fifty *versts* from Moscow. This description of life in St.
Petersburg and Moscow is bathed in the roseate glow of a national
epic; or as Akhmatova might have said (she used these words to
criticize a different Russian writer), 'no swords flash'.[27] In Tolstoy's
final version – the work was continually revised – he cut the amount
of French spoken by his characters in St. Petersburg; in Moscow he
makes Count Rostov speak 'very bad but self-confident' French; and
apart from the opening paragraph of the novel, which is entirely in
French, for most of the dialogue in these early chapters he contents
himself with the occasional interjection of the words *mon cher* or *ma
chère*, together with a reminder to his readers that their 'ancestors'
not only spoke but also thought in refined French.[28] This was indeed
the French that Pushkin, bilingual from childhood, also spoke. Even

when he was dying, the melancholy words, 'I must put my house in order,' were spoken in French, not in Russian.

If the reader of the opening chapters of *War and Peace* can temporarily detach himself or herself from the flowing cadences of Tolstoyan prose and the subtlety of Tolstoy's analysis of character, there will be discerned, often between the lines, a social analysis of the times that has not been subjected to the demands of the nostalgia of a later Russian generation. Thus, with the exceptions of Pierre Bezukhov (whose conversation shows from the outset traces of his being intended by Tolstoy as an embryonic Decembrist) and the younger Prince Bolkonsky (Andrei), cant is talked about Alexander I (the 'lofty destiny of our dear Emperor'); except for Prince Andrei, no one shows much understanding of contemporary political realities; and – leaving aside the very young – the minds of most of them in St. Petersburg and Moscow are concentrated on money, match-making, trading influence and jockeying for position. All this goes on at a round of parties given on the eve of the Battle of Austerlitz. But for the war, what would all of them have been doing, with no parliament, no free press and (except in private) no freedom of assembly to absorb their energies? Tolstoy leaves his readers to imagine the answer to this question, before hurrying them on to the Austerlitz campaign.

The Battle of Austerlitz was Napoleon's greatest victory, in which he decisively defeated the allied Russian and Austrian armies. On learning of the outcome the British Prime Minister, the younger Pitt, is said to have remarked: 'Roll up that map [of Europe]; it will not be wanted these ten years.' His forecast was right. It did indeed take ten years before the map of Europe could at last be redrawn, at the Congress of Vienna, after Napoleon had, in his turn, met his final defeat. Halfway through this epic period of European history, in 1811, Pushkin left his native Moscow for Tsarskoe Selo, where he spent the next six years of his life.

CHAPTER THREE

School at Tsarskoe Selo, 1811–1817

Смуглый отрок бродил по аллеям
У озерных грустил берегов,
И столетие мы лелеем
Еле слышный шелест шагов.

Иглы сосен густо и колко
Устилают низкие пни ...
Здесь лежела его треуголка
И растрепанный том Парни.

(A swarthy youth used to wander through the avenues, he walked sadly by the shores of the lake. A century later we catch the barely audible crackle of his footsteps.

Thick and thorny pine needles cover the low tree-stumps ... Here his three-cornered hat used to lie and his tattered volume of Parny.)

—Anna Akhmatova, Tsarskoe Selo, 1911

On 9 October 1811 Pushkin arrived at Tsarskoe Selo, which has been called Pushkin since the first centenary of his death. As Akhmatova recalled in her poem written there in 1911,[1] Parny was indeed one of the eighteenth-century French poets who most influenced him at this age; the uniform that he wore during his six years at school did include a three-cornered hat; and he and his fellow-pupils were encouraged to walk in the grounds of the tsar's summer palace at Tsarskoe Selo. Pushkin remained a keen walker (also rider and swimmer) in adult life. The village, twenty miles from St. Petersburg, was first called Tsarskoe Selo (meaning the tsar's village, the adjective being a corruption of the original place-name in Finnish, Saarskoe) after Peter the Great had chosen it as the location for a cottage, a hothouse and a zoological garden. His successors – above all Catherine II – gradually converted Tsarskoe Selo into their summer residence, and, as well as building the palace, created its magnificent gardens.

Indirectly, Pushkin owed the fact that he spent the years 1811 to 1817 as a boarder at Tsarskoe Selo to Mikhail Speransky. Before Speransky's fall from grace (it will be recalled that he was dismissed from St. Petersburg by Alexander I in March 1812), one of the innovative measures of liberal intent that the tsar put into practice was the foundation of the imperial lycée, situated in a wing of the palace, in 1811. Had the original concept been carried to its logical conclusion, this select school would have been attended by the young grand dukes, who would thus have been able to rub shoulders at an early age with their contemporaries among the aristocracy on an equal footing. The conservative influence of the dowager empress (always a major figure in the Russian court) was enough to rule this out, however. Instead, although the officially declared purpose was 'the education of youth especially predestined for important parts of the state service',[2] the first intake of thirty boys in the autumn of 1811 consisted of a cross-section, chiefly drawn from the sons of families not of the high aristocracy, but of the middle nobility. Nevertheless, the fact that this project ever got off the ground at all and that entry into the school depended not entirely upon family connections, but also on an examination, was in itself something of an achievement, especially when the academic impoverishment of the Russian capital at that time is taken into consideration. Three years earlier there were only 294 pupils in the four *gimnazii* of St. Petersburg, which – formally speaking – did not even have a university until 1819.[3] It was, moreover, only in 1803 that it was laid down that courses in Russian schools must be taught in Russian.

The immediate reason for Pushkin's being able to sit the entrance examination for the imperial lycée in September 1811 – instead of being exposed to the stern régime of the Jesuit school that had been his parents' first choice – was the fact that the first director of the lycée, Vasilii Malinovsky, was a friend of his father, his uncle and Alexander Turgenev. It was Turgenev, one of the few men who were aware of the boy's potential from childhood onwards, who intervened decisively to make sure that this door was opened for Pushkin. He also thereby saved the Pushkin finances from a considerable burden; education at the lycée was free.

Accompanied by neither of his parents, but by his uncle, Pushkin set off from Moscow in July 1811. Characteristically, Vasilii L'vovich made his own use of the hundred roubles travel money given to the boy by his family, on the way to St. Petersburg.[4] Pushkin seems to have felt no regret at leaving his parents, whose occasional visits during his school years began only in 1814 – it was not until December 1816 that the pupils were allowed to return home even for Christmas. Perhaps all that he really missed was Zakharovo and his maternal grandmother. However that may be, having sat the entrance examination in September, he passed into the school halfway up the list. As might be expected, his knowledge of Russian and French, but of no other subject, stood him in good stead.

Pushkin grew up to be an exceptionally superstitious man – a trait for which his friends would later tease him – and presumably he was already superstitious at the age of twelve. We do not know. What is clear, however, is that the coincidence that the lycée was opened precisely in his thirteenth year, at the moment when he was due to go to school in any case, was a stroke of luck for him, even though he may not have seen it in exactly that light at the time. The school was formally opened on 19 October 1811 in the presence of the emperor, Speransky and the court. Winter had already begun. The snow that by then covered the ground was illuminated by a firework display in the evening. Pushkin's later feelings about his school days seem to have been mixed. Although he referred in his later years to the 'gaps in his damned education', he attended reunions on the anniversary of 19 October whenever he was able; and at his last attendance, in 1836, he broke down and wept. It was at school that he made some of the most significant friendships of his life, notably those with Baron Anton Delvig (Del'vig), Ivan Pushchin and Wilhelm Küchelbecker.

Of Delvig, Pushkin wrote in a letter immediately after his death in 1831, 'nobody in the world was closer to me'.[5] A precocious poet like Pushkin, though of limited range, Delvig was chiefly important as the editor of the best literary journal of Pushkin's time; and his untimely death at the age of thirty-two may have been hastened by the fact that, for what today seem wholly frivolous reasons, the official censor closed down his journal, the *Literaturnaya gazeta*. A gentle, kind and rather lazy man – he had difficulty in getting up in the morning – he died within a month of the closure of his review, evoking a poem written in Siberian exile by Küchelbecker, which would become well known in our own century as forming the text of the ninth of the songs ('Oh Delvig, Delvig') in Shostakovich's Fourteenth Symphony.

Küchelbecker was also a poet, critic and editor. A clumsy, short-sighted man, who spoke Russian with a German accent, he was teased at school but respected by others, including Pushkin, for his encyclopaedic knowledge. Through the years Pushkin repeatedly disagreed with Küchelbecker on literary matters – they even fought a farcical duel on one occasion – and yet they remained on terms of personal friendship. They managed to correspond with each other while Küchelbecker was in Siberian exile; and Pushkin's early death deeply moved Küchelbecker, as had Delvig's six years earlier.

Unlike most of Pushkin's early friends, Pushchin (nicknamed 'Jeannot') was not a writer, but an administrator. After service as an artillery officer, he became a respected judge, who took a prominent part in the Decembrist Revolt. At school his and Pushkin's rooms were next door to each other, presumably for alphabetical reasons. He is a witness of major importance regarding both Pushkin's character and his relationship with the Decembrists.

Two other close contemporaries of Pushkin at school were its star pupils, Baron Modest Korff and Prince Alexander Gorchakov. The former, who was not a friend, would later pursue a successful career in the imperial bureaucracy typical of the mediocrity of the reign of Nicholas I. The latter was a friend, though never a close one. A professional diplomat, his moves up the ladder were slow; and they may not have been helped by the scant respect that he showed for Benckendorff. (There is also a story – unproven – that he offered Pushchin a chance to escape from Russia immediately after the Decembrist Revolt.[6]) Nevertheless, it was to Gorchakov that Alexander II had recourse when the fiasco of the Crimean War had reduced Russian foreign policy to ruins. Appointed foreign minister – an office that he filled with distinction – he later became chancellor; and he was one of the very few of Pushkin's contemporaries to reach old age.[7]

The quality of most of Pushkin's teachers was not of the kind that might have been expected at a school founded by the tsar. With one important exception, he did not learn much from those who tried to teach him. The refrain in their reports on their unusual pupil becomes so monotonous that two examples will serve. Thus the report of the man who taught Pushkin both geography and history describes Pushkin in these words: 'With slight application, he shows very good results and these must be attributed to one thing only, his wonderful talent.' A second report describes him as 'capable of dealing only with subjects that require little effort, and therefore his progress is very slight, especially in the sphere of logic'.[8]

The one exception to the mediocrity of the teachers was Alexander Kunitsyn, assistant professor of moral and political sciences at the lycée throughout Pushkin's time there. Kunitsyn was the only one of his lycée teachers whom Pushkin afterwards mentioned with thanks in his own writing. (In 1835 Pushkin inscribed his *History of the Pugachev Revolt* to him 'as a sign of the author's deep respect and gratitude'.) He taught the general principles of law at the lycée and subsequently at the University of St. Petersburg, from which he was expelled in 1821, not as a radical – which he was not – but as a victim of the reactionary wave that swept through Russian universities in the last years of Alexander I's reign. At the lycée Gorchakov made notes (since published) of Kunitsyn's course, which he and Pushkin attended. So far as the issue of Russian constitutional reform was concerned, his ideas were cautious: the tsar should be advised by a body of elected representatives. The greater part of his course, however, was devoted to the question of natural law. Although he based his own teaching not on the theories fashionable in western Europe at the beginning of the nineteenth century, but on those of the great philosophers of earlier years, he used them to question the very foundation of Russian autocracy: namely the Russian variant of what in England, in an earlier century, had been called the divine right of kings.

For Kunitsyn, the tsar's authority was based, not on God-given powers, but on a contract between ruler and ruled; and 'when the monarch employs the state power not in accordance with the objects of the state, or deprives the subjects of their original and determining rights, for the preservation of which the state came into being, then the form of government is called despotic'. From this it followed logically that Kunitsyn rejected all forms of serfdom as being contrary to the fundamental principles of natural law. Kunitsyn's influence on Pushkin's thinking can be traced not only in his early, radical period, but also in his later years. The Pugachev Revolt, which engaged Pushkin's attention – and much of his time – towards the end of his life, was the most violent and the longest sustained of the insurrections in Russia during the eighteenth century.[9]

Kunitsyn's teaching apart, Pushkin was largely a self-educated man. In this he was not unique; history offers other famous examples, such as Winston Churchill. The breadth of the range of knowledge of literature and of history that he acquired over the years that followed and stored in his powerful memory, was largely the product of his own reading, begun at home in Moscow and continued in the ample library to which the lycée pupils had free access, leading afterwards to his accumulation of a large library, which he amassed as soon as he could afford to buy books for himself.[10]

Even if the value of the friendships formed by Pushkin while he was at Tsarskoe Selo is left out of account, his years at the lycée at this stage in his process of self-education served a useful purpose, in that they left him ample leisure: leisure to read, to write and, gradually, to think for himself – three things of which a less gifted pupil would not have been capable before reaching university. (Pushkin never attended a university.) Leisure was something of which, in spite of superficial evidence to the contrary, the members of the first intake at Tsarskoe Selo had plenty. Indeed, even a boy temperamentally suited for application to conventional study at school would have found it hard to work seriously during the first years of the imperial lycée. On paper, the school curriculum looks demanding. There were six basic subjects – languages (Russian, Latin, French and German); moral science (including religion and philosophy); mathematics and physics; history (of other nations as well as of Russia); literature (including the rules of rhetoric); and fine arts and gymnastics (including calligraphy, drawing, dancing, fencing, riding and swimming). To these were added, as if there were not enough subjects already, the study of psychology, military strategy, political economy, aesthetics, law, French and German rhetoric and 'if possible' architecture.[11]

It is hard to imagine how this imposing array of lessons could have been accommodated in a school timetable which provided for only six hours spent in the classrooms during a weekday (a number on which there is general agreement among Pushkinists). That both the curriculum and the timetable were in practice honoured as much in the breach as in observance is suggested by Pushkin's own

description of the way in which he was spending his time in early
December 1815.

> *10th December.* Yesterday I wrote the third chapter of 'Fatama, or
> Human Reason: Natural Law', I read it to SS [a fellow-pupil, Simon
> Esakov] and in the evening, with my comrades, I put out the candles
> and the lamps in the hall. A splendid occupation for a philosopher! – In
> the morning I read 'The Life of Voltaire' [probably Condorcet's].
>
> I have begun writing a comedy [an unfinished work, 'The
> Philosopher'] – I do not know whether I shall finish it. The day before
> yesterday I wanted to write an ironical poem 'Igor and Olga'.[12]

Malinovsky died in March 1815. His death was succeeded by a hiatus,
which was filled only when Egor Engelhardt (Engel'gardt) was
appointed director of the school early in the following year. Small
wonder, therefore, that Pushkin afterwards described this period of
his school as one of 'anarchy'.[13] Nevertheless, during Pushkin's time
at the lycée its pupils, even though they were confined to Tsarskoe
Selo, enjoyed some advantages which their opposite numbers at an
English boarding school of that period would have envied. From his
first term onwards, every boy had his own room, simply but decently
furnished. Flogging was not allowed. There is no record of systematic
bullying. Nor, unlike Eton, did any of them die in a duel while at
school.[14] Considering the customs of the era, the boys' day seems
comparatively civilized: from six o'clock in the morning until supper
at nine o'clock in the evening, after which there was a recreation
period until ten, followed by prayers and tea.[15] Moreover, unlike his
predecessor, the new director encouraged his pupils to frequent
houses at Tsarskoe Selo, including the home of his own family, where
– again in striking contrast to the monastic tradition maintained by
English public schools until well into the twentieth century – they
were able to meet members of the opposite sex.

For reasons that are not entirely clear – perhaps Pushkin's attempt
to flirt with a recently widowed young woman who was staying with
Engelhardt's family did not help matters – he and Engelhardt did not
get on while he was at school, although four years later Engelhardt, a
thoroughly decent man, was one of those who sprang to Pushkin's
defence when the tsar considered sending him to Siberia. While
Pushkin was at Tsarskoe Selo two diametrically opposed views about
him were held. Engelhardt wrote of Pushkin (in notes made for
himself, while Pushkin was at school) that his mind was completely

superficial. 'This moreover is the very best that can be said of Pushkin. His heart is cold and empty; there is neither *love* nor *religion* in it . . .'[16]

Writing forty years later, Korff, having recalled Pushkin's nickname of 'Frenchman' and his 'exceptional knowledge of the French language', went on to maintain that, at the time of the French invasion of Russia, anyone bearing a French name was hated. He then concluded: 'It is clear that this nickname did not include anything flattering. Hot-tempered to the point of fury, with ungovernable, African (like his maternal ancestry) passions; always distracted, always buried in his poetic dreams, spoiled from childhood onwards by praise and flattery . . .'[17] and so on.

The picture drawn by Pushchin in his memoirs is very different:

> We all of us saw that Pushkin was ahead of us, he had read a lot of which we had not even heard, everything that he read – he remembered; but what was creditable was the fact that he never remotely thought of boasting or giving himself airs, as often happens at that age (each of us was then 12 years old).

Pushchin also recalled the talks that he often had with Pushkin at night, through the wall of their adjoining bedrooms. Pushkin would shed 'bitter tears', lamenting 'both his own conduct and that of others', and make 'outraged admissions', express 'contrition' and, finally, 'discuss plans of how to put right his position among his comrades or how to avoid the consequences of a false move or an unintentional action'.[18]

Pushkin's years at Tsarskoe Selo included the great year 1812, when – following Napoleon's capture of Moscow, at the moment when it still seemed conceivable that he might attempt to march northwards on the capital – preparations were made for evacuating the school from Tsarskoe Selo. Nor is there any doubt about the national fervour that enabled the Russians to survive their narrow defeat at the bloody battle of Borodino, where they suffered 40,000 and the French 30,000 casualties. (Afterwards – it was a warm day – over 87,000 corpses were burned: 56,811 human and 31,664 horses.)[19] The boys, who had watched the regiments marching to the front through Tsarskoe Selo, studied the military communiqués of the campaign right through 1812. They would have been aware of, even if they did not themselves attend, the *Te Deum* celebrated in St.

Petersburg after the receipt of the first news of Borodino, which was
initially reported as a Russian victory. Napoleon was left in possession
of the battlefield, but he failed to consolidate his victory, with results
that later proved fatal for him and his *Grande Armée*. And the lycée
pupils certainly did attend the festivities, organized by the dowager
empress at Pavlovsk, to celebrate the return of the victorious
Alexander from Paris two years later, saluted as the Russian
Agamemnon and the Liberator of Europe.

What earned Pushkin the nickname of 'Frenchman' in the first
instance was indeed his perfect command of the French language. In
the feverish political circumstances of the following years, to carry
this nickname might have been an embarrassment for a sensitive boy
like Pushkin. The fact is, however, that the many French nationals
resident in Russia at the time (Madame de Staël was a visitor then)
incurred little or no Russian resentment. The French regiments
formed only one part of Napoleon's multinational *Grande Armée*. In
this Fatherland War, as it was called, Pushkin was as much of a
patriot as any other Russian schoolboy; and so he remained in later
life. On this score, therefore, Korff's snide remarks may be
dismissed.[20]

As for Pushkin's 'African passions', if the only evidence that the
biographer had to work on, so far as this aspect of Pushkin's
development as a boy was concerned, were Korff's, taken in
conjunction with a number of love poems that Pushkin wrote while at
school, he could perhaps dismiss Korff as a witness once again.[21]
These early love poems, however, were not written in the abstract but
to specific women. 'To a young widow' (including the words 'Is it for
ever that you are going to shed tears? For ever call your dead husband
back from the grave?') refers to the Engelhardts' guest; 'To Natasha'
to one of Princess V. M. Volkonskaya's maids; and 'To an actress' to
one of the domestic serfs performing in the private theatre of Count
V. V. Tolstoy in Tsarskoe Selo.[22]

There is no reason to doubt that, on one occasion, in the corridor
connecting the school with the palace, Pushkin mistook Princess
Volkonskaya, who was of a certain age and not good-looking, for
Natasha. His attempt to embrace her was reported to the tsar.
Though privately amused by the episode, he gave Pushkin a stern
warning, via Engelhardt, never to repeat his escapade. There is,
moreover, a foretaste of Pushkin's later powers of ironic self-

observation in his account of a meeting with 'Dear B' – Ekaterina Bakunina, a maid of honour four years older than himself. After a few lines of verse beginning 'And so I was happy, and so I was delighted', Pushkin adds in his notes some prose reflections, quotes two lines by Zhukovsky ('He sang of love but his voice was sad. Alas! he knew only the torture of love') and concludes with the words: 'How sweet she was! How well her black dress suited dear Bakunina! . . . I was happy for five minutes.'[23]

During their last year at Tsarskoe Selo Pushkin and his schoolmates did little work. They were not only free to visit the homes of families in Tsarskoe Selo; they were also able to attend parties given by officers of the hussar regiment stationed there, at which alcohol is unlikely to have been the only attraction for a sensual boy like Pushkin. For sensual he was, from an early age. His voracious reading (before he even went to school) of French books, especially French translations of poets like Propertius, Tibullus and Catullus, is more likely to have prepared him to become a sexually precocious adolescent than the genes of his Gannibal great-grandfather. What has been described in the Introduction as the Leporello approach to Pushkin is of doubtful value even in relation to his adult life, but it cannot be applied to his six years as Tsarskoe Selo. What the evidence of these years does suggest is that Pushkin was easily attracted by women; when this happened, he quickly showed it; he did not waste much time in discrimination; and age was not of great importance. There is even a story – not proven – that he was in love with Ekaterina Karamzina. (Wife of the historian and Vyazemsky's sister, Ekaterina was born in 1780.) To this extent, Pushkin as a boy gave some indication of what he would be like as a man.

The hussar officers, who formed part of the household cavalry, made such an impression on Pushkin that he became eager to join a cavalry regiment after leaving school. On grounds of expense, his father refused and suggested that instead his son should join a guards infantry regiment, thus following in his father's and his uncle's footsteps. Neither suggestion was pursued. For once, Sergei L'vovich's objection was probably right. The officers whom Pushkin met at Tsarskoe Selo, however, were not all typical representatives of nineteenth-century cavalry regiments (of whatever nationality), about whom it used to be said that in battle they lent elegance to what would otherwise be an unseemly brawl. In particular, they included one man, exactly five years older than Pushkin, Petr Chaadaev, with whom he corresponded over the next twenty years. A writer and philosopher, Chaadaev developed ideas such that in 1836 he was officially declared to be insane. (He died, twenty years later, in full possession of his senses.) In that year, three months before his own death, Pushkin wrote Chaadaev a letter setting out his own views on Russia and Russian history for the last time.

Pushkin and Chaadaev first met at the Karamzins' house in the summer of 1816. By that time he had also already been welcomed by one of the two liberal literary societies of St. Petersburg at this period, *Arzamas*, although he did not become a member of it formally until after he left school. The reason for this welcome for a boy only just eighteen years old was not only the fact that Pushkin had, as a child, already met members of *Arzamas*, such as Vyazemsky and Zhukovsky. From 1814 onwards his poems began to be published. The very first – 'To a Poet-Friend' – appeared in the newspaper *Vestnik Evropy* (the *European Herald*) on 4 July 1814, under an anagram, the last letter of which was 'P'.[24] Six months later, on the occasion of a public examination at Tsarskoe Selo attended by the Minister of Education among others, there occurred an event that is famous in Russian literary history. For an account of what happened on 8 January 1815, we are fortunately not obliged to rely on the bombastic record of Pushkin's declaration made long afterwards by the prolific Russian painter, Ilya Repin (*Pushkin v litseiskom akte*), but principally on Pushkin's own recollection. At this ceremony Pushkin recited his poem 'Memories of Tsarskoe Selo' in the presence not only of the minister, but also of the septuagenarian poet, Gavriil Derzhavin. Derzhavin, until that point barely awake, was moved to tears. After finishing his recitation of his poem, written in the high flown French heroic style, Pushkin fled from the room and hid. For reasons of which we cannot be certain, he refused to return. Afterwards Derzhavin is said to have remarked, in reply to the minister's suggestion that the boy should be taught to write prose, that he should be left as a poet. He himself later spoke of Pushkin as 'the second Derzhavin'.[25]

The number of poems Pushkin wrote while at school totalled one hundred and thirty-six, all but four of them in Russian. Fifty-six were published during his lifetime. Thus, although his first major poem, on which he began preliminary work while still at school, did not appear until 1820, the early establishment of his reputation was virtually assured in advance. Or, as Pushkin himself later put it in one of the stanzas of *Evgenii Onegin*:

> В те дни когда в садах Лицея
> Я безмятежно расцветал.
> Читал охотно Апулея,
> А Цицерона не читал,
> В те дни в таинственных долинах,
> Весной, при кликах лебединых,
> Близ вод, сиявших в тишине,
> Являться муза стала мне.
> Моя студенческая келья
> Вдруг озарилась . . .

In those days, when in the gardens of the Lycée I quietly blossomed, I eagerly read Apuleius, but I did not read Cicero, in those days in the secret valleys in spring, to the cries of the swans, near the waters gleaming in the stillness, my muse began to appear to me. My student cell was suddenly lit up . . .[26]

After a public examination held on 9 June 1817, Pushkin and the intake of 1811 left the lycée three months early. Once again the tsar attended the ceremony, as he had in 1811. Pushkin passed out nineteenth, with a school leaving certificate signed by Engelhardt, which turned out rather better than one might have expected from Pushkin's performance during the previous six years: excellent in Russian and French literature and also in fencing, very good in Latin literature, political economy and financial law and good in other subjects. For his part, Pushkin wrote a charming farewell note in Engelhardt's album.[27] The result entitled Pushkin to enter the ministry of foreign affairs with the rank of collegiate secretary in the Petrine Table of Ranks, which was equivalent to that of a subaltern: a grade carrying an annual salary of seven hundred roubles.

There are no extant portraits of Pushkin at the age of eighteen. He described himself in one of his poems as 'the ugly descendant of negroes brought up in savage simplicity'.[28] Pushkin's use of hyperbole here was deliberate; but although he was not handsome, he had the makings of a *beau laid*. Less than five foot six inches in height (perhaps as short as five foot three), he was a muscular, agile young man, with blue eyes, dark, curly hair, full lips and gleaming white teeth. Two other aspects of his physical appearance that struck most people in later life – his large sideburns and his long, claw-like, carefully cultivated fingernails – were not yet in evidence.

In his farewell poem, 'To my Comrades', written on leaving Tsarskoe Selo, Pushkin contrasts with their embarkation on active careers in the service of the state, whether military or civilian, his own character in the words: 'obedient to fate in everything, the loyal son of happy idleness, carefree at heart and indifferent'.[29] In this spirit he prepared to plunge into the life of St. Petersburg. The reason that he did not do so at once was that his post in the ministry of foreign affairs was a nominal one; and the first thing that he did after being sworn in on 15 June was to ask for leave until the middle of September. His request granted, he set out for his parents' estate at Mikhailovskoe.

CHAPTER FOUR

St. Petersburg, 1817–1820

Pétri de vanité il avait encore plus de cette espèce d'orgueil qui fait avouer avec la même indifférence les bonnes comme les mauvaises actions, suite d'un sentiment de supériorité, peut-être imaginaire.

(Filled with vanity, he had even more of that kind of pride which makes a man admit good actions with the same indifference as bad, the consequence of a perhaps imaginary feeling of superiority.)

—The epigraph to *Evgenii Onegin*

Mikhailovskoe, Pushkin's mother's property in Pskov province, where he later spent two years in exile and where he wrote some of his finest verse, was a modest estate. It lay in the middle of a varied landscape, far removed from the conventional idea of the monotonous Russian plain – a range of low hills, meadows, woods, rivers and lakes. Its small manor house, wholly destroyed in the Second World War, was afterwards painstakingly restored. Of Mikhailovskoe, Pushkin wrote:

> Я твой: люблю сей темный сад
> С его прохладой и цветами,
> Сей луг, уставленный душистыми скирдами,
> Где светлые ручьи в кустарниках шумят.
> Везде передо мной подвижные картины:
> Здесь вижу двух озер лазурные равнины,
> Где парус рыбаря белеет иногда,
> За ними ряд холмов и нивы полосаты,
> Вдали рассыпанные хаты,
> На влажных берегах бродящие стада,
> Овины дымные и мельницы крилаты;
> Везде следы довольства и труда.

I am yours: I love this shady garden with its coolness and its flowers, this meadow, covered with fragrant stacks, where clear streams murmur in the bushes. Everywhere before me there are swift-moving pictures: here I see the azure surfaces of two lakes, where sometimes the sail of a fisherman gleams white, behind them there is a row of hills and striped cornfields, in the distance peasants' huts are scattered, on the wet shores there are wandering herds, smoky barns and windmills; everywhere there are signs of contentment and of labour.[1]

Pushkin wrote several poems about Mikhailovskoe in the course of his life. Much as he loved the house and the surrounding countryside, on this first visit it was, as he later recorded, not long before his love of 'noise and the crowd' drew him back to St. Petersburg, in the last week of August 1817.[2]

In the sparkling opening chapter of *Evgenii Onegin* Pushkin's hero is depicted as converting morning into midnight, sleeping peacefully until after midday. When he awakes, he is brought three invitations for the forthcoming evening. He dresses in morning clothes, goes out for a walk, takes a sleigh to Talon's (a fashionable French restaurateur). He has hardly sat down to a sumptuous meal when he learns that a new ballet has begun and he rushes off to the theatre (the centre of social life at the time), where he arrives late. After an entrancing description of Istomina's steps (she was the leading ballerina of the period, over whom a four-cornered duel was fought, in which Alexander Griboedov, the diplomat and author of *Gore ot uma* (*Woe from Wit*), was wounded), Pushkin reverts to his hero's boredom. Onegin leaves the theatre and goes home to dress – a ritual taking up at least three hours – for a ball. By the time the ball is over, he is half asleep. In this fashion his life continues and 'tomorrow is the same as yesterday'.[3]

These opening stanzas are based on Pushkin's recent memory of the life that he had led during his first phase in St. Petersburg, from 1817 to 1820, with some embroidery and some over-simplification. Nevertheless, the similarities between Onegin – intelligent, restless, idle, bored – and Pushkin aged eighteen to twenty-one are greater than their differences. An obvious difference lies in the fact that, whereas Onegin's way of life described in the poem was not that of a poor man even before he inherited a fortune,[4] Alexander Sergeevich lived on seven hundred roubles a year in a room on the top floor of his parents' house in the unfashionable Kolomna district of the capital, whither Sergei L'vovich and Nadezhda Osipovna had by then moved from Moscow. On the other hand, the fictional Onegin and the real Pushkin had one important characteristic in common at that age: each was on the way to what looked like a dead end. What saved Pushkin was the fact that, in the midst of a frenetic pursuit of the pleasures of life in the Russian capital, he somehow found time to continue to write poems. Their style was still mainly derivative, strongly influenced by French poetry of the eighteenth century, although there were occasional gleams of what was to come – for example, his imaginative poem 'The Water Nymph'[5] (the nymph lures a hermit to his death in the river from which she suddenly arises one morning, combing her hair).

Another important difference between Pushkin and Onegin as young men about town was that, formally speaking, Pushkin was a servant of the Russian state, even though he seldom set foot in the foreign ministry. (Had he done so, he would have found that even the undemanding office hours of that epoch 'rather cut into his day'.[6]) Instead – with the exception of the time that he spent writing – the primary object of these three years of Pushkin's early life was dissipation (rather like Byron's during his time at Cambridge, at about the same age). These were by no means the only dissipated years of Pushkin's life, but they may have been the ones that he had in mind when he wrote in one of his later poems – the 'Elegy' already mentioned in the Introduction – of the 'extinguished gaiety of crazy years' weighing upon him 'like a confused hangover'.[7]

That Pushkin's early life in St. Petersburg did not affect him as much as it might have done is attributable not only to the fact that he still went on writing, but also to his iron constitution: physically, he was a very strong man. The pleasures that he pursued were conventional for a man of his class and his time – wine, women and cards. Taking these three pursuits in reverse order, it was his passion for gambling that never left him. Already during these St. Petersburg years, Pushkin staked and lost a thousand roubles at a sitting: a debt which he was obliged to settle with the manuscript of his own verses, then ready for publication. (This kind of episode would be repeated later in his life, when he had to buy back a whole chapter of *Evgenii Onegin* lost in the same way.) In this respect Pushkin was not alone among nineteenth-century Russian writers. Tolstoy gambled away his family house at Yasnaya Polyana; the building in which he afterwards lived – what a visitor to Yasnaya Polyana sees today – was the lodge, which alone remained. It was, however, well said by a young man whom Pushkin himself taught how to play cards that 'until his death Pushkin was a child at gambling and in the last days of his life he lost even to men from whom everyone but himself used to win'.[8] Pushkin's temperament made him unsuited to play anything more dangerous than a family game of whist, which he sometimes did, but only when he was in the country. His obsession with playing for high stakes, however, right up to the end of his life, seems to have reflected a fundamental aspect of his character.

As for the second pursuit, the early pointers of Tsarskoe Selo were confirmed. It has been suggested that while living in St. Petersburg he fell deeply in love; if so, nobody knows with whom.[9] There is no evidence that when he first met Anna Kern at the house of the Olenins he did more than admire this nineteen-year-old wife of a general more than twice her age, although he did have an affair with her several years later.[10] The lady for whom he does seem to have fallen seriously, though only platonically, if the so-called Don Juan list is to be regarded as accurate,[11] was known as the *princesse nocturne*. This was Princess Evdokiya Golitsyna, who was nearly twenty years older than himself. Separated from her husband, she was noted for her habit of sleeping most of the day, for her classical poses and for the elegance of her salon. Pushkin's sexuality at this stage of his life seems to have been chiefly directed at prostitutes. Indeed, *vivent les grisettes* remained a slogan for him up to the late 1820s: a point made in 1819 with a wit characteristic of Pushkin's juvenilia:

> Ольга, крестница Киприды,
> Ольга, чудо красоты,
> Как же ласки и обиды
> Расточать привыкла ты!
> Поцелуем сладострастья
> Ты, тревожа сердце в нас,
> Соблазнительного счастья
> Назначаешь тайный час.
> мы с горячкою любовной
> Прибегаем в час условный,
> В дверь стучим – но в сотый раз
> Слышим твой коварный шепот,
> И служанки сонный ропот,
> И насмешливый отказ.

Ради резвого разврата,
Приапических затей,
Ради неги, ради злата,
Ради прелести твоей,
Ольга, жрица наслажденья,
Внемли наш влюбленный плач –
Ночь восторгов, ночь забвенья
Нам наверное назначь.

O. Masson

Olga, goddaughter of Cypris, Olga, miracle of beauty, how you have grown accustomed to lavish caresses and insults! Quickening our heart-beats, with a voluptuous kiss, you appoint the secret hour of seductive happiness. Amorously feverish, we run up at the agreed hour, we knock on the door – but for the hundredth time we hear your cunning whisper and the sleepy grumbling of your maid and your mocking refusal.

For the sake of sportive dissipation, of Priapic fun, for the sake of voluptuousness, for gold's sake and for the sake of your charm, Olga, priestess of delight, pay heed to our amorous lament – appoint a genuine night of rapture, a night of oblivion for us.[12]

That Pushkin contracted venereal disease more than once during these first St. Petersburg years is an established fact. Like the young Disraeli twelve years later, he was treated with mercury (rubbed into the skin), about which he wrote flippant letters at the time.[13] Mercury treatment would have caused his scalp hair to fall out and it was common practice to shave the patient's head in such cases. Pushkin certainly did wear a wig after his head had been shaved; and he flaunted it in public, using it as a fan in the theatre on one occasion. His own autobiographical notes also make it clear that he suffered a serious illness early in 1818, which nearly proved fatal. Pushkin comments that the court physician, Dr Leyton, 'would not answer for him' and that his parents were 'in despair'. His illness was a fever described in Pushkin's notes as *gnilaya*. The literal translation of this word is putrid (it has been translated as *une fièvre gangreneuse*). The exact cause of Pushkin's febrile illness remains uncertain. It may have been either typhus or the expression of the secondary stage of syphilis. Irrespective of the cause, what is certain is that in 1818 his constitution pulled him through. In just six weeks he made an excellent recovery.[14]

Alcohol: Pushkin did not depend on this stimulant as much as many artists. True, he drank wine all his life and he liked champagne to be ice-cold, but when he was working long hours at a stretch, often at night, he preferred iced water or lemonade. His early years inevitably included drinking bouts and drinking wagers, however. There is a story that on one such occasion he drank a whole bottle of rum, but although lying full length on the floor by the end, he claimed that he had not passed out because he was still capable of moving the little finger of his left hand – a signal of consciousness. Two societies where wine flowed opened their doors to him in succession. Meetings of the first of these, *Arzamas*, he had already attended while still at school. As soon as he left Tsarskoe Selo he was formally admitted to this society, whose members included his uncle, Vasilii L'vovich, Zhukovsky and Vyazemsky. Every member was given a nickname. Pushkin's was *Sverchok*, 'the Cricket': an insect some of whose characteristics – noisiness, fierceness, restlessness and nocturnal activity – accurately summarize Pushkin's way of life at this time. This name did not stick, partly because *Arzamas* had already fulfilled its literary purpose by the time Pushkin left school; it lasted only three years and it was dissolved in 1818.

Whatever the antics of *Arzamas'* meetings – members had to wear red caps – men did not join it just for dilettante motives. At the time it was formed, there was a literary dispute of real significance for the future of Russian writing. On the one hand stood the followers of the 'Slavonic' movement of Admiral Shishkov, whose 'Society of Lovers of the Russian Word' sought to oppose all importation of words from the west and instead to maintain old Church Slavonic as the foundation of the Russian written word – in effect, the literary forms handed down from the Middle Ages. Ranged against Shishkov and his society were the members of *Arzamas*, whose purpose was to support the literary changes already begun by the historian Karamzin and to foster the ideas of modern writers: the party of the new wave, bent on exploring 'new roads in life as well as in literature'.[15]

Red caps were also part of the uniform of the *Green Lamp*, which was founded one year after *Arzamas* was dissolved. Both Pushkin and Delvig became members, but Küchelbecker did not, on the grounds that it was too frivolous. (Actresses and ballet dancers were among those who attended its evening parties.) Some members of the *Green*

Lamp also belonged to the Union of Welfare, the precursor of the Decembrist movement. Their political overtones, such as they were, did not amount to a great deal, however.

Pushkin himself was never regarded by the future Decembrist conspirators as sufficiently reliable to be invited to join them, either during his three St. Petersburg years or in the 1820s.[16] Nevertheless, what he did contribute was a number of poems which became in effect the rallying cries of the future rebels of 1825. As Alexander I himself remarked, without exaggeration, by 1820 all the younger generation knew these poems by heart.[17] Politically speaking, the three most important of these poems were *The Country*, whose idyllic opening stanzas have already been quoted, the 'Ode to Freedom' and 'Noel'.[18] The latter part of the first of these poems is an indictment of serfdom. The 'Ode to Freedom' is, as its title suggests, a ringing tirade against autocratic rule, including the unenigmatic words 'Tyrants of the world! Tremble! ... Arise, fallen slaves!' 'Noel' begins with the ironical words, 'Hurrah, into Russia gallops [the tsar]'. And, for good measure, Pushkin aimed epigrams both against Arakcheev and – albeit later on – at Alexander's personal courage at Austerlitz.[19]

It was the fact that some of Pushkin's unpublished verses (circulated in manuscript) reached the disapproving eyes and ears of the tsar that brought his three years of dissipation to an abrupt conclusion. By April 1820 the political clouds over Pushkin's head were thickening. The governor-general of St. Petersburg, General Mikhail Miloradovich, failed to obtain copies of the 'Ode to Freedom'; a government detective is said to have tried to bribe Pushkin's manservant, Nikita Kozlov, in the poet's absence to hand over the manuscript for fifty roubles, but met with a refusal. Pushkin then burned many of his papers – not for the last time in his life, as later events proved. He was summoned to see Miloradovich; and although he conducted himself in his interview with the governor-general with such skill that Miloradovich himself was inclined to recommend a complete pardon, the tsar disagreed. In the end, instead of exile to Siberia, Alexander I was prevailed upon by Pushkin's friends to approve his appointment to the staff of Lieutenant-General Ivan Inzov, whose headquarters at that time were at Ekaterinoslav (today Dnepropetrovsk), although shortly afterwards Inzov moved to Kishinev, in Bessarabia.

Before leaving for the south on 6 May 1820, Pushkin had enjoyed one immense satisfaction. On 26 March Zhukovsky gave him his own portrait as a present inscribed with the words: 'To the victorious pupil from the defeated teacher on that triumphant day on which he completed his poem, *Ruslan and Lyudmila*, 26 March 1820, Good Friday.'[20] This poem was a long epic fairy-tale, still indebted to French models, on which he had already been working at Tsarskoe Selo. Pushkin was not yet twenty-one years old. About five years later he added a short prologue, in verse, which has become far more famous than the poem itself. It almost certainly reflects a story told to Pushkin by Arina Rodionovna at Mikhailovskoe, where he wrote it.

> У лукоморья дуб зелёный;
> Златая цепь на дубе том:
> И днём ночью кот учёны
> Всё ходт по цепи кругом;
> Идёт направо – песнь заводит,
> Налево – сказку говорит.
>
> Там чудеса: там леший бродит,
> Русалка на ветвях сидит;
> Там на неведомых дорожках
> Следы невиданных зверей;
> Избушка там на курьих ножках
> Стоит без окон, без дверей;
> Там лес и дол видений полны;
> Там о заре прихлынут волны
> На брег песчаный и пустой,
> И тридцать витязей прекрасных
> Чредой из вод выходят ясных,
> И с ними дядька их морской;
> Там королевич мимоходом
> Пленяет грозного царя;
> Там в облаках перед народом
> Через леса, через моря
> Колдун несёт богатыря;
> В темнице там царевна тужит,
> А бурый волк ей верно стужит;
> Там ступа с Бабою Ягой
> Идёт, бредёт сама собой;
> Там царь Кащей над златом чахнет;
> Там русский дух ... там Русью пахнет!
> И там я был, и мед я пил;

У моря видел дуб зелёный;
Под ним сидел, и кот учёный
Свои мне сказки говорил.
Одну я иомню: сказку зту
Поведаю теперь я свету ...

Prologue to Ruslan and Lyudmila

In a cove there stands a green oak tree; there is a golden chain on that oak; and all the time, day and night, a learned cat walks round and round on the chain; it goes to the right – then it strikes up a song, to the left – then it tells a tale.

There are wonderful things there: there a wood goblin wanders, a mermaid sits in the branches; there on the mysterious paths there are the tracks of unseen beasts; a little hut stands there on hen's legs without windows, without doors; there wood and valley are full of visions; there at dawn the waves surge over the sandy and deserted shore, and thirty fine knights come one by one out of the clear waters, and with them their sea-tutor; there, on his way, a king's son takes a terrible king prisoner; there a magician bears a knight up in the clouds through woods and through seas, in sight of the people; there in a dungeon a princess grieves; there, a mortar with Baba Yaga strolls by itself; there King Kashchey withers away over his gold; there is a Russian scent there ... it smells of Rus'! And there I was, and I drank mead; by the sea I saw the green oak tree; I sat beneath it, and the learned cat told me its tales. One of these I remember: this is the tale that I will now tell the world ...[21]

Pushkin, who had left Moscow as a boy with a hundred roubles as travel money, was given a thousand as travel money by the government when he left St. Petersburg nine years later. This enforced transfer from the capital, however, may be seen as the first blow dealt against Pushkin in his long battle with the imperial establishment, which was to continue for much of the remaining seventeen years of his life. (Pushkin's years in southern Russia are generally referred to as his southern exile, although – strictly speaking – his exile did not begin until 1824, when he was dismissed from the imperial service and banished to Mikhailovskoe.) At the same time this transfer may also be considered as a further stroke of luck for the poet. Not only was Inzov in many ways an ideal man for Pushkin to work for, but it is open to question how far and how fast he would have been able to progress with his writing and – equally important – his reading, had he stayed on in St. Petersburg, living more or less the same kind of life as he had from 1817 to 1820. As it was, what he wrote during the next six years ensured that by the time when he returned from exile to Moscow in September 1826, he had become the most famous poet in Russia and that – at least temporarily – he was lionized both in Moscow and in St. Petersburg.

This question is not the only one that hangs over the story of Pushkin's first years in St. Petersburg. His pride in his own ancestry and his contempt for the newly-created, *nouveau riche*, aristocracy masked the fact that, whatever may have been the date on which the very first Pushkin arrived in Russia, by the second decade of the nineteenth century his was a family only of the middle nobility, in visibly straitened circumstances. Pushkin's parents lived in, if anything, an even more chaotic style of gentility in St. Petersburg than they had previously done in Moscow. For a man of Pushkin's character this was sooner or later bound to present a problem. His sensitivity is also reflected in the numerous duelling challenges which he issued during these three years in St. Petersburg, although all of them either did not end seriously or were patched up in good time by seconds. In St. Petersburg he found the doors of the small literary group within the nobility flung wide open for him. But the doors of the other members of the *haut monde* were not. Towards this problem Pushkin's attitude seems to have been ambivalent.[22] He was hurt and repelled and yet at the same time somehow also challenged and attracted by this upper crust of the Russian Empire, much of it composed precisely of the 'new' aristocracy which he himself later ridiculed in his ironical poem, *My Genealogy*. Although this poem was written with the specific purpose of countering aspersions cast on Pushkin's black great-grandfather by a hack literary critic, it shows how sensitive he remained, even at the age of thirty-one, not just about his Gannibal ancestry but also about his general position in Russian society. Its opening lines are:

> Смеясь жестоко над собратом,
> Писаки русские толпой
> Меня зовут аристократом.
> Смотри, пожалуй, вздор какой!
> Не офицер я, не асессор,
> Я по кресту не дворянин,
> Не академик, не профессор;
> Я просто русский мещанин.

Понятна мне времен превратность,
Не прекословлю, право, ей:
У нас нова рожденьем знатность,
И чем новее, тем знатней.
Родов дряхлеющих обломок
(И по несчастью, не один),
Бояр старинных я потомок;
Я, братцы, мелкий мещанин.

My Genealogy

A crowd of Russian scribblers, laughing cruelly at a fellow-writer, call me an aristocrat. Look, please, what rubbish! Neither an officer nor an assessor [a civil service rank], I am not a nobleman by virtue of a decoration, nor an academic nor a professor; I am simply a Russian bourgeois.

I understand the vicissitude of the times, I do not indeed contradict it: we have an aristocracy that is new in lineage, and the newer it is, the more aristocratic. A fragment of decaying stock (and, unfortunately, not the only one), I am the scion of ancient boyars; I, my friends, am a petty bourgeois ...[23]

In reality Pushkin never thought of himself as bourgeois by birth, even in his wildest moments. Yet this poem reflects a paradox in his character of which some of his friends became aware. Later on perhaps he too became conscious of this personal weakness, for Pushkin's self-insight grew with the passage of the years. As evidence of this, although the French epigraph to *Evgenii Onegin* nominally refers to the character of Onegin – 'filled with vanity' – it could equally well be applied to Pushkin's own character; and it is significant that the epigraph is not an extract from a letter written by somebody else (as the text maintains), but was drafted and redrafted by Pushkin himself with considerable care.[24]

In Kishinev, situated on the far south-western salient of the Russian Empire, the minutiae of social distinctions did not greatly matter. As soon as Pushkin was transferred to the relatively civilized city of Odessa in 1823, to the staff of Count Mikhail Vorontsov, a very different man from Inzov, they began to take on serious significance for Pushkin's life. When he was once again living in St. Petersburg, in the 1830s, he and his wife became accepted members of the *vysshii svet*. Yet, even after every door was open to him, he never felt fully at home in this world.

CHAPTER FIVE

The South

Овидий, я живу близ тихих берегов,
Которым изгнанных отеческих богов
Ты некогда принес и пепел свой оставил.

(Ovid, I am living near the quiet shores to which you once
brought the exiled gods of your fathers and where you left your
ashes.)

—Pushkin, *To Ovid*[1]

Cum maris Euxini positos ad laeva Tomitas
Quaerere me laesi principis ira iubet.

(When the anger of an offended prince orders me to seek the
people of Tomi, on the left-hand shore of the Euxine [Black]
Sea.)

—Ovid[2]

At the time when Pushkin set out from the capital, three weeks before
his twenty-first birthday, his knowledge of the Russian Empire was
limited to its two principal cities, the village of Tsarskoe Selo and two
country estates: Zakharovo, where he had spent summers only as a
child, and Mikhailovskoe, which he had visited for the first time just
after he left school. In the course of the next four years he got to know a
vast tract of the south, extending from the Caucasus through the
Crimea and the Ukraine to Bessarabia. Kishinev, the town where he
spent most of his time in Bessarabia, is situated not far inland from
classical Tomi, the Scythian town near the mouth of the Danube
where Ovid spent his exile. Pushkin could therefore hardly resist
comparing his own situation to that of the Roman poet banished by the
Emperor Augustus; hence the poem 'To Ovid' which forms part of the
epigraph to this chapter. Pushkin himself was well aware that,
geographical proximity apart, the analogy was inexact. The two poets

did not have much in common and the reason why Augustus sentenced Ovid to end his days in Tomi was quite different from that for which Alexander I had Pushkin appointed to the staff of General Inzov.[3]

Aged fifty-one, Ivan Inzov was a humane and experienced officer. Brought up by Prince Nikita Trubetskoi, he was rumoured to be of (illegitimate) royal descent.[4] He was a freemason at a time when membership of masonic lodges was not yet frowned on by the Russian government. (Pushkin himself became a mason – a member of the 'Ovid' lodge in Kishinev – in 1821.) The reason why Inzov's headquarters was at first located at Ekaterinoslav, on the Dnepr river, was that he was head of what was officially entitled the Committee for the Protection of [Russian] Colonists of the Southern Region of Russia. Having been additionally appointed Viceroy of Bessarabia, he moved his headquarters to Kishinev shortly after Pushkin's arrival in Ekaterinoslav. Towards Pushkin Inzov's attitude became like that of a benevolent uncle. In particular, he gave him little work to do and he allowed him long periods of leave. The first of these, which began almost at once, took Pushkin to the Caucasus.

The origin of this journey was pure chance. Soon after his arrival at Ekaterinoslav, Pushkin (always a keen swimmer and accustomed to cold baths) bathed in the Dnepr and developed a feverish cold afterwards. By a coincidence, while he was sitting in a 'nasty little *izba* ... unshaven, pale and thin', writing poetry and sipping iced lemonade, General Nikolai Raevsky and his family were passing through Ekaterinoslav on their way to take the waters in the Caucasus. The general's younger son, also called Nikolai, was one of the hussar officers whom Pushkin had got to know at Tsarskoe Selo. It was he who brought the doctor accompanying the Raevskys, Evstafii Rudykovsky, to see Pushkin. It is clear from Rudykovsky's own account (published twenty-one years later) that Pushkin was quite ill, although he himself made light of it both at the time and afterwards. There is, however, no evidence for supposing, as has been suggested, that this attack of fever had any connection with the illness that had come close to killing him in St. Petersburg.[5]

General Raevsky invited Pushkin to join his party; and he was well enough to travel south with the Raevskys when they set out from Ekaterinoslav on 28 May. Because of his obstinate refusal to follow Rudykovsky's advice or to take the medicine that he prescribed, he had one relapse, but by the time they reached the spa town of

Goryachevodsk, Pushkin was completely recovered – so much so that he at once played a practical joke on the doctor, who held a senior rank in the army hierarchy. He wrote down Rudykovsky's name in the local commandant's visitors' book as *Leib-medik* (physician in ordinary) and against his own name he put the word 'adolescent'. General Raevsky reproved Pushkin; and, after reading *Ruslan and Lyudmila* Rudykovsky forgave him.[6]

The journey from the Ukraine led to the northern shore of the Sea of Azov and across the steppes to the sub-tropical foothills of the great Caucasian divide: the mountain range running diagonally from north-west to south-east for six hundred miles. In that period, even for well-equipped travellers such as the Raevskys, this journey was never an easy one. Travelling there sixteen years later the British ambassadress wrote that after eight hours in a *telega* her 'face was cut to pieces', she was 'bruised all over' and 'could hardly stand'.[7] The latter part of the journey required a military convoy – in the case of the Raevskys, sixty mounted Cossacks and a field gun. Any traveller willing to put up with these multiple hazards was rewarded on arrival by the sight of one of the most spectacular scenes of natural beauty – perhaps the most spectacular – in the whole of Europe.

As Pushkin put it in a letter to his younger brother Lev, 'the magnificent chain of these mountains, their peaks icy, which look from a distance, in the clear light of dawn, like strange clouds, multi-coloured and motionless' formed the 'sultry frontier of Asia', where the 'ancient daring' of the wild Circassians was 'disappearing', although he added that they could not be relied upon, because they liked ransom money.[8] Had Pushkin been able on this occasion (as he was ten years afterwards) to visit the whole turbulent Caucasian region, including Georgia, he would have described in rather different terms the precariousness of Russian rule over savage peoples who would not be subdued for many more years, and then at the cost of thousand of lives. At this meeting place of three empires – the Russian, the Ottoman and the Persian – the Russians had found natural allies in the ancient Christian people of Georgia. From the time of Peter the Great, who mounted the first major Russian expedition into Transcaucasia, the tide of war had flowed back and forth. In 1795 a Persian army had sacked and occupied Tiflis (today Tbilisi), massacring the population, which already included some Russians at that date. Finally, Georgia was annexed by Russia in

1801; and a Russian governor-general established his headquarters in Tiflis. Yet even as late as the year of Pushkin's death, by which time the Russians had also annexed eastern Armenia, the two main focuses of Muslim resistance to the expansion of Russian power – Circassia to the west of the Caucasus and Daghestan to the east – still remained, quite apart from the running series of Russo-Turkish wars, which would last for another half century. And from this ethnic cauldron would then arise the most extraordinary man ever to rule Russia.[9]

Like other Russian nineteenth-century writers who followed in his footsteps, notably Lermontov and Tolstoy, Pushkin was profoundly impressed by the Caucasus. In his case the effect was reinforced by the fact that it coincided with the first impact of Byron's poetry upon him. This influence would last for roughly the next four years (coincidentally, the final years of Byron's life). *The Captive of the Caucasus*, begun while the Caucasus was fresh in Pushkin's mind and completed early in the following year, was published in September 1822.[10] Received by the public as well as, if not even better than, *Ruslan and Lyudmila*, it soon became a ballet, in which Istomina danced; but its first edition earned Pushkin only five hundred roubles. He himself preferred *Ruslan and Lyudmila* and his feelings about *The Captive* were mixed. To his publisher he wrote in 1822: 'Your observations about its defects are completely right and too generous, but what is done, is done.'[11] Seven years later, however, when he reread *The Captive* while on his visit to Transcaucasia he found all of it 'weak, young, incomplete', but he also regarded much of it as 'imagined and expressed with truth'.[12] Pushkin's later opinion is as good a verdict as any on this poem of seven hundred lines: the story of a Russian who is taken prisoner by Circassians, but escapes thanks to a Circassian girl who falls in love with him. As he escapes by swimming across the river, she commits suicide by throwing herself into it; and after the Russian looks back from the further shore and realizes for the first time that the girl is dead, Pushkin adds three laconic words: 'he understood everything'. Leaving the reader to form his own judgement of what it was that suddenly became clear to his hero, he resisted the temptation to point a moral or adorn a tale. Why, objected Vyazemsky, did the Russian not try to save her? Pushkin's response, in a letter written in 1823, was: 'I have swum in Caucasian rivers ... my captive is a clever, sensible man, he is not in love with the Circassian girl – he was right not to drown himself.'[13]

In Pushkin's personal development during the second half of 1820, what counted for more than writing *The Captive of the Caucasus* was the glimpse that the weeks spent with the Raevsky family gave him of something that he had never been given an opportunity to enjoy before – family life. General Raevsky, then commanding II Corps, with his headquarters at Kiev, was a hero of the 1812 campaign. As well as his younger son, two of his four daughters were travelling with him: Sophia, who was fourteen years old, and Maria, who was thirteen. Maria later married one of the Decembrists, Prince Sergei Volkonsky, whom she joined in his Siberian exile. In her memoirs Princess Volkonskaya described this journey to the Caucasus and how, on the way there, she had paddled on the shore of the Sea of Azov. 'In no doubt that the poet was following us, I amused myself by running towards the waves and fleeing from them when they approached me; they finished by washing my feet . . .'[14] There is no reason to doubt the accuracy of this recollection, but she then goes on to ascribe to this particular occasion Pushkin's lines, 'How I longed then to touch the dear feet with my lips, together with the waves!' What these memoirs fail to mention is that these two celebrated lines form part of the so-called pedal digression of *Evgenii Onegin.*[15] The identity of the girl whose feet Pushkin admired so much – if indeed there was just one such girl at all – has provided Pushkinists with a fascinating field of speculation, complicated by the fact that in 1820 it was in reality not Maria, but the eldest Raevsky daughter, Ekaterina, who struck Pushkin most forcibly.[16]

Pushkin was to meet Maria six years later, on a melancholy evening – her last in Moscow. All this, however, has little bearing on his twenty-second year. In the summer months of 1820 his horizon was simultaneously extended by the breath-taking beauty of the Caucasus, the initial impact of Byron and the company of the Raevsky family as a whole. Of the Raevskys Pushkin wrote immediately afterwards:

I have spent the happiest minutes of my life in the midst of the family of the admirable Raevsky. In him I have loved a man with a clear mind, a fine spirit, a generous and protective friend, in every way a dear, affectionate host. A witness of the age of Catherine, a monument of the year 1812, a man without prejudices, with a strong character and sensitive, he attracts without seeking to do so everyone to himself, provided that they are worthy to understand and value his high qualities. His elder son will perhaps be more famous. All his daughters – charming; the eldest – an unusual woman. Judge how happy I was.[17]

Pushkin met all the other members of the Raevsky family on the southern shore of the Crimea, after a naval brig had brought him and the general's party to the Tartar village of Gurzuf on 19 August. There they spent three weeks in a rented house near the village. During this time Pushkin and Nikolai Raevsky visited Bakhchisaray (due east of Sebastopol), where a ruined Tartar palace inspired another Byronic poem, *The Fountain of Bakhchisaray*, the story of a khan who falls in love with a Polish girl captured by the Tartars, with disastrous consequences for her, for the khan's Georgian mistress and ultimately for himself.

Pushkin wrote *The Fountain* in 1822 at Kishinev, but he did not publish it until two years later, with a preface written by Vyazemsky.[18] This was the first of Pushkin's poems to earn him an appreciable sum of money – 3000 roubles. *The Fountain* and *The Captive* were for a time his most popular works. In the year in which *The Fountain* was published, however, he himself described it to Vyazemsky as 'trash' apart from its epigraph, which was a quotation from a medieval Persian poet.[19] By the time Vyazemsky wrote his preface to this Byronic poem,[20] the battle lines between the romantic and classical schools had been drawn up in Russia; and the preface took the form of a romantic manifesto. At any rate at this early period of Russian nineteenth-century literature, the issue at stake was still mainly a contest between two generations, centring on the question of how the Russian language itself should be developed and how it should be used in literature from then on. As an innovative writer of the new generation, Pushkin inevitably lent his name to the romantic school. Yet his considered attitude towards the romantic versus classical argument was fundamentally agnostic. In an unpublished article, drafted in 1828, he wrote:

Following the heated arguments about Romanticism, I imagined that we had indeed tired of the decorum and perfection of classical antiquity and the pale, monotonous copies of its imitators . . . I frankly admit that I . . . see nothing shameful . . . in following the spirit of the age. This first admission leads me to a second, more important one: so be it, I confess that in literature I am a sceptic (to say no worse) and that to me all its sects are equal, each exhibiting both good and bad sides.[21]

By that time Pushkin had become entirely his own man. In so far as he was then under anybody's literary influence, the most significant impact on his poetry was that of Shakespeare.

Pushkin finally reached Kishinev on 21 September 1820. As in St. Petersburg, his official duties there were slight; he translated into Russian the French texts of Moldavian legislation. For much of his time in Kishinev he stayed in General Inzov's house. For Pushkin, Inzov became 'Inzushka'. Pushkin was largely free to do as he pleased. Only when his passionate and excitable temperament took him too far even for Inzov's kindly indulgence, did the general resort to his ultimate sanction: house arrest, which simply meant confining Pushkin to his room – on one occasion for three weeks – by ordering him to be deprived of his boots. Once again, as had happened five months earlier, Inzov gave Pushkin frequent leave of absence: in the first instance to visit the Ukraine, where Lieutenant-General Lev Davydov had his estate at Kamenka (General Raevsky's mother had married Davydov, a future Decembrist, as her second husband). Although his original leave was intended to last only a fortnight, with Inzov's permission he did not return to Kishinev until March 1821, having also visited Kiev, where Ekaterina Raevskaya had become engaged to the commander of 16 Division, Major-General Mikhail Orlov (a former member of *Arzamas* and a member of the Union of Welfare), and Tul'chin, a small town at which the headquarters of Second Army was located. First in the Ukraine and subsequently at Kishinev, Pushkin came into close contact with future Decembrists and men on the fringes of the movement that succeeded the Union of Welfare, whose dissolution was decided in January 1821. Of these men, the one who impressed Pushkin most – 'one of the most original minds that I know' – was the formidably intelligent colonel Pavel Pestel, who became the head of the secret Decembrist society of the south, and was one of the five conspirators hanged in 1826.[22] Once again, as in St. Petersburg, Pushkin was not admitted to the inner circle of conspirators.

Asked by Capodistria, who took the trouble to write from Laibach (today Ljubljana), where he was attending an international conference, for a report on Pushkin in April 1821, Inzov replied that he was certain that 'the years and time will teach him reason', and that meanwhile Pushkin was behaving well and that he was 'taking no part whatever in the present troubled circumstances'.[23] Like the

Caucasus and the Crimea, Bessarabia was a recent Russian conquest. Having changed hands between the Ottoman and Russian empires five times during the hundred-year period ending in 1812, it was then annexed by Russia. The imperial administration was still carried on by the viceroy through a council of indigenous *boyars*. Inzov's instructions, received from Capodistria, were to reorganize Bessarabia on the basis of 'the conservation of the laws and the customs, of the languages and the privileges of the country'.[24] The population of the province was a cocktail of almost every Balkan race, including gypsies; Russians were comparatively few; there were many Greeks; and the largest ethnic ingredient was Moldavian. Thus the atmosphere of Kishinev was – to a Russian – that of a frontier town: exotic like the Caucasus, but without the extra Caucasian dimension of physical danger.

At Kishinev Pushkin witnessed at close quarters two dramatic political events: one national and one international. General Orlov's 16 Division was distrusted by the authorities in St. Petersburg, who were aware of the liberal opinions held by its commander and by several of his officers.[25] When the storm broke over the division, whose headquarters was in Kishinev, Orlov was conveniently on leave. (His powerful family connections in the capital preserved him on this occasion and even four years later he suffered nothing worse than a temporary exile to the Caucasus.) The principal scapegoat of the police was a twenty-seven-year-old major of artillery, Vladimir Raevsky (no relation of General Raevsky), who had fought at the Battle of Borodino at the age of seventeen. Wounded and decorated, he was now serving on the staff of 16 Division. On the morning of 6 February 1822 Raevsky was arrested. For the next five and a half years he was taken from one prison to another, tried and retried (including a trial presided over by the Grand Duke Konstantin) until finally, in October 1827, just at the moment when it looked as though he might be permitted to live as a free man in his native province of Kursk, Nicholas I personally directed that he should be exiled to Siberia 'as a man harmful to society'. He died there in 1872.[26]

Raevsky has gone down to history as 'the first Decembrist'. Strictly speaking, he could not be a Decembrist at this early date. A mason and a member of the Union of Welfare, however, he would certainly have become a Decembrist had he not been in prison at the time of the 1825 revolt. An outspoken man of remarkable strength of character (and a poet, among other things), he had made no secret of his liberal views in Kishinev. Like many other young officers of his generation, he disapproved of flogging soldiers and believed in teaching them instead. He and Pushkin were personal friends – so much so that, after overhearing a conversation about Raevsky in Inzov's house on 5 February, Pushkin was able to forewarn him, thus giving him time to burn his papers.

Raevsky's fate illustrates with an especial vividness the prodigal waste of talent which was one of the results of the rigidity of the Russian regime during this period: an age in which Russia needed the services of all the talented young Russians that it could possibly enlist. So far as Pushkin was concerned, this was the first time that he was brought up against the decision that sooner or later he would have to make: how far could he work within such a system himself? (It also served as a warning of the importance of burning incriminating papers.) Historically, one of the immediate consequences of the episode of 16 Division was the banning of membership of masonic lodges by the Russian government in August 1822. The episode may also have contributed indirectly to the manner in which the Decembrist Revolt was carried out nearly four years later, in that it highlighted the need for secrecy, which in turn contributed to the fact that the revolt was unco-ordinated between the secret societies of north and south. Indeed, it was unplanned until five minutes to midnight, with disastrous results.

The second event in Kishinev, which occurred in the previous year, reached far beyond the frontiers of Russia: the initial flame of the Balkan conflagration, which was at first snuffed out dismally, but led to the independence of Greece by the end of the decade. Early in 1820 an emissary of *Philiki Etairia* arrived in St. Petersburg with the object of persuading Capodistria to accept the leadership of the *Etairia*, the secret Greek organization first founded in 1812 by Greeks resident in Odessa. After he had refused, the same invitation was extended to Prince Alexander Ypsilantis (Aleksandr Ipsilanti). Aged twenty-seven, the son of a former *hospodar* of Vallachia, and an aide-de-camp to Alexander I, Ypsilantis was a brave soldier, but he soon showed that he had no ability whatever as a commander. Appointed leader of the *Etairia* on 12 April 1820,[27] by the autumn of that year he had travelled from St. Petersburg to Kishinev, where his family estate was situated.

Exactly how far the Russian government was involved in the planning of the Greek insurrection at this stage is a matter of debate, but there is no doubt that men like Inzov and the governor-general of Odessa, Count Langeron, did rather more than turn a blind eye to the preparations for revolt against Ottoman rule that were being made under their noses. The original Greek plan had been to launch their revolution in the Peloponnese in December 1820. Believing that a simultaneous rising of Romanian and Serbian nationalists made the Principalities west of the River Prut (Moldavia and Vallachia roughly, modern Romania) a more promising focus of revolt for his own movement, Ypsilantis crossed the river frontier – bribing the Cossack guards – on 21 February 1821. From Jassy he issued stirring proclamations, first to the Moldavians and Vallachians and then to the Greeks. A series of humiliating defeats followed. The Principalities were soon re-occupied by Turkish forces. By the end of June Ypsilantis had fled into Austrian territory, where he was interned. Released from captivity in Bohemia only towards the end of his life, he died in Austria six years afterwards.

In his proclamations Ypsilantis had declared that the insurgents would 'see a mighty Power defend their rights'; and he wrote to Alexander I offering his resignation from the imperial service and at the same time seeking his support. Not only was no Russian support forthcoming, but the tsar's reply (drafted by Capodistria) described the revolt against Ottoman rule as the 'disgraceful and culpable action of a secret society' and dismissed Ypsilantis from his service.[28] Pushkin had met Ypsilantis in Kishinev and he studied his proclamations. The fiasco of the brief occupation of the Principalities and the appalling atrocities (notably, the Turkish massacre of the population of Chios) in the campaign that followed in Greece and in the Aegean, filled him with contempt for the Greeks as people, as opposed to Greece in the abstract. 'We imagined', he wrote to Vyazemsky shortly before leaving southern Russia, that 'a nasty people, consisting of bandits and shopkeepers, were by birth the legitimate descendants and heirs of their fame in school textbooks.' Pushkin added that Vyazemsky would reply that he had changed his mind.[29] Indeed he had. Pushkin's papers make it clear that in his first flush of enthusiasm for the Greek cause his attitude towards Ypsilantis had been one of boundless enthusiasm.[30] Neither view was well founded. Both his initial enthusiasm and his subsequent contempt provide an example of the shallowness of Pushkin's understanding of some aspects of nineteenth-century international relations. This is hardly surprising, given that he was never allowed to travel abroad, although it forms an odd contrast with the quality of his historical knowledge, which was of a different order.

Ypsilantis' disaster may well have had an indirect effect on Pushkin's personal fate, although this cannot be proved. What is certain is that one of the direct consequences of this initial Greek failure was Capodistria's departure from St. Petersburg in August 1822, on extended leave abroad (by a coincidence, within a few days of the suicide of the British Foreign Secretary, Castlereagh). This left Nesselrode, never a supporter of Pushkin, in sole command of the Russian Foreign Ministry for the next thirty-two years. In the words of Metternich, who detested Capodistria, the 'reign of Capodistria' was over.[31] So far as Pushkin was concerned, Capodistria's departure left no one at senior level in the foreign ministry who might put in a good word for him. In the circumstances in which he would find himself two years later, and again in St. Petersburg at the end of his life, this was unfortunate.

Pushkin's mood in Kishinev was so variable that in effect 'he lived a double life'.[32] On the one hand, he continued to play cards, issue challenges to duels, flirt and wench – all within the confines of Kishinev.[33] Since these confines were extremely narrow, he longed for St. Petersburg; and he let everybody know it, including Nesselrode, to whom he unsuccessfully applied for home leave in January 1823.[34] On the other hand, he was able both to read more widely and write far more than he had done during his three hectic years in the capital. For this, the other half of his life, the Bessarabian years formed a period of experimentation and transition. Thus he wrote interesting historical notes (preserved) and autobiographical notes (later destroyed), as well as another politically dangerous poem: 'The Dagger'.[35] This turned out to be his last radical poem. It could not be published in Russia until over half a century after it was written (1821) because of the censorship, although Herzen published it in 1856 in London. It resembles the 'Ode to Freedom' both in substance and in style. He amused himself by trying his hand at two poems, one wittily blasphemous, a satire on the Annunciation,[36] and the other pornographic. Like 'The Dagger', both these were circulated in manuscript. The latter poem ended with the disarming lines: 'Many ... will ask: why do I make this silly joke? What business is it of theirs? I want to.'[37] The former would later land him in political trouble.[38]

The Robber Brothers (telling a story suggested by the escape of two actual bandits, who swam across the River Dnepr chained together) was Pushkin's third, and virtually his last, Byronic poem. True, when he came to write the opening lines of *Evgenii Onegin* on the night of 9 May 1823, he himself believed that it would be something 'in the style of' Byron's *Don Juan*.[39] He soon reversed this opinion, however. By early 1825 he maintained – with justice – that *Don Juan* had nothing in common with *Evgenii Onegin*.[40] And during the eight years that he took to complete *Evgenii Onegin* – by far his longest poem – he left Byron behind. Moreover, before individual chapters of *Evgenii Onegin* began to be published, *The Gypsies*, a poem begun in the south and completed at Mikhailovskoe, had already marked the halfway stage in the development of Pushkin's own poetic style.[41] The significance of the melodramatic story told in this poem – the hero (or anti-hero), Aleko, goes to live with a gypsy tribe, murders his gypsy mistress, Zemphyra, and her lover and is then himself banished by the tribe – has been hotly disputed by Russian critics. For Dostoevsky, who half a century later claimed Pushkin for the slavophile cause, the poem marked the antithesis between the individualist intellectual (Aleko) and the *narod* (represented by the gypsies). This view was subsequently clothed in Marxist ideology by Soviet critics.[42] Ideology apart, *The Gypsies* is notable as Pushkin's first truly polyphonic work[43], in the sense that the storyis carried along by four distinct voices, to one of which, Zemphyra's old father, Pushkin gives the most memorable lines of his poem:

> Меж нами есть одно преданье:
> Царем когда-то сослан был
> Полудня житель к нам в изгнанье.
> (Я прежде знал, но позабыл
> Его мудреное названье.)
> Он был уже летами стар,
> Но млад и жив дуфой незлобной –
> Имел он песен дивный дар
> И голос, шуму вод подобный –

... There is a legend among us: Once upon a time a southerner was sent to us in exile by an emperor. (I used to know his strange name before, but now I have forgotten it.) He was already advanced in years, but young and lively in his mild spirit – he had the wonderful gift of song and a voice like the sound of the waters ...[44]

For Pushkin's biographer, the chief interest of this poem, which was probably based on an actual visit to a gypsy tribe in the Bessarabian countryside, is the fact that it is the first in which Pushkin dealt with the violent theme of jealousy and revenge. These feelings would combine to hit him with catastrophic force in the last year of his own life.

It was thanks to intensive efforts deployed on his behalf by his friends in St. Petersburg that Pushkin was transferred from Inzov's staff in Kishinev, where, towards the end of his stay, he had described himself as 'wallowing in mud',[45] to that of Count Mikhail Vorontsov. In July 1823 Vorontsov had established his headquarters in Odessa, as governor-general of the south and viceroy of Bessarabia. Pushkin arrived in Odessa to join his staff in the first week of August. From a distance, it doubtless looked to Pushkin's friends as though the move would suit him well.[46] Fewer than twelve months afterwards he was dismissed from the imperial service.

In spite of this outcome, Pushkin's months in Odessa were not wasted. Not only did his writing progress. He completed the first chapter of *Evgenii Onegin* on 22 October, the second chapter had been written by the beginning of December and two months later he began the third, including Tatyana's famous letter to Onegin. He also began to collect books for what would in time become a large library; and he started to learn to read English and Italian. It was in Odessa that he came to recognize for the first time in his life that he was capable of becoming a professional writer. He had, he wrote in a draft of a letter in June 1824, already conquered his repugnance for writing and selling verses in order to live – 'the biggest step has been taken'.[47] Moreover, Pushkin liked Odessa. Before his transfer he had already visited the town more than once. Coming from Kishinev, he felt that he had arrived 'in Europe'.[48] Nor did time alter this first impression. The affectionate picture of the bustling, cosmopolitan, liveliness of 'dirty Odessa ... dusty Odessa' later drawn in the unpublished stanzas of *Evgenii Onegin* is avowedly autobiographical.[49] Pushkin's two epithets for Odessa reflected the fact that at that time it still had hardly any paved streets and that it also had no supply of drinking water. Such development as had been undertaken since Odessa was founded in the last decade of the eighteenth century, on the site of what had been a Turkish fishing village, was due largely to the energy of two successive French émigré governors, the first of whom was the Duc de Richelieu. Thanks to them, by the time Pushkin arrived in Odessa a population of little more than thirty thousand enjoyed an opera house, French restaurants and a bookshop. Pushkin took a room in a hotel overlooking the Black Sea.

Vorontsov, aged forty-one at the time of his appointment to the south, would end his long career as a prince and a field marshal. A man of broader horizons than Inzov, he had been brought up in London, where his father had been ambassador and his sister married the Earl of Pembroke, with the result that the British Secretary of State for War at the time of the Crimean War, Sidney Herbert, was half-Russian. Mikhail Vorontsov had distinguished himself in the French campaign; he had the reputation of anglophilia (several members of his personal household were English); and he also had a good library. His thirty-one-year-old wife, Elizaveta (in the Russian form of her name), whom he had married five years earlier, was a Polish aristocrat. By common consent she was one of the most attractive women of her generation – perhaps even a beauty.[50]

It is an open question whether Pushkin and Vorontsov might have got on at least tolerably well if Pushkin had not fallen in love with Countess Vorontsova, who arrived in Odessa early in September 1823. (Nor was he the only man in Odessa to do this; so too did the younger Nikolai Raevsky, whose part in the intrigues that followed is not clear, but was probably unhelpful to Pushkin.) To begin with Vorontsov seems to have received Pushkin well. Even after relations between the two men became strained, Vorontsov continued to invite Pushkin to parties at his house and allow him to use his library. Their characters, however, were 180 degrees apart. This in itself was a source of trouble which Vyazemsky and Turgenev ought to have foreseen. Assuming that they did, they presumably regarded it as a risk worth running as the price of getting Pushkin out of Kishinev. Moreover, perhaps they had in mind not only Pushkin's own dislike of Kishinev, but also rumours (which must surely have reached them) that he was keeping politically dangerous company – not only future Decembrists, but also Caroline Soban'skaya, an attractive woman closely linked with the government's intelligence services?

Vorontsov's temperament was as cold as Pushkin's was hot. From the time of his first appointment to Odessa, and during his many years in the south thereafter, Vorontsov's behaviour developed in a manner comparable with that of senior members of the British Raj later in the century. Unlike Inzov, moreover, Vorontsov expected Pushkin to be prepared to absent himself from Odessa not on leave, but in order to work. When the Kherson district was attacked by a plague of locusts in May 1824, Pushkin regarded it as a personal insult that he was one of those instructed by Vorontsov to travel 180 *versts* (eastwards from Odessa) and report. Having asked to be excused this duty, without success, he did go, but he returned after spending only three days in the affected areas without having done anything.

Tempers on both sides mounted steadily. Two months after his visit to Kherson Pushkin described Vorontsov as a 'vandal' in a letter to Alexander Turgenev.[51] His attitude towards his chief is summed up in an epigram which may be roughly rendered : 'Half milord, half merchant, half sage, half ignoramus, half rogue, but there is the hope that in the end he will go the whole hog.'[52]

On 8 June Pushkin submitted a formal request, addressed to the head of Vorontsov's chancery, Alexander Kaznacheev, that he should be allowed to retire on grounds of health. He described himself as suffering from an aneurism: a phrase that would recur in later correspondence with the St. Petersburg authorities (in fact varicose veins in one leg).[53] It cannot have been altogether a coincidence that on 8 March he had received part of his 3000 roubles for *The Fountain*, enclosed in a letter from Vyazemsky.[54] Kaznacheev advised Pushkin against pursuing his request for retirement.

In the event it was Vorontsov himself who made the break. As early as March 1824 he had begun a series of letters to St. Petersburg preparing the ground for this; and by the beginning of May he was explicitly asking Nesselrode to ensure Pushkin's removal from his staff.[55] He therefore had no difficulty in deciding to forward Pushkin's request to St. Petersburg. Here the police had intercepted a letter written by Pushkin, which was open to the interpretation that he was soft on atheism. This letter, written in light-hearted vein in the spring of 1824, included the remark that as well as writing lines of

Alexander Sergeevich Pushkin in 1822, an engraving by E. I. Geitman.

Abram Petrovich Gannibal, Pushkin's maternal great-grandfather, whose extraordinary career Pushkin described in his unfinished *The Blackamoor of Peter the Great.*

Sergei L'vovich Pushkin, Pushkin's father.

Nadezhda Osipovna Pushkina, Pushkin's mother, known as the 'beautiful creole'.

Tsar Alexander I,
by George Dawe.

Alexander Turgenev, whom Nicholas I
authorized to accompany Pushkin's
body from St. Petersburg to its burial
place near Mikhailovskoe in 1837.

The Imperial Lycée, Tsarskoe Selo, where Pushkin studied between
the ages of twelve and eighteen.

Petr Vyazemsky, one of Pushkin's
closest friends.

Vasilii Zhukovsky, one of the first to
admire Pushkin's poetic talent and
one of his few friends at court –
a drawing presented by him to
Pushkin in 1820.

Anton Delvig, drawn by Pushkin,
who wrote after Delvig's premature
death in 1831: 'Nobody in the world
was closer to me.'

Ivan Pushchin, like Delvig, a close
schoolfriend of Pushkin. Pushchin was
one of the Decembrists exiled to
Siberia in 1826.

Red Square, Moscow, in 1825.

Mikhailovskoe Village, Pushkin's mother's country estate, in 1837.

Kondratii Ryleev, drawn by Pushkin.

Pavel Pestel, drawn by Pushkin.
Both these friends were Decembrists hanged after
the 1825 Revolt.

Tsar Nicholas I, an engraving from a portrait by George Dawe.

Two sketches of hanged men, drawn by Pushkin in the margin of manuscripts following the Decembrist Revolt, suppressed by Nicholas I in 1825, after which five of the conspirators were hanged.

a romantic poem, he was also 'taking lessons in pure atheism' from an 'Englishman, a deaf philosopher, the only intelligent atheist whom I have so far met'. Pushkin was unwise enough to add that the theory of atheism was not as 'comforting as is generally thought, but unfortunately the most probable'.[56] In reality, his attitude towards religion was fairly typical for a man of his social class, whether in Russia, or in any other European country, at that time. (He later had a mass said for the repose of Byron's soul.) To make the episode even more absurd, the Englishman with whom he had discussed atheism was in fact William Hutchinson, Vorontsov's personal physician, who spent three years with the Vorontsovs, first in France and then in Russia which he left soon after his meeting with Pushkin. Having become a member of the Royal College of Surgeons at the age of twenty-seven, on his return to England he seems to have settled down to a country practice.[57]

The discovery by the police of this letter came as a stroke of luck for Vorontsov. This time the entreaties of Pushkin's friends could not deflect Alexander I, who had by now entered the final phase of his reactionary period of mystical gloom. The tsar ordered Pushkin to be dismissed from the service altogether. On 29 July Pushkin found himself summoned – Vorontsov himself was away in the Crimea – by the governor of Odessa, who required him to sign a document undertaking to leave Odessa without delay and to travel without stopping to Mikhailovskoe, in the province of Pskov. For this journey he was provided with a carefully calculated sum of just over 389 roubles. Accompanied by Nikita Kozlov, he left on the following day.[58]

Even on the doubtful assumption that Vorontsov and Pushkin might somehow have been able to hit it off together, Pushkin could not have helped matters by falling in love with the wife of his chief. What exactly her feelings were towards Pushkin is not entirely clear (the series of references to Pushkin, in letters written to her husband in the summer of 1824, admit of more than one interpretation).[59] She was not Pushkin's first love in Odessa. Nor did he at once forget his Kishinev loves, one of whom, Calypso Polychroni, was a Greek who was rumoured to have slept with Byron. But whereas Pushkin's relationships during his Kishinev years are rather shadowy, he himself left a vivid record of his love not only of Elizaveta but also of Amalia Riznich, a Viennese whom he had met earlier in Odessa, where she arrived in the spring of 1823 with her husband, a rich businessman. She left the following year and died in Italy of tuberculosis in 1825. Pushkin was for a time passionately in love with her.[60]

How far Pushkin's advances succeeded either with Amalia or with Elizaveta is a matter of opinion. With the latter he had far more opportunity, because they met regularly at the house of Princess Vera Vyazemskaya, who spent some time in Odessa during Pushkin's stay there; and they went for walks by the sea. Just before he left Odessa Elizaveta gave him a medallion with her portrait and a gold ring with an octagonal cornelian stone: the 'talisman'. In a poem bearing this title, written three years afterwards, Pushkin described how this ring was given him by 'an enchantress' on the seashore in the midst of her caresses.[61] Pushkin gave it on his deathbed to Zhukovsky, whence it passed through several hands (including Ivan Turgenev's) until it was stolen from a museum in St. Petersburg in 1917. Elizaveta and Pushkin continued to correspond long after he left Odessa. He drew no less than thirty sketches of her, in a variety of poses. Arguably, no woman other than his wife ever captured Pushkin's inspiration to such an extent.

CHAPTER SIX

Exile at Mikhailovskoe

O rus!

—Horace

(Used by Pushkin as the epigraph to the second chapter of *Evgenii Onegin*: 'Oh country!' [in Latin] – a pun on the medieval word for 'Russia', *Rus*'.)

Not long after Pushkin had left Odessa he wrote an uncharacteristi-cally self-pitying poem, *To the Sea*. 'Bewitched by powerful passion' (an obvious allusion to Elizaveta Vorontsova) he had 'stayed upon your shores'; and the poem's last four lines read:

> В леса, в пустыни молчаливы
> Перенесу, тобою полн,
> Твои скалы, твои заливы,
> И блеск, и тень, и говор волн.

... Filled by you, I shall carry into the woods and the silent wastes, your rocks, your bays, and the glitter, the shadow and the sound of your waves.[1]

Pushkin's enforced departure, not long after his twenty-fifth birthday, seemed to mark an unhappy ending to his four years in the south. He was now to be confined to the province of Pskov and kept under surveillance, religious as well as secular. For the first time since he left St. Petersburg he became an exile in the formal, as opposed to the metaphorical, sense of the word. Yet, as it turned out, this was the beginning of a new stage of his personal and poetic development: a blessing in disguise. This disguise was heavy at first. Pushkin arrived in Mikhailovskoe from Odessa late on the evening of 9 August 1824. He found all his family at home. Summoned by the governor of Pskov, he was obliged to sign an undertaking of good conduct. Once the full dimensions of his disgrace were understood, the initial feelings of the family reunion, following an absence of over four years, gave way to weeks of strain, culminating in a blazing row at the end of October. In desperation, Pushkin even wrote to the governor of Pskov, asking to be imprisoned. Fortunately his letter was not delivered.[2]

According to Pushkin's own account written immediately afterwards, Sergei L'vovich not only took seriously the official charge of atheism levelled against his elder son – even accusing Alexander Sergeevich of attempting to corrupt his elder sister and younger brother with atheistic doctrine – but he also agreed to the governor's request that he himself should assume the responsibility for his son's secular supervision. (A local monk was appointed Pushkin's spiritual supervisor.) This responsibility was interpreted as including the reading of Alexander Sergeevich's correspondence, on which he was now almost entirely dependent for maintaining contact with the outside world. Father and son had never been close at any time. Now insults flew in both directions. Alexander Sergeevich declared that he would never speak to his father again, while for Sergei L'vovich Alexander became '*ce monstre, ce fils dénaturé*', who had, he alleged, threatened to beat him.[3] In the upshot, the family returned to St. Petersburg in November. Although the quarrel was eventually patched up, Pushkin's parents did not visit Mikhailovskoe so long as he was living there. He remained on this dilapidated but beautiful estate, alone except for the serfs and his nanny, Arina, for the next twenty-two months.

In spite of this unpromising beginning, these two years of isolation proved to be providential for Pushkin. Had he been in St. Petersburg in December 1825, he would almost certainly have been caught up in the Decembrist Revolt, with incalculable consequences for the remainder of his life. (Even if he had still been in Odessa, there were enough Decembrists in the town who were his personal friends, such as Prince Volkonsky, to constitute a political risk for him, if only by association.) Equally important, for the first time in his life Pushkin had almost nothing to do but write and read.

Pushkin's friends did not all agree about where the blame for his exile lay. (Vyazemsky was sympathetic; Delvig urged him to be careful for a year or two; and Karamzin observed that Vorontsov was 'no despot'.) But they were united in wanting him to make good use of it. As Zhukovsky put it, 'You are born to be a great poet, be worthy of this!' Ryleev wrote in similar vein.[4] They may have been preaching to the converted, but he certainly followed their advice. The use that Pushkin made of these years may best be judged if an attempt is made to compare the scale of his literary achievement as it actually was by the end of 1826, when he finally returned first to Moscow and then to St. Petersburg, with the kind of assessment of his work which his death might have evoked from literary critics and historians if his life had ended simultaneously with Byron's (in 1824) or at any time during the following six months.

In 1824, ten years after his first poem had appeared in the St. Petersburg press, Pushkin's reputation rested in large measure on three of his longer, published, works: *Ruslan and Lyudmila, The Captive of the Caucasus* and *The Fountain of Bakhchisaray*. On the basis of this evidence, critics would have speculated about the direction that his mature poetry would have taken after the early flowering of his extraordinary talent. Posthumous publication of the draft of *The Gypsies* and the opening chapters of *Evgenii Onegin* might have confused them (as indeed they actually did confuse some critics when they were first published). Misleading comparisons would probably have been drawn between Pushkin and Byron. Abroad, even at this early date, Pushkin's death would not have gone unnoticed. Pushkin's three major poems of the period 1820–4 were already beginning to be translated into German before he left the south; and articles about his work were beginning to appear in English, French and Polish literary journals as well. The *Westminster Review*, for example, devoted several pages to this 'very original' poet at the beginning of 1824.[5] Even in Russia, however, a hypothetical evaluation of Pushkin's work in mid-1824 could not perhaps have gone very much further than this: an original writer of infinite, but still uncertain, promise.

By the time Pushkin left Mikhailovskoe in September 1826 he had written some of the finest lyrics in the Russian language; he had finished *The Gypsies*; and the greater part of *Evgenii Onegin* was either written or drafted. *The Gypsies* was not published until 1827, but the first chapter of *Evgenii Onegin* was published in 1825 and the first edition of Pushkin's collected poems came out in the following year. It was at Mikhailovskoe that he wrote prefaces in verse – very different from one another, but each of them superb – to *Ruslan and Lyudmila*[6] and to *Evgenii Onegin*.[7] His other Mikhailovskoe poems included, at one end of the scale, *Count Nulin*, a poem which if Graham Greene had written it, he might have classified as an 'entertainment': the Rape of Lucrece in Russian nineteenth-century dress, but relating what might have happened if Lucrece had slapped Tarquin's face.[8] At the opposite pole stands *Boris Godunov*, a play written partly in blank verse and partly in prose, set in the period of the Russian 'Time of the Troubles' in the late sixteenth century.[9] Moreover, it was in these two years that Pushkin first developed his power of criticism. Although he never wrote any single work of literary criticism from then until the time of his death, the aggregate of his views on the writing of others, whether of his own or earlier ages, scattered among letters, notes and commentaries of every kind over a period of twelve years, constitutes a variegated corpus of rigorous literary criticism.[10]

Pushkin's reading at Mikhailovskoe was eclectic, ranging across frontiers and centuries. Thus, having already read the earlier volumes of Karamzin's *History of the Russian State* (there were twelve in all), he now read the remainder – required reading for a writer on the 'Time of the Troubles'; and *Boris Godunov* was dedicated to Karamzin. He read Tacitus's *Histories* and *Annals* in French: an interesting choice of historian by Pushkin, not only because of the economy of Tacitus's unique prose style – an economy that Pushkin's prose would emulate – but also because of Tacitus's attitude to history, which was essentially that of a man looking back on the age that had preceded the one in which he himself lived. Of Shakespeare Pushkin wrote in 1825: 'What a man this Shakespeare is! I cannot get over him. Compared with him, how poor a tragedian Byron is! This Byron who only ever conceived one single character ... he divided among his characters such and such an aspect of his own personality ...'[11]

Shakespeare's influence on Pushkin should not be assessed only in metrical terms: Shakespeare's blank verse and sonnet metres.[12] It would be hard to improve on Pushkin's much later comparison of Shakespeare and Molière:

Characters created by Shakespeare, unlike Molière's, are not models of a particular kind of passion or of a particular kind of vice; on the contrary, they are living beings complete with many passions, many vices. Circumstances unfold to the spectator their varied and many-sided personalities. Molière's miser is miserly – and that is all;

Shakespeare's Shylock is not only miserly, but resourceful, vindictive, child-loving and witty. Molière's hypocrite courts his bene-factor's wife in a hypocritical fashion, takes on the custody of an estate as a hypocrite, and asks for a glass of water hypocritically. Shakespeare's hypocrite pronounces judgement with arrogant sever-ity, but justly; he justifies his cruelty by the profound arguments of a statesman; and he seduces innocence, not with a ridiculous mixture of piety and philandering, but with powerful, fascinating sophistry.[13]

Pushkin wrote *Boris Godunov* with Shakespeare very much in mind. When he had finished it, he read it out aloud to himself from beginning to end; he clapped his hands and congratulated himself – 'Bravo! You son of a bitch!'[14] As it turned out, this work proved to be, in a sense, his Waterloo.[15] Planned as the first part of a dramatic trilogy, it was one of Pushkin's first works to fall foul of the censorship after his political rehabilitation. For that reason it was not printed until 1831; it was first staged as a play nearly forty years later; and even today it is generally thought of in the form of Musorgsky's fine opera.[16]

By contrast, *Evgenii Onegin* survived the censorship, thanks to some judicious omissions and to Pushkin's physical destruction of his politically incriminating Chapter 10. So effectively did he burn the manuscript of this chapter in 1830 that today all that remains is a collection of fragments, later reconstructed mainly from memory, which prove that it dealt with the Decembrists, but not much more than that.[17] Of all Pushkin's works, *Evgenii Onegin* is the best known in the west; and it has become better understood since a path was cut through its forest of allusions, literary and topical, by Nabokov's three volumes of commentary. Yet even in Russia it has been subject to virtually every conceivable interpretation, some of them diametri-cally opposed to each other.[18] In this welter of conflicting opinion it is easy to overlook the fact that Pushkin himself described *Evgenii Onegin* on the title page as a 'novel in verse'. And as a novel it would affect the great evolution of the Russian prose novel for the rest of the nineteenth century.

The bare essentials of the story of *Evgenii Onegin* are deceptively simple. Tatyana, the elder daughter of one of Onegin's neighbours in the country, falls in love with him at first sight; she declares her love, which he does not return. He later leaves the district, having killed a friend in a duel. After a long time spent travelling, Onegin returns to

St. Petersburg, where he again meets Tatyana, now married. He falls in love with her; she rejects him, although she still loves him. The plot of *Evgenii Onegin* appears romantic in Tchaikovsky's operatic version (written half a century later), but as Pushkin originally wrote it, its form is severely classical: a double chiasmus. Its framework depends on two balls – one rural and the other grandiose, in the capital – and two letters, the first, early on, from Tatyana to Onegin, and the second, at the very end, from Onegin to Tatyana. (Onegin's letter – not drafted by Pushkin until 1831 – disappears in the sentimentality of the last act of the opera.) Moreover, it took Pushkin eight years to complete this poem. Its characters developed as the novel went forward. Tatyana's marriage seems to have taken Pushkin himself by surprise; and Pushkin's own character developed over the same period. *Evgenii Onegin* provides many autobiographical nuggets: Chapter 1 relating to his first years in St. Petersburg, Chapter 2 to his exile at Mikhailovskoe and Chapter 8 to his time in Odessa, while Chapter 10 was presumably an attempt to do homage to the Decembrists.

Yet Pushkin is a writer who anticipated Flaubert's principle: '*Il ne faut pas s'écrire.*'[19] As his style grew more mature, so the distance between himself and his heroes and heroines increased. And in *Evgenii Onegin* he even introduced himself as one of the characters of the novel, a friend of Evgenii, so much so that he drew a sketch of the two of them deep in conversation by the side of the river Neva, opposite the Petropavlovsk Fortress (complete with detailed instructions), which he inserted in the first chapter of the poem.[20] Unlike Pushkin, Onegin is a man who never takes a risk if he can avoid it. It is only at the very end of the poem that he realizes that Tatyana, the girl whom he turned down at the beginning, would indeed have proved to be not only, as she modestly put it in her letter to him, a 'true wife and a good mother',[21] but the love of his life. Again, unlike Pushkin, he also took care to fire the first shot in his duel. Arguably, Pushkin was a gambler not only in the literal sense of the word. He was certainly not Onegin.

It was while Pushkin was working at Mikhailovskoe that he became a fully professional writer, entirely dependent upon his writing for the next eight years as his only source of income. It would not be long before each line of his verse would command a price of ten roubles. That he wanted every rouble he could lay hands on is evident from a recurring refrain in his correspondence: 'Some money, for God's sake, some money!'[22] Nevertheless, as a writer he was a perfectionist. Although his power of concentration was such that he could and sometimes did write at an almost unbelievable speed, his drafts are a mass of corrections. He even drafted his letters to his friends, let alone his official correspondence. For once in his life, Pushkin was able at Mikhailovskoe to spend what he earned on what he needed, because while he was living there, he was seldom exposed to the temptations of the green table. His needs during these two years consisted first and foremost of books. His correspondence is full of requests for books of every kind (including the Bible in French) to be sent to him from St. Petersburg. His brother Lev also had to send him during the first few months things as diverse as writing paper, plain paper, wine, cheese, a corkscrew, boots and braces.[23]

In order to reduce the cost of heating at Mikhailovskoe, Pushkin lived in a single room, which served as his study, dining room and bedroom. Arina's room was nearby, on the opposite side of the corridor; he used to call her 'mama'; and their long talks took place in the evening. An early riser and a late luncher, his first act on waking up was to swim in the river in summer and take an ice-cold bath in winter. He usually read or wrote either after his first cup of coffee in the morning or at night, or both. Walking or riding around the estate, he wore a red shirt belted with a sash, broad trousers and a white straw hat; and he always carried an iron stick weighing nine pounds (a habit that he had acquired in the south). This he sometimes threw in the air, catching it as it fell; while sometimes he just threw it in front of him. He maintained that his object was to strengthen his pistol hand (he practised pistol shooting as well). In the evening, if he had nothing better to do, he would play billiards against himself.[24]

Such was Pushkin's normal pattern. Not surprisingly, it was not enough for a man of his restless energy. Off and on throughout his Mikhailovskoe years, he devoted time to plans to get away, with or without official permission. He soon took Olga Kalashnikov, the (serf) daughter of the estate steward, to bed. Their son, Pavel, was born in June 1826 at Boldino, where Olga and her father had moved after Pushkin had sent her, pregnant, to St. Petersburg with a letter to Vyazemsky, seeking his help.[25]

Although Pushkin described Olga to Vyazemsky as a 'very sweet and good girl',[26] the chief pole of emotional attraction for him during these two years was not at Mikhailovskoe, but at the neighbouring estate of Trigorskoe, the property of a distant relation, Praskov'ya Osipova. (She was also a cousin of the Decembrist, Sergei Murav'ev-Apostol.) A competent and intelligent lady in her early forties, twice widowed, she knew how to run her estates (there was another one at Malinniki, in the province of Tver (Tver'), where Pushkin stayed later on. She was devoted to Pushkin and she was present at his burial in 1837. Whether she was ever in love with him or whether – in the words of Alexander Turgenev – she 'loved him like a mother',[27] is a matter of speculation. What is certain is that Pushkin was a frequent and welcome visitor at Trigorskoe, where there was a good library and a bevy of girls of all ages, with whom he flirted right, left and centre. His principal targets during 1825–7 and later in the 1820s, sometimes simultaneously, were Anna (Annette) Vul'f (Praskov'ya's daughter by her first marriage), Evpraksiya Vul'f (Zizi, Anna's younger sister) and Aleksandra (Aline) Osipova (Praskov'ya's stepdaughter). Praskov'ya, moreover, was the aunt of Anna Kern, whom Pushkin had met fleetingly in St. Petersburg and who in 1825 came to Trigorskoe. This time Pushkin fell in love with her.

Although there is enough evidence, in the form both of correspondence and of poetry, to enable a fairly clear picture to be formed of the criss-cross of relationships that developed from 1825 onwards (complicated by the fact that Praskov'ya's son, Aleksei Vul'f, was both Pushkin's rival and his confidant), it is now nearly seventy years since it was first observed that Pushkin's biographers had 'acquired the habit of regarding it as their duty to explain every one' of Pushkin's lyrics 'biographically and using them as direct historical evidence. This is silly.' – wise advice that has not been heeded by all subsequent biographers.[28] Neither the voyeurism of some nor the censoriousness of others has added much to our understanding of Pushkin's sexuality in relation to his Mikhailovskoe years.

This aspect of Pushkin's character seems to have changed remarkably little during the first thirty years of his life. As late as 1828 *les femmes comme il faut et les grands sentiments* were, according to Pushkin himself, what he feared most in the world. Later, Anna Kern described him as 'charmed by brilliance and outward beauty' rather than by 'dignity and simplicity in a woman's character', which she attributed to 'his low opinion of women, entirely in keeping with the spirit of the age'.[29] Generalizations in this field are dangerous. But until his marriage Pushkin seems to have related to women – prostitutes apart – either as mature and intelligent interlocutors, but physically unattractive, or as silly but attractive, although he was usually not attracted by them for long. (Elizaveta Vorontsova may have been an exception.)

This said, the biographer who declines to pursue Pushkin from one embrace to another during this period must make an exception of two of his Trigorskoe loves, Zizi Vul'f and Anna Kern – each for a different reason. Anna met Pushkin for the first time for six years when she came to stay at Trigorskoe. On the last day of her visit, the party drove over to Mikhailovskoe, where Pushkin walked with her down the avenue of trees alone. Before she left Trigorskoe next day, Pushkin gave her a copy of the opening chapter of *Evgenii Onegin*, the pages uncut, but enclosing a poem, 'I remember the wonderful moment'. These twenty-four lines, unquestionably addressed to Anna, did not melt her heart. She seems to have preferred the advances of Aleksei Vul'f – 'Lovelace' in Pushkin's correspondence with him – at the time. It was not until they met again in St. Petersburg three years later that she yielded to Pushkin's insistence.[30]

Я помню чудное мгновенье:
Передо мной явилась ты,
Как мимолётное виденье,
Как гений чистой красоты.

В томленьях грусти безнадежной,
В тревогах шумной суеты,
Звучал мне долго голос нежный
И снились милые черты.

Шли годы. Бурь порыв мятежный
Рассеял прежние мечты,
И я забыл твой голос нежный,
Твои небесные черты.

В глуши, во мраке заточенья
Тянулись тихо дни мои
Без божества, без вдохновенья,
Без слёз без жизни, без любви.

Душе настало пробужденье:
И вот опять явилась ты,
Как мимолётное виденье,
Как гений чистой красоты.

> И сердце бьётся в упоенье,
> И для него воскресли вновь
> И божество, и вдохновенье,
> И жизнь, и слёзы, и любовь.

K * * *

I remember the wonderful moment: you appeared before me like a transient vision of the spirit of pure beauty.

To me, languishing in hopeless sadness, among the cares of the noisy, restive world, a tender voice sounded and beloved features formed my dreams.

The years passed. The storms' wild gust scattered my earlier dreams, and I forgot your tender voice, your heavenly features. I dragged out my days slowly, in distant, dark confinement, cut off from God, uninspired, without tears, without life, without love.

My soul's awakening began: and behold! you appeared again, like a transient vision of the spirit of pure beauty.

And my heart is beating, enraptured, and in my heart all that is godlike, inspiration, life, tears and love, has risen once again.[31]

'I remember' and the even shorter, more poignant, poem 'I loved you', written in 1829, are perhaps the best known among Pushkin's many love lyrics. Of the two, it is the second which tells us – more frankly, even if still ambiguously – how *les grands sentiments* seemed to Pushkin, in reflective mood, at the age of thirty:

> Я вас любил: любовь ещё, быть может,
> В душе моей угасла не совсем;
> Но пусть она вас больше не тревожит;
> Я не хочу печалить вас ничем.
>
> Я вас любил безмолвно, безнадежно,
> То робостью, то ревностью томим;
> Я вас любил так искренно, так нежно,
> Как, дай вам Бог любимой быть другим.

I loved you; perhaps my love is not yet quite extinguished in my soul. But let it not trouble you any more; I do not want to sadden you in any way. I loved you without words, without hope, torn now by timidity and now by jealousy; I loved you as truly and as tenderly as may God grant you to be loved by another.[32]

The identity of the woman to whom the second of these poems was addressed has not been established, although more than one candidate has been advanced: Olenina and Vorontsova are both possibilities. For the biographer, what is striking both about 'I loved you' and about 'I remember' is the contrast that they form with the way in which Pushkin casually mentioned his conquest of Anna in 1828, in the course of a letter written to a friend primarily about gambling debts.[33] His casualness and the four-letter word that he used (replaced by asterisks in the Russian Academy edition), set side by side with these two poems, illustrate two aspects of his character in relation to women, of which he was himself well aware.

Neither with Anna nor with Zizi did Pushkin's love affair last for long. Zizi's biographical importance lies in the fact that, during the last critical days of Pushkin's life, she visited St. Petersburg (by then married, Baroness Vrevskaya) in order to stay with her sister. She thus became one of the few friends to whom Pushkin then unburdened himself. Unlike most of the others, she was aware of his impending duel. She will therefore recur in the last part of this book.

During 1825 Pushkin saw three of his school-friends: Gorchakov, Delvig and Pushchin. The first of these he visited at the home of Gorchakov's uncle, sixty-nine *versts* from Mikhailovskoe. The other two came to Mikhailovskoe. Pushkin and Gorchakov had drifted apart since Tsarskoe Selo and their short meeting in 1825 did nothing to bring them closer to each other. Pushkin read a part of *Boris Godunov* to Gorchakov, who criticized the everyday language (a reference to 'spit') that Pushkin used in the dialogue. Pushkin thought that Gorchakov was 'terribly dried up'.[34] He played no further part in Pushkin's life.

Delvig spent at least a week at Mikhailovskoe in April, but little has been recorded about his visit, to which Pushkin had been eagerly looking forward for a long time. On the other hand, Pushchin, who spent less than twenty-four hours in Mikhailovskoe at the beginning of the year, described his visit in detail in his memoirs.[35] As a present for the poet Pushchin brought a copy of Griboedov's *Woe from Wit*; he also bought three bottles of Veuve Clicquot on the way. He arrived at Mikhailovskoe in deep snow at about eight o'clock on the morning of 11 January. Bare-footed and in his shirt, Pushkin greeted him on the steps of the house. After embracing each other there, they went inside, as Pushchin put it, 'the one almost naked and the other covered in snow': a scene which even after thirty years Pushchin found it impossible to write about without tears blurring his spectacles. Pushchin found Pushkin's appearance little changed, except for the sideburns that he had grown since he had last seen him

in St. Petersburg. He also seemed a little more serious, although he
had lost none of his gaiety and liveliness. Toasts were drunk. They
discussed everything under the sun: the reasons for Pushkin's
dismissal from the imperial service; what people in St. Petersburg,
particularly the tsar, thought about Pushkin; the chances of his exile
coming to an end; and finally, the secret society. Of this Pushchin
wrote:

> When I said to him that I was not the only one to have entered into this
> new service of the fatherland, he leapt from his chair and exclaimed:
> 'Probably all this is connected with Major Raevsky, who has been held
> for five years in the Tiraspol prison and they can get nothing out of
> him.' Afterwards he quietened down and continued: 'By the way, I am
> not compelling you, my dear Pushchin, to talk. Perhaps you were right
> not to trust me. Probably I do not deserve that trust – because of my
> many foolishnesses.' In silence, I kissed him warmly; we embraced
> and went for a walk; we both of us needed some air.

Introduced to Arina, Pushchin noticed one of the seamstresses in her
room (presumably Olga), but said nothing about her to Pushkin,
who 'smiled significantly'. While Pushkin was reading *Woe from Wit*
aloud, they were interrupted by a visit from the monk who was
Pushkin's spiritual supervisor; he drank some glasses of rum as well
as the coffee that was offered to him. After he had left Pushkin simply
continued reading where he had left off and he went on to read part of
his *Gypsies*. It was long after midnight when Pushchin finally left on
his sleigh. They never met again. Pushkin's poem, 'My first friend,
my priceless friend', drafted soon afterwards and finished in 1826,
was later handed to Pushchin across the palisade at Chita (the
Decembrists' place of imprisonment in Siberia) by the wife of a
fellow-prisoner, on the day of his arrival there.[36]

Pushkin's plans for getting away from Mikhailovskoe took several
different forms as time went on. At the very beginning, in December
1824, he was to go abroad disguised as Aleksei Vul'f's servant.[37] This
project never got off the ground; and almost simultaneously he wrote
an imaginary conversation with Alexander I in which Pushkin
sought to explain his atheistic letter as 'a schoolboy joke', two empty
phrases of which should not be judged as though they were 'an
address to the whole nation'. The final paragraph, however, reads:
'But here Pushkin would have got angry and said much more to me
[to Alexander] that was superfluous, I [Alexander] would have lost

my temper and sent him off to Siberia, where he would have written a poem . . .'[38]

In the following spring the idea of treatment for his aneurism was resurrected. Pushkin drafted a letter himself to the tsar in April asking for permission to travel abroad.[39] In June his mother wrote to the tsar on his behalf, asking for permission for him to travel to Riga to consult a specialist there. The outcome was official permission for Pushkin to travel to Pskov, which he at first refused. In the autumn, however, he finally did visit Pskov, where he saw a doctor, whom he consulted again in the following year.

These manoeuvrings were brought to an end by a piece of news that did not reach St Petersburg until 27 November 1825 and Mikhailovskoe at the very end of that month. On 19 November Alexander I died suddenly at Taganrog, on the Sea of Azov. There is no first-hand evidence of Pushkin's immediate reaction to this wholly unexpected event (the reason for the tsar's journey was his wife's ailing health, not his own). The account that we have of what Pushkin then did is based on the recollection of a letter written by him at the time to his brother, which has not survived. Nevertheless there is no reason to doubt that, in the heat of the moment, on 1 or 2 December, Pushkin set out for St. Petersburg under the name of one of Praskov'ya Osipova's servants. Nor, given his superstitious nature, is it improbable that the sight of a brace of hares and a priest soon after he left home were enough to convince him that the journey would not have a happy outcome. He returned to Mikhailovskoe. He was still there when, a little over a fortnight later, he learnt the news of something even more dramatic: the Decembrist Revolt in St. Petersburg.[40]

CHAPTER SEVEN

The First Caesura, 1825–1826

If you would work any man, you must either know his nature and fashions, and so lead him; or his ends, and so persuade him; or his weakness and disadvantages, and so awe him; or those that have interest in him, and so govern him. In dealing with cunning persons, we must ever consider their ends, to interpret their speeches; and it is good to say little to them, and that which they least look for.

—Francis Bacon, *Essays*, XLVII, 'Of Negociation'

As tsar, Alexander I had always preferred multiple options. This preference held good from the moment in 1801, when he lay in his bed while his father was being assassinated, right up to the end of his life – indeed beyond. For the secret instructions that he drew up in August 1823 about the succession to the throne in the event of his own death were of such a kind as almost to guarantee indecision, if not chaos, in advance.

The problem that Alexander had to face was this. He himself had no surviving child. The eldest of his three brothers, Konstantin, who was generally expected to succeed him, had married a commoner, who was moreover a Polish Roman Catholic, whereas the Grand Duke Nicholas, the second of Alexander's three brothers, had a son who had been baptized in the Orthodox faith. With Konstantin's consent, Alexander signed a 'manifesto' declaring Nicholas the heir apparent. This document, which was written by the metropolitan of Moscow, was not published. On the contrary, sealed copies were lodged with the Uspensky Cathedral in the Kremlin, the Council of State, the Senate and the Holy Synod, with instructions that, in the event of Alexander's death, they should be opened before any other action was taken. To make confusion worse confounded, Nicholas, who was far from popular with the army, had not yet made up his mind to accept the throne; nor did he do so even immediately after his brother's death.

At the moment of Alexander's death Konstantin was in Warsaw, where he was in effect Russian viceroy (he was commander-in-chief of the Polish army). Unlike Nicholas, he enjoyed a reputation for liberalism, although this was probably not well founded. At first Nicholas took the oath of allegiance to Konstantin and ordered that the oath should be administered throughout the empire. Konstantin refused to accept the throne, but he also refused either to come to St. Petersburg or to issue a statement that would clear the public mind. Nicholas hesitated. Finally, impelled by police reports of a conspiracy in both north and south, he announced that he would himself be proclaimed emperor and the oath of allegiance administered on 14 December 1825.

Thus the members of the two secret societies (see Chapter 1), who had previously been unable to agree on a common policy, were given a sudden opportunity to fill the power vacuum that Alexander's death had left at the heart of the Russian Empire. Even now, however, the pressure of events did not persuade the conspirators to work out a joint plan. In judging this failure, several factors have to be borne in mind. In the first place, the extreme slowness of communications, coupled with the fact that the police were already watching the southern society closely, was a severe constraint. Both societies, especially the conspirators in St. Petersburg, greatly over-estimated the degree of military support on which they would be able to count, once they had announced their opposition to Nicholas. Finally, Prince Trubetskoi, whom the northern society planned to proclaim the provisional head of state if he had – as intended – taken military command of the uprising, was a lightweight. He lost his nerve and took refuge in the Austrian Embassy on 14 December.

In these circumstances the Decembrists' decision to act in St. Petersburg was taken at five minutes to midnight, in Ryleev's flat, where Pushkin would in all probability have been staying, had he persisted in his journey to St. Petersburg at the beginning of the month. The conspirators did not leave the flat until the small hours. Their plan was summed up in a single sentence attributed to Ryleev: 'Nevertheless we must make a beginning, something will come out of it.'[1] The highly motivated, well-balanced Pushchin (who had recently arrived from Moscow) said much the same; he was out on the square early the following morning.

Beyond this, nothing seems to have been planned beyond bringing out the maximum number of troops as a demonstration against Nicholas. Even so, it is arguable that the situation on the morning of the 14th was still so fluid that, with the number of troops whom the Decembrists did succeed in persuading to march out on to Senate Square, they could have attempted to occupy the Winter Palace, which was only ten minutes away. Instead, by the middle of the day some three thousand troops in all had assembled with flags flying – ironically in the square dominated by the equestrian monument of Peter the Great. There they stood for five hours in the freezing cold, waiting for others to join them. It gradually became apparent that the great majority of troops stationed in St. Petersburg, by whom the three thousand were heavily outnumbered, were remaining loyal to Nicholas. Attempts were made to settle matters peacefully – among others, by Miloradovich, the governor-general of St. Petersburg, who tried to persuade the rebels to return to their quarters, until he was shot dead by one of the conspirators, Petr Kakhovsky. In the end artillery was deployed. When Nicholas finally gave the order to open fire, the rebel square broke.

Late on the night of 14 December Nicholas wrote a triumphant letter – in French – to his 'dear, dear' brother, reporting: 'Your will has been done, I am Emperor, but at what a cost, Great God! At the cost of the blood of my subjects!'[2] In spite of the fiasco in the capital, however, there was a sequel in the Ukraine. Pestel just had time to bury his *Russkaya pravda* constitution before his arrest on the eve of the St. Petersburg revolt (the investigating committee obliged him to dig it up again later). The two Murav'ev-Apostol brothers, both serving at corps headquarters at Zhitomir at the time, were arrested soon afterwards. They were freed by other members of the secret society, including Ivan Sukhinov. Joined by Mikhail Bestuzhev-Ryumin, on New Year's Eve they led the Chernigov Regiment, stationed near Kiev, in revolt. As in St. Petersburg, they were unable to persuade other troops to rally to their cause. On 3 January 1826 a battle group arrived, sent by the government to suppress the revolt. It included cavalry and artillery. The encounter was soon over. Both the Murav'ev-Apostol brothers, one of them wounded, and Bestuzhev-Ryumin were taken to St. Petersburg; Sukhinov escaped but was

soon captured. All the conspirators were confined to the Petropavlovsk fortress in St. Petersburg.[3]

The interrogation of the conspirators themselves and of hundreds
of others, in which Nicholas himself took a prominent part, was
extremely thorough. The depositions and statements of the accused
were frank and detailed.[4] The process lasted until June 1826, when a
Supreme Criminal Court, consisting of seventy-two members,
including three members of the Church, was appointed. By the end of
the month they had voted in favour of death by hanging, drawing and
quartering for five of the accused, all of whom Pushkin knew
personally: Pestel, Ryleev, Sergei Murav'ev-Apostol, Bestuzhev-
Ryumin and Kakhovsky. Nicholas commuted the sentence to
hanging. This sentence was carried out on 13 July. Early on the
morning of the same day, over one hundred of the finest officers of
the Russian army were led out to hear their sentence: penal servitude
and exile in Siberia. As for the Chernigov Regiment, 376 men,
stripped of their medals and insignia, but avoiding the strokes of the
birch that killed or maimed another 120, left in carts destined for the
Caucasus. Their journey did not take quite as long as that of the 121
Siberian exiles, which lasted over a year.

It does not greatly matter whether or not Nicholas I assured the
Duke of Wellington that his clemency would astonish Europe. He
probably thought so himself; and others may well have agreed with
him. Not only was the memory of the horrors of the French
revolutionary terror still fresh in everyone's mind, in England as well
as in Russia. It was also only five years since the so-called Cato Street
Conspiracy in London, where five men were hanged for treason.
Except for the number five and the fact that the conspiracy helped to
justify the British government in passing the repressive Six Acts, the
parallel breaks down, however. Unlike the Decembrists, the men of
Cato Street were old-fashioned Jacobins. There was, moreover, a
difference regarding the death sentences handed down in the two
countries. In Russia, the decision to commute the sentence of
hanging, drawing and quartering passed on the five was exclusively
that of the tsar. In England, it was the outrage of public opinion that
ensured that the five men were spared this barbarism and were
executed by hanging.[5]

Half a century after these melancholy events Tolstoy managed to
obtain a copy of the document signed by Nicholas I, giving his

instructions for the execution of the five Decembrists. This copy disappeared for seventy years, but was rediscovered in 1948. Its words speak for themselves:

> A guard is to be mounted in the crownwork. The troops shall assemble at 3 a.m. First those condemned to penal servitude and degradation shall be brought out under escort and lined up facing the flag. The escort shall stand behind them, two to each. When everyone is assembled, the order to present arms shall be given, and the drums shall sound the first part of the signal to march. Then the general in command of the squadron and the artillery shall read out the sentence, after which the second part of the signal to march shall be played, followed by the command to shoulder arms. Then the executioners will remove the uniforms and the crosses, break the swords, and throw them all on to a prepared bonfire. When the sentence has been executed, they are to be led back to the crownwork in the same manner as they were led out. Then those condemned to death shall be led up onto the ramparts, accompanied by a priest carrying a cross. The drums will then sound the signal for running the gauntlet until all has been completed, after which the troops will wheel about to the right in sections and march past, and then be dismissed.[6]

In the event, the hangings were bungled. Only two of the five died straightaway and the other three had to be hanged all over again. Sergei Murav'ev is said to have exclaimed: 'Poor Russia! We cannot even hang properly!' There was a sixth hanging later, in Siberia. The reckless Sukhinov, having failed in an attempt to escape across the Chinese frontier, hanged himself.[7]

The news of the Decembrist revolt reached Pushkin at Trigorskoe three days after its failure in St. Petersburg. His first reaction was to return home at once and spend the next two or three days burning the most sensitive of his papers, including his autobiographical notes. Isolated in Mikhailovskoe, he seems to have taken some time to come to grips with the realities of the new situation which the suppression of the revolt had produced. True, there are the five Russian words that he wrote on a page of the manuscript of Chapter 5 of *Evgenii Onegin*, on which he drew a sketch of the hanging, which are the equivalent of the English 'there, but for the grace of God'. Yet as late as August 1826 he could still believe in the possibility of an amnesty for those of the conspirators who had been sentenced to Siberia.[8] And the first letter that he was able to send to Zhukovsky by safe hand, towards the end of January 1826, suggests that he believed that it was

entirely up to the Russian government to decide how to treat him and
that the outcome did not require any special effort on his own part.
The key paragraph of this letter reads:

> And so it remains for you to rely on my good sense. You can ask for
> proofs from me of this new quality. Here they are.
>
> In Kishinev I was on friendly terms with Major Raevsky, with
> General Pushchin, and with Orlov.
>
> I was a mason in the Kishinev Lodge; i.e. in the one on account of
> which all the lodges in Russia were done away with. Lastly, I had
> connections with the greater part of the present conspirators.
>
> The late emperor, when he exiled me, could reproach me only with
> agnosticism.
>
> This letter is of course unwise, but one must sometimes put one's
> trust in luck.[9]

In a letter of 12 April Zhukovsky was obliged to remind Pushkin of
something that he must have known already, namely, that although
he was not involved in anything, his poems had been found in the
papers of every one of those who took part. They were indeed; and
Pushkin's name recurs in their depositions.[10] Finally, at some point
between the middle of May and the middle of June 1826, Pushkin
wrote a letter to Nicholas I, enclosing an undertaking not to belong to
any secret societies 'under whatever name they may exist' and also
certifying that he had not belonged and did not belong to any secret
society, nor had he ever had any knowledge of them. The language of
the covering letter ate very humble pie. In 1824 he had had the
misfortune to incur the anger of the late emperor by an ill-considered
opinion about atheism included in a letter. Relying now on his
successor's magnanimity, Pushkin expressed both remorse and the
intention not to let his opinions clash with the generally received
order. On grounds of his health, which he described as 'shattered in
early youth', and of his aneurism, Pushkin ended this letter by asking
the tsar's permission to go for medical treatment to Moscow, St.
Petersburg or abroad.[11]

It was perhaps just as well that Pushkin was unaware of the danger
in which he remained right up to the beginning of August 1826. It
was not until almost half a century afterwards that it was discovered
from the governmental archives that a secret agent, Alexander
Boshnyak, left St. Petersburg on 19 July, bearing with him an open
letter providing for the arrest of Pushkin in the event that he found

evidence justifying this step. Boshnyak was an agent of Witte. An intelligent man, he was a genuine botanist and was therefore able to travel around the countryside with excellent cover. (He also maintained surveillance over Mickiewicz, who wrote a telling description of him, as he did of Witte.)[12] Fortunately for Pushkin, Boshnyak was unable to find incriminating evidence from any quarter, although he asked a lot of people in Pskov province about Pushkin's behaviour during his rural exile. His report, which seems to have amounted virtually to a nil return so far as Pushkin was concerned, was submitted to Nicholas on 7 August in Moscow, where he had gone for his coronation. For this and other services Boshnyak was awarded the Order of St. Anne (second class) and five thousand roubles per annum.[13]

On 28 August the tsar sent instructions to the governor of Pskov ordering Pushkin to be sent, accompanied by a government courier, to report to him at once in Moscow. At first, when the courier arrived at Mikhailovskoe on the night of 3 September, Pushkin does not seem to have realized the implications of the fact that he was free to travel in his own carriage, and specifically not as a man under arrest. By the time he reached Pskov, he was able to read a reassuring letter from Baron Ivan Dibich, Chief of the General Staff. On the strength of this, he wrote to Praskov'ya Osipova on the following morning that he supposed that his sudden departure from Mikhailovskoe had surprised her as much as it had himself. According to Dibich's 'very friendly letter', however, it was 'up to me to be wholly proud of it'.[14] Whatever Pushkin may have felt about this letter, he now set out on a journey that would end in a meeting which would radically change the course of the last ten years of his life.

The meeting between Pushkin and Nicholas I took place at four o'clock on the afternoon of 8 September 1826 in the tsar's study in the Chudov Palace (originally a monastery) in the Kremlin. Nicholas I was the elder of the two men, who had probably never met before,[15] by almost three years. He was also the taller of the two by nearly a foot. Nearly twenty years afterwards Queen Victoria would find him *'magnificent* still, and very *striking'*. A more detailed description of him, also written later on, would have applied in 1826. The homosexual overtones are, however, attributable to its author, the Marquis de Custine.

He has a Greek profile: a high forehead, but sloping backwards, a straight and perfectly formed nose, a very beautiful mouth, a noble face, oval but rather long, a military air and German rather than Slav.

His walk, his attitudes are intentionally imposing.

He always expects to be looked at, he does not forget for one instant that people are looking at him: indeed you would say that he wants to be the object of the gaze of everybody's eyes.[16]

Pushkin, who was taken straight to the imperial study from the office of the general on duty, was dishevelled, dusty and cold after travelling for four days. What he looked like in relaxed mood at the age of twenty-seven may be judged from his portrait painted by Orest Kiprensky in the following year (although the commonest reproduction fails to make clear that in the original, which hangs in the Tretyakov Gallery in Moscow, the artist correctly painted Pushkin's eyes blue). Of this portrait Pushkin himself said: 'This mirror flatters me.'[17] Another, less flattering, description is that by Mikhail Pogodin, who was one of those present when Pushkin read his *Boris Godunov* in the house of friends in Moscow in October 1826:

The high priest of high art expected by us – this was an almost small man of medium build, restless, with long hair, rather curly at the ends, without any pretensions, with lively darting eyes, with a quiet, pleasant voice, in a black frock coat, with a black waistcoat, tightly buttoned up and a loosely tied neck tie.[18]

At first sight the cards at this encounter in the Kremlin were heavily stacked against Pushkin. His formal letter of May/June to the tsar, which Nicholas had received before leaving St. Petersburg, put him firmly in the position of *demandeur* – never a good approach to a critical negotiation. For a negotiation is what this meeting became. For Pushkin it was crucial, whereas for Nicholas I it was only one of a mass of problems, external as well as domestic, that he had suddenly inherited from his brother, Alexander I, less than a year before. Indeed we cannot even be quite sure why he felt it necessary – in the midst of the preparations for his coronation – to deal personally with Pushkin, except that Russia was an autocratic state, ruled by a tsar who had no talent whatever for delegating decisions. Certainly he had little or no interest in literature, unlike Alexander (a far better educated man). On the contrary, though a competent linguist, he was uncultivated and unimaginative. None the less Nicholas was no fool. However conservative he might be, he could scarcely fail to realize that to make a liberal gesture by lifting his brother's sentence from Pushkin – in 1826 a man fast approaching the peak of his fame in his own lifetime – would not oblige him to make any major concession of principle.

Having just gone to the limits of severity in his treatment of the Decembrists, with adverse repercussions through a large section of the leading Russian families, Nicholas stood to gain nothing by antagonizing more members of Russia's small educated class than he already had at the outset of his reign. Thus, by the time he summoned Pushkin to Moscow, he had already dispensed with the services of the odious Arakcheev; and the universities were rid of the grotesque figures of Magnitsky and Runich (even though some ministers remained in office whom Russia could have done without, such as the German finance minister, Count Egor Kankrin, whose reason for distrusting the building of railways was not the burden that they would impose on the state's finances, but the fact that they would encourage Russians to travel). During the first half of 1826 Nicholas' primary concern had been the investigation and sentencing of the Decembrists, but by the autumn of that year he had much else on his mind.

Moreover, the pressure of problems in the Balkans, the Caucasus and Poland was mounting. Although Nicholas was anything but a philhellene, the Anglo-Russian Protocol, signed in St. Petersburg in April 1826, was a milestone on the road towards Greek independence.[19] Two months later Persian forces crossed the Transcaucasian frontier once again and they almost succeeded in capturing Tiflis. Russian expansion in Transcaucasia would soon follow, involving war with Persia and yet another major war with the Ottoman Empire. However, the most serious danger to Russian imperial power lay near the Russian heartland: in Poland. Here, in the wake of the Congress of Vienna, a Kingdom of Poland had been established with its own parliament and army. Nicholas was one of the Russian conservatives who most regretted what Alexander I had said during his speech at the inaugural session of the new Parliament in Warsaw in March 1818, which included a celebrated sentence: 'The results of your work in this first assembly will teach me what the motherland should expect in future from your devotion to her, as from your good feelings towards myself, and whether, faithful to my resolve, I can extend what I have done for you.'

What Alexander had said on this occasion to the *Sejm* disappointed liberals but alarmed conservatives, even though in the event he did nothing to 'extend' the relative freedom of Poland to Russia proper. Nevertheless, Nicholas had to accept the compromise settlement of the Polish Question which the Kingdom of 'Congress' Poland (the successor to the Napoleonic Grand Duchy of Warsaw) represented; and he was duly crowned in Warsaw in 1828. From the very beginning of his reign he was at loggerheads with the Polish parliament about the treatment to be given to members of the Polish Patriotic Society (linked with the Russian Decembrists). The seeds of the Polish revolt and the full-scale Russo-Polish war that followed it were already in the making.

Against this political background, it seems probable that Nicholas had made up his mind how to deal with Pushkin before he met him in the Chudov Palace. Only one thing might have given him pause: if Pushkin had flown off the handle. In the event, Pushkin played such cards as he held with skill, except that – forgetting protocol – he stood with his back to the fire warming his feet. No one knows how long this tête-à-tête meeting lasted: by general consent, over an hour – perhaps as much as two hours. Neither man made any kind of record. Yet there is little disagreement among historians about the essence of what passed between them, even though this became known only from what each of them related to other people afterwards. Pushkin appears to have made no attempt whatever to deny his friendship or his sympathy with the leading Decembrists. In reply to the tsar's question, whether or not he would have taken part in the revolt if he had been in St. Petersburg on 14 December, Pushkin said that he would certainly have joined his friends on Senate Square on that morning. Would he write against the government in future? This question Pushkin was able to answer obliquely. His last poem of this kind had been 'The Dagger', written five years before. For the future he gave the tsar his 'word of honour as a Russian nobleman to conduct himself in an honourable and decent manner'. This undertaking ensured that Pushkin could now travel freely within the Russian Empire, including St. Petersburg, provided that he gave the government advance notice of his intentions. There remained the critical question of his freedom to publish. Nicholas said to Pushkin: 'I myself will be your censor,' a promise repeated in a letter written, on the tsar's behalf, by Benckendorff three weeks later.[20]

Like all oral agreements, this one was open to misinterpretation on both sides. Pushkin would gradually find that he was no less obliged than he had been in the past to submit what he wrote to the government censor. Indeed, his writing was from now on complicated by the fact that the tsar would read what he wrote as well. Nor did the surveillance of Pushkin by the secret police come to an end after his meeting with the tsar. As early as 17 September 1826 one of Benckendorff's agents, Maksim von Fok, ended an adverse report to his chief on Pushkin with the words: 'They say that the tsar gave him a gracious reception and that he is not showing himself worthy of the kindness which His Majesty shows him.'[21] Nevertheless, there is no doubt about the immediate reaction of both men to the outcome of their meeting. In a letter written to Praskov'ya Osipova a week later Pushkin described Nicholas I as having received him 'in the most kind way'.[22] On the evening of 8 September itself, at a ball given by the French Ambassador, Nicholas remarked that he had just had a long talk with the most intelligent man in Russia.[23] At any rate to begin with, Pushkin's relationship with Nicholas did offer him certain advantages.

Whether Pushkin would have derived any advantages at all from this meeting if he had left with the tsar the manuscript of his poem 'The Prophet', which he is said to have stuffed into his pocket at the last moment, is open to question. In the manuscript's original form the last lines are believed to have read: 'Arise, arise, prophet of Russia, clad yourself in ignominious raiment, go, and with a noose around your neck, appear before the foul murderer.' The exact wording is uncertain and has given rise to much controversy among scholars – still more so the story that Pushkin dropped the manuscript on the palace staircase, but managed to retrieve it before leaving the building.[24] In its final form, one of Pushkin's most admired poems (it was greatly admired by Mickiewicz, among others, at the time), 'The Prophet' reveals a violent aspect of his character that is seldom visible in his earlier work. Its high-flown Biblical language, with strong Church Slavonic overtones, makes it hard to render in a plain prose translation. Exceptionally, therefore, a verse translation is quoted below, that of Maurice Baring:[25]

> Духовной жаждою томим,
> В пустыне мрачной я влачился,
> И шестикрылый серафим

На перепутье мне явился;
Перстами лёгкими как сон
Моих зениц коснулся он:
Отверзлись вещие зеницы,
Как у испуганной орлицы.
Моих ушей коснулся он,
И их наполнил шум и звон:
И внял я неба содроганье,
И горний ангелов полёт,
И гад морских полводный ход,
И дольней лозы прозябанье.
И он к устам моим приник,
И вырвал грешный мой язык,
И празднословный и лукавый,
И жало мудрыя змеи
В уста замершие мои
Вложил десницею кровавой.
И он мне грудь рассек мечом,
И сердце трепетное вынул
И угль, пылающий огнём,
Во грудь отверстую водвинул.
Как труп в пустыне я лежал,
И Бога глас ко мне воззвал:
«Восстань, пророк, и виждь, и внемли,
Исполнись волею Моей,
И, обходя моря и земли,
Глаголом жги сердца людей».

With fainting soul athirst for Grace,
I wandered in a desert place,
And at the crossing of the ways
I saw the sixfold Seraph blaze;
He touched mine eyes with fingers light
As sleep that cometh in the night:
And like a frightened eagle's eyes,
They opened wide with prophecies.
He touched mine ears, and they were drowned
With tumult and a roaring sound:
I heard convulsion in the sky,
And flights of angel hosts on high,
And beasts that move beneath the sea,
And the sap creeping in the tree.
And bending to my mouth he wrung
From out of it my sinful tongue,

And all its lies and idle rust,
And 'twixt my lips a-perishing
A subtle serpent's forked sting
With right hand wet with blood he thrust.
And with his sword my breast he cleft,
My quaking heart thereout he reft,
And in the yawning of my breast
A coal of living fire he pressed.
Then in the desert I lay dead,
And God called unto me and said:
'Arise, and let My voice be heard,
Charged with My Will go forth and span
The Land and Sea, and let My word
Lay waste with fire the heart of man.'[26]

If Pushkin really did drop this poem on the stairs of the Chudov Palace, the outcome of his audience with the new tsar must be reckoned to have been a close-run thing. As it was, immediately after the meeting in his study the tsar is said to have taken Pushkin by the hand and led him into the antechamber, which was full of courtiers. 'Gentlemen,' he announced, 'here is the new Pushkin for you, we will forget about the old Pushkin.'[27] Whether or not Nicholas used this exact expression, this was a turning point in Pushkin's relationship with the government on the one hand, and, on the other, with his Decembrist friends.

It is arguable that Pushkin's political views had begun to change at the time when he was still in the south. The fact that he talked a lot and was therefore regarded as a security risk by most of the Decembrists is not the only explanation for his exclusion from the inner circle of their movement. By 1824 his correspondence shows the extent of his disillusion about the future of the liberal cause beyond Russia's borders, particularly in Greece; and there were poems that he wrote before 1825–6, such as his politically pessimistic 'A sower of freedom in the wilderness', which support the view that, well before the failure of the revolt, he was already beginning to give up hope for the liberal cause within Russia as well.[28] Moreover, it is a striking fact that in Lunin's Siberian writings in 1836–40 (that is to say, including the year of Pushkin's death) he never once mentioned either Pushkin or his poetry. And the memoirs of another Decembrist, which were not published in full until 1913, stated flatly that Pushkin was already distrusted by the southern society while he was in Kishinev and

Odessa. True, the Decembrist in question, Ivan Gorbachevsky, was a radical, but there is some evidence in Pushkin's own draft of the second chapter of *Evgenii Onegin* to suggest that he himself was aware of accusations of disloyalty as early as 1824.[29]

Some important evidence is missing. For example, Pushchin is believed to have written to Pushkin telling him that he was going to St. Petersburg from Moscow at the beginning of December 1825, but it is not certain that the letter ever reached its destination.[30] If only Chapter 10 of *Evgenii Onegin* had survived intact, Pushkin's considered view of the Decembrists and his own relationship with them might have been established beyond reasonable doubt. As it is, although there are several other references to the Decembrists in Pushkin's poetry after 1826, there must remain room for speculation, with rather more light and shade than the hagiographical view of Pushkin may allow. For such a fallible, complex, human being, 1826 was a year of exceptional difficulty : a conflict between Pushkin's personal loyalty to his friends and the needs of his own professional life. Those who prefer to take a simple view of the way in which he resolved this conflict can point to one well-attested remark made by Pushkin himself soon afterwards, and also to Pushchin's considered judgement, recorded in his memoirs thirty years later. Both speak for themselves.

When paying a farewell visit to Alexandra Murav'eva in St. Petersburg, before she left for Siberia to join her husband there in 1827, Pushkin is said to have remarked: 'I quite understand why these gentlemen did not want to receive me into their society ; I do not deserve that honour'[31] – an echo of what he had said to Pushchin during their talk at Mikhailovskoe two years earlier. In his memoirs, Pushchin wrote that he had more than once put to himself the question, 'What would have happened to Pushkin, if I had drawn him into our Union and if it had fallen to his lot to experience a life completely different from the one which did in fact become his destiny?' Pushchin went on: 'It was only after his death that all these apparently insignificant circumstances took on, in my eyes, the appearance of the manifest operation of Providence, which saved Pushkin from our fate and preserved him as a poet for the glory of Russia.' Had Pushkin shared the Decembrists' exile in Siberia, 'even if this had not completely dried up his powerful talent, then it would have been far from giving him the possibility of attaining the development which, in a different sphere of life, was unfortunately cut short before his time.' Pushchin's conclusion was : 'In one word, in sad moments I consoled myself with the thought that a poet does not die and my Pushkin was always living for those who, like myself, loved him and for all those able to seek him out, alive in his immortal works . . .'[32]

Pushkin did not live to read these words. Even if he had, it would have been surprising if a man of his sensibility and intellectual integrity had not suffered from unease at the very least, and perhaps worse, while he was enjoying the fruits of the tsar's patronage (by whatever disadvantages this patronage was later accompanied) during the years in which his Decembrist friends were leading a very different kind of life in Siberia. Just over a year after his Mikhailovskoe exile came to an end, Pushkin had an extraordinary, accidental, meeting at a staging post on the road to St. Petersburg. He was, by his own account, in a bad mood at the time, having lost 1600 roubles at cards the previous evening. As he was sitting there, reading Schiller, four *troikas* drew up, with a government courier. Having gone out to have a look, Pushkin noticed a 'tall, pale, young man with a black beard, in a shabby overcoat'. Suddenly they recognized each other. It was Küchelbecker, on his journey from one prison to another. The two school-friends embraced, but were parted by the accompanying policemen. The courier upbraided Pushkin. Küchelbecker nearly fainted. The policemen gave him some water. They then drove off.[33]

Although Pushkin was in no sense one of the initiators of the Decembrist movement, to which he did not even belong, it is none the less hard to imagine the movement without the accompaniment of Pushkin's early radical verses. For Pushkin, moreover, the friendship of other men was an essential part of his life. This said, if the Decembrist revolt had not been precipitated by Alexander's death in 1825 and if the absurd interregnum had not followed, would not the intellectual gap between Pushkin and the Decembrists have been likely to widen as time went on? Some of the Decembrists – certainly Pestel – could have said with Brutus:

> – Stoop, Romans stoop,
> And let us bathe our hands in Caesar's blood
> Up to the elbows, and besmear our swords:
> Then walk we forth, even to the market-place;
> And waving our red weapons o'er our heads,
> Let's all cry, 'Peace! Freedom! and Liberty!'[34]

Pushkin could not.

CHAPTER EIGHT

'The New Pushkin'

Так, полдень мой настал, нужно
Мне в том сознаться, вижу я.
Но, так и быть: простимся дружно,
О юность легкая моя!
Благодарю за наслажденья,
За грусть, за милые мученья,
За шум, за бури, за пиры,
За все, за все твои дары:
Благодарю тебя. Тобою,
Среди тревог и в тишине,
Я насладился ... и вполне;
Довольно! С ясною душою
Пускаюсь ныне в новый путь
От жизни прошлой отдохнуть.

(So my noon has begun and I see that I must acknowledge this. But, so
be it: let us say a friendly farewell, oh my light-hearted youth! I am
thankful for the delights, the sorrow, the sweet sufferings, the noise,
the storms, the feasts, for everything, for all your gifts; I thank you. I
took delight in you in the midst of alarms and of silence ... to the full;
enough! With a clear mind I now set out on a new path, to rest from
my past life.)

—Pushkin, *Evgenii Onegin*, Chapter 6, Stanza XLV

The three and a half years that elapsed between September 1826 and
Pushkin's engagement to Natalya Nikolaevna Goncharova in May
1830 formed a watershed in his life. Of this Pushkin himself, who was
almost thirty-one when his proposal of marriage was accepted, was
fully aware. It was a watershed that he crossed neither with the
single-mindedness nor with the calm expressed in the resigned
farewell to his youth to which he gave such eloquent expression in
stanza XLV of the sixth chapter of *Evgenii Onegin*.[1] This stanza was

written just four weeks before Nicholas I introduced 'the new Pushkin' to his courtiers, in the anteroom of his study in the Kremlin. These years of Pushkin's 'new path' are notable for their sudden zig-zags; for his self-doubt and sometimes violent swings of mood. Over the first few weeks after his arrival in Moscow, however, there were no such shadows cast. The effect of his return from exile was electric.[2] At balls, in the theatre, in gatherings at private houses, Pushkin's name was on the lips of everyone in Russian society, assembled in Moscow in the autumn of 1826 for Nicholas I's coronation.

One of the houses frequented by Pushkin was that of Princess Zinaida Volkonskaya, which was a meeting place both of the aristocracy and of writers and musicians. Here her sister-in-law, Princess Maria Volkonskaya (Maria Raevskaya before her marriage to the Decembrist Sergei Volkonsky) spent her last evening – 26 December 1826[3] – before leaving for Siberia to join her husband. Pushkin was among the guests. Later, in St. Petersburg, when he gave Alexandra Murav'eva his poem to deliver to Pushchin in Siberia, he also gave her a poem for Maria Volkonskaya, ending with the words: 'The heavy fetters will fall, the dungeons will crash to the ground – and freedom will receive you with joy at the gate, and your brothers will return your swords.'[4] Pushkinist scholars are not unanimous in deciding for whom Pushkin intended the dedication of his long narrative poem *Poltava* (celebrating in its climax Peter the Great's decisive victory over Charles XII of Sweden), which was written in 1827 during a single fortnight. It is hard, however, not to believe that it was for Maria:

Посвящение

Тебе – но чоıлос музы темноц
Коскется ль уха твоеıо?
Поймешь лц ты душою скромной
Стремленье сердча моеıо?
Иль посвящснце поэта,
Как некоıда еıо любовь,
Перед тобою без ответа
Пройдет, непрцзнанное вновь?

Узнай, ио крайней мере, звукц,
Бывало, мцлые тебе –
И думай, что во днц разлукц,
В моей цзменчцвой судье,

Твоя, печальная пустыня,
Последнцй звук твоцх речей
Одно сокровцще, святыня,
Одна любовь душц моей.

Dedication

To you* – but will the voice of the dark muse reach your ear? Will your modest spirit understand the striving of my heart? Or will the poet's dedication, like his love formerly, pass before you without a response, unacknowledged once again?

At least recognize the sounds that once were dear to you – and think that, on the day of parting, in my fickle fate your sad wilderness, the last sound of your words, were the one treasure, the shrine, the one love of my soul.[5]

* In Russian, the second person singular is used.

During the succeeding winter Pushkin's popularity reached the zenith of his own lifetime. To the general welcome accorded to him there was only one notable exception: his own father. There was no question of killing the fatted calf. Instead it was only in 1828 that Sergei L'vovich (as before, living in St. Petersburg) finally joined the rest of his family in burying the hatchet, to which he clung for four years after the dispute with his son at Mikhailovskoe in October 1824. After leaving the Chudov Palace on the evening of 8 September 1826, Alexander Sergeevich went straight to the house of his uncle Vasilii (who lived for only four more years – his nephew was with him when he died). A few weeks after this visit Vasilii L'vovich received a letter from his brother that was both bitter and sanctimonious:

No, dear friend, do not think that Alexander Sergeevich will ever feel his injustice towards myself ... He is completely convinced that it is I who must ask his pardon, but he adds that were I to decide to do this, he would then jump out of the window rather than grant me his forgiveness ... I have not yet ceased for one minute to offer up prayers for his happiness and, as the Bible enjoins, in him I love my enemy and I pardon him, if not as a father – since he rejects me – then as a Christian.

He concluded another letter, written on the same day, with the sentence: 'Finally, may he be happy, but let him leave me in peace.'[6] Pushkin appears to have had no difficulty in complying with the second part of his father's wish; even in his last years, when he too was living in St. Petersburg and their quarrel was over, he did not see much of either of his parents.

When Pushkin arrived in Moscow, the work uppermost in his mind (other than *Evgenii Onegin*, on which he was still working) was *Boris Godunov*, completed less than a year earlier at Mikhailovskoe, with high hopes that its publication would revolutionize the Russian theatre. During his first month in Moscow he read it through on more than one occasion, each time in a private house.[7] Pogodin, who was a near-contemporary of Pushkin, recorded his recollection of the second of these readings nearly forty years afterwards. 'What effect that reading produced on all of us – it is impossible to convey . . . the first scenes we listened to quietly and peacefully or, to put it better, with some perplexity.' As Pushkin read on, however:

> We all simply felt as though we were fainting. One of us was thrown into a fever, another into a shivering fit. Hair stood up on end. No one had the strength to restrain himself. One of us suddenly leaped from his place, another cried out. For example, at the lines of the Pretender 'the shade of [Ivan] the Terrible has adopted me', now there was silence, now a burst of exclamation. The reading ended. We looked at each other for a long time. And then we rushed at Pushkin. Embraces began, a din arose, laughter broke out, tears were shed, congratulations were offered . . . champagne appeared and Pushkin was excited, seeing that he had made such an impact on a select group of young people. Our emotion pleased him . . . Oh, what an amazing morning that was, leaving its traces for the rest of my life. I do not remember how we parted, how the day ended, how we went to bed. But hardly any of us slept that night. Our whole organism had been so shaken.[8]

Unfortunately the delicate relationship just established between the poet and the sovereign was also shaken by Pushkin's reading of *Boris Godunov* – in a different way. Almost at once Pushkin found himself obliged to explain to Benckendorff whether or not it was true that he had read his new tragedy at this party, that is to say, without previously submitting the text to the tsar. On 29 November Pushkin sent Benckendorff a tactful reply, confirming that he had indeed read *Boris Godunov* to 'certain persons in Moscow', and excusing the fact that he had not submitted the text by his wish first to delete some 'indecent expressions' from it. However, he now sent Benckendorff his own copy, unamended.[9]

The imperial reply was prompt. On 9 December Benckendorff wrote to Pushkin quoting the tsar's marginal comment, namely, that he considered that Pushkin's object would be fulfilled if, with the cleaning up required, he were to 'convert his comedy [a 'comedy' was what Pushkin originally called it] into a historical tale or a novel modelled on Walter Scott'. This bizarre suggestion, which appears to have been Nicholas' own idea, may conceivably be attributable to the fact that he had visited Scotland ten years earlier, as part of his grand tour as a young man. Once again Pushkin had recourse to a tactful reply: 'I agree that it resembles a historical novel more than a tragedy, as His Majesty the Emperor has been kind enough to observe. I regret that I do not have the ability to rework what I have already written.'[10]

This was not a good beginning. Moreover, Pushkin soon found himself picking his way through the minefield of the imperial censorship. The first mine which he ran into in 1827 was not one laid by himself, but the second, for which he began by denying all responsibility as long as he dared, was entirely his own work. While he was living at Kishinev, Pushkin had written a poem entitled 'André Chénier'. This, together with other poems, was published in October 1825 (that is to say, well before the outbreak of the Decembrist Revolt). Although the subject of 'André Chénier' was the guillotining of the French poet during the French Revolution thirty years earlier, the addition by a third party of the title 'The Fourteenth December' was enough to suggest to suspicious minds that Pushkin intended a parallel with Ryleev's execution in St. Petersburg. This gave rise to a judicial investigation that dragged on for nearly two years. Even when the Council of State finally laid it to rest in July 1828, a rider was added: Pushkin was to be kept under secret surveillance.[11]

Immediately afterwards, in August 1828, Pushkin was confronted with another work also written at Kishinev, which had been circulated only in manuscript: the blasphemous *Gavriliada*. Pushkin began by giving the authorities the lie direct about his authorship of the poem; and in a letter written to Vyazemsky on 1 September he described the affair as 'a preposterous joke hung around my neck'. Within a matter of weeks he was obliged to acknowledge the poem as his own in a personal letter written to Nicholas I. Pushkin's letter has not survived, but on the last day of 1828 the tsar simply minuted that the affair was closed.[12]

In the midst of his disappointing exchanges with Benckendorff and the tsar about *Boris Godunov*, Pushkin had to fulfil a request put to him by Nicholas I, which may at first sight seem curious. It was perhaps seriously intended, given that Pushkin was one of the first pupils to pass out of the imperial lycée; and it may also have been regarded as a test of Pushkin's suitability for some kind of public service. The tsar's request was that Pushkin should submit to him a report on his ideas about public education. Pushkin's dilemma on receiving this commission to write on such a sensitive subject becomes clear in the light of the educational slogan of the man who later became Nicholas' Education Minister, Sergei Uvarov. Although Uvarov was a scholarly figure, who had been President of the Academy of Sciences since 1818 and before that a member of *Arzamas*, his triple slogan consisted of the words 'Orthodoxy, autocracy and *narodnost*'. The last of the three is a Russian word that can only roughly be rendered in English as 'nationalism'. Benckendorff himself later defined it in this sentence (ironically, written in French): 'Russia's past is admirable, her present more than magnificent: as to her future, it is beyond the grasp of the most daring imagination; this is the point of view ... from which Russian history must be conceived and written.'[13]

By Pushkin's own standards, he pulled his punches in the report on education that he submitted to the tsar. Some of his recommendations, however – corporal punishment to be abolished, no need to fear foreign education, explain comparative political theory (including republican principles) to pupils in an objective manner, spend less time on teaching languages – were advanced enough to draw down imperial exclamation marks. In vain, Pushkin did what he could to soften the force of his report by ending it with a modest disclaimer: 'Of myself I would never have ventured to present for the government's consideration such inadequate observations on such an important subject.' Nicholas' opinion of Pushkin's report and indeed his attitude towards much else besides was summed up for Pushkin by Benckendorff in three sentences:

> Your principle, according to which education and genius can alone serve as a basis for moral perfection, is a doctrine that is dangerous for public security, which has already led you yourself to the edge of the precipice and has thrown a large number of young people over it. Morality, exemplary devotion, zeal, deserve to be preferred to education which is untried, immoral and useless. It is on these foundations that well-ordered education ought to be founded.[14]

In spite of the distractions of imperial patronage and imperial censorship, Pushkin accomplished a lot during these years. Considered as a period of creativity, they do not match either the sustained work of the years of his Mikhailovskoe exile or the brilliant products of the three Boldino autumns in the 1830s. Thus, the second chapter of *Evgenii Onegin* was published in 1826 and the third in the following year, as was *The Gypsies*; he wrote *The Blackamoor of Peter the Great* in 1827; 1828 saw Chapters 4–6 of *Evgenii Onegin* in print and a new edition of *Ruslan and Lyudmila*, complete with its magical prologue; and in 1829, *Count Nulin* and *Poltava* both came out, as well as a second edition of the first chapter of *Evgenii Onegin* (first published in 1825) and a second edition, in two volumes, of Pushkin's collected poems. The first edition of his collected poems, most of which had been published individually beforehand, was produced only in the last days of 1825. The reason for this late date – it was not as if Pushkin could not have used the money – was the complexity of his commitments to different publishers in the early 1820s. For five years a major part in his publishing arrangements was played by his brother Lev, whose excellent memory enabled him to recite Pushkin's poems at parties in St. Petersburg (not always an advantage for Pushkin, living far away from the capital at the time). More seriously, in 1820 Pushkin had gambled away for a thousand roubles the manuscript of his poems to Nikita Vsevolozhsky, a fellow-member of the foreign ministry at the time when Pushkin was first enrolled in its ranks and a founder of the *Green Lamp*. It took much time and effort for all this to be sorted out. From 1826 onwards, however, Pushkin enjoyed the good fortune of having Petr Pletnev as his publisher and also one of his closest friends.[15]

In addition to this literary activity, Pushkin received an offer in a field that would continue to attract him right up to the last day of his life: journalism. As events would prove, he did not have the right temperament to become a successful journalist. A new journal, the *Moskovskii vestnik* (the *Moscow Herald*) had recently been founded. Pogodin became editor and its contributors included many of Pushkin's friends. He stood to earn as much as ten thousand roubles a year, had it succeeded. Unfortunately, in spite of a brilliant start, it did not. Too highbrow for the public, by 1828 it was already beginning to founder, although Pushkin went on contributing to it from his poetical works as late as 1830. By then, however, he had transferred his allegiance to the St. Petersburg *Northern Flowers* and the *Literaturnaya gazeta*, founded by Delvig.[16]

This relative failure apart, for the first time in his life Pushkin was now earning steadily and well. Had it not been for his passion for gambling – he temporarily lost the fourth chapter of *Evgenii Onegin* at faro in November 1828[17] – he was now able to live with a fair degree of comfort, almost of luxury. Thus, in the course of a thinly disguised autobiographical fragment written towards the end of his bachelor existence, he described a typical day in his life in these words:

> ... In the morning I get up when I want to, I receive whomever I want to, I think of going out – they saddle my clever, quiet Jenny ... I arrive home – collect my books, my papers, I get my dressing-table in order, I dress carelessly if I am invited out, with all possible diligence if I am lunching at a restaurant, where I either read a new novel or the newspapers; if Walter Scott and Cooper have written nothing and if there is not some criminal trial in the papers, then I order a bottle of champagne on the ice, I check to see that the glass is ice-cold, I drink slowly, rejoicing that lunch is costing 17 roubles and that I am able to allow myself this fun. I go to the theatre, I seek out in one of the boxes a remarkable dress and black eyes; a relationship between us begins, I am taken up with it until we leave. The evening I spend either in noisy society, where the whole city is crammed, where I see everybody and everything and where nobody notices me, or in a select circle of friends, where I talk about myself and where they listen to me. I return home late; I go to sleep reading a good book.[18]

During his visits to the country he had virtually no expenses at all. Whenever he was in St. Petersburg he contented himself with a modest room at his favourite hotel, the *Demuth*, and in Moscow he did the same at the *Evropa*. As time went on, however, he also stayed with friends, such as Vyazemsky, and in Moscow with one particular friend whom he frequented more and more during the last seven years of his life, Pavel Nashchokin. Nashchokin had been a contemporary of Pushkin's younger brother at the Tsarskoe Selo lycée, where Pushkin first met him. After only four years in the army he retired. Wealthy, generous, extravagant and raffish – he had a gypsy mistress – and at the same time a heavy gambler, he appealed to one side of Pushkin's character, although Pushkin also seems to have turned to him for financial advice. What such advice may have been worth is an open question. There is, however, no doubt that Pavel and his wife Vera, whom he married in 1834, were genuinely devoted to Pushkin and deeply mourned his death.

At about the same time as Pushkin renewed his friendship with Nashchokin, he met in Moscow a very different man, a Pole of almost exactly the same age as himself, of whom he quickly became both a friend and an admirer: Adam Mickiewicz. Mickiewicz left Russia for ever two and a half years after he and Pushkin met for the first time; and the bitterness which was the legacy of the Polish Revolt and the Russo-Polish War prevented their friendship from being maintained at a distance. None the less it was one of the most significant relationships in Pushkin's life. For Mickiewicz was the only poet of remotely equal stature whom Pushkin ever met. Their brief encounter was the result, on the one hand, of the Russian imperial government's decision to prevent Pushkin from travelling abroad, and, on the other, of Mickiewicz's expulsion from his native Lithuania to Russia in 1824, at almost the same moment as Pushkin was banished to Mikhailovskoe.

A Lithuanian Pole, Mickiewicz was a graduate of the University of Vilno, whose rector was Prince Adam Czartoryski, who had been a member of Alexander I's inner circle of liberal advisers in the early years of his reign. Mickiewicz wrote in his native Polish; but he spoke elegant French and – unusually for a Pole – good Russian as well. Alexander's opening speech to the *Sejm* in Warsaw in 1818 notwithstanding, by the time Mickiewicz graduated in the following year he had become a radical. Arrest in 1823 and expulsion to Russia in the autumn of 1824 were the consequences. Thus, Mickiewicz arrived in southern Russia just as Pushkin left it. He was universally liked as a man, even though few Russians knew enough Polish to appreciate him as a poet. When he and Pushkin first met two years later, therefore, they had many acquaintances in common. In whose house they met in Moscow is uncertain. It could well have been that of Princess Zinaida Volkonskaya or that of one of the founders of the *Moskovskii vestnik*, to which Mickiewicz became a contributor. What is well attested is Pushkin's own remark, after he had listened to one of Mickiewicz's improvisations (for which he had a remarkable talent): '*Quel génie! Quel feu sacré! Que suis-je auprès de lui?*'[19]

The rivalry of the two poets was at first a friendly one. Vyazemsky later recounted how, at a chance meeting in the street, Pushkin said to Mickiewicz: 'Out of the way, two, the ace is coming!'

Mickiewicz's reply was: 'The two of trumps beats even an ace!' Mickiewicz gave Pushkin an English copy of Byron, inscribed 'Mickiewicz, an admirer of you both, presents Byron to Pushkin.' Each man translated some of the other's verse into his own language. Mickiewicz translated, as *Przypomnienie*, a fragment of Pushkin's *Remembrance* – the poem from which Tolstoy makes Levin quote in *Anna Karenina* – soon after Pushkin had written it.[20]

Their personal exchanges in poems written in the 1830s were less happy.[21] The most famous and most important interaction between the two poets relates to Peter the Great (see page 37). In the opening lines of 'Before the Monument of Peter the Great' in his *Forefathers' Eve, Part III*, Mickiewicz described Pushkin and himself 'standing in the twilight dew, arm linked in arm, one cloak about the two', both looking up at Etienne-Maurice Falconet's monument to the founder of St. Petersburg. The verses continue:

> Like two great Alpine crags, born one,
> Which, riven by deep-hidden streams since birth,
> But little heed the Enemy's dull roar,
> As each towards each their craggy summits soar.[22]

On receiving the news of Pushkin's death, Mickiewicz wrote this about him in the Paris newspaper *Le Globe* on 25 May 1837:

> I knew the Russian poet fairly closely and for quite a long time; I found in him a character that was too impressionable and sometimes frivolous, but always sincere, noble and capable of pouring out his heart. His faults seemed to be the fruit of the circumstances in which he lived: everything that was good in him flowed from his heart.[23]

These were restless years for Pushkin. Lionized in Moscow immediately after his return there in September 1826, and in spite of the presence there both of old friends and of new ones, such as Mickiewicz, within two months he wrote to Vyazemsky that Moscow had made 'an unpleasant impression' on him; and he returned to Mikhailovskoe.[24] Not for long, however. By 1 December he had left his 'damned village' for Pskov,[25] on his way back to Moscow. In May 1827 he returned to St. Petersburg, where he stayed only a month before spending the summer at Mikhailovskoe, partly working and partly renewing his Trigorskoe liaisons. The winter of 1827–8 he spent in St. Petersburg, where Vyazemsky described him to Alexander Turgenev as leading 'the most dissipated possible life';

and he added that 'St. Petersburg may destroy him'.[26] It was, however, to this period that Pushkin owed his friendship with Elizaveta Khitrovo. Twice widowed and over fifteen years older than Pushkin, Elizaveta was Field-Marshal Kutuzov's daughter and she presided over one of the principal political, social and literary salons of St. Petersburg. Well-informed and well-read, she took a close interest in Pushkin's work – sometimes too close for Pushkin's comfort. His correspondence makes it clear that she sometimes bored him. But she also helped him greatly in practical ways. Her feelings for him were afterwards described by Vyazemsky as 'the most tender, passionate friendship'. These feelings towards Pushkin were mirrored by those of Elizaveta's daughter, Dolly Fiquelmont (Dar'ya Fikel'mon), who was the wife of the Austrian Ambassador. The story about an adventurous night spent with her by Pushkin, however, afterwards recorded by Nashchokin (a story regarded by some as the origin of an episode in *The Queen of Spades*), may well be no more than a Casanova's tale.[27]

In the spring of 1828 Pushkin asked to be allowed to join the army in the Caucasus, then fighting the Persians. After receiving the predictable refusal, on 21 April he wrote seeking the tsar's permission for a stay of 'six or seven months' in Paris, a request that does not seem to have been passed on to Nicholas by Benckendorff.[28] Instead, Pushkin was a guest at Praskov'ya Osipova's Malinniki estate for most of the time from October of that year until early 1829. Thence he travelled back via St. Petersburg, to Moscow. For this relentlessly peripatetic existence there is more than one possible explanation. Pushkin may be regarded as having resumed at this stage of his life the pursuit of dissipation more or less where he had left it a few years earlier – apparently the view taken by Vyazemsky in his letter to Turgenev. On the other hand, it may have been in part a reaction to the depression which begins to become apparent in Pushkin during these years. A melancholy poem written at the very end of 1829 included the lines:

> День каждый, каждую годину
> Привык я думой провождать,
> Грядущей смерти годовщину
> Меж их стараясь угадать.

Each day, each year I have grown accustomed to a parting reflection, trying to guess, among them, the anniversary of my approaching death.[29]

It goes without saying that Pushkin never used the modern word 'depression' himself, but the Russian words for 'spleen' and 'bile' recur increasingly during the last ten years of his correspondence. In the late 1820s he already had cause to be depressed. His nanny, Arina Rodionovna, died on 31 July 1828. Moreover, not only did Pushkin become embroiled with the imperial censorship almost immediately after his initially cordial reception by the new tsar, but he also began to fall foul of the literary critics, for the first time in his life.

The most notorious onslaught on Pushkin's work was conducted in the St. Petersburg journal, *Northern Bee*, by a hack journalist, Faddei Bulgarin. Ten years older than Pushkin, a Pole and originally a liberal, by the mid-1820s he had turned his coat. He actually became one of Benckendorff's agents; and it was probably he who read *Boris Godunov* for Benckendorff in 1826. Pushkin also distanced himself from Nikolai Polevoy, the editor of the *Moscow Telegraph*, a journal which Pushkin had at first supported after his return to Moscow. All this in the atmosphere of what could perhaps be described as a literary conflict of 'gentlemen versus players'.[30] This conflict was partly social and partly ideological. Ranged against the 'bourgeois radicalism' of Polevoy, who later found a tactical ally in Bulgarin, was the 'literary aristocracy' of Pushkin and Vyazemsky. It was against this inauspicious background that Pushkin's *Poltava* was published in the following year. It was not a success. The new, metallic quality of Pushkin's poetic style, evident both in the composition and in the metre of this poem, baffled the public as well as the critics at the time. The *Vestnik evropy* (*European Herald*), which had published Pushkin's very first poem in St. Petersburg when he was a schoolboy, described this new style as 'parody';[31] and an influential critic wrote in the same journal that the poem *Poltava* was a veritable Poltava for Pushkin. 'Thanks to his poem he has undergone the very fate of Charles XII.'[32]

Nor did Pushkin at this juncture confine his praise of Russian autocracy to Peter the Great. His poem 'Stanzas', written in the last days of December 1826, at a time when he seems still to have hoped that Nicholas I might prove a less reactionary tsar than he in fact did, concluded with the lines:

> Во всем будь пращуру подобен:
> Как он, неутомим и тверд,
> И памятью, как он, незлобен.

Be proud of your family likeness; in everything be like your ancestor
[Peter the Great], like him, tireless and firm, and, like him, forgiving.

Aware of the effect that this naïveté must have on some of his friends,
he then wrote another poem, 'To my friends', beginning with the
words, 'No, I am not a flatterer when I lay free praise before the tsar.'
On the latter poem the tsar commented that it could be circulated,
but not printed.[33]

To all this criticism Pushkin's response was essentially what he
would write near the end of his life, in the last two lines of his *Exegi
Monumentum*: 'Accept praise and slander with indifference, and do
not quarrel with a fool.' Pushkin's attitude to what he referred to as
the *tolpa* (the crowd) is abundantly clear from a stanza of his poem
'Ezersky': 'Do not share with the crowd either anger or surprise or
melody, needs, laughter or labour ... Your work is your reward – by
that you breathe, but its fruit you throw to the crowd – the slave of
vanity.' Nevertheless, it is equally clear how much he smarted within
himself under criticism of his writing. On another occasion he wrote:

Recently I spent intolerable hours of quarantine [in the autumn of
1830] seclusion, having with me neither a book nor a companion. It
occurred to me to spend the time writing a refutation of the critics who
might just recall their own observations on my own works. I dare
assure my reader (if God sends me a reader) that never in my life have
I been able to think of a stupider occupation than that.[34]

During these years the idea of marriage came gradually to the fore in
Pushkin's mind. He did not abandon his advocacy of *grisettes: 'bien plus
court et bien plus commode'* ('much quicker and much more conven-
ient'). He resumed some old affairs, such as with Anna Kern, and he
also began some new ones, notably with Countess Agrafena Zakrevskaya. Two of his short lyrics are proof of his feelings for Agrafena.
In 'The Portrait' he compares her, outshining every other woman in
St. Petersburg, with 'a lawless comet among the heavenly bodies in
their foreordained path'; while another poem ends with the lines:

> Твоей тоскливою мечтой,
> При ком любовью млеешь явно,
> Чьи взоры властвуют тобой;
> Но жалок тот, кто молчаливо,
> Сгорая пламенем любви,
> Потупя голову ревниво,
> Признанья слушает твои.

> Happy is he who, capriciously chosen by your bored fancy, in whose presence you plainly melt with love, whose glances hold sway over you; but unhappy is he, who silently burning with the flame of love, bowing his head in jealousy, listens to your admissions.[35]

Agrafena, a married lady of exactly Pushkin's age, had many other admirers as well as Pushkin. Known in St. Petersburg society as the Bronze Venus, she appears in the last chapter of *Evgenii Onegin* sitting next to Tatyana at the ball. Pushkin thinly disguises her as 'Nina Voronskaya, this Cleopatra of the Neva'.

Pushkin also knew himself well enough to wonder, right up to the last possible moment, whether marriage would really solve his problems. Moreover, he did not appear an ideal suitor in the eyes of the parents of eligible daughters, in spite of his fame, although he could, if he chose, be very attractive to women. The reasons for this are obvious: he had no property; he spent every rouble that he earned (and more); and his way of life for the past ten years had been erratic. There was, however, an additional reason of some importance. The fact that Pushkin's writings were under judicial investigation was not a closely kept secret in Russian society; indeed one of his prospective fathers-in-law was a member of the Council of State when it took the decision that Pushkin should be kept under secret surveillance.

Between his return from exile and his first, unsuccessful, proposal of marriage to his future wife, Pushkin made three false starts. The first was with a distant relation, Sofia Pushkina, whom he probably met in the house of her brother-in-law, Vasilii Zubkov, during his first weeks in Moscow in 1826. By 3 November she had become his 'good angel'; and four weeks later he wrote Zubkov a long letter in French, simultaneously wondering, on the one hand, whether his own 'life, until now so wandering, so stormy' and his 'unequal character, all at once jealous, susceptible, violent and weak' qualified him to make Sofia as happy as he wanted her to be; and, on the other hand, seeking Zubkov's aid in removing her suitor, Valerian Panin, from the running. In vain – Sofia married Panin in April 1827.[36]

A further attempt was more serious, in that it seems to have included an actual proposal of marriage. Pushkin had frequented the Olenins' hospitable home during his early years at St. Petersburg, when he first met their pretty daughter, Anna, as a child. Ten years later they met there again. By May 1828, according to Vyazemsky's letters to his wife, Pushkin was in love with Anna, who by then was almost twenty years old.[37] Of Pushkin's poems about Anna, the most charming, 'Thou and You', is unfortunately impossible to render in English, because the whole point of the poem was a slip of the tongue, whereby Anna had mistakenly addressed Pushkin in the second person singular.[38] On the following Sunday he brought Anna 'Thou and You', recording her mistake. Another is:

> Город пышный, город бедный,
> Дух неволи, стройный вид,
> Свод иебес зелено-бледный,
> Скука, холод и гранит –
> Всё же мне вас жаль немножко,
> Потому что здесь порой
> Ходит маленькая ножка,
> Вьется локон золотой.

Splendid city, poor city, spirit of bondage, harmonious look, pale green vault of the heavens, boredom, cold and granite – none the less I am a little sorry for you, because here from time to time there treads a little foot, there waves a golden curl.[39]

There are two variants of the reason for the rejection of Pushkin's proposal. According to one, he failed to arrive in time at what was intended as his engagement party. According to the other, this coincided with the decision about Pushkin taken by the Council of State, of which Olenin was a member. One explanation does not necessarily exclude the other.

The girl with whom Pushkin fell in love at first sight – at a ball given in Moscow towards the end of 1826 – whom he saw again and again over the next four years, to whom he dedicated poems, in whose album he wrote and drew repeatedly, but to whom he apparently never proposed marriage, was Ekaterina Ushakova. When reading the last lines of his poem 'The Answer', it must be recalled that Pushkin greatly preferred St. Petersburg to Moscow:

> Пора! в Москву! в Москву сейчас!
> Здесь город чопорный, унылый,
> Здесь речи – лед, сердча – гранит;
> Здесь нет ни ветрености милой,
> Ни муз, ни Пресни, ни харит.

It's time! To Moscow! To Moscow at once! Here the city is dour, cheerless, here their talk is like ice, their hearts are like granite; and here there is no dear frivolity, nor muses, nor Presna, nor graces.[40]

Almost up to the last moment (the spring of 1830) Pushkin's friends still believed that they might marry. At any rate, to begin with Ekaterina clearly reciprocated Pushkin's initial feelings and it is possible that she agreed to marry him, but later changed her mind.[41] The Ushakovs' house in Moscow was frequented by writers and musicians. When Pushkin himself was in Moscow, he sometimes went there as much as three times in a day. It is understandable that those who knew both Pushkin and Ekaterina Ushakova went on thinking that the two might marry. Both Ekaterina's background and her character suggest that she would have made him a good wife. Ten years younger than Pushkin, she also seems to have been a determined girl. Her determination showed itself many years later, when she insisted on destroying her correspondence with Pushkin on the grounds that the secret of her and Pushkin's mutual love must die with her. It did. Ekaterina destroyed her correspondence.[42] Apart from the album containing the celebrated Don Juan list,[43] there is not enough evidence on which to judge what really happened. Once Pushkin had revealed the identity of the family into which he was seeking to marry, both Ekaterina and her parents may well have felt that she had had a fortunate escape. We simply cannot tell.

One year before this point of no return had been reached (in the spring of 1830) Pushkin took one of his least explicable decisions. Without informing Benckendorff, whose disapproval he was bound to incur, he suddenly set off for the Caucasus on 1 May 1829, apparently on the spur of the moment, although in order to undertake this long journey, he had to order horses nearly two months earlier. According to his own papers, he wanted to take the waters and, Tiflis being not far away on the other side of the Caucasus range, also to take the opportunity to visit his brother Lev and some of his friends, in particular Nikolai Raevsky, now commanding a cavalry brigade. This does not, however, explain why he first went two hundred *versts* out of his way to Orel, in order to visit General Aleksei Ermolov. Pushkin was well received by Ermolov, who had previously been a popular commander-in-chief in the Caucasus, but was now living on his estate in retirement. He had been relieved of his command by Nicholas I (who may have suspected him of sympathizing with Decembrist officers) and replaced in the Caucasus in 1827 by Nicholas' intimate friend, Field Marshal Ivan Paskevich. One of Pushkin's characteristics was that he never became street-wise.

It is also not clear why Pushkin waited until 1835 before publishing his *Journey to Erzerum at the Time of the Campaign of the Year 1829*.[44] In his foreword to this account, which was based on the diary that he had kept at the time, Pushkin describes Paskevich as 'a distinguished commander, who received me affectionately under the shade of his tent and also found time among his other major preoccupations to show me the most flattering attention'. At the same time Pushkin wrote that he did not travel to the war in order to sing of future exploits, since that would have been for him 'on one hand, too proud and on the other hand, too indecent'. Be that as it may, these five chapters of descriptive prose do not add a great deal to our knowledge of Pushkin's personality, except that, had he lived until later Russian wars, he might have become a remarkable war correspondent. Having reached Tiflis after nearly a month's travel, he found neither his brother nor Raevsky there. By 8 June, however, he had received permission to visit the army in the field (Paskevich had been briefed well in advance by Benckendorff) and on the 10th he left Tiflis. He finally caught up with Raevsky and his brother on the 13th, not far from the fortress of Kars (in Turkish Armenia), which had already been captured. Pushkin witnessed the Russian army's subsequent capture of Erevan on the 27th.

Here he spent a few weeks before setting out on his return journey on 19 July. According to Pushkin's own published account, on that day Paskevich suggested that he should remain to witness further military operations, but he himself wanted to hurry back home. It seems equally possible that once Paskevich realized that he could not expect an instant eulogy from Pushkin's pen, he was not sorry to see him go. Nevertheless, he presented him with a Turkish sabre, which Pushkin kept as a memento of his journey. Two incidents made this journey memorable, apart from the fact that it was the only time in Pushkin's life that he set foot on non-Russian soil. The first he described himself in his published account. Near the frontier between Georgia and Armenia Pushkin was crossing a river when:

Two oxen, yoked to a cart, were climbing up the steep road. A few Georgians were accompanying the cart. 'Where have you come from?' I asked them – 'From Tehran' – 'What are you carrying?' – 'Griboedov' – It was the corpse of the murdered Griboedov, whom they were escorting to Tiflis. [Griboedov, appointed Russian Minister in Tehran, had been murdered there by the mob in January.][45]

The second episode took place when Pushkin was in the middle of eating a meal with Raevsky, his brother Lev and other officers. Word was brought that the Turks were attacking and had reached the Russian outposts. Everyone present rushed to mount their horses, which had been saddled since the morning. In fact the Turkish attack did not amount to very much, but in the course of the pursuit the other officers lost sight of Pushkin. He was eventually found, having pursued the Turks himself with his sabre and a lance that he had picked up (perhaps from a dead Cossack) on the way. He must have been an extraordinary sight, so much so that, according to another account, the troops mistook him, in his frock coat and top hat, for a Lutheran chaplain.[46]

Pushkin's return journey was uneventful, except for heavy gambling losses incurred on the way. Towards the end of September he was back in Moscow. Benckendorff took some time to give him the inevitable wigging. Pushkin's reply, dated 10 November 1829, said that he believed that he had the right to travel to Tiflis; and once he had reached the army in the field:

> it seemed embarrassing to avoid taking part in the engagements which were about to take place and it is in this way that I was present during the campaign, half as a soldier and half as a traveller. I realize how false my position has been and how thoughtless my conduct; but at least it was nothing more than thoughtlessness. The idea that my conduct might be attributed to any other motive would be intolerable for me.[47]

Pushkin's first concern on his arrival in Moscow had nothing to do with either the tsar or Benckendorff, however. He went straight to No. 50 in Bol'shaya Nikitskaya Street – the house of the Goncharovs. Natalya Nikolaevna Goncharova's mother, Natalya Ivanovna, was not yet up and received him in bed. The reason for this call was that, just before leaving for the Caucasus, Pushkin had received from Natalya Ivanovna a non-committal reply to a proposal of marriage to Natalya Nikolaevna, which he had delivered through an intermediary. It looked very much as though Natalya Ivanovna had decided to incur the expense of a further Moscow season for her daughter, in the hope of securing for her a better marriage than Pushkin could offer. Nevertheless he did not take this half-no for an answer. Instead, on 1 May 1829 he wrote a letter to Natalya Ivanovna that remained on the record, so to speak. Written in the stilted French which a Russian gentleman used in writing to a lady older than himself, it is best left in its original form:

C'est à genoux, c'est en versant des larmes de reconnaissance que j'aurais dû Vous écrire, à present que le Comte Tolstoy m'a rapporté Votre réponse: cette réponse n'est pas un refus, Vous me permettez l'espérance. Cependant si je murmure encore, si de la tristesse et de l'amertume se mêlent à des sentiments de bonheur, ne m'accusez point d'ingratitude; je conçois la prudence et la tendresse d'une mère! – Mais pardonnez à l'impatience d'un coeur malade et privé de bonheur. Je pars à l'instant, j'emporte au fond de l'âme l'image de l'être céleste qui Vous doit le jour – Si Vous avez quelques ordres à me donner, veuillez les adresser au comte de Tolstoy, qui me les fera parvenir.

Daignez, Madame, accepter l'hommage de ma profonde considération.

Pouchkine[48]

It is on my knees, shedding tears of gratitude that I should have written to you, as soon as Count Tolstoy brought me your answer; this answer is not a refusal, you allow me to hope. If I still murmur, however, if sadness and bitterness are mixed with feelings of happiness, on no account accuse me of ingratitude; I can imagine the prudence and the tenderness of a mother! – But pardon the impatience of a sick heart, deprived of happiness. I am leaving at this moment, I bear with me in the depth of my soul the image of the heavenly being who owes her existence to you – If you have some orders to give me, please be good enough to address them to Count Tolstoy, who will pass them on to me.

Kindly accept, Madame, the homage of my deep respect.

Pushkin

In spite of this tactfully expressed suggestion that any further letter might be sent to him through Count Fedor Tolstoy, not a word had been forthcoming during the four months of Pushkin's absence, nor did he make any mention of the Goncharovs in a letter to Tolstoy, which he drafted in Tiflis, on his way southwards.[49] His reception at the Goncharovs' house in September was icy.

Undeterred by this further rebuff, in the autumn of 1829 he turned his attentions elsewhere. In the first instance he resumed his visits to Ekaterina Ushakova, in whose album he drew a sketch of a severe woman, 'Kars Mamma'. (The joke was a comparison with the fortress Kars, captured from the Turks by Russian troops during the campaign that Pushkin had recently witnessed.) However, he also

wrote an inscription on the cover of a volume of his poems, dated 21
September 1829, which suggests that he was still far from indifferent
to Ekaterina.[50] By 12 October he was once again off to St. Petersburg,
by way of the ladies of Malinniki. From St. Petersburg he wrote to
Benckendorff on 7 January 1830, seeking permission – 'while I am
still neither married nor attached to the service' – either to travel to
France or Italy or to visit China with the Russian mission that was
about to go there. Neither request was granted.[51] Towards the end of
the month a letter from Pushkin to Vyazemsky, who was then in
Moscow, asked him for news – equally – of Natalya Nikolaevna
Goncharova and of Ekaterina Ushakova.[52] On 12 March he returned
to Moscow, where he ran into Natalya at a concert. On 5 April he
returned to the charge at Bol'shaya Nikitskaya Street for the third
time.

CHAPTER NINE

The Second Caesura: Marriage

I learned about his [Pushkin's] marriage and his [subsequent] appointment as *Kammerjunker*; both one and the other somehow fitted badly in my mind: I could not imagine Pushkin as a family man and as a courtier of the tsar; a wife who was a beauty and service at court made me fearful on his behalf. All that taken together, according to my conception of him, did not promise to secure his happiness

—Ivan Pushchin

Pushkin did not marry Natalya Nikolaevna Goncharova until 18 February 1831. He first met her at one of the balls given in Moscow during the winter of 1828–9 – the season in which, aged just sixteen, she made her début. Two of his letters written in April 1830, one to his mother-in-law and the other to his parents, suggest that this was a case of love at first sight on his part. Their date, however, and the circumstances in which they were written – just before his official engagement to his future wife – make these letters doubtful indicators of his true feelings, especially if they are compared with the evidence of the way in which he actually spent the years 1828–30.[1] By contrast, there is no doubt whatever that later on Pushkin fell deeply in love with Natalya. A single sentence in a letter that he wrote to her two and a half years after their marriage could hardly have said more: 'Nothing in the world can be compared to your face – but I love your soul more than your face.'[2]

Natalya's feelings towards Pushkin, both before and after their marriage, are a matter of debate, as is her character. After her death in 1863 it was inevitable that her reputation should become vulnerable, especially once Pushkin's letters to his wife had been published (on the initiative of his younger daughter, who in 1877 persuaded Ivan Turgenev to edit them for publication). Pushkin's first biographer,

Annenkov, who was the outstanding Russian memoirist of the century, did not address this problem at all, for understandable reasons. If, moreover – as was at first generally assumed – the only things that Natalya was taught before her marriage were French, dancing and riding, this was nothing out of the ordinary at the time. In her memoirs, published in *Novoe vremya* in 1907–8, Natalya's daughter by her second marriage, Alexandra Arapova, took up the cudgels on her mother's behalf, but her double bias – in her mother's favour and against Pushkin – taken in conjunction with the fact that her evidence was second-hand, make her an unreliable source. The first detailed study of the circumstances of Pushkin's death, Pavel Shchegolev's *The Duel and Death of Pushkin* published in 1917, dismissed Natalya as having 'romanticism of society love affairs' as her sole aim in life. Writing nearly half a century later, by which time further documentary evidence had come to light, Anna Akhmatova launched this swingeing attack : 'Pushkin did not have the slightest influence on his wife, she did all that she wanted, never taking any account of him whatsoever, she ruined him and deprived him of his spiritual tranquillity . . .' In recent years, however, a revisionist trend has counter-attacked on Natalya's behalf in Russia.[3]

What has never been called in question is Natalya's beauty. The standard portrait, constantly reproduced in books about Pushkin, does not do her full justice. Moreover, it is hardly relevant to the present study, because it was painted (by V. Gau) at the time of her second marriage. Nevertheless, it shows us a strikingly elegant woman, by then in her early thirties. Some idea of what she looked like in her first youth is conveyed by Pushkin's own sketch and by the watercolour of Natalya in the Pushkin Museum in St. Petersburg, which is attributed to the fashionable (oil) painter Karl Bryullov. (In Pushkin's later letters to Natalya there are several references to Bryullov and to his wish – unfulfilled – that Bryullov should paint her portrait.) Perhaps the most convincing description of her beauty in early youth is that of Count Vladimir Sollogub:

> In the course of my life I have seen many beautiful women who were perhaps more attractive, but I have never met a woman who presented a perfection that was almost complete, classical both in her features and in her body. She was tall [about 5 feet 6 inches – therefore two or three inches taller than Pushkin] with a deliciously thin waist and marvellous bosom, above which her fine head was balanced like a lily;

I have never had the opportunity to contemplate such a beautiful and such a regular profile, and what colouring, what eyes, what teeth, what ears! Yes, she was a real beauty, and it was quite natural that her presence made all other women fade away, even the most charming. She always seemed reserved almost to the point of coldness and she talked little.[4]

Natalya Nikolaevna's education now seems to have been less sketchy than was originally supposed. Although not a single one of her letters to Pushkin has survived, she clearly had Russian as well as French. This was not always the case in those days. (In *Evgenii Onegin* Pushkin reminds the reader that Tatyana's letter to Onegin could in reality have been written only in French.)[5] She also rode well. Nothing, however, in her education could have prepared her for the multiple role that she had to try to perform in the six years of her marriage to Pushkin, as the wife of a man who was simultaneously poet, scholar, gambler, man of the world and father of a family, who was himself called upon increasingly to look after the affairs of other members of the family as well.

This then was the girl, not yet aged eighteen, to whom Pushkin, who was almost thirty-one, was formally engaged on 6 May 1830. Pushkin still had reservations. He was frank about them; but his reservations related largely to himself, not to Natalya Nikolaevna and her family. Thus, in a letter that he wrote to her mother a month before the official engagement, he reflected at some length on the possibility that, instead of marrying him, she might have had the good fortune to 'form other links more equal, more brilliant, more worthy of herself'. He then went on to reveal his anxiety about what would, in the event, dog the whole of their married life: the problem of money.

Let us speak of money; I don't mind about it myself. My fortune has been enough for me so far. Will it be enough for me once I am married? I shall not tolerate it for anything in the world that my wife should experience deprivations, that she should not be where she is called upon to shine and to enjoy herself. She has the right to demand it. In order to satisfy her I am ready to sacrifice all the tastes, all the passions of my life, an existence that has been completely free and completely adventurous. Nevertheless, will she not murmur if her position in the world will not be as brilliant as the one she deserves and which I would have wished for her? Such are, in part, my anxieties. I tremble to think that you may find them reasonable.[6]

About the same time Pushkin wrote to his parents, asking not only for their blessing, but also for financial help. This was, for once, forthcoming. His father made over to him a small part of the Pushkin family estate in the Nizhnii Novgorod province; this estate comprised the adjacent villages of Kistenevo and Boldino. It was the former, with 200 'free' (that is to say, unmortgaged) serfs, which now became Pushkin's. According to Sergei L'vovich's calculations, this would give his son an annual income of at least 4000 roubles. The transaction was formally completed on 27 June 1830.[7]

The fact that Pushkin's future mother-in-law was aware of his troubles with the government made it prudent – perhaps essential – for him to write to Benckendorff. This he did on 16 April, explaining Natalya Ivanovna's anxiety on this score and declaring: 'my happiness depends on a word of goodwill expressed by him for whom my devotion and my gratitude are already pure and without limit'.[8]

Benckendorff's reply, written twelve days later, ended with this remarkable paragraph:

> As for your personal position in regard to the government, I can only repeat to you all that I have said to you so many times; I find it entirely in your own interest; there can be nothing in it either false or doubtful, unless you wish to make it such yourself. His Majesty the Emperor, with a completely paternal care for you, sir, has been good enough to give me, General Benckendorff, the duty, not as chief of police, but as a man in whom he is good enough to put his confidence, to watch over you and to guide you with his advice; the police have never been given the order to keep you under surveillance. The advice which I have given you from time to time, as a friend, can only have been useful to you, and I hope that you will become ever more convinced of this yourself. What is the shadow that anyone can find in your position in this respect? I authorize you, sir, to have this letter shown to those to whom you believe that you ought to show it.[9]

In parenthesis, Benckendorff's letter also brought Pushkin a welcome piece of news: that the tsar would now allow him to have *Boris Godunov* published in its original form, although this must be done on Pushkin's 'personal responsibility' – a decision which he at once communicated to his publisher, Pletnev, in a letter beginning with the triumphant words 'My dear fellow! Victory!'[10]

Pushkin's friends reacted in different ways to news of his engagement. Vyazemsky wrote at once to say that while having dinner with Pushkin's father in St. Petersburg he had been able to read through Pushkin's letter to Sergei L'vovich, which had convinced him that he really was engaged to be married. But what convinced him most of all of the truth of the engagement was the fact that Sergei L'vovich opened a special bottle of champagne in honour of the occasion. As Vyazemsky put it:

> It was then that I saw clearly that this was no joking matter. I could have disbelieved your letters and your father's tears, but I had to believe his champagne. I congratulate you from the bottom of my heart ... It is fitting that you, our first romantic poet, should marry the first romantic beauty of the young generation.[11]

When Pushkin visited St. Petersburg in the summer of 1830, Anna Kern found him looking 'a completely different man'.[12] On the other hand, Elizaveta Khitrovo warned him about what she described as the 'prosaic side of marriage', saying that she had always thought that 'genius could sustain itself only in complete independence and that it developed only in a series of misfortunes, that a perfect, stable, continual and, in the long run, rather monotonous, happiness killed the means, made a man fat and a contented fellow rather than a great poet!'[13] To this letter Pushkin replied light-heartedly that Elizaveta's reflections about his marriage would be 'perfectly just, if you had judged me less poetically. The fact is that I am a good fellow and that I do not ask for anything better than to grow fat and to be happy – the one is easier than the other.' But he added at the end of his letter three inaccurate sentences: 'My wife's parents pay very little attention to her and to me. I return this to them with all my heart. This relationship is very agreeable and I shall never change it.'[14]

Pushkin's inner feelings were expressed in a passage in the almost certainly autobiographical document which has already been quoted in the preceding chapter:

> I am getting married, that is to say, I am sacrificing my independence, my carefree, self-indulgent independence, my luxurious habits, my aimless passions, my seclusion, my inconstancy. And so I am now doubling my life which was previously incomplete, I am beginning to think: 'we'. I never bothered about happiness: I was able to do without it. Now I have to have happiness for two, but where am I going to get it from?[15]

As events would prove, Pushkin had good reason for his doubts (repeated in a letter written on the eve of his wedding). However, these doubts should not have focused only on himself, but at least equally on the family into which he was going to marry. True, the opinion expressed by Ivan Pushchin (quoted in the epigraph to this chapter) was written a quarter of a century after Pushkin's marriage.[16] Pushchin, moreover, was in Siberia at the time that Pushkin married. Nevertheless, the Russian nobility was so small a class that almost everybody who was a member of it knew everybody else, at any rate in St. Petersburg and Moscow. At the time of Pushkin's marriage, therefore, Pushchin would have retained a good idea of what the Goncharov family was like. Being a sensible man as well as one of Pushkin's oldest friends, he would also have understood the reason why, Natalya Nikolaevna's beauty notwithstanding, most of Moscow's eligible young bachelors might have preferred to give the Goncharov family a wide berth.

Socially, the Goncharovs belonged to much the same stratum of Russian society – the middle nobility – as Pushkin's parents, although they had arrived there by a different route from that followed by both sides of Pushkin's family. The Goncharovs' route is one easily recognizable by social historians of eighteenth- and nineteenth-century England: success in business combined with marriage into the aristocracy. The Goncharov fortune was founded early in the eighteenth century by an enterprising member of a family which had long been engaged in the pottery business near Kaluga. Here Afanasii Abramovich Goncharov established a linen factory and a paper mill on the River Suchodrev. By the time that he died, having supplied sails not only for Peter the Great's newly created fleet, but also – it is said – for foreign navies, his estimated worth was three and a half million roubles. By special ukase issued in 1789 Catherine II conferred hereditary nobility on his grandson, Afanasii Nikolaevich, who was the grandfather of Pushkin's future wife. Both he and his son, Nikolai Afanasevich, married well; Nikolai's wedding in St Petersburg – to Natalya Ivanovna Zagryazhskaya – was attended by the imperial family.[17]

Thereafter, although the Goncharov factory and estate were entailed and it took some years to get through the multimillion fortune, the family went gradually downhill. In 1815, after a long stay in Paris, Afanasii Nikolaevich brought home a lady known as

Madame Babette; and when he died seventeen years later he left one and a half million roubles of debt. He seems, however, to have doted on his grand-daughter, Natalya Nikolaevna ('Tasha' in her own family, although Pushkin rarely called her by this name); and he spoiled her during the first five or six years of her life, which she spent on the family estate. By the time Pushkin met her, she – like her two elder sisters – was living in Moscow with her parents, whose grandeur was now a thing of the past. According to family tradition, Nikolai Afanasevich suffered from a severe form of mental illness as the result of a riding accident towards the end of 1814. More recent research suggests that he took to the bottle. Either way, every problem that Pushkin's engagement and wedding involved – and there were to be many – had to be dealt with exclusively through Natalya Nikolaevna's mother, Natalya Ivanovna, who had by then become an exceedingly difficult lady, seeking solace in exaggeratedly pious religiosity from the (relative) poverty that she had never expected to experience in her life. Worse than that, however, was her *poshlost'*; a Russian word which includes so many disagreeable characteristics – vulgarity, meanness, small-mindedness, banality, pettiness – that it is best left untranslated.[18]

Had there been an equivalent of Oscar Wilde's Lady Bracknell in Russian society at that time, she might have observed that to lose one parent to alcoholism might be regarded as a misfortune, but to lose the other as well – to religious mania – looked like carelessness. In the extraordinary saga that followed Pushkin's engagement to Natalya Nikolaevna, it is not clear how much they saw of each other, whether they had any opportunity to discuss their own future, or whether Pushkin ever received a letter from his fiancée that had not been dictated by her mother. Natalya Ivanovna's iron grip on her family does not seem to have been relaxed by a single iota after her youngest daughter became engaged to be married – if anything, rather the reverse. What is certain is that Pushkin was plunged almost immediately into a prolonged financial haggle with Natalya Ivanovna; and he also allowed himself to be used as an intermediary with the St. Petersburg authorities for a preposterous proposal that the government should, for 25,000 roubles, buy from Afanasii Nikolaevich a huge bronze statue of Catherine II that had been languishing in the cellars of the Goncharov country house since the eighteenth century. Pushkin's diplomacy, for which Afanasii

Nikolaevich was not in the least grateful, did not succeed; in the end the statue fetched 7000 roubles, well after Pushkin's death.[19]

Since Natalya Nikolaevna had no dowry, Pushkin's small estate was swiftly swallowed up. The mortgage to which he at once had recourse, yielded 38,000 paper roubles – the equivalent of nearly 11,500 silver roubles. Of this sum, 11,000 roubles went straight to Natalya Ivanovna, for her daughter's trousseau; 10,000 went to Nashchokin 'in order to extricate him from difficult circumstances: certain money'; and 17,000 remained 'for settling down and living on for a year'.[20] The sum of 10,000 roubles given to Nashchokin – by coincidence, exactly the same as the single payment that Pushkin received from his publisher for *Boris Godunov* – is curious, even allowing for the fact that Nashchokin's finances were notorious for their steep ups and downs. Were the 'difficult circumstances' in reality Pushkin's own, which he asked Nashchokin to deal with, out of the 10,000 roubles? He and Pushkin certainly concluded a triangular deal later on, designed to liquidate simultaneously one of Pushkin's major card debts and a debt owed by Nashchokin to Pushkin. In any event, by September 1831 we know that Nashchokin had no money whatever of Pushkin's at his disposal.[21]

In order to give an idea, for purposes of rough comparison, of the kind of annual income that was needed by a man of Pushkin's social standing in St. Petersburg or Moscow, it may be useful to recall that twenty years earlier – soon after joining the imperial service – Capodistria estimated that he needed 6000 roubles a year to live on, although by exercising severe economy he kept his expenses for the year 1810 down to 4500 roubles.[22] Capodistria was a frugal bachelor. In Pushkin's breakdown of his financial position in the run-up to his marriage there is one significant omission: his card debts. His correspondence during these months makes it clear that these debts were heavy; that his only hope of paying them off was to spread repayment over a period of years; and that he was desperately in need of money throughout 1830. Caught halfway between the erratic generosity of Nashchokin and the unfailing meanness of his future mother-in-law, Pushkin received no contribution from Natalya Ivanovna to the expenses of the wedding except perhaps in the form of jewellery, although it is not clear whether she herself mortgaged her jewels and then gave Pushkin and his wife the power to redeem them or whether she gave the jewels to them and they were mortgaged afterwards – probably the latter.[23] Only this degree of desperation can fully explain two sentences at the end of a letter that Pushkin wrote on 24 August to his fiancée's grandfather: 'My hope rests on you alone. It is on you alone that the decision of my fate depends.'[24] It was not until many months later that reality took over and Pushkin accepted the critical difference between assets and cash flow. Quite simply, there was no money whatever forthcoming either from his mother-in-law or from the Goncharov estate.

Meanwhile the wedding was delayed. Originally fixed for September, it had to be delayed for six weeks because Pushkin was in mourning for his uncle Vasilii, who died on 20 August 1830. Far more important, however, was the further row with Natalya Ivanovna that exploded at the end of the month. This seems to have come close to breaking off the engagement altogether. In his own words, Pushkin left Moscow 'uncertain of his fate'. Nevertheless, the storm was shortlived. By 9 September he was able to write to Natalya Nikolaevna from Boldino both apologizing and thanking her for a letter which has not survived, but which he found 'charming', adding that it 'has completely reassured me'.[25] (This letter to his fiancée was written in French, since they were not yet married and therefore etiquette precluded writing in Russian.) Pushkin did not return for over three months.[26] The reason for this delay was not a wish – understandable though this might have been – to put off yet another argument with his future mother-in-law for as long as possible, but the spread of the cholera epidemic. Asiatic cholera reached Astrakhan in 1830 and from there spread rapidly as far as Moscow. In the following year it reached St. Petersburg and spread as far north as Archangel and westwards to Poland, where both the Grand Duke Konstantin and the commander-in-chief of the Russian army then fighting the Poles were among the victims. In these two years the epidemic killed over one hundred thousand people in the Russian Empire (there were even more serious epidemics in 1847 and 1848).

Pushkin wrote a vivid description in his letters of his repeated attempts to break through the quarantine posts that were established barring the way from Boldino westwards to Moscow. Nevertheless, this, the first of his three 'Boldino autumns', proved to be one of his most remarkable strokes of good fortune. For over a year he had done virtually no literary work. He now found himself without any distractions whatsoever, not even of the kind that had so often made him ride over to Trigorskoe from Mikhailovskoe. Thus, with an astounding spurt of previously pent-up energy, he suddenly embarked on three of the most creative months of his whole life. Thereafter almost all Pushkin's serious writing, with the exception of notes based on his historical researches, would be done at Boldino. (The Boldino autumns therefore form the subject of a separate chapter in this book – 11.)

When Pushkin finally got through to Moscow on 5 December, he found his future mother-in-law no easier to deal with than when he had left in August. Indeed he actually had to reassure both his friends and his own family that his engagement had not been broken off.[27] After such a long delay Pushkin did not approach his wedding day, which was fixed for 18 February 1831, in a sanguine frame of mind. In January, moreover, he had received a personal blow that hit him with a force at least as great as his running fight with Natalya Ivanovna – the news of the death of Anton Delvig.[28] Less than a week before his wedding Pushkin summed up his feelings about it in a letter in which he admitted that he was suffering a day of 'spleen':

> I am married – or nearly married. Everything that you might be able to tell me about the advantages of bachelor life and the disadvantages of marriage, all that I have already thought over carefully. I have cold-bloodedly weighed up the advantages and disadvantages of the existence that I have chosen. My youth has passed noisily and fruitlessly. Until now I have lived differently from the way people live as a rule. I have had no happiness. *Il n'est de bonheur que dans les voies communes.* I am past thirty. At the age of thirty people usually get married. I am acting like other people and probably I shall not regret it. Moreover I am marrying without enthusiasm and without childish infatuation. The future does not appear to me to be a bed of roses, but in its severe nakedness. Sadnesses will not astonish me. They have entered into my domestic calculations. Any happiness will be an uncovenanted bonus.[29]

In all the circumstances, the most notable thing about these months of Pushkin's life is the fact that his wedding ever took place at all. Nevertheless it did, at the old Church of the Assumption in Bol'shaya Nikitskaya Street, which is today Herzen Street. His stag party on 17 February was a miserable occasion; and the evening before that he had wept after Nashchokin's gypsy mistress had sung for him. That there was an atmosphere of some tension during the service is scarcely surprising; and there were some minor mishaps, including one of the wedding rings being dropped on the floor – so much so that as Pushkin left the church his innate superstition overcame him and he is said to have exclaimed: '*Tous les mauvais augures!*'[30] Nevertheless, a week after the wedding Pushkin wrote to his publisher that his only wish was that nothing in his life should change, adding that the memory of Delvig was the only shadow cast upon it. He and Natalya gave what sounds like a highly successful ball in the house that they had rented in the centre of Moscow, on the Arbat, which lasted until nearly three o'clock in the morning.

Pushkin soon changed his mind. Within six weeks of his wedding he had decided that he and his wife must leave Moscow; and it suddenly occurred to him that renting a *dacha* at Tsarskoe Selo might offer a temporary and inexpensive refuge.[31] The Pushkins left Moscow for Tsarskoe Selo on 15 May. It was not until over a month later that Pushkin wrote to his mother-in-law explaining their departure. This time he did not mince words. The reason for leaving Moscow was, he wrote, 'in order to avoid worries which could in the long run compromise more than my peace of mind'. He accused his mother-in-law point-blank of saying to his wife things about himself that were tantamount to 'preaching divorce'. And he concluded with an icy paragraph about the sum of 11,000 roubles that he had lent to Natalya Ivanovna: 'I do not ask for payment, nor am I pressing you in any way. I only want to know exactly what are the arrangements that you consider it right to make, so that I can make my own in consequence.'[32]

It has been observed already that, however much Pushkin's manners may have been those of a man of the world, one of his most endearing characteristics was his lack of street wisdom. Nevertheless, by this time he must have dismissed from his mind any idea of receiving a single rouble either from his mother-in-law or from any other member of her family. It has been also suggested that his wife may have prevented his letter of 26 June from reaching her mother.[33] Be that as it may, on this occasion there was no humble follow-up letter from Pushkin. For the time being the break was decisive, although a tolerably good *modus vivendi* with Natalya Ivanovna and her family was eventually established. Whether it was wise of Pushkin ever to allow anything further than purely formal relations with his in-laws is, in the light of later developments, a debatable question.

At Tsarskoe Selo Pushkin now walked with his wife, in the imperial gardens, where he had walked many years before as a schoolboy. So it came about that one day in July 1831 they met the tsar out for a similar walk. The empress was, according to Pushkin's sister, enchanted with Natalya. The tsar, moreover, offered to take Pushkin back into the imperial service, with the rank of councillor in the foreign ministry and a salary of 5000 roubles a year. Reporting this news in confidence to his publisher on 22 July, Pushkin wrote that the tsar had given him permission to use the imperial archives, without any obligation to do anything in particular while he was studying them. According to Pushkin, the tsar had remarked to a third party: '*Puisqu'il est marié et qu'il n'est pas riche, il faut faire aller sa marmite*'; and he described the tsar's decision to help him financially, now that he was married, as 'very kind'.[34] This decision is also open to interpretation as the deliberate first move in the melancholy series of events that would later bind Pushkin hand and foot to St. Petersburg and to the imperial service there for the last years of his life. It should, however, be borne in mind that moving in and out of government service was nothing unusual. (Vyazemsky, for example, was readmitted to the service – in his case to the Ministry of Finance – at about the same time.) There is no doubt that this offer of the tsar, which was confirmed on 14 November 1831, when Pushkin formally re-entered the imperial service, in effect became the first link in Pushkin's chains. On the other hand, there is no convincing evidence that this is how Nicholas himself saw his offer when he made it.

Just as Pushkin's friends had been divided in their views about his engagement, so too were they now divided in their initial reactions to his marriage. Elizaveta Khitrovo, who had previously been rather sceptical, now wrote to Vyazemsky in terms that were – for her – enthusiastic, whereas her daughter, Countess Fiquelmont, included a prophetic passage in a letter that she wrote to him at almost the same time: 'The appearance of husband and wife does not foretell either calm or tranquil joy in the future ...'[35] What everybody agreed on, however, was that Pushkin had married an extraordinarily beautiful girl.

The conventional wisdom today is that, once Pushkin had shaken off his mother-in-law, the early months of his marriage to Natalya were among the happiest – perhaps the happiest – of his entire life. It is not easy to judge. By the time that the Pushkins moved to St. Petersburg for good, in the middle of October 1831, Natalya was expecting her first child. Clearly, any judgement depends to a large extent on how Pushkin's personal relationship with his wife developed during this first phase of their marriage (as opposed to how they appeared together as a couple to outside observers at the time). Of Natalya's feelings immediately after their marriage there is no real evidence.[36] But there are two poems – both published long after Pushkin's death, for obvious reasons – that are relevant to his feelings towards Natalaya. They also throw some light on their relationship with each other; certainly far more than Pushkin's poem 'Madonna', which he did publish and which has often been quoted in this context.[37] The two unpublished poems raise questions to which there can be no definite answers, but – by the standards of that age – each of them makes sexually explicit statements. Since they became known, they have been variously interpreted.[38] The interpretation that follows is my own.

If the two poems are taken together, although they were not written in the same year, they suggest that – at least at first – Pushkin derived a sexual satisfaction from this 'shy-cold' (his own description) girl of nineteen; the candour with which he describes it in the second poem is vivid. Undoubtedly, moreover, Natalya exerted an enduring fascination on him. If this interpretation is right, it goes some way towards explaining – in conjunction with other factors described in the next chapter – why Pushkin was unable to extricate himself from the imbroglio that gradually engulfed him in St. Petersburg during the rest of his life.

Of these poems, the first was written some time in 1830:

> Когда в объятия мои
> Твой стройный стан я заключаю
> И речи нежные любви
> Тебе с восторгом расточаю,
> Безмолвна, от стесненных рук
> Освобождая стан свой гибкои,
> Ты отвечаешь, милый друг,
> Мне недоверчивой улыбкой;
> Прилежно в памяти храня
> Измен печальные преданья,
> Ты без участья и вниманья
> Уныло слушаешь меня . . .

Кляну коварные старанья
Преступной юности моей
И встреч условных ожиданья
В садах, в безмолвии ночей.
Кляну речей любовных шепот,
Стихов таинственный напев,
И ласки легковерных дев,
И слезы их, и поздний ропот.

When I clasp your slender form in my embraces and I pour out tender words of love to you with rapture, you silently free your supple body from my constraining arms, and you respond to me, dear friend, with a mistrusting smile; carefully preserving in your memory sad recollections of betrayals, you mournfully listen to me without concern or attention.... I curse the cunning endeavours of my wicked youth and the vigils spent in garden trysts, in the silence of the nights. I curse the whispering of amorous words, the mysterious melody of verses, and the caresses of gullible girls, their tears and their tardy reproaches.[39]

The date of the second poem has not been established, but it was probably written in 1831 or 1832. Some copies are headed 'To my wife':[40]

Нет, я не дорожу мятежным наслажденьем
Восторгом чувственнім, безумством, исступленьем,
Стенаньем, криками вакханки молодой,
Когда, виясь в моих объятиях змией,
Порывом пылких ласк и язвою лобзаний
Она торопит миг Последних содроганий!

О, как милее ты, смиренница моя!
О, как мучительно тобою счастлив я,
Когда, склоняяся на долгие моленья,
Ты предаешься мне нежна без упоенья,
Стыдливо-холодна, восторгу моему
Едва ответствуешь, не внемлешь ничему
И оживляешься потом всё боле, боле –
И делишь наконец мой пламень поневоле!

No, I do not value stormy delights, the rapture of the senses, madness, frenzy, the groans, the cries of a young Bacchant, when, writhing in my serpent's embraces, she hastens the instant of final shudders with a rush of fiery caresses and stinging kisses.

Oh, how much dearer, my meek love, oh, how agonizingly happy I am with you, when, yielding to long prayers, you give yourself to me without delight, shyly-cold you hardly respond to my rapture, you pay no heed to anything, and then you are all the time more and more enlivened and at last you share my flame, against your will![41]

CHAPTER TEN

Imbroglio in St. Petersburg, 1831–1835

И всюду страсти роковые,
И от судеб защиты нет.

(And everywhere there are fatal passions, And from Destiny
there is no defence.)

—Pushkin, *The Gypsies*, the last two lines

In describing Pushkin's early years the biographer has to accept the
fragmentary nature of some of the evidence. In the work of
reconstruction, therefore, gaps need to be left where there are no
reliable sources. During the last ten years of Pushkin's life, however,
this difficulty progressively diminishes, as the sources multiply, and
in the last six it is actually reversed. The evidence, including over
sixty letters written by Pushkin to his wife and the diary which he
began writing again at the end of 1833, becomes a flood. In
consequence, from 1831 onwards the main problems are of
interpretation rather than of fact.

The St. Petersburg imbroglio of 1831–5 – that is to say, stopping
short of Pushkin's final year – has lent itself to a variety of emotive
descriptions: Pushkin a grey-haired *Kammerjunker*, a prisoner of the
tsar, a bankrupt obliged to live at the mercy of the imperial treasury, a
man no longer master in his own house and – the cruellest cut of all –
a poet deserted by his muse. To eschew such phrases is not to deny
some of them an element of truth. Nevertheless, this imbroglio is best
understood as a complex concatenation of mounting pressures from
more than one quarter, which steadily weighed Pushkin down. At
one level, these pressures may be regarded as illustrating the
conclusion earlier drawn by Pushkin himself in the final lines of his
poem *The Gypsies*.[1] Yet, at another level, their consequences appear
to have been possible to foresee; and if they were foreseeable (as Ivan

Pushchin appears to have foreseen them), can the pressures themselves be regarded as having been impossible to ward off?

An attempt to assess this period of Pushkin's life must weigh in the scales additional factors, which have not always been given the weight that they deserve; and some attempts have been spoiled by the temptation either to embroider or to oversimplify. These additional factors include the paradoxes inherent in Pushkin's character, the nature of his relationship with his wife, the deterioration in his health observable towards the end of his life and – last but by no means least – the attitude taken towards him by others during these years. The latter factor does not concern only the hostility of the court and of the *haut monde*, but also the attitudes of his friends. Even though Pushkin's friends all closed ranks firmly behind him after his death, while he was alive they seem to have shown a striking lack of concern about a man so manifestly riding for a fall well before the d'Anthès affair came to a head in November 1836.[2] Even a young friend who saw Pushkin often recorded in his memoirs that it was not until a chance meeting in the Nevsky Prospekt in the winter of 1836–7 that he became aware of what was for him 'the first sign of unfolding drama'.[3]

In 1831 Pushkin wrote what was arguably his most deplorable poem and also one of his best, in each case for political reasons. The year of Pushkin's marriage was memorable in Russian history both for the ravages of the first great cholera epidemic in Russia and for the first outbreak of Russo-Polish warfare since the large Polish contingent serving under Napoleon had crossed the River Niemen in June 1812 together with the rest of his *Grande Armée*. The 'Congress' Kingdom of Poland (briefly described in an earlier chapter) was a compromise settlement of the Polish Question, reached with difficulty at the Congress of Vienna after the British Foreign Secretary, Castlereagh, had reminded Alexander I:

> The Emperor insinuated that the question [of Poland] could only end in one way, as he was in possession. I observed that it was very true His Imperial Majesty was in possession, and he must know that no one was less disposed than myself hostilely to dispute that possession; but I was sure His Imperial Majesty would not be satisfied to rest his pretensions on a title of conquest in opposition to the general sentiments of Europe.[4]

The constitutional essence of this settlement was that the Emperor of Russia should also be the King of Poland. This compromise collapsed at the end of November 1830, when an uprising obliged the Grand Duke Konstantin to flee from the Belvedere Palace in Warsaw. Nicholas I responded with a manifesto, condemning the revolution and ordering the Polish commanders to concentrate their forces at Plock. This done, those who submitted would be pardoned; but if there were bloodshed, it would be the Poles' fault. The mood in Warsaw was such that there was no hope whatever of Nicholas' terms being accepted, and by the end of January 1831 a National Government had been elected, with Adam Czartoryski as President, after the Polish Parliament had signed an act deposing Nicholas as King of Poland. Thus the two countries drifted into a state of war. Partly because of the effects of the cholera epidemic on the Russian army, the weaker side in this unequally matched contest was not finally defeated until 4 October, when the last remnants of the Polish army fled across the Prussian frontier. In August 1831 the capital had surrendered to Field Marshal Paskevich, transferred to the Polish front after his southern victories.[5] Under the terms of the settlement imposed upon Poland following the Russian victory, the Polish army ceased to exist. Paskevich, now given the title of Prince of Warsaw, became viceroy of a country whose regime henceforward did not differ greatly from the remainder of the Russian Empire.[6]

In London, and still more in Paris, sympathy for the Polish cause was strong. Although Lord Palmerston received Czartoryski several times at the Foreign Office, however, his response was that Britain could not send an army to Poland and that to burn the Russian fleet would be about as effectual as the burning of Moscow. In Paris Czartoryski established a kind of exiled court at the Hotel Lambert; and the French Chamber of Deputies even discussed active intervention, but in the event neither the French nor the British government expressed its support more forcefully than in words. Nevertheless, as Talleyrand wisely foresaw, many years would pass before Russia forgot the moral support that France gave to the Poles.[7] This moral support was deeply resented by Russians, particularly because Polish aims included the recovery of the so-called eastern territories (broadly, the western Ukraine, incorporated in the Russian Empire by Catherine II as her share of the partition of Poland). True, there were Russian liberals who had the wisdom to

realize that Nicholas' repressive policy against the Poles could
succeed only in the short term. Vyazemsky was one such Russian,
having himself served from 1818 to 1821 as a member of the Russian
mission in Warsaw (where he learned Polish) after the Congress of
Vienna. On the other hand, Pushkin took a simple Russian chauvinist
view: a further illustration of the contrast between his sure
knowledge of history and the relative naïveté of his understanding of
the international relations of his own time. (It is striking that his
writings in 1830–1 do not contain a single reference to the final
establishment of Greek independence, guaranteed by Russia among
other European powers.[8])

On 1 June 1831, by which time the tide of war had turned in the
Russians' favour, Pushkin wrote to Vyazemsky a letter in which he
complained of the Russian army's slowness in suppressing the Polish
rebellion, which he described as 'a family affair'.[9] Two months later
he went further, with a poem entitled 'To the slanderers of Russia'.
Written ten days before the fall of Warsaw, this poem was one of
three contributed by Pushkin to a political pamphlet entitled *On the
capture of Warsaw* published in September 1831 with an epigraph:
Vox et praeterea nihil.

КЛЕВЕТНИКАМ РОССИИ

О чем шумите вы, народные витии?
Зачем анафемой грозите вы России?
Что возмутпо вас? волнения Литвы?
Оставьте: это спор славян между собою,
Домашний, старый спор, уж взвешенный судьбою,
Вопрос, которого не разрешите вы.

    Уже давно между собою
    Враждуют эти племена;
    Не раз клонилась под грозою
    То их, то наша сторона.

Кто устоит в неравном споре:
Кичливый лях, иль верный росс?
Славянские ль ручьи сольются в русском море?
    Оно ль иссякнет? вот вопрос.

    Оставьте нас: вы не читали
    Сии кровавые скрижали;
    Вам непонятна, вам чужда
    Сия семейная вражда;

Для вас безмолвны Кремль и Прага;
Бессмысленно прельщает вас
Борьбы отчаянной отвага –
И ненавидите вы нас ...

За что ж? ответствуйте: за то ли,
Что на развалинах пылающей Москвы
Мы не признали наглой воли
Того, под кем дрожали вы?
За то ль, что в бездну повалили
Мы тяготеющий над царствами кумир
И нашей кровью искупили
Европы вольность, честь и мир? ...
Вы грозны на словах – попробуйте на деле!

To the slanderers of Russia

What are you making a row about, you orators of the people? Why are you threatening Russia with your anathema? What has aroused you? The Lithuanian disturbances? Let it be: this is a quarrel of Slavs between themselves, an ancient family quarrel, already weighed up by Fate, a question that you will not solve.

These tribes have already been at loggerheads for a long time; more than once, now their side, now ours, has bowed beneath the storm. Who will prevail in the unequal conflict? The arrogant Pole or the true Russian? Will Slav streams flow together in the Russian sea? Will it dry up? That is the question.

Leave us alone: you have not read these bloody annals; this family enmity is incomprehensible to you, to you it is strange, for you the Kremlin and Praga [a suburb of Warsaw] are silent; there is no sense in your being attracted by the bravery of this desperate struggle: and you hate us ...

And for what? Answer: is it because, in the ruins of burning Moscow, we did not acknowledge the impudent will of the man beneath whom you trembled? Is it because we threw down into the abyss the idol whose threats hung over kingdoms and with our blood we redeemed the freedom, the honour and the peace of Europe? You threaten us with words – just try deeds!...[10]

Vyazemsky pulled Pushkin's poem to pieces: 'Why write nonsense and moreover against conscience and above all counter-productively?'[11] Europeans who have witnessed, one hundred years later, the historical consequences of Russo-Polish enmity, have good reason to know which of these two Russians was right in 1831.[12]

Pushkin's pen found better employment in 1831 putting the finishing touches to *Evgenii Onegin*. The completion of this work had been one of the signal achievements of Pushkin's first Boldino autumn. However, not only did Pushkin himself destroy Chapter 10, as has already been described, but in addition Chapter 8, which tells of Onegin's travels between the time when he left his country estate and his return to St. Petersburg, was little less politically dangerous, in particular the observations that it included about Arakcheev's notorious military settlements, which he had created as a kind of state within the Russian state.[13] Although Arakcheev had been out of office for six years, such public criticism of the policies for which the *Arakcheevshchina* in the previous reign was most remembered, was not yet admissible. Pushkin himself decided that, rather than rewriting Chapter 8 to suit the censorship, it was better to omit it altogether. This in turn required further work on what thus became the final chapter. In this complicated way it came about that on 5 October 1831 Pushkin added to this now renumbered Chapter 8 Onegin's letter to Tatyana: one of the few examples of brilliant writing in verse undertaken by Pushkin away from Boldino after his marriage.[14] Three months later *Evgenii Onegin* was published as a whole work for the first time.

Hardly had the Pushkins settled into their St. Petersburg flat – their second, because they moved out of their first almost at once – than Pushkin travelled to Moscow, where he stayed with Nashcho-kin: the first of several such visits. Pushkin's purpose was twofold: namely to work in the imperial archives and to attempt to sort out the continuing disorder of his financial affairs. It had now been decided that, so far from doing nothing in the imperial archives (as Pushkin had suggested in his first letter about this to his publisher), he should write a history of Peter the Great. The volume of paper relating to this reign was enormous; and the archives were divided between St. Petersburg and Moscow; Pushkin therefore had to work on the papers in both cities, which he began to do in the winter of 1831–2. His salary was indeed the five thousand roubles a year offered him by the tsar at Tsarskoe Selo, but he received it many months in arrears.

As Pushkin put it succinctly in a letter written to Nashchokin just before his visit to Moscow: 'In marrying, I thought that my expenses would be treble those before marriage, they have turned out to be ten times as much.'[15] The business of sorting out Pushkin's affairs had several aspects: his own card debts, the redemption of the Goncharov diamonds and the proposal, which he pursued for some time, that his two hundred Boldino serfs might be remortgaged more profitably – at fifty roubles per head more – than they had been in 1830. Neither of Pushkin's two objectives was attained during this Moscow visit; and by the middle of January 1832 he was seeking a fresh private loan of twenty-five thousand roubles for a period of two or three years, or at least for two.[16]

These few weeks spent by Pushkin in Moscow at the end of 1831 have left us a precious legacy in the shape of his first letters written to Natalya Nikolaevna as his wife. The Russian in which Pushkin wrote to Natalya is as different from his formal French as it is possible to imagine. As a young man ten years earlier he had already decided what must be the essentials of prose: 'precision and brevity'. Prose, he wrote then, 'demands ideas and ideas – without them brilliant expressions serve no purpose ...'[17] From then on he never swerved from this rule. His letters to his wife are no exception. Written in crisp, colloquial Russian, their freshness recalls the style of the opening chapter of *Evgenii Onegin*.

These early letters, like most of his later letters to his wife, steer clear of any serious intellectual subject. They are on the whole light-hearted, with none of the melancholy of letters to her written in later years, but they do already suggest that some of his wife's letters to which he was replying expressed annoyance with him; and they also foreshadow some of his concerns that would overflow later on. Thus, his second letter from Moscow, as well as telling Natalya that he missed her, added: 'Since I left you I am somehow afraid on your account. You will not be sitting at home, you will drive to the palace, and just see, you will have a miscarriage on the hundred and fifth step of the grand staircase.' His next letter explained the reason why he had not visited the Goncharovs' house – to avoid a scene with his mother-in-law – and ended with the words: 'I kiss you and I beg you to walk up and down in the drawing-room, not to drive to the palace and not to dance at balls. God bless you.' By mid-December he had decided that he had been foolish to leave St. Petersburg: 'Don't be angry that I am angry ... I love you, my angel, more than I can say; ever since I have been here I have only been thinking of how to slip away to Petersburg – to you, my little wife.'[18] Partly because of the chaotic state of Nashchokin's affairs and the confusion in his house, Pushkin finally set out from Moscow for St. Petersburg in time to arrive there for Christmas.

By the beginning of January 1832 Pushkin was reporting to Nashchokin that on his return he had found Natalya well – 'she dances at balls, flirts with the tsar and jumps off the front steps'.[19] Natalya's beauty was bound to ensure instant success in St. Petersburg society, especially after the impression that she had already made on Nicholas I and the empress at Tsarskoe Selo in the summer of 1831. At this early stage of the Pushkins' married life, what seems to have concerned her husband was not so much the fact that Natalya accepted invitations to balls in his absence, as the possible effect on her pregnancy. That she did indeed go to balls in St. Petersburg while Pushkin was in Moscow in December 1831 is clear not only from his subsequent letters to Nashchokin, but also from other contemporary evidence.[20] Later on, however, he resented her accepting invitations to balls where he himself was not present. An outstanding example of this was Natalya's going to a ball at the Anichkov Palace, probably towards the end of 1833: without his knowledge, she was taken there by Countess Nesselrode, the wife of the foreign minister. Pushkin took strong exception to this, which contributed to the coldness, developing into hostility, between him and the Nesselrode family that continued for the remaining years of his life.[21] If this episode has been correctly dated, it may also have been a factor contributing to his appointment as *Kammerjunker* shortly afterwards.

In fairness to Natalya, what else was there for a young and beautiful girl to do in the capital? Nor was money at first the main problem in this respect. From the outset Natalya was taken under the wing of her Zagryazhkaya aunt, Ekaterina. Rich and a lady-in-waiting, she appears to have paid for her niece's dresses, which must have been very expensive.[22] Outside the revisionist school, there is general agreement that Natalya's interest, if any, in Pushkin's writing and in the historical research in which he was increasingly engaged from 1832 onwards, was minimal. There is, moreover, some evidence – albeit anecdotal – that she did not take much trouble to conceal her boredom when he was reading or reciting his work to his friends in his own home; and if these anecdotes[23] are based on fact, they suggest that Natalya may have inherited some of her mother's characteristic of *poshlost'* (as her two sisters seem to have done, judging from some of their surviving correspondence). In any case, there can be no doubt that, however reserved Natalya's manner may have been in public, in private she was capable of speaking her mind on occasion. The lengths to which Pushkin went in his letters written to her from Moscow to explain exactly why his wife had not received word from him as soon after his arrival as she considered it to be her due, are significant in this respect; and they are reinforced by the tone of her letters to her elder brother Dmitrii (discovered comparatively recently), the first of which, written on 31 October 1832, is remarkably forceful for a girl just twenty years old.[24]

Natalya gave birth to her first child – a daughter, christened Maria – on 19 May 1832. By the end of that year she was expecting her second child – their elder son, Alexander, who was born in July 1833. Nevertheless, her social whirl was hardly abated at all. By the winter of 1832–3 Pushkin's life in St. Petersburg had become: 'Neither one thing nor the other. Concern about living prevents me from getting bored. But I have no leisure . . . I whirl round in the social world, my wife is extremely fashionable – all this requires money, I get money from work, but work requires solitude.'[25]

Pushkin's own account is borne out by the observation of his young friend, Nikolai Gogol (Gogol'), that the only place that one could meet Pushkin at that time was at balls. Gogol was well placed to make this observation, because at the end of 1832 he was living not far from the Pushkins' flat in St. Petersburg. He had already tried to make his first contact with Pushkin when he himself was only twenty years old. By his own account it was probably in 1829 (when Pushkin was staying in the capital) that he suddenly decided that he must call on his hero, whom he had never met. So shy was he then that, just as he reached the doors of Pushkin's flat, his nervousness overcame him; he ran off to a café and fortified himself there with a glass of rum. Returning to Pushkin's flat, he rang the doorbell, only to be told that Pushkin was still asleep. To his enquiry whether Pushkin had worked all night, Pushkin's servant replied: 'What do you mean, "worked"? He was playing cards.'[26]

After Pushkin had moved to St. Petersburg towards the end of 1831, his relationship with Gogol developed in a way that shows both his power of literary criticism and his character at their best. Knowing already from his early works what kind of writing Gogol was capable of, Pushkin gave him the central idea both of *Dead Souls* and of *The Inspector General*. For the first, he suggested a scheme whereby a fictitious property could be acquired by buying the rights to dead serfs at nominal prices; and, for the second, he told Gogol the story of a man who had posed as a government inspector in a provincial town. Both a manuscript note written by Pushkin in 1832 – the outline of the story of Krispin, a confidence man who arrives at a town where he is taken for a grandee by the governor of the town, the governor's wife and the governor's daughter, to whom he becomes engaged to be married – and also a note written by Gogol himself are proof of Pushkin's generosity.[27]

So far as Pushkin's finances were concerned, 1832 became a repetition of 1831. He made a further attempt to sell the Goncharov statue of Catherine II to the government for twenty-five thousand roubles. By June 1832 this statue had been transported all the way from the Goncharov estate to the Pushkins' flat in St. Petersburg, where – apart from the embarrassment of obliging Pushkin to write another letter to Benckendorff, which must have raised a horselaugh in the palace – it can only have taken up a great deal of space.[28] A second visit paid by Pushkin to Nashchokin in Moscow, lasting three weeks in September–October, yielded no better results than his visit at the end of the previous year. He returned to St. Petersburg, suffering from a severe bout of rheumatism. He found 'great disorders' in his house;[29] and on 1 December 1832 he rented a twelve-roomed flat at three thousand three hundred roubles a year – over two-thirds of his salary, which he was now at last beginning to receive from the tsar.

To counterbalance Pushkin's growing financial anxieties, his relationship with the palace in 1832 developed reasonably well. True, his poem 'The Upas Tree', written at Malinniki in November 1828 but not published until four years later, caused him some trouble. The English epigraph of this powerful poem – 'It is a poison-tree that ... weeps only tears of poison' – suggests that it was inspired by Coleridge. (Pushkin's library included Coleridge's works.) After twenty lines setting the scene 'in the bare, barren desert, where the upas tree stands, like a grim sentinel alone in the entire universe, in soil scorched by the heat', the poem goes on:

> Но человека человек
> Послал к анчару властным взглядом;
> И тот послушно в путь потек
> И к утру возвратился с ядом.

Принёс он смертную смолу
Да ветвь с увядшими листами,
И пот по бледному челу
Струился хладными ручьями;

Принёс – и ослабел и лёг
Под сводом шалаша на лыки,
И умер бедный раб у ног
Непобедимого владыки.

А князь тем ядом напитал
Свои послушливые стрелы
И с ними гибель разослал
К соседам в чуждые пределы.

But with a powerful glance a man sent a man to the upas tree and he obediently set out on his journey and towards morning he returned with the poison. He brought the lethal resin and a branch with withered leaves, and the sweat poured down his pale forehead in cold streams; he brought it – and he went limp and lay on the matting beneath the entrance of the cabin, and the poor slave died at the feet of the invincible sovereign. But the prince impregnated with this poison his obedient arrows and with them he showered death among his neighbours across foreign frontiers.[30]

In the version first published (together with other poems by Pushkin, in *Northern Flowers*) the word used in the final lines was not 'prince', but 'tsar'. Presumably the first version somehow got through the censorship unscathed, because, once Nicholas I had read the poem himself, Benckendorff wrote Pushkin an official reprimand, to which Pushkin wrote a suave reply on 7 February.[31]

This episode apart, Pushkin succeeded in securing permission to publish a periodical. It was to be called *Diary*. By the end of the year this project petered out, once Pushkin had realized the full political implications – that he would be obliged to publish articles and news favourable to the government. It would be revived, in a non-political form and with a different title, in the last year of his life.[32] He also took his historical research seriously, walking every day to the general staff building in Palace Square, where the archives were housed. The tsar took the work seriously as well, because he readily granted two requests made by Pushkin arising from this work: that he should be allowed to examine Voltaire's immense library of books and manuscripts (bought by Catherine II and housed in the Hermitage) and to recruit an assistant for his researches.[33]

In the event, however, he continued to work on *Peter the Great* alone.

In 1832 Pushkin wrote scarcely a dozen poems. But it was probably in the course of that year that, although he did not abandon his work on the Petrine archives, he first began to be interested in the history of a major event in the reign of Catherine II: the revolt of the Cossack Emel'yan Pugachev. This project was to occupy much of his time in the following year, without damaging his relationship with the tsar. In 1832 Pushkin also consolidated another relationship that was to prove increasingly important for his work: that with the principal St. Petersburg bookseller, Alexander Smirdin. The two men got on well together; and Pushkin was one of those who, on 19 February 1832, attended a dinner given by Smirdin on the occasion of the removal of his bookshop, which served almost as a literary club, to new premises on the Nevsky Prospekt. Smirdin had already entered into agreements with Pletnev regarding the sale of Pushkin's works, and from 1832 until the end of Pushkin's life the royalties that he received from Smirdin would be considerable – of the order of two thousand roubles a year.[34] It is one of the paradoxes of Pushkin's character that he took so much trouble about the exact scale of his remuneration for what he wrote and so little about how he spent what he earned by his writing.[35]

The year 1833 began with Pushkin becoming a member of the Imperial Russian Academy, whose president was Admiral Shishkin. His elder son Alexander was born on 6 July. In the autumn of 1833 – his second autumn spent at Boldino – he wrote two masterpieces, one in verse and the other in prose: *The Bronze Horseman* and *The Queen of Spades*. Beneath the surface, Pushkin's mood was different. In the middle of May he wrote to Praskov'ya Osipova that St. Petersburg did not suit him at all – 'neither my tastes nor my fortune can fit in with it. But for two or three years I must put up with it.'[36] Another of his letters is even more revealing. This long humiliating document, which first came to light in 1970 and has been tentatatively dated May–June 1833 by its discoverers, is a long letter addressed to his brother-in-law, Dmitrii Goncharov. Dmitrii had by then been authorized to take over the management of the Goncharov estate. (His father had been disqualified from doing so on medical grounds.) Having recently discussed with Prince Vladimir Golitsyn the possibility of his making Goncharov a loan, which Pushkin suggests in the letter that Goncharov should discuss with Prince Golitsyn in Moscow, he then goes on:

If you arrange this loan, I would ask you *to lend me for six months* [Pushkin's underlining] 6000 roubles, which I badly need and which I do not know where to borrow. Since it is a matter of no consequence to Prince Golitsyn to lend 35,000 or 40,000 roubles and even more than that, this is a source from which you will be good enough to draw if possible. – I cannot do this myself, because I cannot give him any guarantee other than my word, and I do not want to subject myself to the possibility of receiving a refusal. – Since you are the head of the family into which I have had the honour to enter, and you have shown yourself a really good brother to us, I have decided to bore you by talking about my affairs. My family is growing. My duties oblige me to live in St Petersburg, my expenses are following their own course, and since I saw no possibility of limiting them in the first year of our marriage, my debts have also increased.

The latter part of this letter also reverts once again to the possibility of Pushkin's mother-in-law doing something to help Natalya financially. Pushkin makes reference to the fact that his wife was due to receive three hundred serfs from her grandfather and that Natalya Ivanovna had initially said that she would give Natalya Nikolaevna two hundred. He ends by leaving it open to Dmitrii to show the letter to his mother or not, as he thinks fit.[37] Pushkin knew Golitsyn, a very rich man, reasonably well; Dmitrii Goncharov did not. Nothing appears to have come of Pushkin's suggestion.

Little more than a fortnight after Natalya gave birth to his son, Pushkin was drafting a formal request for permission to spend two or three months away from St. Petersburg, in order to visit his estate and also to take the opportunity to make a journey to Orenburg and Kazan related to his work on the Pugachev revolt. By the end of July he explained his reasons for making this journey in detail:

In the course of the last two years I have been exclusively occupied with historical research, not having written a single line of a purely literary nature. I need to spend about two months in complete solitude, in order to rest from my important tasks and also to finish the book which I began some time ago, and which will earn me some money of which I have need. I am ashamed to waste time on trivial occupations, but what is to be done? They alone can provide me with independence and the means of living with my family in St. Petersburg, where my work, thanks to the sovereign, has a more important and a more useful purpose. Apart from the salary which has been allocated to me through His Majesty's generosity, I have no steady income; in the meantime life in the capital is expensive and with the growth of my family, my expenditure has increased as well.[38]

Pushkin's statement that he had not written a single line, although true by comparison with the outstanding output of his first Boldino autumn (1830), was not strictly accurate. He had in fact recently completed the nineteenth chapter of a short novel, *Dubrovsky*. The novel, never finished, was not published until after Pushkin's death. It tells the story of a violent quarrel in the eighteenth century between a rich landowner and a poor one; and it includes a verbatim quotation from the transcript of an actual law suit between landowners which took place in the province of Tambov not long before *Dubrovsky* was written.[39]

Having received permission for his journey, Pushkin set off from St. Petersburg on 18 August. Remarkably, considering how recent his quarrel with his mother-in-law had been, Pushkin broke his journey at Yaropolets, the Goncharov estate, where Natalya Ivanovna was now living. He even persuaded his mother-in-law to let him take away some thirty books from the house library. A few days in Moscow followed – 'Boring Moscow, empty Moscow, poor Moscow – there are even very few coachmen in its boring streets.'[40] He reached Nizhnii Novgorod on 2 September, Kazan on the 8th, Orenburg on the 19th; and by 1 October, having accomplished a journey of three thousand five hundred *versts* and steeped himself in the history and in the local colour of the Pugachev revolt, he was at Boldino, where he spent six highly productive weeks.

Pushkin's journey in eastern Russia and his stay at Boldino were punctuated by long letters to his wife, twelve in all. Towards the end of the series Pushkin begins to lecture Natalya. For example:

> Now, my angel, I kiss you as if nothing were wrong; and I thank you for describing in detail and with candour your wayward life. Have a good time, little wife; only don't do this too much and don't forget me ... Describe for me your appearance at balls, which, as you write, have probably already begun. But, my angel, please do not flirt. I am not jealous ... But you know how I dislike anything that smacks of a Moscow lady, everything which is not *comme il faut*, everything that is vulgar ... If on my return I found that your dear, simple, aristocratic style has changed, I shall divorce you, by Christ, and I will go for a soldier in my grief.

Pushkin began a letter written a few days afterwards by saying that he felt that he had been over-severe and that he had been annoyed at the time. Nevertheless, he repeated that 'flirting never leads to any good;

and although it may be pleasant in its own way, nothing so quickly deprives a young woman of that without which there cannot be family happiness, nor peace of mind in relationships with society – respect'.[41]

On 20 November 1833 Pushkin returned to St. Petersburg. According to a story later related in her memoirs by Nashchokin's wife, when Pushkin got back, he found that Natalya was not at home, but at a ball being given by the Karamzins. He immediately drove to the Karamzins' flat and found Natalya's carriage outside it. He sat down in it and sent a manservant to tell his wife that she must come home on a very important matter, but gave instructions that she should not be told that her husband was in the carriage. The emissary came back and reported to Pushkin that his wife had asked him to say that she was dancing a mazurka with Prince Vyazemsky. Pushkin sent the manservant back for a second time to say that she should return home without delay. She then came out to the carriage and 'fell straight into the embraces of her husband'.[42] The memoirs containing this account of Pushkin's reunion with his wife after his three-month journey were published well over half a century after the event. Although the account – allegedly Pushkin's own – may be apocryphal, it has a certain ring of truth; and soon afterwards Natalya became pregnant again. By contrast, on his return from leave Pushkin received two unwelcome communications from the tsar: a string of question-marks in the margins of the manuscript of his *Bronze Horseman* and a ukase published in the court circular on 31 December 1833 conferring on him the court rank of *Kammerjunker*.

Both Nicholas I's decision to make this appointment (the news of which, it will be recalled, filled Ivan Pushchin with foreboding, when it reached Siberia) and Pushkin's own reaction to it were entirely in character. In appointing to the lowest rung of the courtier's ladder a distinguished man of nearly thirty-five – fifteen years older than the youths who normally occupied it on their way up – Nicholas was going strictly by the book of rules. Because Pushkin held only the rank of counsellor in the foreign ministry – and that only since the end of 1831 – he did not qualify for the court rank of *Kammerger* (court chamberlain) conferred, for example, on Vyazemsky in 1831.

As for Pushkin's reaction, two entries made in his diary, which he had just begun again, speak for themselves. On 1 January 1834 he wrote:

The day before yesterday the rank of *Kammerjunker* was conferred upon me (which is fairly disagreeable at my age). But the court wanted Natalya Nikolaevna to be able to dance at the Anichkov . . . People have asked me whether I am pleased with my appointment as *Kammerjunker*. I am pleased because the sovereign intended to single me out, and not to make me look ridiculous – and so far as I am concerned, even as a *kammer-pazh* [court page], so long as they do not compel me to learn French vocabulary and arithmetic.

On 7 January he added in his diary that the tsar had remarked to Vyazemsky: "'I hope that Pushkin has taken his appointment in good part – so far he has kept his word to me and I have been pleased with him" etc. etc. The Grand Duke congratulated me the other day at the theatre: "I thank Your Highness humbly; so far everybody has laughed at me, you are the first to have congratulated me".'[43]

The Anichkov Palace had been Nicholas' residence before his accession. It was there that, as tsar, he gave private balls, official balls being held at the Winter Palace. As the result of Pushkin's appointment, from now on the guests at these private parties would include the Pushkins. Natalya was 'delighted' by the entrée now opened to her by her husband's court appointment; and in a letter written on 4 January 1834 Pushkin's mother described her daughter-in-law as 'dancing everywhere every day'.[44] Ball followed ball, the last official one before Lent being held at the Winter Palace on 4 March. There Natalya was suddenly taken ill and, returning home, she had a miscarriage.[45] As soon as she was well enough to travel, in mid-April, she left St. Petersburg with the two children, in order to spend the summer with her mother and sisters at Yaropolets, leaving Pushkin in the capital, where he remained until he joined his family at the end of August.

During these months almost everything that could go wrong in Pushkin's life did go wrong. As if his own financial affairs were not enough of a burden for one man to bear, in the spring his father's affairs reached such a low point, including a hundred thousand roubles of debt secured on the Nizhnii Novgorod estate, that Alexander Sergeevich felt obliged – against his wife's advice – to take over the management of the whole property for just over a year. He also helped his brother Lev. A laconic postscript to a letter to his brother-in-law setting out the details of his father's indebtedness (based on official information that he had received from the government Loan Office – being unable to rely on Sergei L'vovich's own accounts) reads: 'In one month I have already paid *out of my own money* 866 roubles for Father and 1300 roubles for Lev Sergeevich; more than that I cannot do.'[46]

In parallel with this disagreeable extra responsibility, which took up a great deal of Pushkin's time, at the beginning of 1834 Pushkin made the opening moves in what gradually developed into a crucial financial negotiation conducted on his own behalf with the government, as the lender of last resort. This negotiation continued into 1835. The first step was Pushkin's request, made in a letter to Benckendorff on 26 February 1834, that the imperial treasury should make him a loan of twenty thousand roubles at 'established interest rates', repayable in full in two years, in order to enable him to publish his *History of Pugachev*.[47] The request was at once granted; Pushkin's *Pugachev* was published at the very end of 1834; but it did not find favour with the public. (Pushkin had earlier hoped to make a lot of money out of it, which indeed he needed to do, given the amount of time that he had spent on the research, without which it could not have been written.) Of his two masterpieces written at Boldino in the previous autumn, only *The Queen of Spades* was published, so that Pushkin was at least able to remark in his diary that his *Queen of Spades* was 'very popular – gamblers are punting on the three, the seven and the ace'.

Early in May 1834 Pushkin learnt from Zhukovsky that a frank letter which he had written to Natalya towards the end of April had been opened by the police and shown to the tsar. This letter told Natalya that, in order to avoid meeting the tsar, he had reported himself as being ill; he was spending the Easter holidays at home; and he had no intention of going to offer congratulations and greetings to the heir to the throne. Zhukovsky managed to smooth the episode over, but Pushkin remained furious. As he put it in a letter to his wife on 18 May:

No one ought to know what goes on between us; no one ought to be received into our bedroom. Without secrecy there cannot be family life. I write to you, not for the press; and there is no cause for you to accept the public into your confidence. But I know that is impossible; and yet for a long time past swinish behaviour in anybody whoever has not surprised me.[48]

The passage of time did nothing either to enable Pushkin to afford to live in St. Petersburg in the manner that he considered appropriate or to raise his spirits. In order to counteract his depression, he tried to use gambling. He wrote Natalya a candid letter of apology in the second half of June, saying that he was entirely at fault; he had had some money, but he had lost it at cards. 'What could I do? I had so much bile that I had to divert myself with something or other.' On 25 June he resorted to an extreme step. He wrote Benckendorff a short, stiff letter in French:

> Since family affairs require my presence sometimes in Moscow and sometimes in the interior, I find myself obliged to retire from the service and I beg Your Excellency to obtain permission for me to do this. I would request as a final favour that His Majesty's authorization, which he was kind enough to give me to visit the archives, should not be withdrawn.

He received a predictable reply, namely that the tsar would not wish to retain him in his service against his will, but that he could not give permission for research in the state archives to anybody in whom he did not have complete trust.[49]

The evidence suggests that Nicholas – for whatever reason – was reluctant to see Pushkin retire from St. Petersburg. He therefore spoke to Zhukovsky about Pushkin; and Zhukovsky exerted heavy pressure on Pushkin to withdraw his request, which to him seemed to be an example of extreme stupidity. In response, Pushkin did not withdraw his request at once. Instead, he conducted a slow rearguard action. By the end of August, however, both sides had agreed that his request for retirement should be regarded as in effect *nul et non avenu*. It left an unpleasant taste in everyone's mouth.[50]

Some of the series of letters written by Pushkin to Natalya during their four months' separation in 1834 are revealing. Thus, there are repeated assurances that he is not carrying on any flirtations himself (matched by remarks about Natalya's own temptations) and on one occasion he even claims credit for not yielding to friends' suggestions that they should all go on to a brothel after a bibulous dinner at a restaurant. Again and again Pushkin says how much he misses Natalya and that only the need to see *Pugachev* through the printers and to try to sort out his father's affairs keeps him in the capital, although her absence from St. Petersburg does have the advantage that he is not obliged to doze at balls or glut himself on ice-creams.

More than once Pushkin asks Natalya to forgive him for his spleen (a word that he uses in English) and by 8 June 1834 he begins to touch on the question of retirement:

> Do not be angry, my wife, and do not take my complaints amiss. I never thought of blaming you for my dependence. I had to marry you because without you I would have been unhappy for the whole of my life; but I did not have to enter the service and, what is worse, weigh myself down with financial obligations ... They now regard me as a lackey, whom they can treat in any way they like. Disgrace is easier to bear than contempt.

Among these many letters two stand out because of the shadow that they cast on Pushkin's future. The first, dated 11 June, refers for the first time to Natalya's proposal to bring both her sisters to live in St. Petersburg, which Pushkin initially interpreted as being prompted by a wish on Natalya's part to help to arrange for them to be given court appointments. With this in mind, Pushkin advises Natalya that both she and her sisters should stay as far away from the court as possible.

> I kiss you from my heart – now let us talk business. If you have really taken into your head to bring your sisters here, then it would be impossible for us to stay at Olivio's [the Pushkins' flat]; there is not enough room. But will you really bring both your sisters to live with you? Oh, little wife! Look ... My opinion – a family ought to be *one* under *one* roof: otherwise you will be piling up trouble and there will be no family peace and quiet. However, let us talk about this further.

Pushkin left St. Petersburg on 25 August and after spending a few hours in Moscow on the way, he joined his family at Yaropolets, where he spent two weeks. On 8 September he brought his family to Moscow. He himself went on to Boldino, where he spent the last of his three autumns. It was also the shortest: barely a month. Oppressed by the responsibilities of the estate, he did little literary work, but – remarkably in the circumstances – he did write one poem, *The Tale of the Golden Cockerel*.[51] A poem that may reflect Pushkin's inner world at this time most closely is one which he in fact wrote in the previous year, the first line of which is: 'May God grant that I do not go out of my mind.' In the five short verses that follow this line, Pushkin at first describes how, if he did go mad, he would be free to wander wherever he wanted, but he ends by reflecting that he would in fact be locked up and in the last six lines he foresees:

> А ночью слышать буду я
> Не голос яркий соловья,
>
> 　Не шум глухой дубров –
> А крик товарищей моих,
> Да брань смотрителей ночных,
> 　Да визг, да звон оков.

... But at night I shall not hear the nightingale's clear voice, nor the grove's dull sound – instead, the screams of my companions, the curses of the night wardens, the shrieks and the clanking of chains.[52]

From the autumn of 1834 onwards both Natalya's sisters were installed in the new flat to which the Pushkins had now moved, rented from Vyazemsky. All three sisters now belonged to what Akhmatova called '*la bande joyeuse*' – an expression which can perhaps be rendered in English by the equally outdated 'bright young things'.[53] (Since he received a commission in the imperial household cavalry early in 1834 a young French émigré, Baron Georges d'Anthès, had become a prominent member of this group of St. Petersburg society.[54]) Although the new flat was larger than the one previously occupied by the Pushkins, the confusion in the new one must have been considerable. Certainly expenses increased. The end of a long letter from Natalya to her brother, dated 1 October 1835, begs Dmitrii to send her 'a few hundred roubles . . . in extremely straitened circumstances'. A recent attempt to paint a completely different – happy – picture of the atmosphere prevailing in it (based on several letters written by Natalya's two sisters) is unconvincing.[55]

Pushkin's second daughter was born on 14 May 1835. This was perhaps the only happy event in the whole of that year for him, although, as it happened, he missed the birth by a few hours, having gone to spend a few days at Mikhailovskoe, for reasons that are not wholly clear.[56] On 1 June Pushkin returned to the charge with Benckendorff about his own future. On this occasion he asked for a leave of absence of three or four years, to be spent in the country. Once again he received a reply that was easily predictable: Nicholas wrote that there was no objection to Pushkin going wherever he wished, but that he did not understand how Pushkin could reconcile this with remaining in the service. He should therefore be asked whether he wished to retire, because it would not be possible to give him leave for so long a period of time. On 22 July Pushkin finally bit the bullet. He put the alternatives bluntly to Benckendorff: either he must go and live in the country or he needed to borrow a large sum of money from the government. By this time he admitted to debts of sixty thousand roubles. In the end the imperial treasury lent Pushkin forty-five thousand roubles, on the security of his salary.[57]

Leaving Natalya and the children in St. Petersburg, Pushkin set off in September not for Boldino, but for Mikhailovskoe, in the hope of being able to do some work there. Instead, as he wrote to his publisher in the first half of October: 'I have never spent such a fruitless autumn in my life. I am writing, but I am doing it any old how.'[58] On 23 October Pushkin returned to St. Petersburg, defeated; he had not taken his full leave. From now on there are repeated signs that Pushkin became preoccupied with the onset of age and indeed of death. To his wife he wrote on 25 September that everybody around him said that he was ageing and 'sometimes even in good plain Russian'. That he was not in any way joking is made clear by his nostalgic and resigned poem 'I visited again that corner of the earth' [Mikhailovskoe], which ends with verses that are an unmistakable intimation of mortality.[59] Another depressing factor was the serious illness of his mother, who was just sixty. True, Pushkin had never been close to his parents, but in recent years he had shown himself a dutiful son. His mother's illness was protracted; she did not die until March 1836. If all this were not enough, he ended a letter dated 26 December 1835 to Praskov'ya Osipova with the reflection that exactly ten years had passed since the Decembrist Revolt: 'It all seems a dream. How many events, how many changes in everything, beginning with my own ideas, my situation, etc. etc. In truth it is only my friendship for you and for your family that I find still the same in my soul, always complete and entire.'[60]

With the benefit of hindsight after a century and a half, is it possible to pick out from the dismal chronology of these years any one moment that precisely determined or paved the way for what followed in the final year of Pushkin's life? In the first place, there can be no doubt that by the end of 1835, even though Pushkin still managed both to work on his research into the Petrine archives and to undertake the editing of a new literary journal, he was a man who had reached a low ebb. Among the choice of turning points, his ill-fated appointment as *Kammerjunker* at the very end of 1833 is a strong candidate. Given the combination of snobbishness and vanity that formed part of Pushkin's paradoxical character, he could not be expected to take this appointment lightly. Moreover, he was bored by balls; and he particularly disliked wearing uniform, although most of his friends seem to have done their best to talk him out of making a fuss about it.

Nevertheless, few of Pushkin's friends realized the core of his problem – Gogol was one of the few exceptions – namely, that he simply had to get away from St. Petersburg, not only for financial reasons, although these were powerful enough, but in order to remain a creative writer: to be able – in Vyazemsky's words, already quoted in the Introduction – to retain access to the 'shrine, the font in which sores were healed, courage and freshness overcame the feebleness of exhaustion'. In obliging Pushkin to reconcile himself to staying on in St. Petersburg, which involved accepting a substantial government loan, Nicholas I clearly played a major part. But an at least equally pressing consideration in Pushkin's mind must surely have been that, in order to move to the country, he would have had to be prepared to behave towards his wife in a way of which he was incapable. Nothing proves this inability more conclusively than the lame resistance that he put up to Natalya's determination to bring her sisters from the country to join her in St. Petersburg: by any standards, a preposterous decision, as subsequent events were to prove. Nor does Natalya seem to have shown any understanding of her husband's need to spend at least some time in the country. A revealing letter, written on 31 August 1835 by Pushkin's sister, Olga, to her husband, gives an account of a visit paid to her the day before by the Pushkins, during which Natalya declared categorically that she would not move from St. Petersburg even for a few days, contrary to Alexander's wishes. As Olga's letter put it, '*Madame ne veut pas.*'[61]

Whatever the explanation for the increasing futility of Pushkin's way of life and whenever exactly he reached the point of no return, it remains remarkable that he somehow continued to deploy the internal resources needed for writing for as long as he did. Pushkin's saving grace was his astounding achievement during the three autumns that he spent at Boldino.

CHAPTER ELEVEN

The Boldino Autumns

Now is my season . . .
—Pushkin, *Autumn*

T. S. Eliot's description of April as the cruellest month would not have surprised Pushkin. In his account of his recovery from his serious illness in 1818, Pushkin remarked that his six weeks' convalescence took place in early spring, 'although this time of year usually brings on melancholy and even harms my health'.[1] (The word here translated as 'melancholy' is the Russian *toska*, which could equally be rendered as 'yearning'.) At that early age and for several years thereafter Pushkin seems to have been able to write more or less at any time and anywhere. But in his maturity autumn became his season for writing. And in *Autumn*, an unfinished fragment, unpublished until after his death, he explained exactly why:

Октябрь уж наступил – уж роща отряхает
Последние листы с нагих своих ветвей;
Дохнул осенний хлад, дорога промерзает,
Журча ещё бежит за мельницу ручей,
Но пруд уже застыл; сосед мой поспешает
В отъезжие поля с охотою своей,
И страждут озими от бешеной забавы,
И будит лай собак уснувшие дубравы.

Теперь моя пора: я не люблю весны;
Дни поздней осени бранят обыкновенно,
Но мне она мила, читатель дорогой,
Красою тихою, блистающей смиренно.
Так нелюбимое дитя в семье родной
К себе меня влечет. Сказать вам откровенно,
Из годовых времён я рад лишь ей одной.

В ней много доброго; любовник не тщеславный,
Я нечто в ней нашел мечтою своенравной.

Как зто объяснить? Мне нравится она,
Как, вероятно, вам чахоточная дева
Порою нравится. На смертв осуждена,
Бедняжка клонится без ропота, без гнева.
Улыбка на устах увянувших видна;
Могильной пропасти она не слышит зева;
Играет на лице ещё багровый цвет.
Она жива ещё сегодня, завтра нет.

Унылая пораг очей очарованье,
Приятна мне твоя прощальная краса –
Люблю я пышное природы увяданье,
В баірец, и в золото одетые леса,
В их сенях ветра шум и свежее дыханье,
И мглой волнистою покрыты небеса,
И редкий солнца луч, и первые морозы,
И отдалённые седой зимы угрозы.

И с каждой осенью я расцветаю вновь;
Здоровью моему полезен русский холод;
К привычкам бытия вновь чувствую любовь:
Чредой слетает сон, чредой находит голод;
Легко и радостно играет в сердце кровь,
Желания кипят – я снова счастлив, молод,
Я снова жизнй полн – таков мой организм
(Извольте мне простить ненужный прозаизм).

И забываю мир, – и в сладкой тишине
Я сладко усышлён монм воображеньем,
И пробуждаетсн поэзия во мне:
Душа стесняется лирическим волненьем,
Трепещет и звучит, и ищет, как во сне,
Излиться наконец свободным проявленьем –
И тут ко мнс идёт незримый рой гостей,
Знакомцы давние, плоды мечты моей.

И мысли в голове волнуются в отваге,
И рифмы лёгкие навстречу им бегут,
И палвцы просятся к перу, перо к бумаге,
Минута – стихи свободно потекут.
Так дремлет недвижим корабль в недвижной влаге,
Но чу – матросы вдруг кидаются, ползут
Вверх, вниз – и паруса надулись, ветра полны,
Громада двинулась и рассекает волны.

Плывёт. Куда ж нам плыть? ...

Autumn: a fragment

October has already arrived – already the grove is shaking off the last leaves from its naked branches; the autumnal cold has breathed, the road is beginning to freeze, the water still runs bubbling beyond the mill-stream, but the pond is already icy; my neighbour hastens to the distant fields with his pack, and the winter crop suffers from the wild sport and the baying of the hounds wakens the sleeping forest.

Now is my time; I am not fond of spring . . .

Usually people abuse the days of late autumn, but I, dear reader, respond with affection to autumn's quiet beauty and humble glow. Like a child who is unloved in its own family, she attracts me to herself. To speak with candour, among all the seasons of the year, I welcome her alone. In her there is much good; not being a vain lover myself, with my capricious imagination I have found in her a particular quality . . .

O melancholy season! A delight to the eyes, your leave-taking beauty pleases me – I love the magnificent fading of nature, the woods clothed in purple and in gold, the sound of the wind and the freshening breeze in the treetops, and the skies covered with rolling mist, and the rare shaft of sunlight and the first frosts and the distant threats of hoary winter.

And with every autumn I blossom afresh; Russian cold is good for my health; once again I feel affection for the habits of everyday existence; sleep glides up at its due time and hunger too approaches when it should; the blood in my heart plays lightly and joyfully, desires seethe – once more I am happy and young, and I am full of life again – my organic nature (be good enough to excuse an unnecessarily prosaic usage) is like this . . .

And I forget the world – and in the sweet tranquillity I am sweetly lulled by my imagination and poetry is wakened within me: my spirit is seized by lyrical excitement, it trembles and resounds and, as in a dream, seeks final release in free expression – and now an invisible host of guests comes up to me, old acquaintances, the fruits of my daydream.

And thoughts stir boldly in my head, and rhymes run towards them, light as air, and my fingers demand a pen, my pen demands paper, one minute – and verses will flow freely. Thus a ship slumbers in still water, but listen – the sailors are suddenly on the move – they crawl up and down, and the sails have been puffed out by the wind, the massive shape has moved and is cutting its way through the waves.

It is sailing – but where are we bound for? . . .[2]

It will be recalled that, of the five autumns between 1830 and 1834, Pushkin spent three at Boldino. After the failure of his attempt to spend the autumn of 1835 writing at Mikhailovskoe, he spent the last autumn of his life in St. Petersburg. There could hardly have been a greater contrast than that between Pushkin's way of life in the capital (or in Moscow, during 1830 and the early months of 1831) and the simplicity of Boldino, where he lived alone, in a small, wholly undistinguished house set in a featureless plain. True, some of the work that he managed to do elsewhere during these years is remarkable (examples have already been mentioned), but the great majority of his creative writing in the 1830s was the product of the three Boldino autumns: 1830, 1833 and 1834.

At Boldino, by applying his power of intense concentration in a peaceful environment, at 'his' time of year, for a period amounting – in aggregate – to just a few months, Pushkin was able to write a series of works, in prose as well as in verse, whose execution would have been inconceivable in St. Petersburg or Moscow. In spite of the fact that during most of his time spent at Boldino Pushkin was anxiously looking over his shoulder at Natalya in a constant flow of letters, the harvest of his stays there was one of magnificent variety and richness. This harvest concerns Pushkin's biographer no less than it does anyone assessing his literary achievement. It forms an important part of the evidence of the gradual change in Pushkin that marked the years of his maturity. This is particularly true of the later works written at Boldino. It is for this reason that the general rule established at the outset of this biography (not to offer synopses of Pushkin's works)[3] is twice broken in the account of the Boldino autumns that follows: for *The Bronze Horseman* and for *The Queen of Spades*, not just because they are masterpieces, but because, taken together, they offer clues to understanding Pushkin's character and in particular his state of mind at the time when they were written.

Although much of what Pushkin wrote at Boldino was written at phenomenal speed, it was also written with intense precision. With very rare exceptions (*Poltava*, written in St. Petersburg, may be an example), the idea of lines of verse frenetically dashed off, hot from the poet's pen, familiar to German and other romantic writers of the period, was as foreign to him as the German metaphysics that exercised such a fascination on Russian intellectuals only a few years younger than himself. The way in which he wrote descended from a tradition older than that which inspired the contemporary poets of the great romantic movement, for whom poetic structure and general philosophy were inseparable, as also were the poet and the landscape that he was describing, before which the distinction between self and non-self dissolved.[4] Pushkin's poems *Winter Morning*, *Winter Evening* and *Winter Road* and Coleridge's *Frost at Midnight* might almost have been written on different planets.[5]

For Pushkin, as for Horace, a poem was like a painting; and for him, from an early age, 'the aim of poetry is poetry'.[6] He understood his own variable, volatile and explosive character well enough to be able to define at the age of twenty-five the *sine qua non* for his writing – tranquillity – which demanded solitude such as he enjoyed, albeit briefly, at Boldino during the latter years of his life. In this definition (a commentary on an article that had appeared in a journal in 1824) Pushkin wrote: 'The critic is confusing inspiration with rapture. Inspiration is an attitude of the *spirit* to the most vivid possible reception of impressions and the grasp of concepts, and subsequently their exposition. Inspiration is as necessary in geometry as it is in poetry. Rapture excludes *tranquillity* – the indispensable prerequisite of *beauty*.'[7]

At this point the question presents itself: if Pushkin had been able to travel abroad and, in particular, to meet there some of the English and French romantic writers face to face (instead of being obliged to rely on the books in his library), what might his reaction to their impact have been? Perhaps not very great. Compared with his Russian predecessors of the previous century, Pushkin was – as a writer – revolutionary. But, as a man, he does not strike the present-day reader as typical of the nineteenth century. Pushkin's personality, like Disraeli's, gives the impression rather of a man of the eighteenth century, who might in some ways have felt more at home in the twentieth than in the nineteenth century. In part perhaps because of the fact that he died young, it is easy to forget – for example – that Pushkin's passage about inspiration just quoted was written five years after Queen Victoria was born and that her favourite prime minister was his near-contemporary.

The boundaries of Pushkin's writing during the 1830s are defined by two letters that he wrote to his publisher, Pletnev. Separated by nearly five years, they offer an eloquent contrast. In the second of these letters, written from Mikhailovskoe in October 1835, Pushkin explained the fruitlessness of the autumn that he was spending there by the fact that inspiration required mental tranquillity, adding that he was 'absolutely not at peace'.[8] And in the first letter written from Moscow immediately after his return from his first Boldino autumn, in December 1830, he told Pletnev that he had brought back with him to Moscow:

> The two *last* chapters of *Evgenii Onegin* the eighth and ninth, completely ready for printing. A story . . . (400 lines of verse), which we shall publish anonymously [*The Little House in Kolomna*]. Some dramatic scenes or little tragedies, namely: *The Covetous Knight*, *Mozart and Salieri*, *The Feast in the Time of Plague* and *Don Juan* [*The Stone Guest*]. On top of that I have written about thirty short poems. Good? And that is not all (in strict confidence). I have written five stories in prose [*The Tales of Belkin*] . . . which we shall also publish anonymously.[9]

This outpouring of wholly new writing at Boldino in 1830 is the more remarkable in that Pushkin was at the same time not only engaged in completing *Evgenii Onegin*, the longest poem that he ever wrote, but also in seeing through the printer the work which had held a special place in his personal affection, ever since he finished it five years earlier at Mikhailovskoe – *Boris Godunov*. On the day on which he finished *Evgenii Onegin* at Boldino, he wrote the following words:

> Onegin
> Kishinev, 9 May 1823
> Boldino, 25 September 1830
> 7 years, 4 months, 17 days

As it turned out, Pushkin's work on *Onegin* was not over, because of the troubles with the censorship already described, which required the revision of the final chapters in 1831. The censorship also required a change at the end of *Boris Godunov*. But – for once in the history of Russian censorship – the line that had to be substituted for what Pushkin had written is at least as good, if not better than the original. Pushkin's original text gave to the 'people' – following the death of Boris Godunov, his wife and son – the words: 'Long live the tsar [Pretender to the throne] Dmitrii Ivanovich!' What the censor insisted on substituting for the crowd's reaction was just two words in Russian: 'The people are silent.'[10]

Pushkin's concept of *Boris Godunov*, both as theatre and as history, was so revolutionary that for the Russian public, its reception would have been helped by a preface, although perhaps not by one including some of the sentences that Pushkin drafted – for example:

I present myself after renouncing my early style. No longer having to make famous an unknown name and my early youth, I no longer dare to count on the indulgence with which I had previously been received. It is not the fashionable style that I seek. I voluntarily withdraw from the rank of fashion's favourites, offering my humble thanks for the favour with which it has received my feeble attempts during ten years of my life.[11]

Boris Godunov was finally published at the very end of 1830, bearing the date of 1 January 1831. Although it sold well enough, it was received for the most part with silence; nor did it lead to the reform of Russian dramatic convention for which Pushkin had hoped while he was writing it. No doubt the equivocal attitude of the government contributed to this outcome, although Nicholas I was dead long before *Godunov* was first performed on stage, nearly half a century after Pushkin had written it. In spite of the rapturous reception given at private gatherings in Moscow in 1826 when Pushkin first read *Boris Godunov* to his friends, few of his contemporaries seem to have seen its point (exhaustively analysed in recent years).[12] Interestingly, given the contrasts between Poland and Muscovy around the year 1600, which Pushkin depicts, one contemporary admirer was Mickiewicz, whose verdict was: '*Et tu Shakespeare eris, si fata sinant!*'[13] ('You too will be a Shakespeare, if the fates allow!') For *Godunov* the Fates did not allow this, reserving Fortune's blessings in Pushkin's lifetime for *Onegin*.

The Tales of Belkin was Pushkin's first attempt to write prose fiction, if his earlier *Blackamoor of Peter the Great* is excluded. It soon became common knowledge that he was the author of these short stories, written with all the economy that was rigorously exercised in everything that he wrote in prose. Nevertheless, at first he was reluctant to admit authorship: hence their half-humorous attribution by Pushkin to an imaginary 'The late Mr Ivan Petrovich Belkin'. Like *Boris Godunov*, the *Tales* broke completely fresh ground. To a foreign reader they may even appear slight and indeed in a sense they are, since they contain a strong element of parody.[14] Published in the summer of the following year, they were at the time criticized by some writers, such as Vyazemsky, whose opinion Pushkin normally valued. As in the case of *Boris Godunov*, there were exceptions: for example, Gogol, although he also remarked that 'we cannot repeat Pushkin'.[15] But – unlike *Boris Godunov* – the eventual influence on later Russian writers of the flashes of brilliance that partially illuminate *The Tales of Belkin* was immense.[16] Those who acknowledged the debt owed by their own prose to Pushkin's even included Tolstoy, although their prose styles stand at opposite poles.

Pushkin's second, slightly shorter, stay in Boldino was even more impressive than his first. When he arrived there on 2 October 1833, he had just completed his long journey to eastern Russia, which had taken him from St. Petersburg to the Urals. He brought with him the notes that he had made both of the topography and of the reminiscences of the people of the region, where from 1772 to 1774 the Don Cossack Emel'yan Pugachev had led the bloodiest revolt of the entire eighteenth century in the Russian Empire – the atrocities committed on both sides were appalling – proclaiming himself to be the (murdered) Tsar Peter III. Pushkin had done preliminary work on the Pugachev Revolt at the beginning of 1833, based on his research in the imperial archives, including some documents not previously published, although even he was not allowed access to all of them.

The resulting book, presented to the tsar on 1 January 1834 and published in two volumes in December of that year, was called not *The History of Pugachev*, but *The History of Pugachev's Revolt*, in deference to Nicholas I, who maintained that a rebel could have no history. *Pugachev* did not earn Pushkin the large sum of money that he had hoped for. Was its objectivity too near the bone for most members of the Russian nobility? Even though the additional notes written for the tsar's eyes only were not published until after Alexander II had abolished serfdom in Russia, Pushkin's final summing up was ahead of his time:

> Thus ended a revolt, begun by a handful of unruly Cossacks and strengthened by the inexcusable negligence of the authorities, so that it shook the state from Siberia to Mosow and from the Kuban to the Murom forests. It was a long time before complete peace was re-established. Panin and Suvorov remained for a whole year in the pacified provinces, restoring their weakened government, rebuilding towns and fortresses and eradicating the last traces of the broken revolt. At the end of 1775 a general amnesty was proclaimed and it was decreed that the whole affair should be consigned to perpetual oblivion. Catherine, wishing to extirpate all recollection of that dreadful time, abolished the ancient name of the river whose banks had first witnessed the revolt. The Yaitskii Cossacks were renamed 'Ural

Cossacks' and their town was called Uralsk. But the name of the terrible rebel still resounds in the lands where he raged. The people vividly recall the bloody time which – so expressively – they called the *Pugachevshchina*.[17]

Pushkin himself described his *Pugachev* as a fragment, like much else that he wrote. Certainly it was a by-road down which he travelled, turning off from what had by then become his primary historical interest – the reign of Peter the Great – or, as the brilliant historian Klyuchevsky put it nearly fifty years later, Pushkin was an unintentional historian.[18] If Pushkin could write a historical monograph as good as this one, however, what might his history of Peter the Great have been like? To this question there are – Marxist theoreticians apart – broadly two possible answers. On one view, the clarity of Pushkin's early observation about the founder of the Russian state ('he believed in his own power and despised mankind perhaps more than Napoleon did'[19]) had by the 1830s given way to such ambivalence that he could never have accomplished the daunting task which he had accepted from Nicholas I. As he himself put it in a letter written as late as 1834, 'I am approaching Peter with fear and trembling, just as you are approaching your professional chair of history.'[20] Moreover, even if he had somehow succeeded in squaring the circle, what would Nicholas I have made of the result?

The second – preferable – view is supported by at least two pieces of hard evidence, one related to Pushkin's reading of ancient history and the other consisting of his own *Preparatory Text of the History of Peter*.[21] For reasons already pointed out (in Chapter 6), Tacitus' influence on Pushkin is highly significant. As for his *Preparatory Text*, which has never been translated into English, these are indeed notes prepared for his own future use. But a total of over 100,000 Russian words – that is to say, the equivalent of not less than 125,000 words in English – cannot be dismissed (as it was in a chapter written by a critic in the 1930s) as a few fragments.[22] The 'Introduction' at the very beginning shows clearly on what a large scale Pushkin planned his *History of Peter*:

> Russia from without
> Russia from within
> Taxes
> Trade
> Military strength

The Nobility
The People
Laws
Education
The Spirit of the Time[23]

Pushkin's early death leaves the choice between these two views open. There can be no doubt, however, that he had at any rate the potential ability to become a great Russian historian.

What makes the Boldino autumn of 1833 especially memorable in Pushkin's life is the fact that, while he was there, he wrote both his masterpiece in verse and his masterpiece in prose. The first of these works is *The Bronze Horseman*. The introductory part of this poem begins by presenting to the reader Peter the Great as the founder of the new capital, St. Petersburg. From the city's foundation Pushkin carries his reader a hundred years forward with his long invocation of contemporary St. Petersburg (quoted in the Introduction to this biography). The tone then suddenly changes – 'there was a dread time ... my tale will be sad' – a warning that is followed in Part 1 by a further presentation, this time of another Evgenii, whose family name, once famous, is now 'forgotten by the world and by fame'; he 'works in an office somewhere, he shuns the aristocracy and grieves neither for deceased relatives nor for forgotten times of old'. Evgenii has just returned home on the night of the great St. Petersburg flood of 1824, which Pushkin vividly describes, depicting Evgenii sitting behind Falconet's bronze equestrian monument of Peter the Great, looking not at the water lapping his feet, but towards 'one distant point' and wondering how his beloved Parasha, living on the opposite side of the river, has fared on this wild night.

The second part of the poem begins with another change of tone. The flood waters subsiding, Evgenii persuades a ferryman to carry him across the swollen river (whose bridges are still up) for a few kopeks. He is thus able to reach the site where the 'small ramshackle house' of Parasha and her widowed mother had stood. He finds no trace either of them or of the house. After walking round, he bursts into hysterical laughter. Deranged, he does not return home, but becomes a tramp, sleeping on the embankment of the Neva. (Pushkin imagines an intervening summer.) One autumn night Evgenii again finds himself standing by Peter the Great's monument, as he had on the night of the flood. His confused thoughts become terribly clear.

One of many self-portaits by Pushkin. This one was stuck into the album of
Ekaterina Ushakova, whom he came close to marrying.

One of thirty sketches by Pushkin of
Elizaveta Vorontsova, the wife of his
chief in Odessa in 1823-4.

Anna Olenina, whom Pushkin had
courted a decade earlier, painted
in 1839.

Elizaveta Khitrovo, a devoted admirer of
Pushkin, drawn by Orest Kiprensky.

Ekaterina Ushakova (and her feet),
drawn by Pushkin in 1829.

Above: Natalya Goncharova, Pushkin's fiancée, drawn by Pushkin between October and November 1830 while he was working at Boldino.

Right: Natalya Nikolaevna Pushkina, a portrait painted not long after their marriage in February 1831.

Above: Monument to Peter the Great, in St. Petersburg – the 'Bronze Horseman' of Pushkin's poetic masterpiece.

Left: Adam Mickiewicz, the great Polish poet, drawn by Pushkin, who was his exact contemporary and briefly his friend.

Peter the Great's monument, the horse imagined riderless, drawn by Pushkin.

View of the Moika Canal, St. Petersburg. The last flat rented by Pushkin, in which he died, was on this canal and is now a museum.

Les Grands Croix Commandeurs et
Chevaliers du Sérémssime Ordre des
Cocus réunis en grand Chapitre sous la
présidence du vénérable grand-Maive
de l'Ordre, S. E. O. L Narychkine, ont
nommé à l'unanimité Mr Alexandre
Pouchkine coadjuteur du grand Maître
de l'Ordre des Cocus et historiographe de
l'Ordre.

Le secrétaire perpétuel: Cte J. Borch

Copy of the anonymous and insulting letter
received by Pushkin in November 1836,
which led ultimately to the duel fought on
27 January 1837.

Georges d'Anthès, who challenged Pushkin to the duel in 1837 in which Pushkin received the mortal wound from which he died two days later.

A portrait of Pushkin, of very doubtful attribution (? painted by A.L. Linev, 1836-7). If the dating and the attribution are accurate, this is the last portrait of Pushkin.

Statue of Pushkin in Moscow, unveiled in 1880.

He recognizes the square which the flood had reached and the monument. He wanders round the monument until he whispers, 'trembling with wrath: "All right then, builder of marvels! Just you wait!"' The tsar's response, imagined by Evgenii, is to gallop after him across the square. Evgenii runs away 'at break-neck speed' and 'all night long, wherever the poor madman turned his step, the Bronze Horseman galloped after him with ponderous clatter'.

The brief conclusion is calm by comparison with what has gone before it. Pushkin describes a desolate island off the shore, sometimes visited by 'some civil servant, while boating on a Sunday', where the flood had 'in its play driven a ramshackle little house' which had remained above the water 'like a black bush'. When it was taken away 'last spring on a wooden barge . . . by the threshold, my madman was found and on that very spot his cold corpse was buried out of charity.'[24]

In *The Bronze Horseman* Pushkin's reluctance to point a moral or adorn a tale – already noticeable at the end of his *Captive of the Caucasus*, written thirteen years earlier[25] – reaches its apogee. It is therefore hardly surprising that, in consequence, few poems written in the nineteenth century have evoked so many diverse interpretations, both from Russian and from foreign critics, as this deceptively simple 'St. Petersburg Tale' (*povest'*).[26] Given the relationship between Mickiewicz and Pushkin, which has other reflections in Pushkin's verse, it is virtually certain that at least in part *The Bronze Horseman* was Pushkin's response to Mickiewicz's recently published *Monument of Peter the Great* and to his attack on Russia's 'historical desert' and the 'cosmopolitan masquerade of St. Petersburg, a city without a past, lacking a real national life'.[27] What is much less certain, although Pushkin's earliest biographer had no doubts whatever on this score, is the relationship between *The Bronze Horseman* and *Ezersky* (the fragment of an unfinished poem begun a little earlier). Annenkov was convinced that these two poems originally formed a single whole, which Pushkin divided into two, not having decided by the time of his death on the exact form that *The Bronze Horseman* should take.[28] Since then successive generations of Russian critics have concentrated largely on the question of the significance of the role of the two protagonists: Peter the Great and Evgenii – the tsar and the decayed nobleman, a clerk who now becomes a pauper. Is it significant that in *The Bronze Horseman* he chose as the site of Evgenii's final encounter with Peter the Great the very square in which the Decembrists stood for hours eleven years after the flood? Did he intend Evgenii's furious, but futile, reproach to the monument of the greatest Russian autocrat as a symbol of the botched revolt of 14 December 1825? Did Pushkin also foresee a different outcome for the autocracy the next time round, whenever that might be? Among his papers a drawing was found of Falconet's monument of Peter the Great – riderless – the bronze horse has lost its horseman.[29]

There can be no single 'authorized version' of an unfinished poem, unpublished in Pushkin's lifetime and not even published in an un-bowdlerized form until 1904, which – on close inspection – has so many facets and so many layers of meaning. In spite of its apparently detached style, moreover, it is the most personal and the most intimate poem that Pushkin ever wrote (a few of his lyrics excepted). And it has one striking link with the prose story which he wrote during the same autumn at Boldino – *The Queen of Spades*.[30] Again the apparent simplicity of the plot of *The Queen of Spades* is deceptive. A detailed account of this plot would require an explanation of the rules of the game of faro (in Russian, *shtos*), a card game then in fashion throughout the capitals of Europe, in which very high stakes could be placed and correspondingly large sums won and lost. Just such a summary is provided by Nabokov in his commentary on a reference to the game in *Evgenii Onegin*.[31] For present purposes, therefore, a broad synopsis of the plot of *The Queen of Spades* will suffice.

The Queen of Spades both begins and ends quietly and quickly: Pushkin at his most succinct, leaving his reader to fill in the picture sketched with broad strokes of his brush. On the other hand, his description of what lies between the two is detailed and dramatic. The story (of about 10,000 words) opens with a group of officers sitting down to a champagne supper at five o'clock in the morning after playing cards. Over supper one of them tells the story of his grandmother, Countess ★★★ (Pushkin gives only her first name and patronymic, Anna Fedotovna). In her youth in Paris, after losing half a million francs borrowed from the Duc d' Orléans, the countess was able to repay him only thanks to the secret of three unfailingly winning cards revealed to her by the legendary Count St. Germain, to whom in her desperation she had recourse. The secret of the three cards had been passed on by her in her long life – she was now over eighty – only once: to a young gambler, this time in Russia, who had just lost three hundred thousand roubles, on the strict condition that he would never play again. Once again the secret saved the gambler from ruin.

On one of the officers listening to this tale it makes an immediate and profound impression. This is Hermann, a young, frugal, engineer officer of Russianized German origin, who has never touched a card in his life. His presence in the opening scene of *The Queen of Spades* is explained by the fact that he is so fascinated by the drama of the card table that he is willing to sit up for nights on end watching others play. Socially he is an outsider in the company of the other characters who appear in *The Queen of Spades*, all of whom are members of the *haut monde*. (Pushkin assumes throughout that the reader is familiar not only with the world of gambling, but also with the *haut monde* of St. Petersburg in general.) Nevertheless, Hermann is later – flippantly but significantly – described by the officer who related his grandmother's story as a romantic with a Napoleonic profile and a Mephistophelean soul.

In Pushkin's development of the central part of *The Queen of Spades*, Hermann first succeeds in establishing contact with the countess' young companion and ward, Lizaveta, whom he eventually manages to persuade of his love, to the point where she writes giving him an assignation shortly after two o'clock in the morning, following a ball at which she knows she will be in attendance on the countess (the countess still follows the social round in St. Petersburg). Lizaveta's letter to Hermann contains careful instructions on how he should walk up from the hall of the countess' house to the countess' bedroom and then up a narrow winding staircase leading to her own bedroom.

Hermann follows Lizaveta's instructions, except that instead of meeting Lizaveta he waits until the countess has dismissed her servants, but has not yet gone to sleep, and then accosts her in her bedroom. He pleads with her for the secret of the three cards. Her only remark in the whole of the ensuing conversation is that the story related by her grandson was a joke. At last Hermann draws his pistol (in fact unloaded). The countess dies of shock. Hermann then goes up to Lizaveta's bedroom; he tells her what has happened, making it clear that what he has done was for money, not for love; and although she calls him a monster, she gives him the key to a door of the house leading out on to the street from a secret staircase. He lets himself out calmly and without remorse.

Three days later Hermann attends the countess' funeral service. As he bends over the open coffin (for the ritual of the *poslednyi potselui*, 'the last kiss'), the dead woman appears to wink at him. In the small hours of the next morning he is visited in his bedroom by the dead countess, who tells him that the three, seven, ace, played in that order, will win for him, on condition that he does not play more than one card in twenty-four hours; and that he will never play again for the rest of his life. She adds that she will forgive him for causing her death if he marries her ward Lizaveta.

Hermann loses little time in using his (hitherto untouched) patrimony of forty-seven thousand roubles in order to follow the countess' instructions to the letter. He wins on the three on the first night. The following night he stakes ninety-four thousand on the seven, with the same result. On the third night he stakes everything – an enormous sum even by the standards of the professional gambler who is holding the bank – on the ace. Through an unexplained mistake, however, he loses everything by playing not the ace, but the queen of spades. It seems to him that the card winks at him and smiles. 'The old woman!' he shouts in horror.

The conclusion – Pushkin calls it just that – is:

> Hermann went mad. He is now sitting in room 17 at the Obukhov Hospital; he answers no questions whatever, but merely mutters with unusual rapidity: 'three, seven, ace! three, seven, queen!' Lizaveta Ivanovna has married a very agreeable young man; he has a good position in the service somewhere; he is the son of the former steward of the old countess. Lizaveta Ivanovna is bringing up a poor relation.
>
> Tomsky [the countess's grandson] has been promoted to the rank of captain and is going to marry Princess Polina.

The Queen of Spades, related in Pushkin's most deadpan style of narrative, is not open to the same infinite number of interpretations as *The Bronze Horseman*. But they still cover a broad range: varying from straight melodrama to a dazzling display of intricate symbolism.[32] Autobiographically speaking, *The Queen of Spades* and *The Bronze Horseman* are linked by one common feature: namely, the fact that in both works protagonists go out of their minds. Taken in conjunction with Pushkin's poem (quoted in the preceding chapter)

'May God grant that I do not go out of my mind', they suggest the possibility that in 1833, in addition to the material concerns by which he was beginning to be weighed down, he also had to contend with this frightening anxiety. True, it may be objected that neither Evgenii in *The Bronze Horseman* nor Hermann in *The Queen of Spades* has anything else in common with Pushkin (nor have the two works anything else in common with each other). If so, the answer may be that Pushkin was at pains to depict both characters in colours which were in all other respects far removed from his own.

Pushkin's *annus mirabilis*, 1833, had two not unworthy pendants: *The Tale of the Golden Cockerel* and *The Captain's Daughter*.[33] Both may be regarded as sharing a common political theme: the exercise and abuse of power. The former, a *skazka* (fairy-tale) in verse, was written during Pushkin's last autumn spent at Boldino, which was by far the shortest of the three. The latter, a short historical novel set in the context of the *Pugachevshchina*, was not published until two months before Pushkin's death. In effect it was a Boldino product, in that it arose directly from his *Pugachev*, with which the first draft of *The Captain's Daughter* was virtually simultaneous. Indeed, in Klyuchevsky's epigram about Pushkin he described the history of *Pugachev* as one long explanatory note to the novel. Posthumously, *The Captain's Daughter* earned far more than *Pugachev* ever did. *The Golden Cockerel*, which has received high praise in recent years, baffled the public at the time.[34]

These two works are not only pendants to Pushkin's output of the years 1830–3. They are also the final important works of a bruised – not to say, exhausted – man, who by 1835 had reached the point where, at least for the time being, he no longer enjoyed either the tranquil environment or the peace of mind that his imagination needed for inspired writing. Instead he turned to a different field. Long after he had first advocated the need for a Russian *Edinburgh Review*, he now revived the idea. The outcome, approved by the censorship, was the literary journal, the *Sovremennik*, in whose editorial chair he would spend what turned out to be the last months of his life. This chair provided Pushkin with work, which he took seriously, but not the healing and restorative 'shrine' and 'font' that his spirit needed now more than ever before. How much more might he have written if he had been able to spend more time at Boldino, or somewhere equivalent, in the 1830s? Probably a great deal. And, had

he lived longer, how many other masterpieces might he have
written? To this question there can be no certain answer, but perhaps
Pushkin might have been able to say of himself what an English poet
wrote two hundred years earlier:

> I once more smell the dew and rain,
> And relish versing. Oh, my only light,
> It cannot be
> That I am he
> On whom thy tempests fell at night.[35]

CHAPTER TWELVE

Ambiguous Relationships

Seal up the mouth of outrage for a while,
Till we can clear these ambiguities

—Shakespeare, *Romeo and Juliet*, Act V, Scene iii.

The 'mouth of outrage' has been wide open ever since Pushkin's death – with justice – but most of the efforts made to explain the circumstances of his death have either been overtaken by later archival discoveries or created more heat than light – or both. Recent Russian scholarship has brought about the beginning of a change: in particular the assembling of the bulk of the documentary evidence, some of which is comparatively new, in chronological order.[1] The modern biographer no longer needs to detain the reader with detailed discussion of earlier studies of what happened in St. Petersburg between the beginning of January 1836 and the end of January 1837, such as that written by Pavel Shchegolev nearly eighty years ago;[2] and certainly not with two accounts that have since appeared in English, one of which reflected what Robert Hughes has called, in another context, the 'priggishness of the Puritan school-marm',[3] while the other resorted to use of the technique of the unsupported assertion, clad in embarrassingly purple prose.[4]

This said, much of what happened during Pushkin's final year is still shrouded in ambiguity and it seems likely to remain so. In part this is because of the difficulty of reconstructing Pushkin's state of mind with a measure of certainty at any point during his last, critical months.[5] Uncertainty becomes outright ambiguity when account is taken of the nature of the multiple network of personal relationships, whether proven or unproven, at the centre of which Pushkin lived during – roughly – the last two years of his life. Even the timespan of these relationships is still a matter of opinion. The two years just mentioned are measured from the autumn of 1834 to the autumn of

1836. This timespan is supported by a phrase in one of Pushkin's letters: *'une persévérance de deux années'.*[6] – his own description of the attentions paid to his wife (and, he might have added, to his sister-in-law) by Baron Georges-Charles d'Anthès – although it has been argued that in reality 'the whole romance' between Natalya and d'Anthès lasted only one year.[7] However that may be, there is a consensus that it was sometime during 1834 that the Pushkins first met d'Anthès: whose place in French history – such as it is – is that of a man who did well both in business and in politics under the Second Empire, living almost to the end of the nineteenth century, whereas in Russian works of reference he is simply described as Pushkin's murderer.

D'Anthès arrived in St. Petersburg in the autumn of 1833, having left France after the bloodless revolution of 1830.[8] Born at Soultz in 1812 (as it happened, in the same year as Natalya Goncharova) he was a member of a family that had been established in Alsace since the late seventeenth century and was ennobled in 1731. At the age of seventeen he entered the French military academy of St. Cyr, where his studies were cut short by the overthrow of Charles X, whose cause he espoused – in vain. There being no future in the France of the new bourgeois monarchy for a youth of his legitimist political opinions, d'Anthès decided to try his luck as a soldier of fortune in Prussia. On arrival in Berlin, he soon discovered that the professional standards of the Prussian Army were beyond or, as he might have seen them, beneath him, because he would have been obliged to begin his military service in Prussia as a non-commissioned officer. However, the close family links between the royal houses of Prussia and Russia ensured that, armed with a valuable letter of introduction, he was able to leave Berlin for St. Petersburg in 1833 hoping for acceptance by the Russian army instead. Travelling by road, d'Anthès met in a German inn a Dutch diplomat, who was returning to his post in St. Petersburg. This complete stranger, who would soon exercise a lasting effect on his own future and, as it turned out, a profound influence on the fate of Pushkin, was Baron Louis Borchard van Hekkeren. Hekkeren was forty-one at the time of this encounter. His family was one of the oldest in Holland; in his youth he had served in the French navy; and after Napoleon's final defeat in 1815 he joined the Netherlands diplomatic service. In St. Petersburg, where he served for ten years from 1823, first as chargé d'affaires and then as minister, he aroused mixed feelings in the diplomatic world, although he was an intimate of the Nesselrode circle. Although Nesselrode was known ironically in St. Petersburg as 'the Austrian Minister for Russian foreign affairs', it was the Austrian Ambassadress who described Hekkeren in her diary as 'cunning, false and *peu sympathique*'.[9]

In the euphemistic language of the early twentieth century, Hekkeren might have been described as 'a confirmed bachelor'. In the nineteenth century the idea that a government could not safely entrust its representation abroad to a man of homosexual leanings – provided that he was reasonably discreet – was not one to which much attention was paid. And up to 1834 Hekkeren was discreet with one exception: he grossly abused the privilege of the diplomatic bag. He used this to import – duty-free – goods of all kinds in quantities far exceeding the requirements of personal use and therefore intended for the market. Hekkeren was by no means the first head of mission to err in this way, either in his century or in our own. In avoiding trouble with the officials both of the Russian customs and of the ministry of foreign affairs, he doubtless relied on his friendship with Nesselrode and on the value set in St. Petersburg on his own ultramonarchist convictions. Once the future of Belgium had been internationally agreed, at the London Conference in 1831 (under the Vienna settlement, Belgium had formed part of the Kingdom of the Netherlands), Hekkeren cannot have had much of importance to do in St. Petersburg; his leaves of absence were of extreme length even by the standards of those days. But for what happened in 1836–7, he might have been remembered only as a malicious, though harmless, busybody, a familiar type in the diplomatic services of all ages.

From the turn of the year 1833–4 an extraordinary change, triggered by Hekkeren's meeting with d'Anthès in Prussia, came about. Hekkeren had given d'Anthès a lift in his carriage, so that the two men left the inn together and arrived in Russia together on 8 September 1833. In the course of the following year Hekkeren travelled to Alsace in order to meet Georges d'Anthès' family. By February 1836 Georges' father, who was not well off, wrote to Hekkeren authorizing him to adopt his son; and on 22 May the Russian foreign minister received from the Netherlands minister formal notification of the fact that, by decision of the King of the Netherlands, Georges d'Anthès was entitled to bear his name, his title and his coat of arms. Hekkeren had had some legal difficulty in his own country in bringing this remarkable operation to a successful conclusion. He was obliged to overcome the fact that the French *code civil*, which was still in force in the Netherlands, did not allow an adoption of this kind. This obstacle was circumvented by means of a royal decree which did not mention the word adoption, but did lay down that both d'Anthès and his descendants were authorized to bear the name of Hekkeren.[10] From then on Russian documents tend to refer to the elder Hekkeren and the younger Hekkeren, but since this is confusing to a present-day reader, the use of the name d'Anthès is retained throughout the rest of this book, except in quotations.

Was Hekkeren's affection for – not to say, obsession with – this handsome blond man, half his age, platonic and was d'Anthès actively bisexual? Both are questions to which no definitive answers can be given. At the time, the general reaction in St. Petersburg was one of astonishment, but the candid expression of this astonishment seldom went outside the privacy of confidential correspondence. Long afterwards, however, two pieces of evidence came to light, both of which point in the same direction. In his account of the events of 1836–7, one of d'Anthès' brother officers in St. Petersburg, Prince Alexander Trubetskoi, wrote that there was one exception to d'Anthès':

> youthful mischief . . . about which we learned much later. I do not know whether to say that he lived with Hekkeren or that Hekkeren lived with him. At that time buggery was widespread in high society . . . It must be assumed that, in his relations with Hekkeren, he [d'Anthès] played only the passive role.[11]

Like all memoirs, this account, which was written fifty years after d'Anthès had left Russia, cannot be relied upon. On the other hand, there is only one reasonable explanation of the fact that when writing (in French) to Hekkeren from St. Petersburg, d'Anthès used the second person singular throughout. No Frenchman who was born a member of the *noblesse* – or, for that matter, the upper bourgeoisie – would have addressed his father as anything but '*vous*' in the nineteenth century – and indeed well into the twentieth.[12]

Pushkin's first reference to d'Anthès is an entry in his diary of 26 January 1834, where he remarks that the guards are not happy with the decision to accept two French émigrés, one of them Baron d'Anthès, 'as officers straight away'.[13] In February of that year d'Anthès, without knowing a word of Russian (a language that he never troubled to learn during his three and a half years in St. Petersburg), was indeed gazetted cornet in the household cavalry; and two years later he was promoted to the rank of lieutenant. He retained his French citizenship, however. He seems to have got on well enough with his brother officers. He also enjoyed the financially important patronage of the Empress Alexandra (Nicholas I's Prussian wife), who was his regiment's colonel-in-chief; and it was not long before he became a familiar figure in St. Petersburg society.

It is possible that d'Anthès first met the Pushkins soon after the entry in Pushkin's diary, although the date of Natalya's miscarriage (March 1834), after which she spent over five months in the country, fixes a *terminus ante quem*.[14] A more probable dating is sometime in the autumn of 1834, by which time d'Anthès was a member of *la bande joyeuse* and Natalya had brought both her sisters, Alexandra and Ekaterina, to live with her in St. Petersburg. The consequences of Natalya's insistence on importing her sisters to St. Petersburg, against her husband's wishes, were much as Pushkin had feared, although he turned out to be wrong in his forecast that neither of them would receive a court appointment, because the elder of the two, Ekaterina, became a maid of honour at the age of twenty-five, two months after arriving in the capital. The gushing letters written home by these two provincial ladies in October–November 1834 report a swift plunge into the social round, equipped with ball gowns paid for by their rich aunt, Ekaterina Zagryazhkaya. Well before the end of year holiday season had begun an attack of fever (presumably influenza) cost Alexandra – the middle sister, one year younger than Natalya – 'only one ball and two *spectacles*'. By early December Ekaterina was waxing enthusiastic about the number of balls she had attended. And by the end of 1835 both of them were never at home for a single evening, thanks to 'Tasha and her husband'.[15]

Even before the age of the telephone, the amount of noise that all this must have added to a flat which already housed four children and numerous servants, must have been considerable. By day Pushkin, who always ate his main meal late, was able to escape to the privacy of his study, where he would remain well into the afternoon, after which he always went for a walk, whatever the weather. But in the evening there were some invitations which obliged him to accompany all three sisters. Although the jokes to which the sight in public of such an unusual 'harem' gave rise were bad enough, the financial implications were worse. Alexandra (Azya in the family) and Ekaterina (Koko) both had annual allowances of 4500 roubles paid to them from the Goncharov estate, but Pushkin's bills soared, not only because he was obliged to rent a much larger flat – from the Vyazemskys – but also because of what he described in a bitter sentence in a letter written to his wife as *'l'intérêt de Monsieur Durier et Madame Sichler'*.[16] (These were the names of two leading St. Petersburg couturiers.) Natalya herself was obliged to admit in a letter written to her brother: 'We are in such an impoverished condition that there are days when I do not know how to run the house, my head goes round and round in circles.'[17]

It is a moot point at what stage and to what extent financial and domestic confusion in Pushkin's household was worse confounded by the sexual behaviour of its members, perhaps including Pushkin himself. Three interrelated questions are involved. The simplest way to address them is separately: the first question concerning d'Anthès, the second Pushkin himself and the third d'Anthès and Natalya jointly. Taking these questions in that order – the fact that d'Anthès flirted with Ekaterina as well as with Natalya is well attested. In the St. Petersburg society of the mid-1830s there is nothing surprising about this. D'Anthès had the good looks, the ready wit and – as a foreigner – the lack of inhibitions which guaranteed him success in this field. However, given the dramatic turn of later events which culminated first in d'Anthès marrying Ekaterina and then in his fighting a duel with Pushkin in January 1837, this first question cannot be left hanging in the air so far as Ekaterina is concerned. Tall, short-sighted and three years older than d'Anthès, she was not only flattered by his attentions, but fell in love with him. The letter that she wrote to her brother on 9 November 1836 – that is to say, five days after Pushkin had issued his first challenge to d'Anthès – includes the sentence: 'Happiness for all my family and death for myself – that is what I need and that is what I continually pray for to the Almighty . . .'[18]

What long remained a matter of controversy is whether Ekaterina's first child by d'Anthès was conceived as early as mid-1836. In order to reach the opposite conclusion, namely that she was not already several months pregnant at the time of her marriage to d'Anthès, it is necessary to suppose that a letter written to her by her mother, bearing the date 15 May 1837 (first published by Shchegolev) was in reality written one year later, on 15 May 1838. This letter includes the following sentence: 'In your last letter you speak about your journey to Paris; to whom will you entrust the looking after of your little girl during the time of your absence? Will she remain in safe hands? Your separation from her must be distressing for you.' To accept the supposition of a twelve-months' error in the dating of this letter requires a considerable effort, but recent research in the Goncharov family archives indicates that Natalya Ivanovna's letter was indeed written in 1838, in which case the official date of the birth of the d'Anthès' first child – October 1837 – may be accepted.[19]

Of the first two questions, the more important is whether Pushkin slept with Alexandra, in addition to flirting with her at parties, which he certainly did. Predictably, Arapova was the principal prosecutor and Akhmatova a passionate advocate in Pushkin's defence. If it could be proved, which it cannot, Arapova's story about a ring belonging to Alexandra which Pushkin's servants were obliged to search for high and low, and which was eventually discovered in Pushkin's bed, might be regarded as a clear pointer.[20] This story was related seventy-one years afterwards, by a heavily biased narrator, but there were those who were close to Pushkin at the time, such as Zhukovsky, who might not have found it impossible to believe – witness, for example, the entry in Zhukovsky's notes, where he recorded in November 1836: 'What I said [to Pushkin] about his relationships (*otnosheniya*)' and '*Les révélations d'Alexandrine*'.[21] (Soviet readers sometimes had to be reminded by editors of such documents that *otnosheniya* was the term used for sexual relationships as well as for relationships in general.) As against this, it seems well established that, to the end of her days, Alexandra kept a portrait of d'Anthès hanging in her dining room, where it remained until 1940.[22] The case remains open. What is certain is that Alexandra was unattractive (she had a pronounced squint); she married sixteen years later, when she was over forty. She was genuinely devoted to Pushkin and, according to earlier accounts, she alone of the three sisters played the role of Martha in his household, which Natalya neglected. These accounts have since been challenged; and it is now accepted that, at any rate towards the end of Pushkin's life, his wife played her full part at home. In all probability, however, Alexandra was the only member of his family to whom Pushkin revealed the fact that he had written the fatal letter that finally led to his duel with d'Anthès.

There remains Arapova's statement, made at the beginning of our own century, that Pushkin frequented brothels after his marriage. Pushkin's views about *grisettes* are a matter of record and they have already been quoted in this book. But if he did visit them in 1836–7 he would have been running a considerable risk at the hands of his 'empress', as he now referred to Natalya.[23] For almost all the time from the end of 1835 onwards he and Natalya were together in St. Petersburg. Arapova's allegation remains pure speculation.[24]

The third question, about Natalya and d'Anthès, is the one that is critical to any assessment of the circumstances of Pushkin's death. Was she, as Pushkin publicly maintained, as pure as driven snow? Did she, as d'Anthès claimed privately, return his love? Or was the Russian poetess Marina Tsvetaeva right when she wrote over half a century ago:

> Just as Helen of Troy was the occasion, but not the cause, of the Trojan war (which itself was nothing else but the occasion of the death of Achilles), so also Goncharova was not the cause, but the occasion, of the death of Pushkin, predestined from the cradle. Destiny chose the simplest, the most futile, the most guiltless weapon: a beautiful woman . . .[25]

Once again there can be no simple answer to this question. But no attempt to answer it can afford to overlook two letters from d'Anthès to Hekkeren. These were published only in 1946, after they had been discovered among the d'Anthès family papers at Soultz.[26] (Even the Goncharovian revisionists have felt obliged to devote several pages to these letters, whose authenticity they have made a lonely and unconvincing attempt to demolish.[27]) The flavour of these crucially important letters is as significant as their content. In attempting to form a judgement, it is important to bear in mind the effect of his use of the French second person singular, which cannot be rendered in English at all.

St. Petersburg, 20th January 1836

Mon très cher ami

I am truly guilty of not having replied straight away to the two good and amusing letters that you have written to me, but, you see, the night spent dancing, the morning at riding school and the afternoon asleep, this has been my existence for the past fortnight, and I have just as much of this ahead of me, and what is worse than all this, is the fact that I am madly in love! Yes, madly, because I do not know where to turn my head, I shall not give you her name, because a letter can get lost, but recall to yourself the most delicious creature in St. Petersburg and you will know her name. And what is most horrible in my position is the fact that she also loves me and that we cannot see each other, something that has been impossible so far, for the husband is a man of revolting jealousy: I confide all this in you, *mon bien cher*, as to my best friend, and because I know that you will take part in my grief, but, in God's name not a word to anybody nor any information to find out to whom I am paying court, you would destroy her without wishing it and I myself would be inconsolable. For, you see, I would do everything in the world for her, only in order to please her, for the life that I have led for some time is a torture at every moment. To love one another and not to be able to say so to each other except between two ritornellos of a counter-dance is an awful thing: I am perhaps wrong in confiding all this to you and you will treat it as nonsense, but I have a heart so heavy and so full that I need to pour it out a little. I am certain that you will excuse me this folly, I agree that it is a folly, but it is impossible for me to use my reason, although I need to do so badly, because this love is poisoning my existence: but rest assured, I am being prudent and I have been so much up to the present moment, that the secret belongs only to her and to me (she bears the same name as the lady who was writing to you about me and who was in despair [for] the plague and the famine had ruined her villages); you must understand now that it is possible to lose one's reason for such a creature, above all when she loves you! I repeat to you again, not a single word to Broge [or Brage?] because he is in correspondence with Petersburg and it would be enough for him to give some indication on his part to his wife to destroy both of us! For God alone knows what might happen: so, my very dear friend, the four months that you and I still have to spend far from each other will appear to me centuries, because in my position one has an absolute need of someone whom one loves in order to be able to open one's heart and to ask for courage. This is the reason why I do not look well, because that apart I have never been in better health physically than I am at the moment, but my head is so excited that I no longer have a moment of rest either by night or by day, it is this that gives me an appearance of illness and sadness and not my health . . . Goodbye, *mon cher*, be indulgent towards my new passion, for I love you too from the bottom of my heart.

In the three and a half weeks that passed between d'Anthès' two letters a significant change appears to have taken place.

> *St. Petersburg, 14th February 1836*
>
> *Mon cher ami,* here the carnival is over and with that a part of my torments: really I believe that I am a bit calmer now that I do not see her every day and then, everyone cannot any longer come and take her hand, her waist and dance and converse with her as I do myself; and that is even better than it is for me, because their conscience is clearer than mine. It is stupid to say this, but it is something that I would never have believed, namely that it is from jealousy that I found myself in a continual state of irritation which made me sound happy. And then, we have had an explanation, the last time that I saw her, which was terrible, but which did me good. This woman, of whom most people suppose that she has little intelligence, I do not know whether it is love that has given it to her, but it is impossible to show more tact, more grace or more intelligence than she did in this conversation, and it was difficult to conduct, for it was a question of nothing less than refusing to violate her duties for a man whom she loves and who adores her; she described her position to me with so much renunciation and asked my understanding with so much naïveté that I was really defeated, and I could not find a word to say in reply to her. If you knew how she consoled me, for she saw clearly that I was choking and that my position was awful and when she said to me: I love you as I have never loved, but do not ask me for more than my heart, for all the rest does not belong to me and I cannot be happy except by respecting all my duties, have pity on me and love me always as you do now, my love will be your only reward; but, you see, I believe that I would have fallen at her feet in order to kiss them if I had been alone and I assure you that since that day my love for her has increased still more, but it is not the same thing now: I venerate her, I respect her, as one respects and venerates a being to whom all your existence is attached. But forgive me, my very dear friend, I am beginning my letter by talking of her: but she and I constitute only one person, for to talk about her is also to talk to you about myself, and in all your letters you reproach me for not expatiating enough about myself. I, as I was saying, am better, much better and am beginning to breathe, thank God, because my torture was intolerable: to be merry, laughing in front of the world, in front of the people who used to see me every day, while I had death in my heart, that is an awful position which I would not wish upon my most cruel enemy . . .[28]

Leaving on one side the implications for d'Anthès' relationship with Hekkeren that his use of the second person singular must involve, not to mention the fact that a worldly man aged twenty-three does not normally feel the need to write to his father about his feelings for a married woman at all, let alone at such length and in such terms, these two letters prove that, at any rate at the date on which the first letter was written, d'Anthès' 'new passion' had swept him off his feet. The way in which he describes his loved one and her 'revoltingly jealous' husband, however guarded, leaves the present-day reader, as it must have been intended to leave Hekkeren, in no doubt which was the married couple in question. In particular, the combination of the words 'the most delicious creature in St. Petersburg' and 'the husband is a man of revolting jealousy' point unmistakably to Natalya Pushkina and her husband. What cannot automatically be accepted at its face value is d'Anthès' conviction, expressed in both his letters, that Natalya returned his love in equal measure. Not that d'Anthès deceived Hekkeren about Natalya's feelings, but the possibility cannot be excluded that, like many another man in a similar position, d'Anthès deceived himself.

The second letter, in which d'Anthès reports that during the 'explanation' between himself and Natalya, she refused 'to violate her duties for a man whom she loves', raises a further problem. By mid-February Natalya was six months pregnant. She gave birth to her fourth child, a daughter, on 19 May and she did not go out again in society until the very end of July 1836.[29] Clearly much depends on the significance attached to the epithet 'new' which d'Anthès adds to the word 'passion' at the end of his first letter. At first sight, this does not square with Pushkin's use of the phrase 'two years' perseverance'. It has been argued that, on the contrary, whereas Natalya may well have continued to harbour the same feelings for d'Anthès at the end of 1836 as she did at the beginning, d'Anthès' love for Natalya was something of a flash in the pan; and that by the fatal autumn of 1836, it was in reality all over, so far as he was concerned, however much he continued to flirt with her in public.[30]

It is easy to make the word 'new' bear too much weight; d'Anthès' use of it is susceptible to more than one explanation. Moreover, there is no evidence of the effect that d'Anthès' letters had on Hekkeren in January and February, nor of what passed between them after Hekkeren's return to St. Petersburg in May 1836, following a long absence abroad. For example, did Hekkeren regard Natalya as a rival in his affection for d'Anthès? Was he perhaps, in his own way, as jealous a man as Pushkin undoubtedly was? We simply do not know. Russian Pushkinists take it as read that Pushkin could not fail to see 'what was thrown in the eyes of everyone'[31] at the beginning of 1836. They may well be right, but there is no hard evidence of the extent to which he was aware of the extreme point then reached by d'Anthès' infatuation with Natalya; nor of what exactly Pushkin believed about the nature of her feelings for d'Anthès at that time. Husband and wife certainly had a frank exchange nine months later, but in quite different circumstances that were deeply humiliating for both of them.

Confronted with this mishmash of conflicting evidence, a British biographer of Pushkin might hope to find some enlightenment from the pen of a shrewd English observer of the St. Petersburg scene at the time: John Lambton, first Earl of Durham, who served as ambassador there from 1835 to 1837. A man of wider vision than most of his British political contemporaries on questions both of domestic and of external policy, Durham was no ordinary ambassador; the value of his judgement on Russian society and the Russian government of the time has since been recognized in Russia.[32] 'Radical Jack' was the leader of the left wing of the Whig Party; and part of the reason for his appointment to St. Petersburg was that when Lord Melbourne (an easy-going, right-wing Whig) was invited by the king to form a government in June 1834 – remarking, before he agreed to do so, 'I think it's a damned bore'[33] – decided to exclude from his cabinet the two leading radical members of the previous Whig administration, one of whom was Durham.[34]

Apart from his intelligence, Durham had other qualifications for this important post. He was immensely rich; it was said of him that he spent nearly a million pounds on doing up his house in Britain. On an earlier visit to St. Petersburg he had got on well with Nicholas I; as Princess Lieven, for twenty years the Russian ambassadress in London, put it, 'we drowned him in courtesies'.[35] Pushkin must have known Durham, as he did other members of the diplomatic corps in St. Petersburg.[36] And the similarities between the characters of the two men are striking. Many adjectives – impatient, hot-tempered, hypersensitive to criticism, vain and prone to take offence at fancied slights, but also generous and never vindictive – could equally well be applied either to Durham or to Pushkin. Some empathy between the two men might perhaps have been expected. Moreover, the British

Embassy's report on Pushkin's death was signed by a man who had himself grown up in the fast Regency set – Durham's first marriage had been at Gretna Green – and it was addressed to a foreign secretary, Palmerston, known in the British press as 'Lord Cupid', who was no stranger either to love affairs or to the ins and outs of Russian society. Although he never went to Russia – indeed he never travelled further than Berlin – he was at one time rumoured to have been Princess Lieven's lover.

In the light of this, there is disappointingly little to be gleaned from Durham's despatch of 3 May 1837. A routine document, probably drafted by a junior member of the Embassy staff, it consists of little more than a covering document to its principal enclosure, the French version of the ukase which published the findings of the governmental enquiry held in St. Petersburg after Pushkin's death. In fairness to Durham (with one important exception), his diplomatic colleagues' reports to their governments did little better;[37] and his despatch does at least leave little doubt that he did not have a high opinion of Hekkeren.

Today, the historian has more material to base his conclusions on than observers in St. Petersburg did in 1837, whether they were Russians or foreigners. In spite of the documents that have gradually come to light since then, however, the evidence remains contradictory and partial; and the lacunae are still large. Yet Pushkin's biographer cannot afford to overlook these complex and ambiguous relationships, because it is only against the background that he can seek to explain the turgid drama that unfolded in St. Petersburg during 1836 and the first month of 1837.

CHAPTER THIRTEEN

A Fighting Withdrawal, 1836

The New Year is upon us. May God grant that it is happier than
the one that has just passed.

—Pushkin to his father, end of December 1836

Writing to his father at the end of December 1836, Pushkin could
scarcely have described the year that was just drawing to a close as
anything but unhappy. Quite apart from the explosion in his own life
that began on 4 November, it was the year in which his mother died.
Nevertheless, an account of his day-to-day activities in 1836, at any
rate during the first ten months, may at first sight appear almost
humdrum if measured against the highly charged emotions described
in the preceding chapter. One way of reconciling these two aspects of
Pushkin's life in 1836 is to regard his conduct throughout that year in
quasi-military terms: a fighting withdrawal.

Thus January 1836 began with a Pushkinian raid into enemy
territory, conducted with characteristic panache. Just three days
after Benckendorff had officially informed the Minister of Education, Sergei Uvarov (who combined this office with presidency of the
Academy of Sciences and of the Censorship Committee), that the tsar
had granted Pushkin permission to publish in the course of 1836 four
issues of his literary journal, the *Sovremennik* (*The Contemporary*),
copies of a poetic lampoon, directed against Uvarov personally,
began to circulate in St. Petersburg. Pushkin's relations with Uvarov,
which had earlier been friendly, deteriorated steadily in the 1830s
(among several other things, Uvarov saw to it that Pushkin never
became a member of the Russian Academy of Sciences – only of the
Academy of Literature). Somehow or other, the Moscow censors
had failed to spot the personal implications for Uvarov of Pushkin's
biting ode entitled 'On the convalescence of Lucullus', written
in November 1835, which was later published in the *Moskovskii*

Nablyudatel' (*Moscow Observer*).[1] St. Petersburg became aware of this poem only when copies of the *Moscow Observer* began to circulate in the capital on 17 January 1836. Uvarov at once complained to the tsar, on whose instructions Benckendorff administered a stern reprimand to Pushkin.[2] Pushkin then drafted a letter attempting to prove that his ode had not been directed against anyone whatsoever.[3] Had he sent such a letter, he would have convinced no one in the aristocratic or official circles of St. Petersburg. Indeed only a few of his close friends supported him on this issue. The affair petered out, but while it lasted it created a furore.

Up to 1836 the epigram 'desperate, but not hopeless' – used many years later to describe the state of the declining Austro-Hungarian Empire – could have been applied to Pushkin's financial circumstances. From the beginning of 1836 onwards Pushkin's financial affairs did indeed become hopeless. Or rather, any hope whatever of his financial recovery depended on one of two doubtful sources: either further indulgence on the part of the government or an increased literary income. Both of these hopes proved to be illusory before the year was out. It will be recalled that the imperial treasury's loan to Pushkin of 45,000 roubles had been secured on his salary. Since repayment of 25,000 of this sum now had to begin under the terms of the loan, the consequence was that from January 1836 Pushkin was no longer receiving a single rouble from the tsar. His attempt to use his share of his father's Nizhnii Novgorod estate in order to repay the entire governmental loan was turned down by the Minister of Finance (Pushkin had no legal right to sell during his father's lifetime).[4] Since this route towards solvency, towards which Pushkin turned only as a last resort, was barred, he pinned his main hope on the success of his venture into journalism. As he put it in a letter written to his wife in May of that year, 'I see that it is essential for me to have an income of 80,000 roubles. And I shall have them'[5] – two sentences providing powerful evidence of the extent to which Pushkin ignored reality in 1836.

The *Sovremennik*, whose first issue appeared on 11 April 1836, did not achieve anything remotely like the success for which Pushkin had hoped and for which he worked hard right up to the last day of his life. (Ironically, long after his death it would become the most famous literary journal in nineteenth-century Russia.) This initial failure was not in any way due to the quality of the contributors, who included Gogol, besides Pushkin himself. It was in the *Sovremennik* that Gogol's short story, *The Nose*, was first published. (His *Inspector General* had its premier performance in Moscow in the same month.) But in order to be successful, this journal had to overcome three obstacles: the nit-picking of the official censorship, which showed itself as capricious as ever in its dealings with Pushkin over the contents of the *Sovremennik*; Pushkin's lack of business acumen (marketing a newspaper was not one of his skills); and his unpopularity with most of the literary critics of the 1830s. From a man like Bulgarin only the worst could be expected, but even Belinsky wrote an article which included the question: 'Who does not know that it is possible to write superb poetry and to be an unsuccessful journalist?'[6]

The loan extended to Pushkin by the imperial treasury in 1835 had enabled him both to pay off some of his debts and to pay a proportion of his household bills. In 1836, however, his bills could be met only by a dismal succession of promissory notes, bearing a 10 per cent rate of interest, and a series of smaller sums obtained from pawnbrokers, in return for silver and other family possessions, all of which came to light when his debts had to be dealt with after his death. By that time the exact amount of his indebtedness, excluding his governmental loan, amounted to 76,505 roubles and 12 kopeks.[7] In absolute terms, this sum may not seem very large when compared, for example, with the gambling debts of leading members of English society in the same period, or even with Disraeli's total indebtedness, which reached £60,000 by the middle of the nineteenth century.[8] In Pushkin's case, however, several factors combined to make his situation worse in reality than it appeared at first sight. He had virtually no security to offer as collateral for the loans he incurred; his regular income from the government – 5000 roubles per annum – had come to a halt; the number of people to whom he owed money, not excluding his own servants, was large; and the curve of his expenditure led in one direction only – upwards. Thus, in May 1836 Natalya still owed the couturier firm of Stichler 3279 roubles for the years 1834–5; Pushkin rented a large *dacha* chosen by Natalya on the *Kamennyi Ostrov* (near the capital) for the summer of 1836 while continuing to pay rent for an empty flat in St. Petersburg; and when the family moved back in mid-September, he rented another flat, the one on the Moika, in which he would die four months later, at an annual rent of 4300 roubles.

As if these anxieties were not enough, Pushkin's mother died on Easter Sunday, 29 March. Her death was soon followed by an acrimonious financial argument about the sale of her Mikhailovskoe estate, which was still unresolved at the moment of his own death. The protracted correspondence about the estate between Pushkin and his brother-in-law, Nikolai Pavlishchev, reached the point where Pushkin was no longer willing to read his letters when he received them. (Nor did Pushkin's brother Lev Sergeevich, serving in the army in the Caucasus, help matters by running up debts of 30,000 roubles.)[9] It fell to Pushkin – not to his father – to make arrangements for his mother's funeral; and he accompanied her body to Mikhailovskoe. She was buried on 13 April within the walls of the neighbouring Svyatogorsk Monastery, next to the graves of Pushkin's Gannibal grandparents.

Pushkin and his wife were in mourning until the end of June. On 29 April, however, he set out on a long-delayed visit to Moscow. Here he stayed for nearly three weeks, as usual with Nashchokin. He enjoyed the company of Nashchokin and his wife Vera (they had married early in 1834) and the visit gave him temporary relief from the trials of his life in St. Petersburg, where (as he put it in a letter written two months later) his 'head' went 'round and round'.[10] But he achieved so little in Moscow that by mid-May he was already writing to Natalya that his work on the Petrine archives would require another visit to Moscow in six months' time.[11] An earlier letter contains the usual admonition to Natalya about flirting. For her part, Natalya urged Pushkin to come back. He did, but he only arrived at midnight on 23 May, a few hours after Natalya had given birth to her fourth child, a daughter, named Natalya after her.[12]

During these weeks a strange, perhaps premonitory, episode was brought to a conclusion – fortunately a happy one – although the fact that it happened at all is in itself an indication of how sensitive Pushkin was in this year of his life. At a ball in St. Petersburg at the turn of 1835–6, Count Vladimir Sollogub made a remark (his exact words are uncertain) to Natalya Pushkina, which she afterwards related to her husband. Pushkin considered it so offensive that he at once challenged Sollogub to a duel: the first occasion on which he had been involved in a challenge since his bachelor days. His written challenge did not reach Sollogub, who by that time had left the capital for Tver (Tver'). Hearing of the letter, however, Sollogub wrote a letter to Pushkin, which Pushkin regarded as unsatisfactory, as we know from a draft letter to Sollogub that has survived.[13] The sequel was described by Sollogub himself many years later. The two men eventually met in Moscow, where Nashchokin succeeded in making peace between them; Sollogub wrote a letter of apology to Natalya; and thereafter he and Pushkin became the best of friends.[14]

At the beginning of this year, and again from the end of July 1836 onwards, the Pushkins' social life was intense. During the first few weeks following Pushkin's return from Moscow, however, while he and his family were living in their *dacha*, he succeeded in doing a lot of work. As well as conducting the correspondence necessitated by editing the *Sovremennik*, he also found the time and the energy to write the final version of *The Captain's Daughter*, which he completed on 22 July. (This was his historical novel written at Boldino, the original draft of which has not survived.) He decided to publish it in the fourth issue of the *Sovremennik*, which came out just before his death. In addition he wrote a few poems, one of which – his proud *Exegi Monumentum* (quoted in the Introduction to this book) – had to wait until the present century for its correct text to be established; Zhukovsky felt obliged to make a number of amendments in order to get it published four years after Pushkin's death.[15]

By the end of the summer the effect of the strains to which Pushkin had been subjected for some time past was beginning to show. He broke down and wept at the twenty-fifth imperial lycée reunion on 19 October, while reciting the poem that he had written for the occasion – 'There was a time'. This may be ascribed to the emotive nature of the evening and in particular to the absence from it – whether through death or because of exile – of Pushkin's closest school-friends,[16] although his poem also showed his awareness that his turn would come. A letter written to his father on the following day ends with the words: 'I had counted on going to Mikhailovskoe. I could not do so. This is going to throw me out for a year at least. In the country I would have worked a lot; here I do nothing except produce bile.'[17] Still more revealing is Natalya's description – in a letter written to her brother – of her husband's state of health: 'I see how sad and dejected he is. He cannot sleep at night . . .'[18] And in a memoir, which is less reliable since it was written later on, but more dramatic, Pushkin's state of health at this time is thus described:

It was with difficulty that he could even conduct a consecutive conversation, he could not sit for any length of time in the same place, he shuddered when he heard loud noises, that of objects falling to the floor; he unsealed letters nervously; he could not tolerate the noise either of children or of music.[19]

All this notwithstanding, on the same day as he attended the lycée reunion, Pushkin managed to write a remarkable letter to his friend, Petr Chaadaev. This letter was never sent, either because Pushkin feared that it might add to Chaadaev's political difficulties if intercepted by the censors, or because he did not want to upset his friend by the differences of historical view expressed in his letter, or both.[20] Pushkin's letter, extracts from which are translated below, begins by thanking Chaadaev for sending him a *'brochure'*. By this he meant the Russian translation, which had been published by *The Telescope* on 3 October, of Chaadaev's *Lettres Philosophiques* (written in French, as was Pushkin's letter of comment), on which Chaadaev had been engaged since the end of 1829. The theme of Chaadaev's letters was two-fold: on the one hand a severe indictment of the serf-based society of contemporary Russia and, on the other hand, a theory of Russian history which stood at the opposite pole to the doctrine of the 'Third Rome'.[21] For Chaadaev, it was precisely because Russian Christianity derived from Byzantium and had therefore taken the Greek Orthodox side in the Great Schism of 1054, thus cutting itself off from the civilization of the Roman Catholic West, that Russia had become a country with no authentic historical tradition or culture of its own (a view similar to that of Mickiewicz, quoted in Chapter 11).

For the Russian government of 1836, what Chaadaev had written was scandalous. *The Telescope's* editor was exiled to Siberia; the censor who had let the translation through was dismissed; and Chaadaev, declared mad, was put under medical supervision. The position taken up by Pushkin was intermediate:

> There is no doubt that the Schism separated us from the rest of Europe and that we took no part in any of the great events which have stirred Europe; but we have had our own mission. It is Russia's immense space which absorbed the Mongol conquest. The Tartars did not dare cross our western frontiers and leave us in the rear. They withdrew towards their deserts and Christian civilization was saved. In order to achieve this we had to lead an existence which was completely on one

side, which while leaving us Christians, left us none the less completely strangers to the Christian world, so that our martyrdom did not in any way distract Catholic Europe from its energetic development ... As for our historical nullity, I decidedly cannot share your opinion ... Peter the Great who all by himself is a universal history! And Catherine II who put Russia on the threshold of Europe? And Alexander who led you to Paris? And (hand on heart) do you not find something impressive in the contemporary situation of Russia, something which will strike the future historian? Do you believe he will put us outside Europe? Although personally my heart is attached to the emperor, I am far from admiring all that I see around me; as a man of letters, I am bitter; as a man of prejudices, I am offended – but I swear to you on my honour that for nothing in the world would I wish to change my fatherland, nor to have a history other than that of our ancestors, such as God has given us ...

An earlier draft of Pushkin's letter, left among his papers, includes this franker paragraph:

What had to be said and what you have said is that our contemporary society is as contemptible as it is stupid; that this absence of public opinion, this indifference to everything which is duty, justice, right and truth; for everything which is not necessity. This cynical contempt for thought and for the dignity of man. It should be added (not as a concession, but as a fact), that the government is still the only European government of Russia and that wholly brutal and cynical though it is, it could be a hundred times worse. No one would pay the slightest attention to it.[22]

If *Exegi Monumentum* is Pushkin's personal poetical testament, his letter to Chaadaev written a few months later is his last attempt to sum up his historical view of Russia. Pushkin read both the poem and the letter aloud to Alexander Turgenev. Taken together, Chaadaev's and Pushkin's exchange – even though Pushkin's letter was never despatched – represents the beginning of what would become later on in the century the Great Debate about Russia. And in our own century viewers of Tarkovsky's film *Mirror* will recall the memorable scene in which the boy's grandmother tells him to go and look in her bookcase for the volume of Pushkin's correspondence which contains his letter to Chaadaev.

Simultaneously, in the autumn of 1836, Pushkin's life moved towards its climax. What was seen as d'Anthès' renewed pursuit of Natalya became a matter of general comment in St. Petersburg.

Writing to her brother, Sofia Karamzina described an evening party held on 17 September, attended among others by the Pushkins and d'Anthès. According to her letter, everybody was enjoying themselves except Pushkin, who was 'sad, thoughtful and preoccupied with something or other'. He never took his eyes off his wife and d'Anthès, who 'continues all the same tricks as previously – not moving a single step away from Ekaterina Goncharova, from a distance he throws tender glances towards Natalya, with whom at the very end he danced a mazurka. It was sad to look at Pushkin's face, who was standing opposite them by the door, silent, pale and threatening.'[23] Describing what went on in October, Countess Fiquelmont's diary contains this shrewd comment: 'Either it was simply the vanity of Madame Pushkina that was flattered and aroused or d'Anthès really moved and confused her heart, however that may be, she was no longer able to reject or to put a stop to the manifestations of his unbridled love.'[24]

On the morning of 4 November 1836 Pushkin received an anonymous letter, posted in St. Petersburg. By the evening of that day he knew that seven of his friends had also received a copy, including Vyazemsky, Sollogub and Elizaveta Khitrovo. Copies were sent only to Pushkin's friends – not to his enemies. The text of the letter, written in French and in a curious squiggly hand, was as follows:

> The Knights Grand Cross, the Commanders and the Knights of the most illustrious Order of Cuckolds, assembled in the Grand Chapter under the presidency of the venerable Grand Master of the Order, His Excellency D. L. Naryshkin, have unanimously elected Monsieur Alexander Pushkin assistant to the Grand Master of the Order of Cuckolds and as historian of the Order.
>
> The permanent secretary: Count I. Borkh.
> 4 November 1836.[25]

Before the day was out Pushkin had what seems to have been a candid talk with his wife. What exactly was said, we shall never know. According to Princess Vyazemskaya's later account, it was then that Natalya revealed that she had been invited to the house of an intimate of the Hekkeren circle, Idalya Poletika, where she had found not Madame Poletika, but d'Anthès, who had renewed to her the appeal that he had made in the previous February, this time threatening to shoot himself. If, as the most recent Russian analysis of all the evidence suggests, this encounter did indeed take place on 2 November, the significance of its timing for the timing of the anonymous letters is clear.[26]

Pushkin was convinced that his wife, however naïve, was guiltless. He also reached the conclusion, as he later put it in a letter addressed to Benckendorff, but intended for the eyes of the tsar, that 'from looking at the paper, the style of the letter, the way in which it had been written, I recognized from the first moment that the letter was from a foreigner, from a man of high society, from a diplomat'.[27] In all the circumstances, Pushkin's belief that Hekkeren and d'Anthès were, in one way or another, behind the anonymous letter was reasonable enough. Proof positive is quite another matter. Who wrote the anonymous letter – as opposed to who inspired it – gave rise to varying suspicions. Two men in particular were obliged to defend themselves against this accusation: Prince Petr Dolgorukov and Prince Ivan Gagarin (both were overt homosexuals). From 1927 onwards Russian handwriting experts sought for over half a century to establish whose really was the handwriting on this letter, the original of which has survived. The reason for the starting point of 1927 is that it was in this year that Shchegolev, in an attempt to end the long speculation and apparently overlooking the lesson of the Dreyfus case, took the misguided step of seeking the opinion of a none too competent forensic expert. This expert decided that, beyond doubt, the letter was written by Dolgorukov. His view held the field for some time, but in 1966 the findings of another expert pointed towards Gagarin. Finally, in 1987 the Russian journal *Ogonek* organized yet another investigation. According to this, the handwriting was neither that of Dolgorukov nor that of Gagarin, but of a third party, whose identity has not been established to this day.[28]

There the controversy about the handwriting rests. What really matters is Pushkin's own reaction: by the evening of 4 November he had sent d'Anthès a challenge to a duel, in a letter, which was sent through the post, but has not survived. Could he have done otherwise? In theory, yes. Vyazemsky's first reaction, on receiving his copy of his anonymous letter, was that he should throw it in the fire. Had he lived in less introverted, more relaxed society than that of St. Petersburg, Pushkin might perhaps have been able simply to treat his own copy in that way. But Pushkin would not have been Pushkin if he had done anything of the kind. His character was such that this would probably have applied at any moment of his life, but certainly in the circumstances of late 1836 he was bound to launch a counter-attack. Pushkin's challenge for some reason (possibly because d'Anthès was now called Hekkeren) was received and opened not by d'Anthès, who was on duty at the time, but by the Netherlands minister. Hekkeren presented himself at Pushkin's flat on the following day and persuaded him to allow twenty-four hours' grace. Simultaneously Natalya, acting on her own initiative, sent for her brother, who was serving with his regiment at Tsarskoe Selo. Dmitrii in turn enlisted the help of Zhukovsky, who was also in Tsarskoe Selo at the time. According to Vyazemsky, Hekkeren tried to persuade Natalya to write d'Anthès a letter asking him not to fight a duel with her husband. She declined. The next step taken by Hekkeren was to ask Pushkin for a further delay – of a week. Pushkin granted two.

Events then took an extraordinary turn. Hekkeren told Zhukovsky, who was now acting as the principal intermediary between Pushkin and himself, that the real object of d'Anthès' attentions was not Natalya but her sister Ekaterina, whom he wished to marry: an assurance confirmed to Pushkin by Hekkeren personally at a meeting between them, which took place on 14 November at Ekaterina Zagryazhkaya's flat. Pushkin decided not to send the violent letter to Hekkeren that he had drafted; the draft survives, however, and Pushkin used it when he finally did write to Hekkeren two months later. Instead, on 17 November he wrote to his second, Sollogub, that in view of the impending marriage of his sister-in-law, he would regard his challenge as 'not having taken place'. Right up to the last moment of this act of the drama, however, it was touch and go. The date of the duel had been fixed for 21 November; and, even after writing his letter to Sollogub, Pushkin was restrained only by Zhukovsky from putting everything back to square one. Zhukovsky left nothing to chance, therefore. On 22 November he informed the tsar. On the following day Pushkin had an audience (almost certainly a private one, it now seems) with Nicholas I at the Anichkov Palace.

What passed between the two men on 23 November is unknown, but it is generally agreed that Pushkin gave the tsar his word that he would not fight d'Anthès.[29] What assurances, if any, he was given by the tsar on this occasion is also uncertain. What we do know is that, around the turn of the year, Benckendorff, acting on the tsar's instructions, sent Natalya a thousand roubles 'on the occasion of the marriage of your sister, [the tsar] being sure that it will give you pleasure to give her a wedding present'.[30] On the face of it, it looked at first as though Pushkin's counterattack had secured its objective. Unfortunately for Pushkin, this was far from being the end of the battle.

The reasons that had led both to Pushkin's issuing the challenge and to his withdrawing it were kept secret between a small circle of people. From this it inevitably followed that outside this circle of St. Petersburg society every kind of rumour rapidly spread by way of explanation for what had happened, not least for the surprising fact that d'Anthès (now a rich bachelor, thanks to his adoption) was about to marry a not very attractive woman, older than himself and without a penny to her name. By many of Pushkin's enemies it was readily believed that the real reason for d'Anthès' decision was in order to cover up some kind of scandal within the Pushkin family – a personal sacrifice on d'Anthès' part. Thus it was Pushkin who came to be represented as the villain and d'Anthès as the hero of the drama.

In order to understand this remarkable reversal of roles, three things need to be borne in mind. In what amounted to a public relations exercise carried out in the St. Petersburg of 1836, Pushkin was in a weaker position than the Hekkeren-d'Anthès clique. True, he had access to the tsar, but the empress was one of d'Anthès' strong supporters. He had many enemies in the *haut monde* – not just those, such as Uvarov, whom he had personally lampooned. The class of the 'new' aristocracy as a whole had been the butt of his sarcasm in *My Genealogy* (p. 65). Hekkeren, moreover, was close to the Nesselrodes, with whom Pushkin was on bad terms. To explain why Pushkin found himself snatching defeat from the jaws of victory at the turn of the year does not necessitate going all the way with Akhmatova's thesis – that Hekkeren, by manipulating those around him, above all d'Anthès and Natalya, engineered and directed what amounted to a personal plot against Pushkin. Nor, if he had been given the chance to do so, could Lermontov have proved his political accusation (quoted at the beginning of this book) against the imperial court. At the same time it is clear that there were political overtones to the whole affair. Hekkeren was a man of the far right and Pushkin was widely – though wrongly – regarded as a radical. The novelist Ivan Turgenev's account of a dinner party given at the Russian Embassy in Paris in June 1858, over twenty-one years after Pushkin's death, is telling. On this occasion Turgenev found that all the other guests were Russian, with a single exception: d'Anthès, who – unless diplomatic protocol was ignored – must have been the Ambassador's principal guest. (Never a strong-willed man, Turgenev did not walk out.)[31] Russian political prejudice against Pushkin certainly died hard. Or, as the poet Alexander Blok put it in his celebrated remark, made long afterwards, what killed Pushkin was not d'Anthès' bullet, but the absence of air.[32]

On 24 December 1836, Pushkin's sister Olga wrote from Warsaw, immediately after receiving the news that d'Anthès was engaged to be married to Ekaterina Goncharova (the wedding was fixed for 10 January 1837):

> His [d'Anthès'] passion for Natalya has never been a secret for anyone. I knew perfectly well about this when I was in St. Petersburg . . . Believe me, there must be something suspicious here, some kind of misunderstanding, so that perhaps it would be very good if this marriage did not take place.[33]

Olga's presentiment was fully justified. There was an icy encounter between Pushkin and d'Anthès at an evening where they were fellow guests on 28 December, Pushkin looking 'dark as night and scowling like Jupiter in wrath'.[34] And much worse was soon to follow.

Explanations of what happened next were written by several Russians who observed events at close hand, including Pushkin's friends, some of whom wrote more than one account. Their value varies. Some of them were written for special reasons. For example, Zhukovsky's double object after Pushkin's death was to secure the best possible treatment of his family by the imperial treasury and to preserve Pushkin's papers from the Third Department. But there is one account which is by far the most important. It relates, at great length, how Pushkin's receipt of the anonymous letter on 4 November 1836 led, step by step, to his death eight weeks later: Vyazemsky's letter written on 14 February 1837, in the immediate aftermath of Pushkin's death, to the Grand Duke Mikhail, who was in Rome at the time. The second part of this letter (not translated here) includes special pleading; and even the first makes some assumptions in Pushkin's favour that are open to question. But the evident sincerity of these opening pages comes close enough to the ring of truth to make a translation of them a fitting transition between the present chapter and the one that follows:

Letter from Prince P. A. Vyazemsky of 14 February 1837 to the
Grand Duke Mikhail Pavlovich

... The mystery which surrounds the final events in his [Pushkin's] life and thereby gives extensive food to popular ignorance and malice, for every kind of guesswork and false rumours, obliges Pushkin's friends to unveil everything whatsoever that they know on this subject and in this way to show Pushkin's personality in its true light. It is with this aim that I venture to address these lines to Your Highness. Would you please be kind enough to devote to them a few minutes of your leisure. I shall tell only the truth.

Your Imperial Highness is not unaware that the young Hekkeren [d'Anthès] was paying court to Madame Pushkina. His excessive and fairly open flirtation gave rise to rumours in the drawing rooms and caused her husband agonizing anxiety. In spite of this, being certain of his wife's devotion to himself and of the purity of her intentions, he did not make use of his conjugal authority in order to forestall in good time the consequences of this flirtation, which in fact led to an unheard of catastrophe, which unfolded before our eyes.

On 4 November last year my wife came into my study with a sealed note addressed to Pushkin, which she had just received in a double envelope by the city post. She suspected at that very moment that this contained something wounding for Pushkin. Sharing her suspicion and exercising the right of the friendship which bound me to him, I decided to unseal the envelope and found in it the certificate enclosed herewith. My first movement was towards throwing the paper into the fire, and my wife and I gave each other our word to keep all this a secret between us. We quickly learned that this secret was far from being a secret for many people had received similar letters; and even Pushkin had not only himself received the letter, but two other similar ones, which friends of his had handed over to him, not knowing their contents and having been placed in the same situation as we had.

These letters led to explanations between the Pushkins in private and compelled his wife, herself innocent in reality, to admit to thoughtlessness and frivolity, which had led her to behave indulgently towards the importunate flirtation of young Hekkeren; she revealed to her husband the whole conduct of the younger and of the elder Hekkeren in relation to herself; the elder Hekkeren had attempted to persuade her to betray her obligations as a wife and to drag her over the precipice. Pushkin was moved by her trust and her remorse and he was alarmed by the danger which threatened her, but, possessing a fiery and passionate nature, he was unable to address with *sang-froid* the situation in which he and his wife had been placed: tormented by jealousy, wounded in his most tender, intimate feelings, loving his wife, seeing that her honour was wounded by some unknown hand, he sent a challenge to the younger Hekkeren, as the only man responsible, in his eyes, for the double insult inflicted on him at the very heart. It is essential to observe in addition that as soon as these anonymous letters were received, he suspected the elder Hekkeren of having written them and he died with this conviction. So we never discovered on what ground this supposition was based, and right up to the moment of Pushkin's death we considered it inadmissible. Only an unexpected chance later lent it some measure of probability. But since in this respect there do not exist any juridical proofs, nor even any positive grounds, this supposition must be left to a divine court, not to a human one.

Pushkin's challenge did not reach its intended addressee. The elder Hekkeren interfered in the matter. It was he who received the challenge, but put off the final decision for twenty-four hours, in order to give Pushkin the possibility to consider the whole thing with greater calm. Finding Pushkin unyielding at the expiry of this time, he related to him his own critical situation and the difficulties in which the affair had put him, whatever its outcome might be; he talked to him about his fatherly feelings towards the young man, to whom he had devoted his entire life, with the object of securing his wellbeing. He added that he saw the whole edifice of his hopes shaken to their foundations at the very moment when he thought his work had been carried to its conclusion. In order to be prepared for anything that might happen, he asked for a further delay of a week. Accepting the challenge that had been intended for a young man, that is to say his own son, as he called him, he nevertheless asserted that his son had absolutely no suspicion about the challenge, about which people told him only at the last minute.

Pushkin, moved by the distress and the tears of the father, said: 'If that is so, then not just a week – I will give you a deadline of two weeks and I give you my word of honour not to take any action in this matter until the prescribed day and if I meet your son, to behave just as though nothing whatever had happened between us.' Thus everything had to remain like that without change until the decisive day. Beginning from that moment, Hekkeren put in motion every possible military manoeuvre and diplomatic stratagem. He rushed to Zhukovsky and to Mikhail Vel'gorsky, in order to persuade them to act as mediators between himself and Pushkin. Their pacific good offices did not have any success whatsoever. After some days Hekkeren the elder spread a rumour about the forthcoming marriage of the young Hekkeren with Ekaterina Goncharova. He assured Zhukovsky that Pushkin was mistaken, that his son was in love not with Pushkin's wife but with his sister-in-law, that for a long time past he had been begging his father to agree to their marriage, but that finding this marriage unsuitable, he [Hekkeren] had not agreed, but now, seeing that the prolonged opposition on his part had led to a mistake which threatened sad consequences, he had finally given his consent. The father demanded that in no circumstances should people talk to Pushkin about this, so that he would not think that this marriage was only a pretext for avoidance of the duel. Knowing the character of the elder Hekkeren, it is easier to suppose that he said all this in the hope of some kind of indiscretion, in order to deceive the trusting and honourable Pushkin.

However that may be, the secret was kept. The deadline approached, but Pushkin did not yield in any way, and the marriage was decided upon between the father and [Ekaterina's] aunt Madame Zagryazhkaya. It would be too long to lay before Your Imperial Highness all the wily intrigues of the younger Hekkeren at the time of these negotiations. I will mention only one example. The Hekkerens, elder and younger, conceived the bold and base intention of asking Madame Pushkina to write a letter to the young man in which she would beg him not to fight a duel with her husband. It goes without saying that she refused this low proposition with indignation. When Pushkin learnt about the marriage that had already been decided upon, he of course was obliged to consider it as sufficient satisfaction for his honour, since it was clear to the whole world, that this marriage was one of reason, and not of love. The feelings, or the so-called 'feelings' of young Hekkeren, received publicity of such a kind that it made this marriage rather ambiguous. In consequence of this Pushkin withdrew his challenge, but he made it clear in the most positive way that he would not tolerate between his family and that of his sister-in-law not only the relationships of family, but even ordinary acquaintance, and that they would never be in his house nor he in theirs. To anyone who approached him with congratulations on the occasion of this marriage, he replied with the remark for all to hear: '*Tu l'as voulu, Georges Dandin.*'

To tell the truth, it must be said that we all of us who were so close to the development of this affair, never supposed that the younger Hekkeren decided on this desperate step, except in order to avoid the duel. He was probably himself misled by the dark intrigues of his own father. He offered himself to him as a sacrifice. At least that was how I understood him myself. However, a section of society wished to look upon this marriage as a triumph of high self-abnegation undertaken in order to save the honour of Madame Pushkina. But of course that was only the fruit of idle fantasy. Nothing in the past of the young man, nor in his conduct in relation to Madame Pushkina, admits the thought of anything remotely of this kind. The consequences proved this well, as

Your Highness will see later in this letter. In any case this wounding and unfounded supposition came to Pushkin's notice and produced a fresh anxiety in his mind. He saw that this marriage was not saving him finally from the false situation in which he found himself. The young Hekkeren continued, in the eyes of society, to stand between him and his wife and threw a shadow over both of them which was intolerable for Pushkin's sensitivity. It was a fantasy not existing in reality, since Pushkin was sure of his wife, but nevertheless this fantasy pursued him. Could a passionate and impressionable poet really judge his own situation and look upon it in the same way as a wise or impartial observer? It is easy for indifferent people to speak in this way, but it is necessary to sympathise with his sufferings, with all the bitterness which had consumed poor Pushkin, before allowing oneself to blame him.

Ekaterina Goncharova's agreement to marry and her entire conduct in this matter are incomprehensible unless this puzzle is explained simply by her wish at all costs to get out of the category of old maids. Pushkin thought the whole time that some chance would prevent the marriage from the very beginning. Nevertheless the marriage took place. This new situation, these new relationships, made little change in the essence of the matter. The young Hekkeren continued, in the presence of his own wife, to emphasise his passion for Madame Pushkina. Gossip in the city was renewed and the wounding attention of society was turned with redoubled strength on the actors in the drama that was taking place before their eyes.

Pushkin's situation became even more tormenting. He became preoccupied, agitated, it was difficult to look at him. But his relationship with his wife did not suffer from this. He became even more attentive, even more tender towards her. His feelings, about the sincerity of which it was impossible to have any doubt, probably blinded his wife to the true situation of affairs and to their consequences. She ought to have withdrawn from society and to have asked this of her husband. She did not have the character for this and once again she began to find herself in the same relationship to the young Hekkeren as before his marriage. In this there was nothing criminal, but there was much inconsistency and imprudence. When Pushkin's friends, wishing to calm him, said to him that it was not worth tormenting himself, if he was certain of the innocence of his wife and this certainty was shared by all his friends and by all decent people in society, then he replied to them that, for him, his own certainty and that of his friends and of a certain circle of people, was not enough, that he belonged to the whole country and that he wished his name to be unsullied everywhere where he was known. A few hours before his duel he said to d'Archiac, Hekkeren's second, in explanation

of the reasons that had compelled him to fight: 'There are cuckolds of
two kinds: one carries real horns; they know perfectly well how to
behave; the situation of the others who have become cuckolds through
the kindness of the public, is more difficult. I belong to the latter
category.'[35]

CHAPTER FOURTEEN

Duel and Death, 1837

Come, come; no time for lamentation now,
Nor much more cause. Samson hath quit himself
Like Samson, and heroicly hath finished
A life heroic, on his enemies
Fully revenged – hath left them years of mourning . . .

—Milton, *Samson Agonistes*

Alexander Blok's remark, that what killed Pushkin was not a bullet, but the absence of air, is one of the rare explanations for Pushkin's death, following the duel that he fought on 27 January 1837, which sums up the surrounding circumstances in one short sentence. Each of the three principal lines of approach traditionally adopted to the complex problems involved – Pushkin, the victim of conspiracy; Pushkin overwhelmed by fate; and Pushkin determined to meet death, weapon in hand[1] – relates to a mass of evidence which is itself open to more than one interpretation. Moreover, to some extent all three lines of approach overlap.

There are two possible clues to Pushkin's state of mind at the end of his life, both of which are arresting. Of these clues, the first is conjectural: what may have been the very last portrait of Pushkin, attributed to an amateur artist, Ivan Linev.[2] Both the portrait and its attribution are a matter of controversy, but if this was indeed how Pushkin's face looked in January 1837, almost any outcome to the dilemma in which he then found himself would have been conceivable. By contrast, the second clue, although it too involves conjecture, is partly factual. During the last days of his life Pushkin was working on an article intended for the fifth issue of the *Sovremennik* (in which it duly appeared, after his death) on 'Milton and Chateaubriand's translation of *Paradise Lost*'. We also know that seven months earlier he had bought a copy of Milton's complete works in English from Dickson's bookshop in St. Petersburg.[3] Describing in this article how Milton had dictated *Paradise Lost* in poverty, persecution and blindness, Pushkin underlined these words that he used about Milton: 'in evil days, the victim of evil tongues.'[4] During the months that elapsed between his buying Milton's works and drafting this article, may Pushkin's eye perhaps have fallen on the penultimate speech in *Samson Agonistes?* His command of English was probably not yet such as to enable him to understand all the subtleties of Milton's verse, but the five opening lines of that speech, which form the epigraph to this chapter, are plain enough.

Contrary to Pushkin's hopes, the wedding of his sister-in-law Ekaterina Goncharova and Georges d'Anthès was celebrated as planned on 10 January 1837. There were two religious services: one Roman Catholic and one Orthodox. Natalya Pushkina attended the latter ceremony, but she did not stay on afterwards for the wedding supper. Thereafter Pushkin adhered vigorously to his ban on all forms of contact between the two families. Thus, when the d'Anthès began the round of calls customary for a newly-married couple in St. Petersburg, they were denied admission to the Pushkins' flat on the Moika; and Pushkin's oral reply to a letter from d'Anthès, written on the insistence of his adoptive father, seeking to persuade him to forget the past and to make peace, was a flat negative. Pushkin's insistence on a kind of Montague–Capulet relationship between his family and that of d'Anthès might have been just sustainable if he had been in a position to persuade at least his friends not to admit Georges and Ekaterina d'Anthès to their houses either. He was not. One of the young couple's first calls, made three days after their wedding, was on the Vyazemskys. At the height of the winter social season, moreover, the d'Anthès and the Pushkins could not avoid meeting at other people's parties: meetings that could have been averted only if what Vyazemsky – perhaps wise after the event – believed should have been done, namely if Natalya had withdrawn from society altogether, at any rate for a time.

The climax was reached at a ball given by Countess Vorontsova-Dashkova, the wife of the palace chief of ceremonies, on the evening of 23 January. Here, according to a number of witnesses (who did not, however, include Pushkin himself), d'Anthès made a pun in poor taste about his wife and Pushkin's which Natalya afterwards related to her husband, for whom this appears to have been the last straw. At any rate on the following day he pawned Alexandra Goncharova's table silver for 2200 roubles; and on 26 January he ordered two pistols.

It was not until 1899 that it became known that, at some point in the second half of January 1837 – these meetings cannot be exactly dated – the tsar again took a hand in the proceedings. According to an account then published, Nicholas I himself told Pushkin's fellow-pupil at the lycée, Modest Korff:

> Towards the end of his [Pushkin's] life, since I often met his wife, of whom I was sincerely fond and of whom I am fond now as a very good woman, I somehow or other talked to her about the gossip to which her beauty was subjecting her in society; I advised her to be as careful as she possibly could and to preserve and guard her reputation, as much for herself as for the happiness of her husband in the light of his well-known jealousy. She obviously related this to her husband, because when he saw me somewhere or other, he began to thank me for the good advice that I had given his wife. 'Surely you did not expect anything different from me?' – I asked him. – 'Not only, Sir, could I indeed expect it, but, I confess candidly, I suspected you personally of paying court to my wife,' – His final duel was three days after this.[5]

Neither intervention by Nicholas I was of much help. Indeed, they may have filled Pushkin's poisoned chalice to overflowing. That the tsar found Natalya attractive, as did many other men, is undoubted. But there is no evidence that she was his mistress during Pushkin's lifetime, although this was an insinuation clearly intended by the writer of the anonymous letters in November 1836, which referred to Naryshkin, whose wife had indeed been the mistress of Alexander I. (The question of Natalya's relationship with Nicholas I later on, after her return to St. Petersburg, is another matter.) Nevertheless, during the immediate run-up to the duel, the attitude taken towards Pushkin by the tsar and his chief of police had something in common with the sentiment expressed in Arthur Clough's couplet: 'Thou shalt not kill; but need'st not strive/Officiously to keep alive.'[6]

In forming a judgement today on this aspect account should be taken of an important question relating to Pushkin's letter to Benckendorff – evidently intended for the eyes of the tsar – which bears the date 21 November 1836. In this letter (briefly referred to in Chapter 13) Pushkin set out his case against Hekkeren and d'Anthès.[7]

Russian Pushkinists now believe that this letter, like Pushkin's draft letter to Hekkeren of approximately the same date, was never despatched; and that, on the contrary, one of Pushkin's last actions before leaving home on the afternoon of his duel was probably to take care to put the letter to Benckendorff in a separate envelope, constituting – as it certainly did – an essential document in the case for his own defence, whatever the outcome of the duel might be. Doubtless the tsar was aware – if from nobody else, through Zhukovsky – at least of the gist of this letter.[8] But if in fact it was not received by Benckendorff until after the duel, when it was found among Pushkin's papers, nor read by Nicholas I, this might go some way, although perhaps not very far, towards explaining the apparently nonchalant attitude that they adopted during the last days of Pushkin's life. We do not know.

On 25 January, although the letter bears the date of the 26th beneath Pushkin's signature, Pushkin wrote a letter in French to the Netherlands minister, which this time was indeed despatched:

Monsieur le Baron!

Allow me to make a résumé of what has just happened. The conduct of your son had been known to me for a long time past and I could not be indifferent towards it. I confined myself to the role of observer, ready to intervene when I judged it appropriate. An incident, which at any other moment would have been extremely disagreeable to me, very fortunately rescued me from the affair: I received the anonymous letters. I saw that the moment had come and I took advantage of it. You know the rest: I made your son play a role so pitiable that my wife, astonished by so much cowardice and banality, could not prevent herself from laughing, and the feeling which perhaps she had felt for this great and sublime passion was extinguished in the calmest contempt and the most well-deserved disgust.

I am obliged to admit, Monsieur le Baron, that your role has not been altogether proper. You, the representative of a crowned head, have acted paternally as the pimp of your son. It appears that all his behaviour (incidentally, pretty inept), has been directed by you. It is you who probably dictated these poor jokes which he has just poured out and the bits of nonsense which he has taken a part in writing. Like an obscene old woman, you would lie in wait for my wife in every corner, in order to talk to her about the love of your bastard, or one who is so called; and when he was confined to his quarters by pox, he said that he was dying for love for her; you murmured to her: 'Give me back my son.'

You realize full well, Monsieur le Baron, that after all this, I cannot endure my family having the slightest relationship with yours. It was on that condition that I had given my consent not to allow this dirty affair to have any consequence, and not to dishonour you in the eyes of our court and of that of the Netherlands, as I could have done and as I intended to do. I do not care for my wife to listen to your paternal exhortations any more. I cannot allow that your son, after his abject behaviour should dare to address a word to my wife, nor – still less – that he should recite regimental puns and play the part of devotion and unhappy passion, whereas he is nothing but a coward and a scoundrel. I am therefore obliged to address myself to you, in order to ask you to put an end to all this scheming, if you wish to avoid a further scandal, before which I shall certainly not shrink.

I have the honour to be, Monsieur le Baron,
    your very humble and very obedient servant,
      Alexander Pushkin.
    26 January 1837.[9]

Pushkin was at pains to make an immaculately written copy of this letter, which he gave to his second on his way to the duel. Written in such terms, it could have only one result: a challenge issued by d'Anthès to Pushkin. For this very reason, Pushkin was careful to let a minimum of those close to him know of the impending duel. Unlike in November 1836, in January 1837 neither Natalya nor Zhukovsky had the slightest inkling. Even Alexander Turgenev, whose diary has many entries about his conversations with Pushkin during the last weeks of his life, knew nothing. On the contrary, in a letter written on 28 January he described how two days earlier he had found Pushkin 'cheerful, full of life, without the slightest signs of anxiety: we talked for a long time on many subjects and he joked and laughed'. This is one of several contemporary accounts, all of which indicate that a weight had been lifted from Pushkin's mind, once he had written his insulting letter to Hekkeren.

So little did the Vyazemskys suspect what was impending that on the evening of 25 January they invited both the Pushkins and the d'Anthès to their house. It was on this occasion that Pushkin let Princess Vyazemskaya into his secret, which she must subsequently have shared with her husband. Pushkin's sister-in-law, Alexandra, must also have known, either directly or at least indirectly, on the day of the duel. But it was to Baroness Vrevskaya (Zizi) that he fully unburdened himself at several meetings, one of which seems to have lasted almost a whole day. Zizi had come to St. Petersburg from the country in order to visit her sister, but also to discuss with Pushkin the problem of the sale of the Mikhailovskoe estate. According to her subsequent account, Pushkin's mind was already closed to any argument about the duel. When she reminded him about the fate of his children, he replied that the tsar would take them under his protection. This was a significant answer, if Pushkin really believed that this was so and if his belief was based on something said to him by Nicholas I at their last meeting.

Even at the time, however, there were those, including Vyazemsky, who believed that Pushkin's talks with Zizi Vrevskaya were a factor of some importance in determining the final outcome; and the publication, in 1962, of a letter written on 16 February 1837 by Zizi's mother, Praskov'ya Osipova, to Alexander Turgenev has suggested the possibility that during their talks Pushkin revealed to Zizi not only the fact that he had decided to fight d'Anthès, but also some piece of vital information which has remained a secret ever since ('I am almost glad', Praskov'ya wrote, 'that you [Turgenev] have not heard what he [Pushkin] said to my daughter Evpraksiya before the fatal day.') To Turgenev's reply, imploring her to let him know what it was that she had remained silent about in her letter, Praskov'ya Osipova did not respond. Was it perhaps something about Natalya which Pushkin told nobody else, as an oblique reference to Natalya by Praskov'ya suggests? On balance, probably not. But this brief correspondence raises tantalizing questions.[10]

It was at least in part in order to avoid compromising any of his Russian friends that Pushkin's first choice as a second for the duel was a foreign diplomat. On this occasion, as in November, d'Anthès' second was an attaché at the French Embassy, Viscount Auguste d'Archiac, who was also a relation of d'Anthès. The man whom Pushkin first asked to act as his second was an attaché at the British Embassy, Arthur Magenis.[11] Magenis did not give Pushkin his answer at once, because he wanted first to discuss the matter with d'Archiac. Their talk together having made it crystal clear that any reconciliation between Pushkin and d'Anthès was out of the question, in the early hours of 27 January he wrote a friendly letter to Pushkin explaining that, for this reason, he felt unable to act as his second.

Pushkin now faced a dilemma. He had to have a second. His first attempt to resolve it on the morning of 27 January was to write d'Archiac a curt letter, saying that he was content for d'Anthès to choose a second for him and that he would accept anyone, even d'Anthès' lackey (*chasseur*). Pushkin must have known that this would not do. Confronted at once with a sharp reply from d'Archiac, he finally resorted to a schoolfriend, Lieutenant-Colonel Konstantin Danzas, who agreed to act for him. After discussion with d'Archiac, at about two o'clock in the afternoon Danzas was able to bring Pushkin the conditions of the duel, which the two seconds had drawn up together in French.[12]

1. The two adversaries will be placed at a distance of twenty paces, each of them five paces from the two barriers [these were not literally barriers, but formed a kind of no man's land demarcated in advance by the two seconds on the ground] which will be separated by ten paces.
2. Each armed with a pistol, when the signal is given, they will be able to use their weapons, advancing one towards the other, without in any event over-stepping the barrier, however.
3. It remains agreed, moreover, that once a shot has been fired, neither of the two adversaries will be allowed to move his position, in order that the one of the two that has already fired first shall in all eventualities meet the fire of his opponent at the same distance.
4. The two opponents having fired, if there is no result, the matter will be begun again as on the first occasion, the opponents being withdrawn to the same distance of twenty paces, and preserving the same barriers and the same conditions.
5. The witnesses will be intermediaries responsible for offering any kind of explanation between the opponents on the duelling ground.
6. The witnesses of this duel, undersigned, having been given full powers, guarantee on their honour the strict execution of the above mentioned conditions, each one on behalf of his own party.

27 January 1837, 2.30 in the afternoon.
Signed: Viscount d'Archiac, Attaché at the French Embassy
Konstantin Danzas, Lieutenant-Colonel of Engineers

This was an age in which duels were common throughout Europe. Even in England, where duelling was by the late 1830s on the decline, politicians of the standing of Pitt, Fox, Canning and Wellington had all been 'out'; and Peel was twice a challenger. Early in the century the American vice-president, Alexander Hamilton, was killed in a duel. And it so happened that the year 1836 saw the publication in Paris of a work entitled *Essai sur le duel*, written by Count de

Chatauvillard, to whose wide acceptance the signatures of no less than eighty senior members of the French army and French society bore witness.[13]

Around the middle of the afternoon of 27 January, Pushkin wrote the last letter of his life, addressed to a lady who had written a Russian history for children, Alexandra Ishimova. This letter began with the sentence: 'I am extremely sorry that it will be impossible for me to accept your invitation today.' Pushkin went on to enclose a book by an English author, in which he had marked in pencil some passages which he greatly hoped Ishimova would translate.[14] He left his home about four o'clock. Natalya was out, but Alexandra was there. The weather had worsened during the day; a cold wind had got up and there were fourteen or fifteen degrees of frost (accounts vary). Soon afterwards he and Danzas met in a pâtisserie, from which they set out on a sleigh. By one of the many coincidences for which Pushkin's life was remarkable, they passed Natalya's carriage going in the opposite direction. They saw her, but being short-sighted, she did not recognize them.

The duellists arrived at about half-past four at the place chosen by their seconds, a secluded spot hidden by thick bushes about a hundred and fifty metres from the road on the northern outskirts of St. Petersburg. It took the seconds about half an hour to level out the snow. Wrapped in his bearskin overcoat, Pushkin was calm, but he remarked in French, 'Try to do all this more quickly.' After Danzas had given the signal to begin – with his hat – Pushkin and d'Anthès both walked towards the 'barrier'. What happened next was in some respects foreshadowed by Pushkin's description of the duel between Onegin and Lensky in his *Evgenii Onegin*, which was also fought in the snow. Pushkin's antagonist, like Lensky's, fired first; and like Onegin d'Anthès fired just before reaching the barrier – at a distance of about eleven paces.

Why did Pushkin, an experienced shot, but out of practice, take the risk of waiting until he reached the barrier before taking aim? Faced by a younger and presumably fitter antagonist, this was a gamble. Was he simply indifferent? Is a Russian Pushkinist right in saying that he had 'tried all genres, they had all revealed their finiteness, he was bigger than any genre, and at the very end even the genre of life seemed to be insufficient. Then he fell silent and – as he did in his verse and in his prose – he compelled silence to speak'?[15]

Nobody can say. But the most logical explanation – albeit in a matter where emotion was stronger than logic – is that Pushkin calculated that his best hope was to fire from the shortest possible distance allowed by the rules: that is to say, from the barrier. True, this carried the risk that d'Anthès would fire the first shot, but had d'Anthès missed or only wounded him slightly, Pushkin would probably have had him at his mercy.

In the event, by firing first, it was d'Anthès who brought Pushkin to the ground; his bullet penetrated Pushkin's right side and lodged in his intestine. (He believed at the time that his thigh had been broken.) Pushkin's pistol fell from his hand into the snow, but he declared that he was still strong enough to fire his own shot. Leaning on his left arm, he did this from the ground with a fresh pistol given him by Danzas (correctly, according to the rules). D'Anthès, who was now standing at the barrier, protecting his chest with his right hand (again, according to the rules), was wounded by Pushkin's shot, for which he took careful aim. 'Bravo!' shouted Pushkin, as d'Anthès in his turn fell. He threw his pistol to one side. He believed that d'Anthès' wound was serious. In fact it was relatively minor.

It was about six o'clock when Pushkin and Danzas returned to Pushkin's flat on the Moika, where Pushkin was carried in by his servants. Both men sought to reassure Natalya, who had returned home in the interval, about Pushkin's wound, although by that time Pushkin had begun to realize the truth. He ordered clean clothes, undressed and lay down on the divan in his study. The court physician, Arendt, was sent for. From then until the moment of Pushkin's death, nearly forty-eight hours afterwards, Pushkin's small study, lined with his books, became a kind of miniature theatre. There were many exits and entrances; a series of doctors came and went; some of Pushkin's closest friends – notably both the Vyazemskys, Ekaterina Karamzina, Zhukovsky, Turgenev and Danzas – were present almost all the time; others came to pay their respects, including the French ambassador. As in all scenes of high drama, the spectators tried afterwards to recapture every word that had been spoken, especially those of Pushkin himself. Even after going to a real play, different members of the audience remember differently what they have seen and heard in the theatre. Not surprisingly, therefore, some recollections of Pushkin's last hours cannot be wholly relied upon. (For purposes of historical comparison, Nelson's famous dying words are familiar to everyone who knows any British history, but these do not include what he is known to have said most often, which was 'water, water!' and 'fan, fan!'.) This said, all accounts are agreed that Pushkin's first words to Natalya were: 'Do not worry. You are not guilty in this matter.' Later, he advised her to go and live in the country for two or three years before remarrying.

Before Arendt could arrive, Danzas brought two other doctors, one of whom Pushkin asked to tell him frankly whether his wound was mortal. The doctor replied that this was his opinion, but this needed the confirmation of others. Arriving at nine o'clock, Arendt did confirm it. Pushkin thanked him, and after a silence, he said in French: 'I must put my house in order.' Whether it was this thought that led him to dictate to Danzas, as best he could, a list of all his debts, which he then signed, is unclear. It also appears to have been his own doctor, Ivan Spassky, whom he asked to summon a priest from the local church, to give him the last rites (confession and holy communion).

About midnight Arendt returned, having come direct from the palace. At this point fact and legend become difficult to disentangle, even though the legend is supported by reputable witnesses. In brief, Arendt is said to have brought with him a pencilled note from Nicholas I, forgiving Pushkin, but advising him to 'die as a Christian' and also undertaking to look after Natalya and the children. On the following day, when Zhukovsky, then about to go to the palace, asked Pushkin what he would like him to say to the tsar, Pushkin's reply is said to have been: 'Tell him that I am sorry to die; I would have been all his.' There is the further tradition, for which Zhukovsky seems to have been responsible, that on receiving the tsar's letter, Pushkin raised his arms heavenwards, as a sign of gratitude. It is hard to say how much of this was elaborated after the event, albeit with the best intentions. Valedictory words strikingly similar to 'I would have been all his' were written by Voltaire in a poem addressed to his former patron, Frederick of Prussia in 1775: '. . ."Mon sort est trop beau:/J'aurai vécu pour lui; je lui mourirai fidèle."'[16] The possibility cannot therefore be excluded that, like Voltaire, Pushkin did not lose his gift of irony even on his deathbed.

Pushkin's naturally strong constitution made him put up a stiff fight for life. Although he suffered great pain, he remained conscious for a large part of these two days. So great was the stream of visitors of all kinds, that Danzas was obliged to ask for police reinforcements outside the house. Pushkin said goodbye to his closest friends one by one; and he even remarked what a pity it was that Ivan Pushchin could not be with him. As Ekaterina Karamzina was leaving, she made the sign of the cross; Pushkin held out his hand and asked her to bless him again; she did so; and he kissed her hand. Pushkin blessed each one of his children in turn. Almost at the last minute on the afternoon of the 29th he asked Natalya to feed him. This she did, giving him spoonfuls of cloudberry syrup. Less than one hour later he said to one of the doctors: 'It is hard to breathe. Something is weighing me down.' He died at a quarter to three.

POSTSCRIPT

If the sequence of events before 29 January 1837 strikes the reader as bizarre, what happened between that day and Pushkin's burial, at the Svyatogorsk Monastery on 6 February, is scarcely less strange. In assessing the reactions to Pushkin's death both of the Russian government and of Russian public opinion – in so far as public opinion can be said to have existed in the Russia of 1837 – it is important to bear in mind that at that time few people in St. Petersburg knew even the majority of the facts about the circumstances leading to Pushkin's death which have since come to light; and most people knew hardly any at all. The text of Vyazemsky's letter to the Grand Duke Mikhail (pp. 208–12) was not published until the beginning of this century, nor was the tsar's.

'Everything is quiet here,' Nicholas wrote to Paskevich on 4 February, 'and only Pushkin's tragic death occupies the public and serves to feed a variety of foolish rumours.'[17] A rather muddled letter written to the Grand Duke Mikhail on the previous day, however, had attempted to strike some sort of balance. 'Although for some time past,' Nicholas wrote, 'it was to be expected that their [Pushkin's and d'Anthès'] awkward situation would end in a duel ... the hope had to be ...' that d'Anthès' marriage and Pushkin's withdrawal of his challenge [in November 1836] were the end of the matter. On the one hand, Pushkin had behaved 'as any man would have done in his place'; d'Anthès' behaviour and especially that of his 'swinish father' could scarcely be justified. On the other, 'the final reason for the duel, which no one comprehends and including Pushkin's very impudent letter to Hekkeren, put d'Anthès in the right in what he did.'[17]

Persuaded by Zhukovsky, the tsar made generous financial provisions, although arguably it would have been impolitic to do much less:

> 1. Pay debts. 2. Clear the mortgaged estate of his father from debt. 3. A pension for his widow and daughters until they marry. 4. The sons to become pages and to receive 1500 roubles for the education of each of them until they enter service. 5. Publish Pushkin's works at public expense for the benefit of his widow and children. 6. Once only, a payment of 10,000 roubles.[18]

In public the government reacted in the opposite direction. For this contrast between private calm and official paranoia, the most likely explanation is that offered by Prince Hohenlohe-Kirchberg, since 1833 Minister in St. Petersburg of the Kingdom of Württemberg. Unlike most of his colleagues in the diplomatic corps, this head of mission sent his government not one despatch about Pushkin's death, but a whole series. In one of them, dated 6 February 1837, he wrote:

> Immediately after the duel between Pushkin and the young Baron Hekkeren [d'Anthès] the majority pronounced in favour of the latter, but not as much as twenty-four hours were needed for the Russian party to change the feeling in people's minds in Pushkin's favour. As regards the two Barons Hekkeren, they certainly did everything for their part to attract general dissatisfaction, and many persons previously according respect to the minister have been obliged at the present moment to regret it.[19]

Doubtless the fact that Hohenlohe was married to a Russian explains why his ear was close enough to the ground to make him aware of this swing of opinion in St. Petersburg.

While Pushkin lay on his deathbed, St. Petersburg had been prepared for the worst by a series of short bulletins signed by Zhukovsky, the last of which consisted of six (Russian) words: 'The patient is in an extremely dangerous condition.'[20] The formal invitation to the requiem mass, to be held at eleven o'clock on the morning of 1 February, was signed by his widow, who referred to her late husband simply as *Kammerjunker* and made no reference whatever either to the reason for his fame or to the cause of his death.

The duel was mentioned in neither of two glowing obituaries that appeared in the press on 30 January. Nevertheless, on Uvarov's instructions, the author of one of the obituaries was reprimanded by the committee of censors. He was even asked ironically: 'Was Pushkin a commander, a minister, a statesman?' Instructions were issued that from then on the tone of all obituaries of Pushkin should be kept as flat as possible. Moreover, the university was forbidden to interrupt its studies to allow professors or students to attend the requiem service.[21]

Even the gentle Zhukovsky, at the conclusion of his report to Benckendorff on his examination of Pushkin's papers, which he completed on 25 February, ridiculed the precautions taken by the police over the arrangements for Pushkin's requiem service and thereafter, as giving the impression that 'the government was admitting before the whole of society that it was afraid of a conspiracy'. At the last moment, at night, the authorities had the requiem mass switched from St. Isaac's Cathedral, to which Pushkin's widow had specifically referred in her invitation, to another church, situated near the Pushkins' flat in the square known as *Konyushennaya* (Stables). Even so, this church was packed, both by Russians and by the diplomatic corps, including the French ambassador, with a few exceptions – Hekkeren was not invited; the Prussian ambassador declined on the grounds of Pushkin's liberalism; and Durham was unwell. As Alexander Nikitenko put it in his diary, 'This was a really national funeral.'

On 2 February, Benckendorff, who had just seen the tsar, had instructions sent to the governor of Pskov province ordering him to forbid anything being done for Pushkin's burial beyond that which would be done in the case of any member of the nobility. It was the tsar who gave Alexander Turgenev the task of escorting Pushkin's coffin to Mikhailovskoe. From Turgenev's diary, we know that it was about one o'clock in the morning of 4 February that, accompanied by a police captain, he set out on his journey from the *Konyushennaya* church. They reached Pskov at nine o'clock in the evening of the same day, resuming their journey on the following morning. Turgenev spent the next night at Trigorskoe; at his request, Praskov'ya Osipova sent serfs to dig the grave at the Svyatogorsk Monastery. Here Pushkin's body was laid to rest early on the morning of 6 February. Turgenev threw a handful of earth into the grave. The few mourners included Praskov'ya Osipova and Pushkin's faithful servant Nikita Kozlov. Afterwards, against the wishes of his police escort, Turgenev visited Mikhailovskoe, which he found deserted, except for the guardian and his wife, both in tears. By the evening of 8 February, after another night's travel, he was back in St. Petersburg.

In Turgenev's absence a twenty-two-year-old cornet in a hussar regiment, Mikhail Lermontov, had added to his poem *Death of a Poet* (written on the day that Pushkin died) sixteen lines of postscript accusing the imperial court of complicity in Pushkin's death. Turgenev admired Lermontov's verses; and curiously, Bencken-dorff's reaction was mild at first. Not so the tsar, who first ordered that Lermontov should be medically examined (was he insane?) and then – on 25 February – had him transferred to a dragoon regiment serving in the Caucasus.[22]

By 19 March the government had recovered its balance. On that day the Ministry of War issued its report on the findings of the court of inquiry, which had been set up after the duel. This report (which formed the enclosure in Durham's despatch, mentioned in an earlier chapter), announced that Hekkeren [d'Anthès] had been reduced to the ranks; the tsar had approved this sentence, but he had added that 'not being a Russian subject, he will be conducted to the frontier after having handed in his officer's commission'. (Durham reported that d'Anthès' journey to the frontier was made in an open *telega*.) Pushkin was also condemned, but – being, so to speak, *in absentia* – he was not sentenced.

The Netherlands minister did all he could to persuade the Russian foreign minister that he had acted correctly throughout; and when he left St. Petersburg – he had no option – he gave out that he was only going on leave. Refused the audience normally given to any head of mission going on leave, he none the less accepted a jewelled tobacco box which the tsar sent him – a present usually given by the sovereign to heads of mission who were leaving St. Petersburg for good. After he had left, Hekkeren arranged for the Netherlands chargé d'affaires to distribute p.p.c. cards (*pour prendre congé*) to his colleagues on his behalf. 'Nobody', wrote Hohenlohe, 'regretted his departure.'[23]

With the signal exception of Pushkin himself, none of those involved in the duel, either directly or indirectly, suffered any lasting consequences. Natalya did indeed withdraw to the country for a time.

After her return to St. Petersburg she made a conventional and apparently happy marriage to an officer who enjoyed the tsar's patronage;[24] and she bore him three daughters, to the first of whom Nicholas I was godfather. After spending a decent period *en disponibilité*, Hekkeren went on to serve his country for over thirty years as ambassador in Vienna. D'Anthès changed political sides in France, abandoning the legitimist cause and espousing that of Louis Napoleon instead. His later career provided a good example of the slogan *enrichissez-vous*. His wife, Ekaterina, became a Roman Catholic and bore him three children; she died young.

There is a story – although the evidence for it has been contested – that at some time in the 1850s a reunion took place in Slovakia, at the country house of Baroness Friesenhoff, as Alexandra Goncharova had now become. In the park of this house, Natalya, on a visit there from Russia, Alexandra and d'Anthès, who had arrived from Vienna (where he was presumably visiting Hekkeren) went for a long walk. They returned reconciled.[25] Whether or not anything like this strange encounter ever occurred is immaterial. Ivan Turgenev's account of the dinner party given by the Russian ambassador in Paris, seen against the background of the 'dark seven years' of the end of Nicholas I's reign, suggests that Pushkin's memory is unlikely to have been uppermost in the thoughts of any member of this trio – Natalya, Alexandra and d'Anthès – nor, for that matter, in that of Hekkeren (or Ekaterina, when she was alive). Nevertheless, all five of them would, in the event, later 'go to their rest in the indexes of editions of Pushkin's works'.[26] Pushkin's posthumous victory still lay some way over the horizon, however. It took many years after his death for the full dimensions of this victory to become clear, even in Russia.

Posthumous Victory

To the tsar's [Peter the Great's] command to the people to become educated, they replied, after one hundred years, with the vast phenomenon of Pushkin.

—Alexander Herzen

Writing a century later, Akhmatova qualified her description of Pushkin's 'resplendent' victory as gradual and 'not without a creaky start'. This was a major understatement. In fact it took almost fifty years to bring about. But once almost everyone in Russia had accepted the fact that Pushkin had indeed won, what he achieved was not just victory, but apotheosis (the word actually used to describe two of the ceremonial events during the three days of the Pushkin celebrations held in Moscow in June 1880). The reasons both for this long time-lag and for the subsequent swing from one extreme to the other are to be found in a peculiarly Russian combination of politics and literary politics. In nineteenth-century Russia the line of demarcation between these two fields was a narrow one, frequently blurred. Just as Pushkin's life in the early years of that century can be fully understood only within its historical context, so too it is only within these parameters that the way in which most Russians treated their greatest poet until the watershed of 1880 – and indeed thereafter – becomes comprehensible.

To take the purely political aspect first – it was not only a question of the ludicrous lengths to which the imperial bureaucracy went in 1837 to play down Pushkin's death. Financially, the tsar did indeed show generosity towards Pushkin's memory, but when Zhukovsky – recalling the precedent of the death of the historian Karamzin eleven years earlier – urged Nicholas to issue a statement proclaiming Pushkin's services to his country or to have a national monument erected that could be worthy both of him and of the tsar, he met with a flat refusal. In Nicholas' eyes, Pushkin had only with difficulty been persuaded to die a Christian death, whereas Karamzin had died like an angel.[1]

So long as Nicholas I ruled Russia, that was that. The next twenty years, so far from being recognized as the 'Age of Pushkin', were, for those who had to live through them, the age of Nicholas I: in Herzen's words, a period of mediocre and repulsive ruthlessness.[2] The accuracy of this description is in no way diminished by the first flowering of the Russian intelligentsia that marked the ten years immediately following Pushkin's death.[3] These first products of Russian universities began to fight out the Great Debate about the role of literature in the Russian body politic and the battle for what were seen as the two models for Russia – the one western and the other slavophile. However passionate their differences of view, what united intellectuals was their reaction against the increasingly dead hand of Nicholas' thirty-year rule.

It was indeed easier to enumerate what this conscientious, industrious, narrow-minded autocrat was against than what he was for. Anti-liberal, anti-Semitic, anti-Catholic, anti-Polish (the Uniate Church was forcibly dissolved in 1839), he bequeathed to his son a country which – demographic growth apart – was almost exactly as he had himself inherited it from his brother in 1825.

Nor was it an accident that Annenkov confined his memoir *The Remarkable Decade* to the years 1837–47. In Austria, Hungary, France, Prussia and Romania 1848 was the year of revolution. Nicholas' immediate response was personally to draft a memorandum which he issued in March 1848, declaring Russia's determination to resist the forces of revolution. In the following year the 'gendarme of Europe' acceded to the Austrian Emperor's request for Russian military intervention in Hungary, where the Hungarian army was in revolt against Vienna.[4] In Russia itself the Year of Revolutions evoked few echoes from the public. Yet it was followed by the *mrachnoe semiletie* (the 'dark seven years'). A special committee, set up in 1848 in order to enforce the strictest possible censorship, was so effective the Nikitenko remarked in his diary that it was becoming impossible to write anything in the press at all.[5] Even Uvarov had to resign. His successor as Minister of Education, Prince Platon Shirinsky-Shikhmatov, prided himself on being a blind instrument of the will of the sovereign. During his tenure of office the number of Russian university students actually declined to a total of 3600 in 1854, 1000 fewer than in 1848.[6] And on the night of 21/22 April 1849 the St. Petersburg police carried out a famous mass raid, arresting forty intellectuals – members of the Petrashevsty, a reformist discussion group. Fifteen of them were sentenced to death. Taken to their place of execution, they were informed at the very last moment that their sentences had been commuted to forced labour in Siberia. One of the victims of this cruel farce was Dostoevsky; his *Notes from the House of the Dead* was the product of his six Siberian years.

In the end Nicholas proved to be more effective as the gendarme of Russia, where opposition to the autocratic regime was still rudimentary, than he did as the gendarme of Europe: a role that led him to pursue a foreign policy that succeeded in uniting virtually the whole of Europe against Russia, notably Britain and France, whose armies found themselves fighting side by side just forty years after Waterloo. The particular issue that undid Nicholas was what was known in the nineteenth century as the Eastern Question: the future, both in the Balkans and in the Levant (the Near East), of the Ottoman Empire, which he himself described as 'the sick man of Europe'. His attempt to divide the Ottoman inheritance, which he had hoped to achieve by means of personal diplomacy, ended in the Crimean War.[7]

There are many 'ifs' about this war, which was described at the time by Disraeli as just, but unnecessary. For example, if Palmerston had not been out of government at the time, the war might never have been fought at all. Nevertheless, Nicholas swam out of his political depth by relying on Russia's military hegemony in continental Europe to address, on his own terms, problems that involved what the other major European powers regarded as their vital interests. That the campaign which gave this war its name was fought on Russian soil – the Crimean peninsula – was a strategic accident. Yet when Sebastopol finally fell to the allied armies on 10 September 1855, the result was not just the destruction of Russian naval power in the Black Sea, but the public proof of the condition of the Russian state and of Russian society.

The issue of serfdom came first and foremost. Among important secondary issues, however, one of the reasons for the comparatively small size of the forces that Russia was able to deploy in the Crimea was the primitive state of communications throughout Russia, where roads hardly deserved the name and where the railway system was still in its infancy (the first train ran between St. Petersburg and Moscow only in 1851). By contrast, the allied troops, however great the privations that they suffered during the campaign, had the advantage of having their backs to the sea, where their fleets ensured reasonably effective communications between the armies on shore and their bases at home.

The terms that Russia was obliged to accept at the Paris Peace Conference in April 1856 were disagreeable for a country that had for over forty years been generally regarded as the first military power in Europe, but they were not severe. Of far greater significance were the political consequences, not only within Russia – where, in 1861, the serfs were at last emancipated – but for Russia's reputation throughout Europe. From 1856 until 1945 Russia was reduced to the status of just one among a number of major European powers. After the Crimean humiliation Russia was no longer the superior of France; she was the inferior of Britain; and from 1870 onwards the inferior of Germany as well. Once again Nikitenko hit the nail on the head: 'We have been at war for thirty years, maintaining an army a million strong and unceasingly threatening Europe. What was all this for? What advantage and what glory did Russia get from it?'[8] One of the indirect casualties of the Crimean War was the tsar himself. Whether he simply succumbed to the attack of a minor illness, suffered a breakdown or actually committed suicide, appalled by the impending defeat, does not greatly matter. The man to whom, less than six years earlier, Paskevich had proudly reported that Hungary lay at his feet, died on 18 February 1855, mourned by few.[9]

That Pushkin's posthumous reputation was not actively fostered by a regime such as that of Nicholas I is scarcely surprising. To make matters worse, however, the government-financed edition of Pushkin's works in eight volumes, published between 1838 and 1841, proved to be a flop. It was so incompetently edited and unattractively produced that by 1845 the whole series was being advertised for sale at less than a third of the original price.[10] Moreover Pushkin's reputation as a writer, above all as a poet, simultaneously became a kind of football in the game of Russian literary politics. The literary critic who did more than anyone else in the 1840s to lay the foundations of Pushkin's ultimate victory was Belinsky – brilliant, erratic and a sick man (he died of consumption at the age of thirty-eight). Nevertheless, he was obliged by his own didactic theory of literature to insist that Pushkin's writing suffered from a lack of what he called social content. In 1865, moreover, this criticism was taken to extreme lengths by the nihilist writer D. I. Pisarev, who maintained that Pushkin's works were the product of a frivolous and socially pernicious aestheticism: a verdict that would not be overturned for the next fifteen years. Thus, when Annenkov's biographical volume on Pushkin (his *Materialy*) was reprinted in 1873, Nikolai Strakhov, a confirmed admirer of Pushkin, could still lament 'the great decline' in the understanding of Pushkin in his time.[11] This, then, was the unpromising background against which the annual reunion on the anniversary of the founding of the imperial lycée was held on 19 October 1869.

Three and a half years earlier an attempt had been made to organize a public subscription for a monument to Pushkin, but this had run into the sand. On 19 October 1869 it was decided to form a committee 'to renew the question of a monument to Pushkin'. During the 1870s, in spite of the adverse effects of the continuing debate between the left and the right wings of the Russian intelligentsia and between westernizers and slavophiles, Pushkin's cause at last began to gain strength from some countervailing factors. In the first place, Alexander II gave the project of the Pushkin monument his personal support; in April 1871 he approved a committee under the nominal presidency of a member of the imperial family, the Prince of Oldenburg; and by June 1872 he had sanctioned the choice of a site for the monument in Moscow, at the end of the Tverskoi Boulevard. Unlike the earlier attempt at a public subscription, this time money did not present much of a problem. The sum that had been collected in the earlier subscription was rapidly surpassed, so that when the time arrived for the unveiling of the monument, the total public subscription, including accrued interest, amounted to over a hundred thousand roubles.[12]

There were indeed problems that delayed the project, such as the choice of the sculptor. He had to be Russian. In the end the winner was N. M. Opekushin. He produced the statue of a pensive Pushkin, standing on a pedestal, on which work was at last under way by the beginning of 1878. What would Pushkin have made of Opekushin's statue? It is hard not to imagine Pushkin making some caustic remark. The organizers of the celebration were also not helped by the bitter quarrels that broke out between left- and right-wing literary figures, notably between Ivan Turgenev and Mikhail Katkov, who had originally been a liberal, but was by now a conservative of the far right.

Most sadly of all, in spite of a personal appeal by Turgenev, who in May 1880 travelled to Yasnaya Polyana for the express purpose of persuading Tolstoy to attend the celebration, Tolstoy declined the invitation. The reasons for his refusal had less to do with Pushkin than with the beginnings of Tolstoy's spiritual Odyssey, which was to lead him step by step from the conclusion that all Russian literature (including his own) of the previous half century had been irrelevant to the Russian people as a whole, towards his own withdrawal from literary work.

Turgenev took Tolstoy's refusal to attend in 1880 very hard. As the 1870s drew towards a close, however, liberals who had never wavered in their admiration of Pushkin, such as Turgenev, suddenly found themselves facing a half-open window of political opportunity. The Russo-Turkish War of 1877–8 and the general settlement subsequently agreed by the European powers (assembled at the Congress of Berlin in June 1878) were followed, within Russia, not only by disillusion at the terms which Russia was obliged to accept at the Congress, but also by a decision taken by the terrorists of the *Narodnaya Volya* (People's Will) organization to assassinate the tsar. After several failures, they finally succeeded in killing him with a bomb thrown in a St. Petersburg street in March 1881. Yet in the final year of his reign Alexander II responded to the terrorist threat, of which he was fully aware, by an attempt to win over moderate public opinion by a series of liberal appointments, which, had he survived, might have paved the way towards a period of real constitutional reform.[13]

Although the tsar's assassination abruptly closed this window, while it was still half-open the brief liberal interlude lasted just long enough to provide the most favourable conceivable circumstances for an act of reconciliation by the Russian intelligentsia, whatever their political or literary opinions might be. Nor could they have found a better way of demonstrating this reconciliation publicly than by a ceremony that would reverse once and for all the neglect to which the genius of Russia's national poet had fallen victim: the unveiling of the monument in Pushkin's honour in Moscow during a public holiday that would last for three days. One of the features that distinguished this liberal interlude from the period of political counter-reaction that followed it was the widespread use of words that would become familiar throughout the world a century later, such as *glasnost*. The Pushkin celebrations were therefore preceded by a wave of publicity, thanks in large measure to the fact that from April 1880 until January 1881 governmental censorship as a whole was greatly relaxed. Journalists who tried to establish the exact spot where Pushkin's duel had taken place outside St. Petersburg were dismayed to report that they had found animals grazing there; Opekushin's ponderous statue became a subject of heated debate; and Pushkin cigarettes and Pushkin vodka appeared in the shops.[14] The cult of Pushkin had begun.

The three 'Pushkin Days' were opened officially at two o'clock on the afternoon of 5 June 1880. Estimates of how many people converged on Moscow for the unveiling ceremony vary wildly: anything from one hundred thousand to over half a million. The enthusiasm aroused by the celebrations went far beyond what even the most sanguine of the organizers had ever dared to hope. Among these organizers, by far the most famous and most authoritative figure was Turgenev. It was natural, therefore, that the organizing committee should ask him to write a special brochure, intended for the Russian people as a whole, which he would deliver as a speech at the first public session held on the day after the unveiling of the Pushkin monument. Less than a month beforehand, however, Turgenev wavered. The writing of his address had gone faster than he had expected, but he decided that it should be intended not for the whole Russian people – the *narod* – but for the cultivated classes. So indeed it turned out. Turgenev's speech might have been well attuned to the English university that had conferred on him an honorary degree – Oxford. Moscow, in the city's ecstatic mood of 6 June 1880, provided a very different audience. Moreover, Turgenev delivered his speech in his weak, high-pitched voice; and in his own words, written in a letter immediately afterwards, it did not make 'a big impression on the public'. At the end of his speech he reached the crucial question: the comparison of Pushkin with the greatest poets of the past – Homer, Shakespeare, Goethe. To this question he fudged his answer. Yes – Pushkin's historical role had been to perform two tasks, which in other countries would have been divided by a whole century or longer : to establish the Russian language and to create a Russian literature. Nevertheless, Pushkin could not do everything. In spite of his greatness and his profound Russianness, he had died young, before fulfilling his potential.

In short, Turgenev was unwilling to grant to Pushkin the rank of a universal (*vsemirnyi*) poet. Up to this point it had been Turgenev who had been at the epicentre of the Pushkin celebrations. His reluctance to accord to Pushkin the ultimate accolade gave Dostoevsky an opportunity which he grasped with both hands. On the morning of 8 June he delivered a speech which earned him an ovation on a scale that put the reception given to Turgenev at the outset of the celebrations completely in the shade. Even Turgenev himself and Annenkov publicly hugged Dostoevsky in the hysterical pandemonium that followed his speech. Instead of presenting an apologia for Pushkin – as Turgenev had done in effect, whatever his intention may have been – Dostoevsky put into words the apotheosis of Pushkin that had so far been expressed only by the formal laying of wreaths on Pushkin's head in the course of the celebrations. In Dostoevsky's slavophile rhetoric, Pushkin became a national hero, leading Russia against the forces of the west : a political interpretation that Dostoevsky made even more explicit in the foreword to the speech, which he published after the speech itself had been delivered.[15]

Not content with offering a questionable exegesis of Pushkin's *Gypsies* (see p. 77) in his speech, Dostoevsky went on to suggest that Pushkin might have done better to have given *Evgenii Onegin* the title *Tatyana*, instead of *Onegin*, on the grounds that Tatyana is 'undeniably the poem's principal character'; and that it is to this 'apotheosis of Russian womanhood' that Pushkin assigns 'the expression of the idea of the poem in the famous scene of Tatyana's last meeting with Onegin'. In Dostoevsky's opinion, Pushkin revealed himself in this poem as 'a national [*narodnyi*] writer such as no other Russian writer had ever been before him'.

As for the comparison of Pushkin with the poets of other nations, Dostoevsky said that in European literature there had indeed been men whose artistic genius had been of 'enormous greatness', such as Shakespeare, Cervantes and Schiller. He at once added this qualification, however : 'But show me just one of those great geniuses who possessed such a capacity for universal empathy as did our Pushkin. And he shared with our people [*narod*] this capacity, our pre-eminent national characteristic, and this is the main reason that makes him our national [*narodnyi*] poet.'

There had, Dostoevsky maintained, 'never been a poet with such a universal empathy as Pushkin', whose almost perfect reincarnation of his own spirit in the spirit of foreign peoples 'was without parallel in any other poet of the entire world'. As a Russian national poet, Pushkin had 'a presentiment of the great future significance of Russian national power' – thereby becoming a prophet.

Summing up Pushkin's genius towards the end of this speech Dostoevsky declared:

> At least we can already point to Pushkin, to the universality and to the universal humanity of his genius. He could surely absorb foreign geniuses in his soul, as his own. In art at least, in artistic creation, he undeniably revealed this universality of the aspiration of the Russian spirit, and in this there is already a great indication. If our thought is a fantasy, then at least Pushkin offers fantasy a basis.

In Dostoevsky's interpretation of Pushkin's genius, Pushkin's poem 'The Prophet' (see Chapter 7) was the key. He recited this poem again and again to audiences during the last years of his life. If ever there was a case of projection by one writer on to another, this must surely be it. It was Dostoevsky who saw himself as a prophet. Pushkin was never a didactic poet in the simplistic manner attributed to him by Dostoevsky. Nor would much of Dostoevsky's eulogy of Pushkin have been spared thrusts of Pushkin's ironic tongue. Nevertheless, it is Dostoevsky's speech about Pushkin in Moscow in June 1880, not Turgenev's, that has been remembered not only by Russian literary historians, but by Russian historians as a whole.

In the right-wing reaction that followed the assassination of Alexander II less than a year after the euphoria of June 1880, the original theme of the Pushkin celebrations – reconciliation – was submerged. Dostoevsky's speech was not. Although the formation of a committee by a group of liberals to celebrate the fiftieth anniversary of Pushkin's death, 29 January 1887, was immediately brought to a halt by the government, on the day that followed this anniversary an event occurred which even the Russian government was powerless to prevent: the fifty-year copyright of Pushkin's works expired. At a well-known St. Petersburg bookshop where the entire stock of

Pushkin's works was sold out by midday, riots took place. It has been calculated that in the course of 1888 well over a million copies of books by Pushkin were sold in Russia.[16] Even if the immediate effects of the Moscow celebrations of 1880 were short-lived, the 1880s none the less proved to be Pushkin's watershed. So resplendent – to use Akhmatova's word again – has his posthumous victory been that it has become necessary to think of Pushkin in three different dimensions: Pushkin the myth, Pushkin the poet and Pushkin the man.

For the next hundred years no Russian government, of whatever political complexion, could afford to ignore the advantages of making use of the writings of a hero whose books were so popular among the Russian people. The tsarist regime led the way, by themselves organizing a massive centennial celebration in 1899. (Many liberals, disgusted by this belated act of repentance, took no part in the celebrations.) Not long afterwards the Soviet regime piled Pelion on Ossa. Against all the evidence of the political views that Pushkin actually held, everything possible was done to claim him as a forerunner of Marxist-Leninist ideology. If this strikes the present-day reader as beyond belief, he or she need only glance at the nauseating conclusion of the Introduction to a book of Pushkinist essays written on the occasion of the first centenary of Pushkin's death, which – as it happened – coincided with the height of Stalin's Great Terror.[17]

Yet there is another side to this coin. Members of Russian families who suffered under the Soviet regime often recount examples of their relations' efforts, which sometimes succeeded, to take with them to prison or to the camps at any rate one volume of Pushkin's works. Years spend in the Gulag by the Russian dissident Andrei Sinyavsky (Abram Terz) were responsible for two books. In one of these, *Progulki s Pushkinom*, he ridiculed Soviet hagiographical writing about Pushkin. In the other, *Golos iz khora*, describing conversations in the Gulag, he relates an astounding story of how Pushkin's personality appeared to some inmates of his camp:

> One day when he [Pushkin] was sitting with a young ruffian by the camp fire, a sergeant came up to them with a revolver and began to drive them to their work. The ruffian snapped back. The pig fired and killed him – 'Ah, you shit' – says Pushkin, and he gropes behind himself, still sitting, for some sort of stick or an axe. But he felt

nothing. And he slowly stands up and slowly he advances against the
pig – 'Scoundrel'.

And in the corner of his mouth a cigarette was still burning.

– 'Do not come near me! I will kill you!' shouts the pig and he takes
aim and backs away, he went pale, as white as this wall, and his hands
are shaking.

– 'You wouldn't dare,' replies Pushkin, moving right up to him.

And taking the cigarette stub out of his mouth, he put it out on the
forehead of the sergeant. He then turned round and calmly went his
way. And the other man did not fire after all.[18]

The celebrations that are due in 1999 – the two-hundredth
anniversary of Pushkin's birth – cannot be expected to ignore the cult
of Pushkin. They will, however, offer an opportunity to concentrate
attention not on Pushkin the myth, but on the heart of the matter:
Pushkin the poet and Pushkin the man. Among some of the
inhabitants of the former Soviet Union there may perhaps be some
reaction against the long years during which Pushkin's poetry was
rammed down the throats of every pupil, whether ethnically Russian
or not, at every school within the Soviet boundaries. But nothing can
alter the magic exercised on every native Russian-speaker by
Pushkin's command of Russian words and by his use of Russian
sounds. For Russians, this power is reinforced by the fact that,
however mixed his ancestry really was, Pushkin was a very Russian
Russian. He lived and wrote, moreover, as this biography has sought
to show, during a crucial period of Russian history. Even more clearly
than his poetry, there is a short passage of Pushkin's prose which
vividly establishes the fact of his Russianness. Taken together, the
letter to Chaadaev of October 1836 and the draft lines which, in the
event, Pushkin omitted from this letter, reveal a characteristically
Russian combination of passionate devotion to Russia as a country
with contempt for its regime.[19]

Pushkin is for Russians, as Shakespeare was for Ben Jonson, 'not of
an age, but for all time'. Or, as Herzen put it in the words that form
the epigraph to this chapter, Pushkin was the Russian people's
response to Peter the Great's command.[20] Moreover, it was a
response lasting little more than ten years. Almost all Pushkin's truly
memorable writing was accomplished between the day in 1823 on
which he wrote the first lines of *Evgenii Onegin* and his *annus mirabilis*,
the Boldino autumn of 1833.[21] Had he been able to work, whether in

verse or in prose or both, for another ten years after 1837, he would still have been under fifty. True, Sappho survives only in fragments and in Latin translations; and argument still rages among critics about which of a small number of marvellous paintings can be definitively attributed to Giorgione, who was even younger than Pushkin when he died. This said, an English-speaker trying to assess Pushkin needs to bear in mind Shakespeare without *The Tempest*, *King Lear*, *Macbeth* and *Troilus and Cressida*. Moreover, as well as writing Russian in such a way that every subsequent Russian writer, whether of verse or of prose, has acknowledged his or her debt to Pushkin, he also formed a cultural bridge between Russia and the rest of Europe, by virtue of the breadth of his knowledge both of classical literature and of European literature. Before Pushkin this bridge scarcely existed; or in so far as it did, it was in poor repair. Since Pushkin's time it has survived the millions of words of nonsense written on both sides, notably during the years of the Cold War.

The final question still remains: in judging Pushkin, who was right – Turgenev or Dostoevsky? Was Pushkin a 'national' or a 'universal' writer? To attempt to answer this question through the fog of indifferent verse translations of Pushkin's poetry is not easy. It has been well said that 'anyone who takes the trouble to learn Russian in order to read Pushkin . . . will never regret it'.[22] Among famous writers who have not made this effort, Flaubert was puzzled by Pushkin (see his remark to Turgenev, quoted on p. 3), whereas Lampedusa put his finger on one of the keys to understanding Pushkin's writing: what Lampedusa called leanness.[23] At any rate the point has at last been reached where neither Russian-speaking foreigners nor foreigners who have no Russian at all can any longer seriously doubt Pushkin's greatness as a poet.[24] Does it really help either Pushkin's legacy or our understanding of his writing to go further than this, by trying to establish, as it were, his precise position in some kind of imaginary Petrine Table of Ranks designed not for generals and civil servants, but for writers? It is, I suggest, an exercise of which Pushkin himself could scarcely have approved: indeed it is in a way an insult to his memory.

There is also no simple answer to the questions raised by consideration of Pushkin the man. As Vyazemsky remarked in his letter of 14 February 1837 to the Grand Duke Mikhail, Pushkin was not understood in his lifetime, either by people who were indifferent towards him or by his friends. If this biography has proved nothing else, it will have shown how paradoxical Pushkin's character was; and that this paradox within himself was something that Pushkin recognized. All countries need heroes. Their mythology may be magnificent – witness the Greeks. Russia is fortunate to have a poet for a hero. With the passage of time, however, a hero's fellow-countrymen usually become more aware of his weaknesses – so to speak, of the hero's 'warts and all' – whether or not these were evident during his lifetime. This recognition may at the same time enhance our admiration of the hero's qualities as a human being. So it is, I believe, with Pushkin. Whatever kind of life Pushkin had led, what he wrote would have been infinitely more important than the way in which he lived. Yet in fact his life demonstrates the human condition in a peculiarly poignant manner. He did not succeed in resolving his inner conflict, which contributed to his destruction. But two lines of his poem 'Elegy' proved to be prophetic:

> Но не хочу, о други, умирать!
> Я жить хочу, чтоб мыслить и страдать.

> But I do not want to die, my friends! I want to live, in order to think and to suffer.[25]

Pushkin did both in equal measure. A far more impressive figure than Pushkin the paragon is Pushkin the man.

A Selective Chronology

Note: All dates are given according to the Julian calendar unless marked★

CHAPTERS 1–14

1796   Catherine II dies; succeeded by
                                              her son, Paul I

1797   Third Partition of Poland (by
                                              Russia, Austria and Prussia)

1799   26 May, Alexander Sergeevich
              Pushkin born in Moscow

1801   11/12 March, Paul I
                                              assassinated; succeeded by his
                                              eldest son, Alexander I

1804   2 December,★ Napoleon
                                              Bonaparte crowned Emperor of
                                              the French

1805   21 October,★ Battle of Trafalgar
                                              2 December,★ Battle of
                                              Austerlitz

1807   25 June,★ Napoleon and
                                              Alexander meet at Tilsit;
                                              Franco-Russian Treaty of
                                              Alliance

1809   Birth of Gogol

1811   19 October, Pushkin enters
              imperial lycée, Tsarskoe Selo

1812	27 August, Natalya Nikolaevna Goncharova born	24 June,* Napoleon invades Russia 5–7 September, Battle of Borodino 14 September, Napoleon enters Moscow 19 October, Napoleon begins retreat from Moscow
1813	Birth of Pavel Annenkov	16–18 October,* Napoleon defeated at Battle of Leipzig
1814	4 July, Pushkin's first published poem appears in St. Petersburg press 4 October, birth of Lermontov	30 March,* Alexander I enters Paris 11 April, Napoleon abdicates Alexander pays State visit to London in June
1814–15		Congress of Vienna (interrupted by Napoleon's escape from Elba – the 'One Hundred Days')
1815		18 June,* Battle of Waterloo; Napoleon exiled to St. Helena; France occupied by Allied armies; Alexander secures adherence of Austria and Prussia to his Holy Alliance
1816–22		The Concert of Europe, directed by the Quadruple Alliance; Austria, Britain, Prussia and Russia (France participates from late 1818 onwards)
1817	11 June, Pushkin leaves school, joins Foreign Ministry	
1818	Birth of (Ivan) Turgenev	Alexander I opens first session of the *Sejm*, the parliament of 'Congress' Poland, in Warsaw
	26 March, Pushkin completes his first major poem, *Ruslan i Lyudmila*; 6 May, expelled from St. Petersburg; appointed to Southern Russia; visits Caucasus for first time	

1820–3	Pushkin in Kishinev; writes *The Captive of the Caucasus, The Fountain of Bakhchisaray, The Robber Brothers*; begins *The Gypsies*	
1821	Birth of Dostoevsky	Greek War of Independence begins
1822	Capodistria leaves St. Petersburg	
1823	In May Pushkin writes first lines of *Evgenii Onegin*; in August, he is transferred to Odessa	
1824	30 July, Pushkin dismissed from imperial service, leaves Odessa	
1824–6	Banished to Mikhailovskoe, under police surveillance: years of intense creativity – lyric poetry, drama (*Boris Godunov*) and he completes *The Gypsies*; continues *Evgenii Onegin*	November 1834 – the great flood in St. Petersburg
1825	Late December, first edition of Pushkin's collected poems published	19 November, Alexander I dies at Taganrog; confusion in St. Petersburg; Nicholas I's proclamation as tsar is followed on 14 December by the Decembrist Revolt in St. Petersburg; revolt suppressed
1826	Writes 'The Prophet' 28 August, Nicholas I summons Pushkin to Moscow 8 September, Nicholas I and Pushkin meet (alone) in the Kremlin; Pushkin's banishment is rescinded	13 July, five Decembrists are hanged in St. Petersburg; over a hundred exiled to Siberia
1826–31	Pushkin's life divided between Moscow, St. Petersburg and the country	

1826	Beginning of Pushkin's friendship with Mickiewicz	
1827		6 July,* Treaty of London paves the way for Greek independence; Capodistria becomes provisional president of Greece
1827–8		Russo-Persian War
1828	Pushkin writes *Poltava*, which is published in 1829; birth of Tolstoy	
1828–9	Pushkin meets Natalya Goncharova for the first time	Russo-Turkish War; Russia acquires eastern Armenia
1829	Pushkin visits Caucasus and Transcaucasia; witnesses campaign in eastern Turkey	
1830	6 May, Pushkin and Natalya Goncharova formally engaged; August–November, Pushkin's first autumn spent writing at Boldino; *Evgenii Onegin* completed; writes 'Little Tragedies' and *The Tales of Belkin*, his first short stories in prose	February,* Greek independence guaranteed by protocol of London
1830–1		Russo-Polish War; first cholera epidemic in Russia
1831	18 February, marriage of Pushkin and Natalya Goncharova, in Moscow October – Pushkins move to St. Petersburg (via Tsarskoe Selo) 11 November, Pushkin readmitted to Foreign Ministry; given access to imperial archives relating to Peter the Great	Capodistria assassinated in Greece 15 October,* London Conference agrees on future of independent Belgium
1832	19 May, birth of Pushkin's first child (three further children born 1833, 1835 and 1836)	

1833	Pushkin visits eastern Russia; during second Boldino autumn his writing includes *The Bronze Horseman* (verse), *The Queen of Spades* (prose), *History of Pugachev*; and the drafts of *The Captain's Daughter* 31 December, Pushkin appointed *Kammerjunker* at court	October, Georges d'Anthès arrives in Russia
1834	25 June, resigns from imperial service; resignation withdrawn by end August; Autumn – Pushkin's last Boldino autumn; writes *Golden Cockerel*; both Natalya's sisters join her in St. Petersburg, where they remain in the Pushkins' flat	January, d'Anthès commissioned in the imperial household cavalry
1835	July, Pushkin requests and receives government loan (45,000 roubles) September–October, Pushkin attempts to spend autumn on leave writing at Mikhailovskoe – failure	
1836	Pushkin's main work now becomes the editorship of the *Sovremennik* (quarterly journal), but he completes *The Captain's Daughter*; his financial position becomes virtually hopeless; his health declines D'Anthès' courtship of Natalya Pushkina; 4 November, Pushkin receives anonymous letter; challenge issued to d'Anthès to duel, but withdrawn after two weeks because of d'Anthès' engagement to Pushkin's sister-in-law, Ekaterina Goncharova	May, Netherlands Minister (Baron Hekkeren) informs Russian Foreign Minister of his adoption of d'Anthès

1837	10 January, wedding of d'Anthès and Ekaterina in St. Petersburg
	26 January, Pushkin sends insulting letter to Baron Hekkeren; challenged to duel by d'Anthès
	27 January, Pushkin mortally wounded by d'Anthès in duel
	29 January, Pushkin dies
	1 February, Pushkin's requiem mass in St. Petersburg
	6 February, Pushkin buried at Svyatogorsk Monastery, near Mikhailovskoe
	19 March, d'Anthès reduced to ranks and expelled from Russia

EPILOGUE

1837		20 June,* Queen Victoria accedes to the throne
1841	Lermontov killed in a duel	
1844	16 July, Natalya Pushkina marries Major-General Petr Lanskoi	Nicholas I pays State Visit to Britain
1848		Year of European Revolutions (Britain and Russia the exceptions)
1848–55	Russia's 'Dark Seven Years'	
1849	Dostoevsky sentenced to death but spends six years in Siberian imprisonment	Russian Army occupies Hungary
1851	21 May, Natalya Lanskaya gives Annenkov Pushkin's papers and grants him right to publish Pushkin's works	

1852		Alexander Herzen (left Russia in 1847) settles in London 2 December,* Louis-Napoleon proclaims himself Emperor of the French (Napoleon III)
1854	7 October, Nicholas I gives permission, subject to strict conditions, for Annenkov's publication of his first (biographical) volume on Pushkin	
1853–6		The Crimean War: Russian defeat marks the end of Russian military hegemony in continental Europe
1855	18 February, death of Nicholas I	
1856		Surviving Decembrists are granted amnesty
1861		February, Alexander II promulgates the emancipation of the serfs
1863	26 November, death of Natalya Lanskaya	Polish Rebellion; suppressed
1864		Marx forms First International in London
1870	Birth of Lenin	The Franco-Prussian War
1877	Pushkin's letters to Natalya published (edited by Turgenev)	Russo-Turkish War
1878		June, The Congress of Berlin
1879	Birth of Stalin	

1880	Monument to Pushkin unveiled in Moscow; speech by Dostoevsky; apotheosis of Pushkin	
1881		17 February, Alexander II assassinated
1889	Birth of Anna Akhmatova	

Note on Sources

Primary sources for Pushkin's life

Not surprisingly, the overwhelming majority is Russian. Among primary sources, Pushkin's own writings are indispensable, even though he destroyed most of his autobiographical notes. By no means all Pushkin's works, whether in verse or in prose, have been translated into English; the gaps are large and important; and the quality of the translation of his verse is extremely uneven (see Preface). The writings of some of Pushkin's contemporaries, whether letters written during his lifetime or recollections thereafter, are also important, those of his friends Petr Vyazemsky and Ivan Pushchin being of especial significance. It is a particular misfortune, however, that not a single letter written to Pushkin by his wife has survived.

In assessing two periods of Pushkin's life – 1825–6 (the year of the Decembrist Revolt and the trial of the Decembrists) and his final year – the biographer must take into account a broader range of sources. In particular, the sources for the twelve months ending in January 1837 now constitute virtually a corpus of documentary evidence on their own, including as they do Russian governmental documents and foreign diplomatic correspondence as well.

Secondary sources in Russian

Like the primary sources, most secondary sources are in Russian. The millions of Russian words devoted to Pushkin, particularly from 1880 onwards, some of them by eminent writers such as Anna Akhmatova, do not include a biography that can be described as 'definitive', or that Russians themselves would recognize as such. The aftermath of the collapse of the Soviet regime can be expected to give rise to a Russian reappraisal of at any rate some aspects of Pushkin's life. Meanwhile there is one biography which no modern biographer of Pushkin can afford to ignore: the very first, that by

Pavel Annenkov, in spite of the mass of fresh evidence that has come to light in the past one and a half centuries. The fact that Annenkov began to write it after Pushkin's widow had sent him two trunks full of Pushkin's papers twelve years after his death, at a time when she and Nicholas I were both still alive, imposed formidable constraints. (These were summed up by Alexander Turgenev in a letter written to Annenkov in October 1852: 'Better to break the legs of the statue than to lessen their height'.) Annenkov's *Materialy dlya biografii Pushkina* must therefore be read in conjunction with his *Pushkin v Aleksandrovskuyu epokhu*, written many years later and hence less subject to these inhibitions and to the rigorous system of censorship of the earlier reign.

Since then every conceivable aspect of Pushkin's life and work has been the subject of exhaustive study by successsive generations of Russian writers. It would be invidious to attempt to list them in order of importance. Most Pushkinists would, however, agree that among this vast array of books there are works of scholarship which, even if some of them include political overtones reflecting the period during which they were written, are each in their own way invaluable as works of reference. Notable examples are S. L. Abramovich, *Pushkin. Poslednyi god*; D. D. Blagoi, *Tvorchesky put' Pushkina*; L. A. Chereisky, *Pushkin i ego okruzhenie*; V. V. Kunin, *Poslednyi god zhizni Pushkina*; M. A. Tsyavlovsky, *Letopis' zhizni i tvorchestva A. S. Pushkina, 1799–1826*; and V. V. Veresaev, *Pushkin v zhizni*. Special mention must also be made of B. V. Tomashevsky's notes on the 1962–6 'Little Academy' edition of Pushkin's works. Finally, B. L. Modzhalevsky compiled a complete catalogue of Pushkin's extensive library in 1910, part of which has been translated into English; and two authors – Abram Efros and T. G. Tsyavlovskaya – have each written excellent notes to accompany a selection of Pushkin's drawings.

In order to do full justice to this *embarras de richesses*, a massive bibliography would be required. For the more modest purposes of the present study, which (although based on Russian sources) is intended for the general reader who may well not know Russian, the simplest solution has seemed to be to compose its bibliography almost entirely from works either quoted from or referred to in the book. The absence of a particular work from this bibliography, however distinguished its author may be and however valuable its contribution to Pushkinist studies, does not necessarily mean that I am unaware of it – only that a line has to be drawn somewhere.

Sources for the 'Age of Pushkin'

Although Pushkin's life was short, its historical context covers a vast canvas of Russian political and social history. Doubtless, not only Soviet but Russian nineteenth-century history will now be subjected to fresh and rigorous study by Russian scholars. Meanwhile, V. O. Klyuchevsky's sparkling prose still offers the most stimulating introduction to the history of Pushkin's times. (Unfortunately only one of his five volumes – that relating to the reign of Peter the Great – has been well translated into English.) In English, Seton-Watson's *The Russian Empire: 1801–1917* gives a painstakingly impartial account, although when it was written (in the 1960s) its author was unable to obtain the benefit of discussion with Russian scholars. It is also important to bear in mind that – as a British historian has recently put it – 'political novels are worth innumerable academic theses about nineteenth-century politics' (Max Beloff, *An Historian in the Twentieth Century*, Yale University Press, New Haven, 1992, p. 24). Gogol's *The Inspector General* and *Dead Souls* are obvious Russian examples of the truth of this observation. So too is the brilliant reconstruction of the opening years of the century in Tolstoy's *War and Peace*. Alexander Herzen's (Gertsen's) writing is important for an assessment of the reign of Nicholas I. Diaries, although they may sometimes mislead, can also illuminate: for example, that of Alexander Nikitenko (born a serf in 1805 and helped by Zhukovsky to buy his freedom, he became Professor of Russian literature at St. Petersburg University).

Secondary sources in English

Within the English-speaking world, Pushkin has recently fared much better in the field of literary assessment than he has in that of biography. The works of John Bayley, A. D. P. Briggs, Paul Debreczeny, John Fennell, Vladimir Nabokov, J. Thomas Shaw and Tatiana Wolff have all contributed biographical insights as by-products of their primary purpose. Biographies of Pushkin in English are another matter, however. Those written during the past sixty years vary in quality, but they all have one thing in common: at the time of writing, they are out of print. So too, unfortunately, is a short, forthright book on Pushkin written in English by the Russian literary historian D. S. Mirsky in 1926. The most scholarly biography (Ernest

Simmons') disappeared from print not long after it was published by the Oxford University Press in 1937; and a quarter of a century passed before it reappeared under a different imprint. David Magarshack's biography (1967) had no notes, no references and a poor bibliography. The sole survivor, in its original French (not in the English translation, which is out of print), is Henri Troyat's *Pouchkine* – in his own phrase, *mot par mot* as he wrote it in 1946. Anyone intending to use this book for scholarly purposes needs to bear in mind Nabokov's description of it (quoted in the Introduction, note 12).

Since this book was written it has been announced that, thanks to a project sponsored by the Prince of Wales, a facsimile version of the whole set of Pushkin's working notebooks will be published for the first time.

Notes to the Chapters

Unless otherwise stated, the ten-volume 'Little Academy' edition of Pushkin's works, produced under the general editorship of B. V. Tomashevsky, Moscow, 1962–6 and the lineal descendant of the sixteen-volume edition timed by the Academy of Sciences to coincide with the first centenary of Pushkin's death, has been used for almost all references to Pushkin's own writing. (Unless specifically stated otherwise, therefore, in the Notes that follow 'Pushkin' – or, in immediately succeeding notes, 'Ibid.' – refers to the Little Academy edition.) In the case of Pushkin's verse, the volume number and the (Russian) name of the poem are supplied in the Notes. For prose, the volume number and either the page number or the full reference of letters are cited; and in the case of letters, the relevant number and volume reference in J. T. Shaw's admirably annotated edition of Pushkin's letters has been added in brackets as well.

To this general system of referencing the Notes one exception has been made: since there are several English versions of *Evgenii Onegin*, which occupies most of Volume V of the Little Academy edition, only the chapter and stanza number have been supplied for quotations from this poem.

Introduction

1 Anna Akhmatova, *O Pushkine: stati'i i zametki* (Sovetskii pisatel', Leningrad, 1977), p. 6.
2 See – for example – the letters exchanged between Nicholas I and Prince Paskevich in February 1837, *Russkii arkhiv*, 1897, I, 19.
3 Marquis de Custine, *Lettres de Russie: La Russie en 1839* (Gallimard, Paris, 1975, first published in 1843), pp. 209 ff.
4 Pushkin, vol. III, 'Ya pamyatnik sebe vozdvig nerukotvornyi' echoed Horace's ode *Exegi Monumentum* – a title which he used for this poem. Although Pushkin was often ironical about himself as well as about other people, the attempt made by some – notably Nabokov – to interpret its first four stanzas as ironical is ingenious, but in my view implausible. Nabokov's

commentary on this poem is in Vladimir Nabokov, *Eugene Onegin*, revised edn (Princeton University Press, Princeton, New Jersey: Routledge and Kegan Paul, London, 1975), vol. II, pp. 310 ff. For a wholly different view, see V. Nepomnyashchy, *Poeziya i sud'ba* (Sovetskii pisatel', Moscow, 1983), pp. 3–29.

5 Letter (not sent) to N. N. Strakhov, cited in A. N. Wilson, *Tolstoy* (W. W. Norton, New York and London, 1988), p. 269.

6 This and the first quotation (V. Solov'ev) in this paragraph are derived from *The Oxford Book of Russian Verse* (Clarendon Press, Oxford, 1st edn, 1924, 2nd edn 1948), pp. xxiv–xxv.

7 Pushkin, vol. X, Pushkin to N. B. Golitsyn, 11 November 1836. Flaubert's remark is cited in John Bayley, *Pushkin: A Comparative Commentary* (Cambridge University Press, Cambridge, 1971), p. 1.

8 Matthew Arnold, 'Count Leo Tolstoi', in *Essays on Criticism*, second series (Macmillan, London, 1954), p. 150. This essay was first published in the *Fortnightly Review*, December 1887.

9 Baring appears to have been heavily influenced by Gilbert Murray, at the height of his fame in the 1920s; and he therefore spoiled the case that he was making for Pushkin by seeking to draw a dubious comparison between Pushkin and classical Greek poetry, seen through Murray's eyes. See *The Oxford Book of Russian Verse*, pp. xiii ff.

10 Ernest J. Simmons, *Pushkin* (Oxford University Press, London, 1937, reprinted 1971 by Peter Smith, Gloucester, Massachusetts). On p. 3 its author observed – with justice – that compared with Turgenev, Dostoevsky and Tolstoy, Pushkin was then 'almost a nonentity outside his native land'.

11 David Grene, Introduction to Thomas Hobbes' translation of Thucydides' *History of the Peloponnesian War* (University of Chicago Press, Chicago and London, 1989), p. vii.

12 Still less anything resembling a psycho-history. In his *Onegin*, vol. I, p. 138, Nabokov dismisses as a '*biographie romancée*, tritely written and teeming with errors' Henri Troyat's *Pouchkine*, 2 vols (Albin Michel, Paris, 1946, reprinted 1976, Librairie Académique Perrin, Paris).

13 Pushkin, vol. X, Pushkin to Elizaveta Khitrovo, August–first half of October 1828, written in French (no. 275 in *The Letters of Alexander Pushkin*, translated by J. Thomas Shaw (Indiana University Press and University of Pennsylvania Press, Bloomington and Philadelphia, 1963), vol. II). In the original the last two words of this quotation are *toutes tiers-état*. I prefer the metaphorical to the literal translation of this expression.

14 Cited in Brian Boyd, *Vladimir Nabokov: The Russian Years* (Chatto & Windus, London, 1990), vol. I, p. 147.

15 Nabokov, *Onegin*, vol. III, p. 256, describes as 'intelligent' Annenkov's *Materialy dlya biografii A. S. Pushkina*, written in the 1850s in exceptionally difficult circumstances (see Note on Sources). The contemporary edition, with a useful introduction by G. M. Fridlender, was published in Moscow by Izdatel'stvo Sovremennik in 1984.

16 Prince Petr Vyazemsky, *Polnoe sobranie sochinenii*, 10 vols, (Izd. Sherem'eteva, St. Petersburg, 1878–86), vol. II, p. 373.

17 'My one hundred and thirteenth love': Pushkin, vol. X, Pushkin to Princess Vera Vyazemskaya, late April 1830 (no. 275 in Shaw, *Letters*, vol. II).

18 For example, Troyat devotes six pages of his *Pouchkine* to '*Initiations Amoureuses*' – an attempt to explore Pushkin's sexuality as a schoolboy.

19 This 'digression' is exhaustively examined by Nabokov in his *Onegin*, vol. I, pp. 120 ff.

20 Well before he became tsar, however: Alexander I to de Laharpe, 27 September 1797, text in N. K. Schil'der, *Imperator Aleksandr I: ego zhizn' i tsarstvovanie* (Izd. A. S. Suvorin, St. Petersburg, 1897), vol. I, pp. 280–82.

21 Pushkin's draft of his reply to Ryleev's letter is no. 163 in Pushkin, vol. X, (no. 152 in Shaw, *Letters*, Vol. I).

22 Ibid., Pushkin to Anton Delvig, first half of June 1825 (no. 126 in Shaw, *Letters*, vol. I).

23 Vyazemsky, *Polnoe sobranie*, vol. I, pp. 322.

24 Strictly speaking Capodistria was quoting the view of Pushkin's 'patrons', in a letter written by himself, but signed by Nesselrode, to Lieutenant-General Inzov, introducing Pushkin (on his departure from St. Petersburg to join Inzov's staff), 4 May 1820.

25 M. Yu Lermontov, *Sobranie sochinenii*, 4 vols (Izdatel'stvo khudozhestvennaya literatura, Moscow, 1964), vol. I, p. 21 – *Smert' poeta*.

26 Wilson, *Tolstoy*, p. 5.

27 Pushkin's description comes from the invocation addressed to the city of St. Petersburg, which forms the opening of his poem, *The Bronze Horseman* (Pushkin, vol. IV, *Mednyi vsadnik*).

28 The concept of the Russian capital as the 'Third Rome' dated from the early sixteenth century. Following the fall of Byzantium – the Second Rome – in 1453, Ivan III married the niece of the last Byzantine Emperor. Ivan IV was the first to be crowned tsar in 1547; and in 1589 the Metropolitan of Moscow received the title of Patriarch. Thereafter it faded, until in the nineteenth century it was revived as part of Russian nationalistic foreign policy.

29 Pushkin, vol. III, *Elegiya*. For Pushkin's definition see the concluding sentences of the Epilogue.

30 Lewis Namier's observation that at the turning point of German history – 1848 – German history failed to turn.

31 Alexander Herzen (1812–70), one of the most prominent dissidents of his time, whose inherited wealth enabled him to live abroad (mainly in London) from 1847 onwards. His remark about Pushkin is quoted in full as the epigraph to the Epilogue; see also Epilogue, note 20.

Chapter One, *Imperial Zenith: The Historical Context*

1 Pushkin, vol. X, Pushkin to his wife, 20 and 22 April 1834 (no. 488 in Shaw, *Letters*, vol. III).

2 David Cairns' Introduction to *The Memoirs of Hector Berlioz, 1803–65* (Spear Books (Cardinal), 1990, first published Gollancz, 1969), p. xvi. Artistically both Pushkin and Berlioz were innovators; both were bowled over by Shakespeare; both had troubles with the Establishment; and both fell in love with and insisted on marrying women ill-suited to be their wives.

3 'A Russian . . . neither knows anything nor wants to know anything, because he does not believe in the possibility of knowing anything' (Lev Tolstoy, *Voina i mir*, 4 vols (Molodaya gvardia, Moscow, 1978), vol. III, Pt 1, p. 52). The text of this edition follows that of vols IV–VII of the twenty-volume edition of Tolstoy's works published by Khudozhestvennaya literatura, Moscow, 1964–8.

4 Ibid., p. 118. In the words of the elder Prince Bolkonsky, however.

5 Pushkin, vol. VII, 'O nichtozhestve literatury russkoi', pp. 306–07.

6 Ibid., vol. VII, 'Puteshestvie iz Moskvy v Peterburg', p. 289. The preceding quotation is from Mikhail Speransky, cited in John Gooding, 'Michael Speransky', *Slavonic and East European Review* (London), vol. 64, no. 1, January 1986.

7 Hugh Seton-Watson, *The Russian Empire, 1801–1917* (Clarendon Press, Oxford, 1967), p. 25. See also V. O. Klyuchevsky, *Sochineniya* (Izdatel'stvo sotsial'vo-ekonomicheskoi literatury, Moscow, 1958), vol. V, pp. 130 ff.

8 Klyuchevsky, *Sochineniya*, vol. V, p. 185.

9 Cited in ibid., p. 184.

10 Pushkin, vol. VIII, 'Zametki po russkoi istorii XVIII veka', pp. 121 ff.

11 Cited in N. Eidel'man, *Pervyi dekabrist* (Izdatel'stvo politicheskoi literatury, Moscow, 1991), p. 47.

12 Pushkin, vol. I, 'Volnost', lines 75–80. The motives of the assassins and the question of their victim's sanity lie outside the scope of this book.

13 Klyuchevsky, *Sochineniya*, vol. V, p. 457.

14 See Michael Jenkins, *Arakcheev, Grand Vizier of the Russian Empire* (Faber & Faber, London, 1967 and Dial Press, New York, 1969), passim. This book examines the qualities that made the services of this singularly unattractive man (1769–1834), valuable for two successive tsars. For the 'barracks' epigram, see Klyuchevsky, *Sochineniya*, vol. V, p. 241.

15 Pushkin, vol. I, 'Na Arakcheeva'.

16 Cited in C. M. Woodhouse, *Capodistria, the founder of Greek Independence* (Oxford University Press, London, 1973), p. 54.

17 Originally a Venetian subject, he joined the imperial Russian service in 1809. During the eighteenth and early nineteenth centuries many foreigners held high office in the service of the tsars.

18 Klyuchevsky, *Sochineniya*, vol. V, p. 444. For Pushkin's description of Alexander, see Pushkin, vol. III, 'K byustu zavoevatelya' (written in 1829).

19 Pushkin, vol. VIII, *Dnevniki*, p. 42.

20 Klyuchevsky, *Sochineniya*, vol. V, p. 458.

21 *The Letters of Queen Victoria*, ed. A. C. Benson and Viscount Esher (John Murray, London, 1908), vol. I, p. 14.

22 Seton-Watson, *The Russian Empire*, p. 201.

23 Klyuchevsky, *Sochineniya*, vol. V, p. 462.

24 Cited in Seton-Watson, *The Russian Empire*, p. 227.

25 Cited in Wilson, *Tolstoy*, pp. 211–12. For a graphic contemporary British account of the barbarity of Russian punishment in the early nineteenth century, see Sir Robert Porter, *Travelling sketches in Russia and Sweden* (London, 1809), Letter XXVIII, reproduced as Appendix I in Jenkins, *Arakcheev*.

26 Countess Jeannette Grudzinska, who received the Russian title of Princess of Lowicz.

27 From a discarded foreword by Tolstoy to *1805*, cited in Henry Gifford (ed.), *Leo Tolstoy: a critical anthology* (Penguin Books, Harmondsworth, 1971), pp. 38–9.

28 A class-mate, but not a friend, of Pushkin at school: see Chapter 3.

29 Cited in N. Eidel'man, *Conspiracy against the Tsar: a portrait of the Decembrists*, trans. Cynthia Carlile (Progress Publishers, Moscow, 1985), p. 226.

30 Ibid., pp. 189 ff.

31 From Mickiewicz's poem 'Do przyjaciól Moskali'.

32 Klyuchevsky, *Sochineniya*, vol. V, p. 249.

33 The 'Spirit of the Age' quotation is from P. I. Pestel; and the statement about the need to 'borrow from Europe' is from Nikolai Turgenev. Both are cited in Leonard Schapiro, *Rationalism and Nationalism in Russian Nineteenth-Century Political Thought* (Yale University Press, New Haven and London, 1967), pp. 24–5.

34 Cited in Klyuchevsky, *Sochineniya*, vol. V, p. 249. Küchelbecker was another school-friend of Pushkin.

35 See Eidel'man, *Conspiracy against the Tsar*, pp. 11 ff. Pushkin, who knew him, found Lunin 'truly remarkable'.

36 For a detailed account of the northern and southern societies' draft constitutions, see Seton-Watson, *The Russian Empire*, pp. 187 ff.

37 Klyuchevsky, *Sochineniya*, vol. V, p. 253.

38 The title of Chapter 7 of this book.

39 Eidel'man, *Conspiracy against the Tsar*, p. 244.

Chapter Two, *Pushkin's Origins*

1 'He [Shakespeare] is the very Janus of poets; he wears everywhere two faces . . . ' (John Dryden, *Essay on the Dramatic Poetry of the Last Age*).

2 Seton-Watson, *The Russian Empire*, p. 239.

3 V. I. Semevsky, *Krest'yane v tsarstvovanii Imperatritsy Ekateriny II* (St. Petersburg, 1901–3), vol. I, pp. 32–3. Other estimates are far higher.

4 Liliana Archibald, *Peter the Great* (a translation of vol. IV of Klyuchevsky's *Sochineniya*) (Macmillan, London, 1958), p. 110.

5 The Russian commander-in-chief in 1812, familiar to readers of *War and Peace*. His daughter, Elizaveta Khitrovo, was devoted to Pushkin.

6 Written in 1830, as a riposte to an article published by the hack journalist, Faddei Bulgarin, alleging that Pushkin's Gannibal great-grandfather had been bought for a bottle of rum by the skipper of a merchant ship (Pushkin, vol. III, *Moya rodoslovnaya*).

7 Ibid., vol. VIII, *Dnevniki*, 22 December 1834 (a remark made in French).

8 Nabokov, *Onegin*, vol. 3, p. 437.

9 Pushkin, vol. V, p. 513: a note added by Pushkin in the first edition of *Evgenii Onegin*, referring to the eleventh line of Chapter 1, Stanza L.

10 Cited in Nabokov, *Onegin*, vol. III, p. 398 – part of a long appendix reconstructing Abram Gannibal's life. Even the exact spelling of his place of birth is uncertain, because of the difficulties in Russian transliteration: probably Lagona or Lahona, however.

11 Pushkin, vol. VI, *Arap Petra Velikogo* (*Arap* does not mean 'Arab' in Russian).

12 Nabokov, *Onegin*, vol. III, p. 438.

13 Annenkov, *Pushkin v Aleksandrovskuyu epokhu*, p. 15.

14 'Medically and morally broken and bankrupt': Annenkov, *Pushkin v Aleksandrovskuu epokhu*, p. 17.

15 Troyat, *Pouchkine*, p. 34, citing Baron M. A. Korff (see Chapters 1 and 3), whose recollection may in this case have been accurate.

16 For the financial details of Zakharovo, see M. A. Tsyavlovsky, *Letopis' zhizni i tvorchestva A. S. Pushkina, 1799–1826*, 2nd edn (Leningrad, Nauka, 1991), p. 36. That Pushkin remembered Zakharovo and his grandmother with affection in later years is clear from his poem, written 1822, *Napersnitsa volshebnoi stariny*, Pushkin, vol. II.

17 Cited in Troyat, *Pouchkine*, p. 43.

18 Annenkov, *Materialy*, p. 42.

19 Pushkin, vol. VIII, *Dnevniki*, p. 74.

20 Ibid., vol. X. Pushkin (in draft) to D. M. Schvartz (Shvarts), 9 December 1842 (no. 95 in Shaw, *Letters*, vol. I).

21 See Annenkov, *Materialy*, p. 41.

22 See E. V. Pavlova, *A. S. Pushkin v portretakh*, 2 vols 2nd edn (Moscow, 1989), pp. 15–20. Whereas there are several theories about the original drawing on which Geitman's engraving was based, there is now a consensus that that earlier portrait of Pushkin as a small boy is really of someone quite different: perhaps of a child, M. A. Mudrov, who in later life became a professor of medicine.

23 Mickiewicz's lines are an extract from his *Introduction to the Forefathers' Eve, Part III*, trans. Arthur P. Coleman, in Cross, S. and Simmons, E. (eds), *Centennial Essays for Pushkin* (Harvard University Press, Cambridge, Mass, 1937), p. 97.

24 Pushkin, vol. IV. For a complete translation of *Mednyi vsadnik*, see John Fennell, *Pushkin: Selected Verse* (Bristol Classical Press, 1991, first published by Penguin Books, 1964), pp. 233–56.

25 Pushkin, vol. VII, 'Puteshestvie iz Moskvy v Peterburg', pp. 273–5.

26 Ibid., *Evgenii Onegin*, Chapter 7, Stanza XXXIV.

27 Cited by Isaiah Berlin, in an interview published by *The New York Review of Books*, 28 May 1992, p. 249. Akhmatova was then talking about Chekhov, but she also had reservations about the influence on Tolstoy's writing of his 'Establishment' aunts.

28 Tolstoy, *Voina i mir*, vol. I, pp. 10 and 49.

Chapter Three, *School at Tsarskoe Selo, 1811–1817*

1 For the influence of Parny (1753–1814) on Pushkin, see D. S. Mirsky, *Pushkin* (Routledge, London, 1926), p. 210.

2 Cited in Seton-Watson, *The Russian Empire*, p. 99.

3 Ibid., p. 98.

4 Although Pushkin remembered the 'loan' many years later, the relationship between uncle and nephew was always a good one. See N. I. Mikhailovna's introduction to her *Vasilii Pushkin: stikhi, proza, pis'ma* (Sovetskaya Rossiya, Moscow, 1989).

5 Pushkin, vol. X, Pushkin to P. A. Pletnev, 21 January 1831 (no. 344 in Shaw, *Letters*, vol. II). For his 'damned' education, see Mirsky, *Pushkin*, p. 13.

6 Eidel'man, *Conspiracy against the Tsar*, pp. 253 and 278.

7 He died in 1883.

8 Cited in Annenkov, *Materialy*, p. 44, fn.

9 Both this paragraph (including the quotation) and the preceding paragraph are indebted to Schapiro, *Rationalism and Nationalism in Russian nineteenth-century political thought*, pp. 48–50.

10 For the lycée library, see Annenkov, *Materialy*, p. 44. The Appendix to Tatiana Wolff's *Pushkin on Literature* (Athlone Press, London, and Stanford University Press, Stanford, California, 1986, first published by Methuen, 1971) is a catalogue of the approximately one thousand non-Russian books in Pushkin's library.

11 Cited in Troyat, *Pouchkine*, p. 44.

12 Pushkin, vol. VIII, pp. 10–11.

13 Ibid., p. 75.

14 For duelling at Eton in the same period (in one duel there a boy was killed), see V. G. Kiernan, *The Duel in European History: Honour and the Reign of the Aristocracy* (Oxford University Press, Oxford, 1988), p. 214.

15 See Tsyavlovsky, *Letopis'*, pp. 43 ff., the source of all unascribed references in this chapter. The timetable is given in full by A. Gessen, *Zhizn' poeta* (Detskaya literatura, Moscow, 1972) p. 31.

16 Engelhardt's assessment of Pushkin as a schoolboy was published in the journal *Sovremennik*, 1863, no. 8, p. 376.

17 Korff's assessment, written in 1852, is cited in full in Annenkov, *Pushkin v Aleksandrovskuyu epokhu*, pp. 41–2.

18 I. I. Pushchin, *Zapiski o Pushkine*, ed. and biographical sketch by S. Ya. Shtraich (Moscow, 1925), pp. 85 and 95–6. Pushchin's assessment of Pushkin as a boy was first published in the journal *Atenei*, 1859, no. 8. See also Annenkov, *Pushkin v Aleksandrovskuyu epokhu*, p. 23.

19 Cited in Eidel'man, *Conspiracy against the Tsar*, p. 34.

20 Tsyavlovsky, *Letopis'*, pp. 46–52 and 77. Troyat, *Pouchkine*, pp. 87 ff., also cites Madame de Staël's account of the excellent way in which she was treated in Russia during the French invasion.

21 Mirsky, *Pushkin*, p. 31, describes Korff as 'a German prig'.

22 All three poems are in Pushkin, vol. I: 'K molodoi vdove', 'K Natashe' and 'K molodoi aktrise'.

23 Pushchin, *Zapiski*, pp. 105–06, relates the corridor episode. Pushkin's account of his meeting with Bakunina is in Pushkin, vol. VIII, p. 10.

24 Pushkin, vol. I, 'K drugu stikhotvortsu'.

25 Repin lived from 1844 to 1930. Pushkin's own account was written twenty years later (Pushkin, vol. VIII, pp. 65 ff.), but it was confirmed by Pushchin, *Zapiski*, p. 103. For Derzhavin's subsequent remarks about Pushkin, see Tsyavlovsky, *Letopis'*, p. 88, and S. T. Aksakov, *Semeinaya khronika i vospominaniya: znakomstvo s Del'vigom* (Moscow, 1856), p. 524.

26 *Evgenii Onegin*, Chapter 8, Stanza 1.

27 Cited in full in Tsyavlovsky, *Letopis'*, p. 133–4.

28 Pushkin, vol. II, 'Yur'evu'.

29 Ibid., vol. I, 'Tovarishcham'. For Pushkin's own judgement of his personal conceit (*tshcheslavie*), see Pushkin, vol. VIII, *Dnevniki*, p. 75 (referring to 1814).

Chapter Four, *St. Petersburg, 1817–1820*

1 Pushkin, vol. I, extract from *Derevnya*.

2 Ibid., vol. VIII, p. 19.

3 Ibid., *Evgenii Onegin*, Chapter 1, Stanzas XV–XXXVI.

4 From his uncle, whose death occurs in the first chapter of *Evgenii Onegin*.

5 Pushkin, vol. I, 'Rusalka', trans. Fennell, *Pushkin: Selected Verse*, pp. 5–6.

6 According to a British Foreign Office anecdote, early in the twentieth century the head of one of its departments observed that his daily schedule (still timed to begin at the hour when, in an earlier age, the mail used to arrive from Dover – mid-morning – and to end promptly at five o'clock) 'rather cut into his day'.

7 Pushkin, vol. III, *Elegiya:* 'Bezumnych let ugasshee vesel'e'.

8 Pavel Vyazemsky, *Sobranie sochinenii* (St. Petersburg, 1893), p. 515.

9 Mirsky, *Pushkin*, pp. 41, 47–8.

10 Aleksei Olenin (1763–1843) was, among many other offices that he held, president of the Academy of Arts. For Anna Kern, see Chapter 6.

11 A man's account of his own sexual successes and failures is notoriously unreliable. Nevertheless, in 1829 Pushkin attempted to write down just such a list, of thirty-seven names, in the album of Elizaveta Ushakova in Moscow. This has since come to be known as Pushkin's 'Don Juan' list: Pushkin, vol. VIII, pp. 73–4.

12 Ibid., vol. I, 'O. Masson'.

13 Ibid., vol. X, Pushkin to Pavel Mansurov, 27 October 1819 (no. 9 in Shaw, *Letters*, Vol. I). For Disraeli, see Robert Blake, *Disraeli* (Methuen, London, 1969, first published Eyre and Spottiswoode, 1966), pp. 62, 73. Mercury remained one of the standard treatments for syphilis well into the twentieth century.

14 See Pushkin, *Polnoe sobranie sochinenii*, Academy edition, 16 vols (Moscow, 1939), vol. XII, p. 305; and Tsyavlovsky, *Letopis'*, pp. 155–6. For the translation of Pushkin's illness as *une fièvre gangreneuse*, see Troyat, *Pouchkine*, p. 139.

15 Annenkov, *Pushkin v Aleksandrovskuyu epokhu*, pp. 112–13.

16 Pushchin, *Zapiski*, pp. 117–18, describes his own decision when both of them were in St. Petersburg.

17 In conversation with Engelhardt, cited by Tsyavlovsky, *Letopis'*, p. 205.

18 All three poems are to be found in Pushkin, vol. I: *Derevnya*, 'Vol'nost' and 'Skazki, Noel'.

19 See Chapter 1.

20 Pushkin, vol. IV, *Ruslan i Lyudmila*.

21 This preface and an epilogue added while Pushkin was in the Caucasus later in 1820 are both in the same volume (IV). Baba Yaga was a wicked magician and King Kashchey was a wicked and rich old man in Russian folklore. For both identifications I am indebted to Dimitri Obolensky.

22 Annenkov assesses this paradox in *Pushkin v Aleksandrovskuyu epokhu*, Chapters III and IV.

23 Pushkin, vol. III, *Moya rodoslovaya*. For a full translation of this poem, see Fennell, *Pushkin: Selected Verse,* pp. 64–7.

24 Nabokov – in his *Onegin*, vol. 2, pp. 5 ff. – proves conclusively that this French epigraph was not a quotation at all, but was written by Pushkin himself.

Chapter Five, *The South*

1 Pushkin, vol. II, 'K Ovidiyu' (in alexandrines).

2 Ovid, 'His Autobiography', *The Oxford Book of Latin Verse* (Clarendon Press, Oxford, 1934, first published 1912), p. 235.

3 See Pushkin's note on *Evgenii Onegin*, Chapter 1, Stanza VIII, in the first edition.

4 Natan Eidel'man, *Pervyi dekabrist* (Izdatel'stvo politicheskoi literatury, Moscow, 1990), p. 126.

5 Annenkov, *Materialy,* p. 87, put forward this suggestion.

6 Rudykovsky published a detailed account – 'Vstrecha s Pushkinom (iz zapisok medika)' – in *Russkii vestnik* (St. Petersburg), 1841, no. 1. *Nedorosl'* – the word that Pushkin wrote against his own name in the visitors' book – has implications not easily rendered in English. The best translation is the French slang word '*ado*'.

7 *Russian Journal of Lady Londonderry, 1836-7,* ed. W. Seaman and J. Sewell (John Murray, London, 1973), pp. 137–8. When the road became impassable for the wheels of comfortable vehicles, travellers were obliged to transfer to a *telega* (a Russian wagon). I am indebted for this quotation to Laurence Kelly, who describes the hazards of Caucasian travel in *Lermontov: tragedy in the Caucasus,* Robin Clark, London, 1983, first published Constable, 1977, pp. 27–8.

8 Pushkin, vol. X, Pushkin to Lev Sergeevich Pushkin, 24 September 1820 (no. 11 in Shaw, *Letters,* vol. I).

9 The Russo-Turkish conflict, resumed in the First World War, was brought to a standstill by the Congress of Berlin (Disraeli's 'peace with honour') in 1878. Joseph Stalin was born (Djugashvili) in Gori, Georgia, a year later.

10 Pushkin, vol. IV, *Kavkazkii plennik.*

11 Ibid., vol. X, Pushkin to H. H. Gnedich, 27 June 1822 (no. 27 in Shaw, *Letters,* vol. I).

12 Ibid., vol. VI, *Puteshestvie v Arzrum vo vremya pochoda 1829 goda* (which records his visit to the front in eastern Turkey), p. 651.

13 Pushkin, vol. X, Pushkin to Vyazemsky, 6 February 1823 (no. 40 in Shaw, *Letters*, vol. I). This refusal (to point a moral or adorn a tale) became an essential Pushkinian device.

14 *Mémoires de la Princesse Marie Volkonsky*, ed. Prince Michel Volkonsky (St. Petersburg, 1904), p. 19.

15 *Evgenii Onegin*, Chapter 1, stanza XXXVIII, lines 5–6 (lines that have evoked some preposterous English verse translations).

16 See Nabokov, *Onegin*, vol. II, pp. 121–2; and for the pedal digression as a whole ibid., pp. 155 ff.

17 A continuation of Pushkin's letter to his brother: see note 8.

18 Pushkin, vol. IV, *Bakchisaraiskii fontan.*

19 Ibid., vol. X, Pushkin to Vyazemsky, 14 October 1823 (no. 48 in Shaw, *Letters*, vol. I).

20 Discussed by John Fennell (ed.), 'Pushkin', in *Nineteenth-Century Russian Literature: Studies of Ten Russian Writers* (University of California Press, Berkeley and Los Angeles, 1976), pp. 14–16. See also Mirsky, *Pushkin*, pp. 61 ff.

21 Translated by Tatiana Wolff, *Pushkin on Literature*, revised edition (Athlone Press, London and Stanford University Press, Stanford, California, 1986, first published, Methuen, 1971), p. 221.

22 Pushkin, vol. VIII, *Dnevniki*, p. 17.

23 Tsyavlovsky, *Letopis'*, pp. 292–3.

24 Cited in Woodhouse, *Capodistria*, p. 236.

25 See Annenkov, *Pushkin v Aleksandrovskuyu epokhu*, p. 196.

26 Eidel'man, *Pervyi dekabrist*, p. 381. This paragraph and the two that follow are both indebted to Eidel'man's book, passim.

27 The letter of his appointment, written in St. Petersburg, is cited in Woodhouse, *Capodistria*, pp. 230–31.

28 Ibid., pp. 252 ff.

29 Pushkin, vol. X, Pushkin to Vyazemsky, 24–25 June 1824 (no. 73 in Shaw, *Letters*, vol. I).

30 Ibid., vol. X, the draft of a letter of early March 1821 (no. 14 in Shaw, *Letters*, vol. I).

31 Cited in Woodhouse, *Capodistria*, p. 291.

32 Annenkov, *Pushkin v Aleksandrovskuyu epokhu*, p. 160.

33 In imperial Russian times the province of Bessarabia was bounded by the River Dnestr to the east and by the River Prut to the west. Its capital,

Kishinev, became the capital of the Moldavian Republic in the Soviet period.

34 Pushkin, vol. X, Pushkin to Count Nesselrode (in French), 13 January 1823.

35 Ibid., vol. II, 'Kindzhal', a poem inspired by the stabbing of a reactionary German dramatist, Kotzebue, by a student in 1819. Kotzebue was thought to be in the pay of the Russian government.

36 Pushkin, vol. IV, *Gavriliada.*

37 Ibid., vol. II, *Tsar Nikita i sorok ego docherei.*

38 See Chapter 8.

39 Pushkin, vol. IV, *Brat'ya razboiniki;* and vol. X, Pushkin to Vyazemsky, 4 November 1823 (no. 51 in Shaw, *Letters,* vol. I).

40 Ibid., vol. X, Pushkin to A. Bestuzhev, 24 March 1825 (no. 111 in Shaw, *Letters,* vol. I).

41 Ibid., vol. IV, *Tsygany.*

42 Views discussed by John Bayley, *Pushkin: A Comparative Commentary* (Cambridge University Press, Cambridge, 1971), pp. 101 ff.

43 For the concept of Pushkin's 'stylistic polyphony', see Fennell, 'Pushkin', in *Nineteenth-Century Russian Literature,* pp. 31 ff.

44 For a full translation of this poem, see Fennell, *Pushkin: Selected Verse,* pp. 77–109.

45 Pushkin, vol. X, Pushkin to Vyazemsky, March 1823 (no. 41 in Shaw, *Letters,* vol. I).

46 See the correspondence between Turgenev and Vyazemsky, May–June 1823, cited in Tsyavlovsky, *Letopis',* pp. 385–7.

47 Pushkin, vol. X, Pushkin to A. I. Kaznacheev, after 2 June 1824 (no. 47 in Shaw, *Letters,* vol. I).

48 Ibid., vol. X, Pushkin to Lev Sergeevich Pushkin, 25 August 1824 (no. 47 in Shaw, *Letters,* vol. I).

49 Pushkin, *Evgenii Onegin,* 'Excerpts from Onegin's Journey', the stanzas beginning with the line: 'I lived then in Odessa . . .'

50 In Pushkin's day the Russian word *krasavitsa* (a beauty) was used to mean little more than a pretty girl.

51 Pushkin, vol. X, Pushkin to Alexander Turgenev, 14 July 1824 (no. 76 in Shaw, *Letters,* vol. I).

52 Ibid., vol. II, 'Polu-milord, polu-kupets.'

53 Ibid., vol. X, Pushkin to Kaznacheev, 22 May 1824, rough draft (no. 69 in Shaw, *Letters,* vol. I).

54 Ibid., vol. X, Pushkin to Vyazemsky, 8 March 1824 (no. 64 in Shaw, *Letters*, vol. I).

55 Tsyavlovsky, *Letopis'*, pp. 445 ff.

56 Pushkin, vol. X, Pushkin to (?) Küchelbecker (a fragment), first half of (?) May 1824 (no. 68 in Shaw, *Letters*, vol. I).

57 On Hutchinson, see L. M. Arinstein, 'Odesskii sobesednik Pushkina', in *Vremennik Pushkinskoi komissii* (Academy of Sciences USSR, Leningrad, 1975), pp. 58 ff. This article makes it hard to accept as accurate the story (recounted by some Pushkinists) that Hutchinson later took holy orders.

58 Tsyavlovsky, *Letopis'*, pp. 488–99.

59 Some are cited in Troyat, *Pouchkine*, pp. 283–4.

60 See, for example, Pushkin, vol. II, 'Prostish' li mne revnivye mechty.'

61 Ibid., vol. III, *Talisman*. For a list of the sources of evidence for the Pushkin–Vorontsova relationship, see Tsyavlovsky, *Letopis'*, p. 413.

Chapter Six, *Exile at Mikhailovskoe*

1 Pushkin, vol. VI, *K moryu*. For a full translation of this poem, see Fennell, *Pushkin: Selected Verse*, pp. 13–16.

2 Pushkin, vol. X, Pushkin to Lev Pushkin, late November 1824 (no. 90 in Shaw, *Letters*, vol. I); and Tsyavlovsky, *Letopis'*, pp. 468–77.

3 Pushkin, vol. X, Pushkin to Zhukovsky, 31 October 1824 (no. 87 in Shaw, *Letters*, vol. I).

4 For the reactions of Pushkin's friends to his exile, see Tsyavlovsky, *Letopis'*, pp. 432–90.

5 *Westminster Review*, January 1824, pp. 80–101.

6 See page 63.

7 The *Conversation of the bookseller with the poet* was originally the preface to *Evgenii Onegin*: see Pushkin, vol. II, *Razgovor knigoprodavtsa s poetom*, pp. 191–7. It later became a poem in its own right.

8 Ibid., vol. IV, *Graf Nulin*.

9 Ibid., vol. V, *Boris Godunov*.

10 Admirably assembled and edited by Wolff, *Pushkin on Literature*.

11 Pushkin, vol. X, Pushkin to Nicholas Raevsky Jr., late July 1825, a draft written in French (no. 139 in Shaw, *Letters*, vol. I).

12 On the question of metre, see Nabokov, *Onegin*, vol. I, pp. 10 ff.

13 Pushkin, vol. VII, 'Table Talk', p. 516.

14 Ibid., vol. X, Pushkin to Vyazemsky, about 7 November 1825 (no. 161 in Shaw, *Letters*, vol. I).

15 So described after Pushkin's death by V. G. Belinsky, *Polnoe sobranie sochinenii* (13 vols, Moscow, 1935–39), vol. VII, p. 505. On *Boris Godunov*, see further in Chapters 8 and 11.

16 Musorgsky's work was first produced in 1874 in St. Petersburg, having been turned down by the Opera there four years earlier.

17 See Nabokov, *Onegin*, vol. III, pp 312 ff.

18 E.g., whereas for Belinsky it was 'an encyclopaedia of Russian life', for Nabokov it was not a picture of Russian life at all. See Fennell, 'Pushkin', in *Nineteenth-Century Russian Literature*, pp. 36–7, for these and other Russian opinions of *Evgenii Onegin*.

19 Cited in Paul Debreczeny, *The Other Pushkin: a study of Pushkin's prose fiction* (Stanford University Press, Stanford, California, 1983), pp. 30, 307.

20 Pushkin, vol. X, p. 107, sketch and letter from Pushkin to Lev Pushkin, 1–10 November 1824 (no. 88(a) in Shaw, *Letters*, vol. I).

21 *Byla by vernaya supruga i dobrodetel'naya mat'*: a beautiful line which illustrates the difficulty of rendering Pushkin's deceptively simple verse into convincing English.

22 Pushkin, vol. X, Pushkin to Lev Pushkin, about 20 December 1824 (no. 96 in Shaw, *Letters*, vol. I) – one of many examples.

23 Ibid., continuation of the same letter; and Pushkin to Lev Pushkin, 22 and 23 April 1825 (no. 118 in Shaw, *Letters*, vol. I). (For 'braces', American readers should read 'suspenders'.)

24 A description compiled from a variety of sources by Tsyavlovsky, *Letopis'*, pp. 449–50.

25 Boldino was part of Pushkin's father's estate, east of Moscow.

26 Tsyavlovsky, *Letopis'*, pp. 487, 501, 628. The letter to Vyazemsky is dated late April/early May 1826, in Pushkin, vol. X (no. 181 in Shaw, *Letters*, vol. I).

27 The best account of this complicated family is that set out in the Osipov and Vul'f entries in Chereisky, *Pushkin i ego okruzhenie*, (Nauka, Leningrad, 1975). The Turgenev quotation is on p. 295.

28 Mirsky, *Pushkin*, p. 77.

29 A. P. Kern, *Vospominaniya o Pushkine* (Sovetskaya Rossiya, Moscow, 1988), pp. 72–3.

30 Anna Kern, *Vospominaniya*, pp. 40 ff. gives her own account of her 1825 meeting with Pushkin in her (not always accurate) memoirs.

31 Pushkin, vol. II, *K* * * *, 'Ya pomnyu chudnoe mgnoven'e'.

32 Pushkin, vol. III, 'Ya vas lyubil.'

33 Pushkin, vol. X, Pushkin to Sergei Sobolevsky, second half of February 1828 (no. 226 in Shaw, *Letters*, vol. II).

34 Ibid., vol. X, Pushkin to Vyazemsky, second half of September 1825 (no. 158 in Shaw, *Letters*, vol. I).

35 I. I. Pushchin, *Zapiski o Pushkine* (Moscow, 1925), pp. 123 ff, the source of this paragraph and the next one.

36 Pushkin, vol. II, 'Moy pervyi drug, moy drug bestsennyi!' See also Eidel'man, *Conspiracy against the Tsar*, pp. 268–9. Chita is situated to the east of Lake Baikal, north of the Mongolian frontier.

37 Tsyavlovsky, *Letopis'*, p. 482.

38 Pushkin, vol. VIII, pp. 69–71.

39 Ibid., vol. X, *Aleksandru I* (in French).

40 Tsyavlovsky, *Letopis'*, pp. 577 and 682–3.

Chapter Seven, *The First Caesura, 1825–1826*

1 Cited in Klyuchevsky, *Sochineniya*, vol. V, p. 254.

2 Text in N. K. Schil'der, *Imperator Nikolai I*, vol. I, pp. 298 ff.

3 There have been many accounts of the Decembrist Revolt. There is general agreement on what happened in St. Petersburg, but the clearest account of the southern conspiracy is that of N. Eidel'man, particularly in his *Conspiracy against the Tsar*.

4 See *Dokumenty po istorii vosstaniya dekabristov*, ed. M. V. Nechkina, 11 vols (Moscow, 1958).

5 For an account of the Cato Street conspiracy see E. P. Thompson, *The Making of the English Working Class* (Penguin Books, Harmondsworth, 1980, first published Victor Gollancz, 1963), pp. 769 ff.

6 Cited in Eidel'man, *Conspiracy against the Tsar*, p. 193.

7 Ibid., p. 85.

8 Pushkin, vol. X, Pushkin to Vyazemsky, 14 August 1826 (no. 188 in Shaw, *Letters*, vol. I).

9 Ibid., vol. X, Pushkin to Zhukovsky (and intended also to be read by Karamzin), 20 January 1826 (no. 172 in Shaw, *Letters*, vol. I).

10 Tsyavlovsky, *Letopis'*, p. 612; and N. Eidel'man, *Pushkin i dekabristy* (Khudozhestvennaya literatura, Moscow, 1979), Chapter 10.

11 Pushkin, vol. X, Pushkin to Nicholas I, 11 May to first half of June 1826 (no. 186 in Shaw, *Letters*, vol. I).

12 Adam Mickiewicz, *Sobrannye sochineniya*, 5 vols (Goslitizdat, Moscow, 1945), vol. III, pp. 386–7.

13 For an account of Pushkin during these critical weeks, see Tsyavlovsky, *Letopis'*, pp. 628 ff.

14 Pushkin, vol. X, Pushkin to P. A. Osipova, 4 September 1826 (no. 189 in Shaw, *Letters*, vol. I).

15 They must have at least seen each other before, either at Tsarskoe Selo or St. Petersburg or both, but this was their first real meeting.

16 De Custine, *Lettres de Russie*, p. 117. (De Custine's homosexuality was well known.) Queen Victoria's remark occurs in her letter to her uncle written in 1844: see Chapter 1, note 21.

17 Cited in V. V. Veresaev, *Pushkin v zhizni* (Moskovskii rabochii, Moscow, 1986), p. 661.

18 M. P. Pogodin, *Russkii arkhiv*, 1865, p. 97. Pogodin was editor of the *Moscow Telegraph*.

19 Under the terms of this agreement (see Seton-Watson, *The Russian Empire*, pp. 295 ff.), the two governments agreed to mediate between the Ottoman Empire and the Greeks.

20 Benckendorff to Pushkin, 30 September 1826, cited in Simmons, *Pushkin*, p. 270. Pushkin's undertaking to the tsar was subsequently spelled out by Benckendorff, in a letter of 3 May 1827 to Pushkin, who did not contest its accuracy: cited in Veresaev, *Pushkin v zhizni*, p. 71.

21 Cited in B. L. Modzalevsky, *Pushkin pod tainym nadzorom* (St. Petersburg, 1922), p. 30.

22 Pushkin, vol. X, Pushkin to P. A. Osipova, 16 September 1826 (in French) (no. 190 in Shaw, *Letters*, vol. II).

23 Recorded – among others – by P. I. Bartenev, *Russkii arkhiv*, 1865, pp. 96, 389.

24 For the staircase story, see Veresaev, *Pushkin v zhizni*, pp. 30–1.

25 First published in the *Slavonic Review*, vol. XVI, no. 34, July 1933, pp. 1–2.

26 On the questions involved in this much discussed poem, see D. D. Blagoi, *Tvorcheskii put' Pushkina, 1813–26* (Izdatel'stvo Akademiya nauk, Moscow/Leningrad, 1950), vol. I, pp. 533 ff. And – in English – see Bayley, *Pushkin*, pp. 145 ff.

27 Pushkin appears to have recounted this incident to his brother, Lev: see Veresaev, *Pushkin v zhizni*, p. 26.

28 Pushkin, vol. II, 'Svobody seyatel' pustynnyi, ya vyshel rano, do zvezdy', written in 1823.

29 Eidel'man, *Pushkin i dekabristy*, pp. 137, 147 ff. (For Lunin, see Chapter 1).

30 Ibid., p. 283.

31 I. D. Yakushkin, *Zapiski, stat'i, pis'ma* (Academy of Sciences, USSR, Moscow, 1951), p. 43.

32 Pushchin, *Zapiski o Pushkine*, pp. 133–4.

33 Pushkin's account is cited in Veresaev, *Pushkin v zhizni*, p. 87.

34 Shakespeare, *Julius Caesar*, Act III, Scene I.

Chapter Eight, '*The New Pushkin*'

1 Stanza XLV – the epigraph to the present chapter – is the penultimate stanza of Chapter 6 of *Evgenii Onegin*, which Pushkin wrote – according to his own note – on 10 August 1826.

2 Of Byron's return to London (aged twenty-four) after his return from the East, his biographer, Thomas Moore, wrote: 'The effect was . . . electric, his fame . . . seemed to spring, like the palace of a fairy king, in a night.'

3 See A. V. Venevitinov, *Russkaya starina*, vol. 12, 1875, p. 822, for an account of the evening in Moscow.

4 Pushkin, vol. III, 'Vo glubine sibirskikh rud.'

5 Ibid., vol. IV, p. 253, *Poltava*.

6 Both letters (dated 17 October 1826 and both in French) are cited in B. L. Modzhalevsky, *Pushkin pod tainym nadzorom* (St. Petersburg, 1922), pp. 31–2.

7 The house of Anna Venevitinova, mother of the brothers Aleksei and Dmitrii Venevitinov, distant cousins of Pushkin.

8 M. P. Pogodin, *Russkii arkhiv*, 1865, p. 97.

9 Pushkin, vol X, Pushkin to Benckendorff, 29 November 1826 (no. 197 in Shaw, *Letters*, vol. II).

10 Ibid., Pushkin to Benckendorff, 3 January 1827; see also Troyat, *Pouchkine*, p. 408.

11 Ibid., vol. II, 'Andrei Shen'e'. Who added the additional title is uncertain, but it was not Pushkin: see the note on p. 429 of this volume.

12 Ibid., vol. X, Pushkin to Vyazemsky, 1 September 1828 (no. 234 in Shaw, *Letters*, vol. II) and vol. IV, notes on pp. 551–2. See also Veresaev, *Pushkin v zhizni*, pp. 115 ff.

13 Cited in Ronald Hingley (quoting the historian Florinsky), *Russian Writers and Society, 1825–1904* (Weidenfeld & Nicolson, London, 1967), p. 101. See also Seton-Watson, *The Russian Empire*, pp. 199 ff.

14 Pushkin, vol. VII, *O narodnom vospitanii*, pp. 42 ff. See also Troyat, *Pouchkine*, p. 411.

15 After Pushkin's death Pletnev described himself as having been 'everything – both relation, friend and cashier' to Pushkin: cited in Chereisky, *Pushkin i ego okruzhenie*, p. 312.

16 For the *Literaturnaya gazeta*, see Annenkov, *Materialy*, Chapter XXI.

17 Pushkin, vol. X, Pushkin to Vyazemsky, 1 December 1826 (no. 199 in Shaw, *Letters*, vol. II).

18 Ibid., vol. VI, pp. 581–2.

19 The account of this occasion, written by a Polish eyewitness, Edward Odyniec, in May 1829, is quoted (in Russian translation) in Veresaev, *Pushkin v zhizni*, p. 43.

20 Pushkin, vol. III, *Vospominanie*. For the encounter in the street, see Vyazemsky, *Sochineniya*, vol. III, p. 309.

21 Notably, a personal attack by Mickiewicz on Pushkin in verses added to Part III of his *Forefathers' Eve*. For Pushkin's reply written in 1831 – 'On mezhdu nami zhil' ('He lived among us') – see Pushkin, vol. III.

22 Translated by Arthur P. Coleman, 'Pushkin and Mickiewicz', in *Centennial Essays for Pushkin*, pp. 97 and 102. The view, once held, that Mickiewicz was referring not to Pushkin in these lines, but to Ryleev, is no longer sustainable: see Walter Lednicki, 'Mickiewicz's stay in Russia, and his friendship with Pushkin', in *Adam Mickiewicz in World Literature* (University of California Press, Berkeley and Los Angeles, October 1956), p. 88.

23 Translated by Vyazemsky, *Sochineniya*, vol. III, p. 315.

24 Pushkin, vol. X, Pushkin to Vyazemsky, 9 November 1826 (no. 194 in Shaw, *Letters*, vol. II).

25 Ibid., Pushkin to V. P. Zubkov, 1 December 1826 (no. 200 in Shaw, *Letters*, vol. II).

26 Vyazemsky to Turgenev, 18 April 1828, *Arkhiv brat'ev Turgenevykh* (Petrograd), vol. VI, 1921, p. 65.

27 Vyazemsky's description of Elizaveta's feelings is in his *Sochineniya*, vol. III, p. 521. For *The Queen of Spades* episode, see Chapter 11.

28 Pushkin, vol. X, Pushkin to Benckendorff, 21 April 1828 (no. 229 and note on p. 391 in Shaw, *Letters*, vol. II).

29 Pushkin, vol. III, 'Brozhu li ya vdol' ulits shumnykh'.

30 For a brief account, see Chereisky, *Pushkin i ego okruzhenie*, p. 318.

31 *Vestnik Evropy*, 1830, no. 7.

32 Nikolai Nadezhdin, cited in Troyat, *Pouchkine*, p. 438.

33 Pushkin, vol. II, 'Stansy', and vol. III, 'Druz'yam', together with note on p. 485.

34 Ibid., vol. VII, pp. 168–9, and vol. IV, p. 347, Stanza XIV of *Ezersky*. For *Exegi Monumentum*, see Introduction.

35 Ibid., vol. III, *Portret* and *Napersnik*. On Pushkin and Agrafena Zakrevskaya, see – for example – Vyazemsky to Alexander Turgenev, 15 October 1828, *Ostafevskii arkhiv*, vol. III, p. 179.

36 Pushkin, vol. X, Pushkin to Zubkov, 1 December 1826 (no. 200 in Shaw, *Letters*, vol. II).

37 Vyazemsky to his wife, 21 May 1828, cited in Veresaev, *Pushkin v zhizni*, pp. 112–13.

38 Pushkin, vol. III, *Ty i Vy*.

39 Ibid., vol. III, 'Gorod pyshnyi'; and see notes, p. 488.

40 Ibid., vol. III, 'Otvet'. Presna is a district of Moscow.

41 E.g. Vyazemsky to his wife, 20 March 1830, cited in Chereisky, *Pushkin i ego okruzhenie*, p. 435; and see also P. I. Bartenev, 'Iz zapiskoi knizhki', *Russkii arkhiv*, vol. III, 1912, p. 300.

42 The reason for this destruction comes from Bartenev's account, cited in the preceding note.

43 See Pushkin, vol. VIII, pp. 73–4.

44 Ibid., vol. VI, *Puteshestvie v Arzrum vo vremya pokhoda 1829 goda*, the source of all subsequent quotations from Pushkin's own account of his journey in the rest of this chapter. See also Annenkov, *Materialy*, p. 207.

45 Pushkin, vol. VI, *Puteshestvie v Arzrum*, p. 666.

46 The accounts of this episode recorded by M. I. Pushchin and N. I. Ushakov are quoted in Veresaev, *Pushkin v zhizni*, pp. 176–7. The onlookers' supposition that Pushkin was a Lutheran chaplain derives from a letter (not preserved) received by Nashchokin from Pushkin at the time: see P. I. Bartenev, *Devyatnadtsatyi vek* (Moscow), vol. I, 1872, p. 402.

47 Pushkin, vol. X, Pushkin to Benckendorff, 10 November 1829 (no. 251 in Shaw, *Letters*, vol. II).

48 Ibid., Pushkin to N. I. Goncharova, 1 May 1829 (no. 246 in Shaw, *Letters*, vol. II).

49 Count Fedor Tolstoy, nicknamed 'the American' because of a visit that he had made to the Aleutian Islands, acted as Pushkin's intermediary for his first proposal of marriage to Natalya, although some years earlier he and Pushkin had come close to fighting a duel.

50 Veresaev, *Pushkin v zhizni*, p. 193.

51 Pushkin, vol. X, Pushkin to Benckendorff, 7 January 1830 (no. 255 in Shaw, *Letters*, vol. II).

52 Ibid., Pushkin to Vyazemsky, end of January 1830 (no. 260 in Shaw, *Letters*, vol. II).

Chapter Nine, *The Second Caesura: Marriage*

1 Pushkin, vol. X, Pushkin to N. I. Goncharova, 5 April and (in draft) to his parents, 6–11 April 1830 (nos. 271 and 272 in Shaw, *Letters*, vol. II). There is, however, no evidence to support the last paragraph of Troyat's *Pouchkine*, p. 471.

2 Pushkin, vol. X, Pushkin to his wife, 21 August 1833 (no. 456 in Shaw, *Letters*, vol. III).

3 Notably, P. Obodovskaya and M. Dement'ev, in their *Natal'ya Nikolaevna Pushkina po epistolyarnym materialam*, 2nd edn (Sovetskaya Rossiya, Moscow, 1987). The two pejorative descriptions are quoted from P. E. Shchegolev, *Duel' i smert' Pushkina: issledovanie i materialy*, 3rd edn (Gosizdat, Moscow/Leningrad, 1928), p. 49; and from Anna Akhmatova, *O Pushkine*, p. 295.

4 Cited in Troyat, *Pouchkine*, p. 477. One year younger than Natalya Nikolaevna, Sollogub first met the Pushkins at Tsarskoe Selo in 1831.

5 *Evgenii Onegin*, Chapter 3, Stanza XXVI.

6 Pushkin, vol. X, Pushkin to N. I. Goncharova, 5 April 1830 (no. 271 in Shaw, *Letters*, vol. II).

7 Ibid., Pushkin to his parents (draft), 6–11 April 1830 (no. 272 in Shaw, *Letters*, vol. II); and see B. L. Modzhalevsky, *Pushkin i ego sovremenniki*, vol. XIII, p. 99, cited in Veresaev, *Pushkin v zhizni*, p. 217.

8 Pushkin, vol. X, Pushkin to Benckendorff, 16 April 1830 (no. 273 in Shaw, *Letters*, vol. II).

9 Cited in Veresaev, *Pushkin v zhizni*, p. 212.

10 Pushkin, vol. X, Pushkin to P. A. Pletnev, 5 May 1830 (no. 280 in Shaw, *Letters*, vol. II). On the publication of *Boris Godunov*, see Chapter 11.

11 Cited in Veresaev, *Pushkin v zhizni*, p. 211.

12 Ibid., p. 220.

13 Ibid., p. 665.

14 Pushkin, vol. X, Pushkin to Elizaveta Khitrovo, 19–24 May 1830 (no. 284 in Shaw, *Letters*, vol. II).

15 See Chapter 8, note 16.

16 Pushchin, *Zapiski o Pushkine*, p. 132.

17 The brief account of the Goncharov family given in this and succeeding paragraphs is indebted to P. Obodovskaya's and M. Dement'ev's book (Note 3).

18 For Natal'ya Ivanovna's *poshlost'*, see the description of her quoted by P. I. Bartenev in Veresaev, *Pushkin v zhizni*, p. 244.

19 Pushkin, vol. X, Pushkin to Benckendorff, 29 May 1830 (no. 287 in Shaw, *Letters*, vol. II); and to A. N. Goncharov, 9 September 1830 (no. 312 in Shaw).

20 Ibid., Pushkin to P. A. Pletnev, about 16 February 1831 (no. 349 in Shaw, *Letters*, vol. II).

21 Ibid., Pushkin to Vyazemsky, 3 September 1831 (no. 395 in Shaw, *Letters*, vol. II); and for the triangular deal, see Pushkin to Nashchokin, 22 October 1831 (no. 405 in Shaw, *Letters*, vol. II and note in Shaw, p. 576).

22 Woodhouse, *Capodistria*, p. 60.

23 The full story, in its two versions, came to light early in the present century: see Veresaev, *Pushkin v zhizni*, pp. 258-9. References in Pushkin's correspondence suggest that if the transaction was eventually successful, it yielded only 5500 roubles.

24 Pushkin, vol. X, Pushkin to A. N. Goncharov (no. 307 in Shaw, *Letters*, vol. II).

25 Ibid., Pushkin to his fiancée, end of August and 9 September 1830 (nos 308 and 311 in Shaw, *Letters*, vol. II).

26 It was at Boldino that the small, single-storey manor house of the Pushkin estate (a far more modest house than that at Mikhailovskoe – it did not even have a garden) was situated. Pushkin always stayed there when visiting the estate in the 1830s.

27 Pushkin, vol. X, Pushkin to his fiancée, 4 November, and to Elizaveta Khitrovo, 11 December 1830 (nos 319 and 332 in Shaw, *Letters*, vol. II).

28 Ibid., Pushkin to Pletnev, 21 January 1831 (no. 344 in Shaw, *Letters*, vol. II).

29 Ibid., Pushkin to N. I. Krivstov, 10 February 1831 (no. 348 in Shaw, *Letters*, vol. II).

30 According to his sister, Olga Sergeevna: see Veresaev, *Pushkin v zhizni*, pp. 256–7.

31 Ibid., p. 258, citing A. Ya. Bulgakov's letter of 28 February 1831 (published in *Russkii arkhiv*, 1902); and Pushkin, vol. X, Pushkin to Pletnev, 26 March, 11 April and about 14 April 1831 (nos 354, 356 and 357 in Shaw, *Letters*, vol. II).

32 Pushkin, vol. X, Pushkin to N. N. Goncharova, 26 June 1831 (no. 371 in Shaw, *Letters*, vol. II).

33 This suggestion is Shaw's: *Letters*, vol. II, note on p. 509.

34 Pushkin, vol. X, Pushkin to Pletnev, 22 July 1831 (no. 381 in Shaw, *Letters*, vol. II).

35 Both these letters, of 21 and 25 May 1831 respectively, are cited in Veresaev, *Pushkin v zhizni*, pp. 263–4.

36 Obodovskaya and Dement'ev, *Natal'ya Nikolaevna Pushkina*, p. 63, state – but without adducing any hard evidence – that Natalya's 'feelings of happiness' at this time are 'easy to imagine'. Troyat, *Pouchkine*, p. 547, similarly resorts to guesswork.

37 Pushkin, vol. II, *Madona: sonet*, written on 8 July 1830. See also Veresaev, *Pushkin v zhizni*, p. 218.

38 Examples of interpretation which I do not share are Troyat, *Pouchkine*, pp. 572–4 and Simmons, *Pushkin*, p. 348.

39 Pushkin, vol. III, 'Kogda v ob''yatiya'.

40 Ibid., B. V. Tomashevsky's note on p. 531.

41 Ibid., *Net, ya ne dorozhu*.

Chapter Ten, *Imbroglio in St. Petersburg, 1831–1835*

1 Pushkin, vol. IV, *Tsygany*.

2 An observation well made by Akhmatova, *O Pushkine*, pp. 110 ff. (The crucial date in the d'Anthès affair is 4 November 1836, when Pushkin received his copy of the famous anonymous letter: see Chapters 12–13.)

3 Pavel Vyazemsky, *Sochineniya*, p. 555.

4 Quoted by C. K. Webster, *The Congress of Vienna, 1814–15* (Humphrey Milford, London, 1919), p. 101.

5 For the Southern victories, see Chapter 8; and for an account of the Polish Rebellion and the Russo-Polish war, see Seton-Watson, *The Russian Empire*, pp. 282 ff. (These events, taking place in Poland, are dated according to the Gregorian calendar.)

6 The middle and lower ranks of the Polish government machinery remained Polish, but the Polish army was abolished. The Polish assemblies which should have been established at district and provincial level, according to the new Organic Statute of February 1832, never materialized.

7 A remark made by Talleyrand – by then French ambassador in London – in January 1838, according to the Vicomte de Guichen, *La Révolution de*

Juillet et l'Europe, 1917 (cited in the Preface to Custine, *Lettres de Russie*, p. 23). For Palmerston, see Jasper Ridley, *Lord Palmerston* (Constable, London, 1970), pp. 143 ff.

8 Under the terms of the London Protocol of 3 February 1830, signed by Britain, France and Russia.

9 Pushkin, vol. X, Pushkin to Vyazemsky, 1 June 1831 (no. 363 in Shaw, *Letters*, vol. II).

10 Pushkin, vol. III, 'Klevetnikam Rossii'. For a full translation of this poem, see Fennell, *Pushkin: Selected Verse*, pp. 69–71.

11 Vyazemsky, *Sochineniya*, vol. IX, p. 158.

12 Talleyrand's celebrated remark '*C'est plus qu'un crime, c'est une bêtise,*' made about Napoleon on learning of the assassination of the Duc d'Enghien, could well be applied to Pushkin on this occasion.

13 For an account of these settlements, see Seton-Watson, *The Russian Empire*, pp. 161–3. Briefly, Arakcheev persuaded the tsar to authorize him to settle troops on the land, subject to military discipline. By 1825 these hated colonies had a total population of three quarters of a million people.

14 This letter is Stanza XXXII in *Evgenii Onegin*, Chapter 8. For the 'Boldino autumns', during which almost all Pushkin's major work was written from September 1830 onwards (with the obvious exception of his *Preparatory Texts* on Peter the Great), see Chapter 11.

15 Pushkin, vol. X, Pushkin to Nashchokin, 7 October 1831 (no. 401 in Shaw, *Letters*, vol. II).

16 Ibid., Pushkin to M. O. Sudienko, 15 January 1832 (no. 419 in Shaw, *Letters*, vol. II). Sudienko was Benckendorff's adjutant from September 1827.

17 Pushkin, vol. VII, 'O proze', pp. 14–16, written in 1822 but not published until 1884.

18 Ibid., vol. X, Pushkin to his wife, 8, 10 and mid-December 1831 (nos. 412–15 in Shaw, *Letters*, vol. II). 'Little wife' is the only, though inadequate, English translation of the Russian diminutive *zhenka*.

19 Ibid., Pushkin to Nashchokin, 8–10 January 1832 (no. 418 in Shaw, *Letters*, vol. II).

20 See Pushkin's subsequent letters to Nashchokin and, for example, the letter cited in Obodovskaya and Dement'ev, *Natal'ya Nikolaevna Pushkina*, p. 73.

21 Chereisky, *Pushkin i ego okruzhenie*, p. 272.

22 Ibid., p. 152. Born in 1779, she must be distinguished from Natal'ya Zagryazhkaya, a distant relation of Pushkin's wife, who (born in 1747) probably served him as the model for the countess in his *Queen of Spades*.

23 Among several examples, see the account of one such incident, recalled by Pushkin's sister Olga, in Veresaev, *Pushkin v zhizni*, p. 292.

24 This letter, reproduced in full in Obodovskaya and Dement'ev, *Natal'ya Nikolaevna Pushkina*, pp. 79–80, is mainly concerned with the documentation required in St. Petersburg to enable Dmitrii Goncharov to take over the management of the entailed Goncharov property. For Pushkin's detailed answers to his wife's 'accusations' about his writing from Moscow, see, for example, Pushkin, vol. X, 22 September and early October 1832 (nos 436 and 440 in Shaw, *Letters*, vol. II).

25 Pushkin, vol. I, letter to Nashchokin, late February 1833 (no. 445 in Shaw, *Letters*, vol. II).

26 Annenkov, *Materialy*, pp. 331–2.

27 Loc. cit.; and see also Veresaev, *Pushkin v zhizni*, notes on pp. 410–12.

28 Pushkin, vol. X, Pushkin to Benckendorff, 8 June 1832 (no. 431 in Shaw, *Letters*, vol. II).

29 Ibid., Pushkin to Nashchokin, 2 December 1832 (no. 441 in Shaw, *Letters*, vol. II).

30 Ibid., vol. III, 'Anchar' on pp. 82–3; and see the note on p. 491.

31 Ibid., vol. X, Pushkin to Benckendorff, 7 February 1832 (no. 422 in Shaw, *Letters*, vol. II), a letter which, by a slip of the pen, Pushkin dated 7 January.

32 Ibid., Pushkin to Benckendorff, 27 May 1832, and to Mikhail Pogodin, 11 July 1832 (nos 429 and 433 in Shaw, *Letters*, vol. II).

33 Ibid., Pushkin to Benckendorff, 24 February 1832, and to Pogodin, 5 March 1832 (nos 425 and 446 in Shaw, *Letters*, vol. II).

34 Chereisky, *Pushkin i ego okruzhenie*, p. 382; and Modzhalevsky, *Pushkin*, p. 360 (the latter quoting Annenkov's notes).

35 As Annenkov rightly observed: *Materialy*, p. 185.

36 Pushkin, vol. X, Pushkin to Praskov'ya Osipova, not later than 15 May 1833 (no. 449 in Shaw, *Letters*, vol. II).

37 This letter is reproduced in full by its discoverers, I. Obodovskaya and M. Dement'ev, in *Natal'ya Nikolaevna Pushkina*, pp. 85–6.

38 Pushkin, vol. X, Pushkin to A. N. Mordvinov (Benckendorff's deputy), second draft, 30 July 1833 (no. 453 in Shaw, *Letters*, vol. III).

39 Ibid., vol. VI, *Dubrovsky*, pp. 217–316; and note on p. 771.

40 Ibid., vol. X, Pushkin to his wife, 27 August 1833 (no. 458 in Shaw, *Letters*, vol. III).

41 Ibid., Pushkin to his wife, 30 October and 6 November 1833 (nos 469 and 472 in Shaw, *Letters*, vol. III).

42 V. A. Nashchokina, 'Vospominaniya', *Novoe vremya*, 1898, no. 8122.

43 Pushkin, vol. VIII, *Dnevniki*, pp. 33–4. All subsequent diary entries by Pushkin quoted in the remainder of this chapter are derived from the same source.

44 Letter of 4 January 1834 from Natal'ya Osipovna Pushkina (Pushkin's mother) to E. N. Vrevskoi, in French, published in *Russkii vestnik*, 1869, p. 90.

45 Pushkin, vol. X, Pushkin to Nashchokin, mid-March 1834 (no. 481 in Shaw, *Letters*, vol. III). See also Pushkin's diary entry of 6 March 1834.

46 Ibid., Pushkin to I. M. Penkovsky, 13 April 1834, and to N. I. Pavlishchev (the husband of Pushkin's sister Olga), 4 May 1834 (nos 484 and 494 in Shaw, *Letters*, vol. III).

47 Ibid., Pushkin to Benckendorff, 26 and 27 February 1834, 5 and 25 March 1834. (Of these three letters, the first is no. 478 in Shaw, *Letters*, vol. III.)

48 Ibid., Pushkin to his wife, 16 and 18 May 1834 (nos 498 and 499 in Shaw, *Letters*, vol. III), confirmed by Pushkin's diary entry of 10 May. All further references in the remainder of this chapter to Pushkin's letters to his wife are derived from Pushkin, vol. X, pp. 473 ff. (pp. 641 ff. in Shaw, *Letters*, vol. III).

49 Ibid., Pushkin to Benckendorff, 25 June 1834 (no. 507 in Shaw, *Letters*, vol. III); and Benckendorff to Pushkin, 30 June 1834, cited in Veresaev, *Pushkin v zhizni*, p. 373.

50 Zhukovsky's letters to Pushkin and to the tsar during the month of July 1834 are cited in Veresaev, *Pushkin v zhizni*, pp. 374 ff. Pushkin's to Zhukovsky and Benckendorff during the same period are in Pushkin, vol. X, pp. 498 ff. (Shaw, *Letters*, vol. III, pp. 665 ff, and note on p. 688). For Pushkin's private summing up at the end of this exchange, see his diary entry of 22 July.

51 Pushkin, vol. IV, *Skazka o zolotom petushke* (trans. Fennell, *Pushkin: Selected Verse*, pp. 223–33).

52 Ibid., vol. III, 'Ne dai mne Bog soiti s uma'. For a full translation of this poem, see Fennell, *Pushkin: Selected Verse*, pp. 72–4.

53 Akhmatova, *O Pushkine*, in her chapter 'Gibel' Pushkina' (more than once).

54 For d'Anthès, see Chapter 12.

55 However the content of Alexandrina and Ekaterina Goncharova's letters (Obodovskaya and Dement'ev, *Natal'ya Nikolaevna Pushkina*, pp. 124 ff) recording their first impressions of life in the capital, may be interpreted, their style cannot seriously be regarded as 'written in beautiful light French ... often wittily' (p. 129). Natalya's letter to Dmitrii Goncharov is quoted in full on p. 149.

56 Several contemporary comments are cited in Veresaev, *Pushkin v zhizni*, pp. 405–10.

57 Pushkin, vol. X, Pushkin to Benckendorff, 22 and 26 July 1835 (nos 568 and 570 in Shaw, *Letters*, vol. III).

58 Ibid., Pushkin to Pletnev, about 11 October 1835 (no. 582 in Shaw, *Letters*, vol. III).

59 Ibid., vol. III, 'Vnov' ya posetil'.

60 Ibid., vol. X, Pushkin to Praskov'ya Osipova, 26 December 1835 (no. 587 in Shaw, *Letters*, vol. III).

61 O. S. Pavlischcheva to N. I. Pavlischchev, 31 August 1835 (in French), cited in Veresaev, *Pushkin v zhizni*, p. 405.

Chapter Eleven, *The Boldino Autumns*

1 Pushkin, *Polnoe sobranie sochinenii*, 16 vols (Academy, 1937), vol. XII, p. 305.

2 Pushkin, vol. III, *Osen'*. For a full translation of this poem, see Dimitri Obolensky, *The Heritage of Russian Verse* (Indiana University Press, Bloomington, USA, 1976, originally *The Penguin Book of Russian Verse*, Penguin Books, 1962).

3 See Preface.

4 See Mario Praz, *The Romantic Agony* (Fontana Books, 1962, first published, Oxford University Press, Oxford, 1933), p. xviii; and M. H. Abrams, 'Structure and Style in the Greater Romantic Lyric', in *From Sensibility to Romanticism*, ed. Frederick W. Hiller and Harold Bloom (Oxford University Press, New York, 1965), pp. 54 ff.

5 Pushkin's three winter poems are 'Zimnee utro' (Pushkin vol. III), 'Zimnyi vecher' and 'Zimnaya doroga' (both vol. II).

6 Ibid., vol. X, Pushkin to Zhukovsky, between 20 and 25 April 1825. The quotation from Horace is from the *Ars Poetica* – *Ut pictura, poesis*.

7 Annenkov, *Materialy*, pp. 241–2; later repeated at greater length by Pushkin in an article published in *Northern Flowers* in 1826 (see the translation of this article in Wolff, *Pushkin on Literature*, pp. 169–70).

8 Pushkin, vol. X, Pushkin to Pletnev, near the end of October 1835 (no. 582 in Shaw, *Letters*, vol. III).

9 Ibid., vol. X, Pushkin to Pletnev, 9 December 1830 (no. 330 in Shaw, *Letters*, vol. II).

10 Pushkin, vol. V, p. 322.

11 Cited in Annenkov, *Materialy*, p. 151.

12 For example, in Russian, by D. Blagoy, *Tvorcheskii put' Pushkina*, vol. I; G. Gukovsky, *Pushkin i problemy realisticheskogo stilya* (Moscow, 1957); and in English, by Bayley, *Pushkin: a comparative commentary*, pp. 108–21 and 165–85.

13 Quoted by Lednicki, 'Mickiewicz's stay in Russia and his friendship with Pushkin', p. 83 (see Chapter 8, note 22).

14 On this aspect, see Paul Debreczeny, *The Other Pushkin: a study of Pushkin's prose fiction*, (Stanford University Press, Stanford, California, 1983), pp. 61 ff.

15 Cited by Bayley, *Pushkin*, p. 354.

16 The text of the *Povesti Belkina* is in Pushkin, vol. VI, pp. 77 ff.

17 The *Istoriya Pugacheva* is in Pushkin, vol. VIII, pp. 143 ff. This summary is on p. 268 and the notes submitted to Nicholas I are on pp. 552 ff.

18 Cited by Michael Karpovich, 'Pushkin as an Historian', in Cross and Simmons (eds), *Centennial Essays for Pushkin*, p. 197.

19 Pushkin, vol. VIII, 'Istoricheskie Zametki', p. 122.

20 Ibid., vol. X, Pushkin to Mikhail Pogodin, about 7 April 1834 (no. 482 in Shaw, *Letters*, vol. III).

21 Ibid., vol. IX, *Istoriya Petra: polgotovitel'nye teksty*.

22 Karpovich, 'Pushkin as an Historian', p. 189; and note on p. 199.

23 Pushkin, vol. IX, p. 70.

24 Pushkin, vol. IV, *Mednyi vsadnik*; trans. Fennell, *Pushkin: Selected Verse* pp. 233 ff.

25 See p. 69.

26 Fennell, 'Pushkin', in *Nineteenth-Century Russian Literature*, p. 27; 'hardly a critic has refrained from giving his own interpretation, or from confirming or rejecting his predecessor's views'. For a modern British assessment of *The Bronze Horseman*, see Bayley, *Pushkin*, pp. 162, 164.

27 Lednicki, 'Mickiewicz's stay in Russia', p. 63.

28 Annenkov, *Materialy*, pp. 342 ff. *Ezersky* is in Pushkin, vol. IV.

29 I am indebted to Mr Kyril Zinovieff for directing me towards this fascinating insight.

30 Pushkin, vol. IV, pp. 317 ff., *Pikovaya dama*.

31 Nabokov, *Evgenii Onegin*, vol. II, pp. 258 ff.

32 Debreczeny, *The Other Pushkin*, p. 200, makes the valid point that 'the question whether the countess's ghost *really* visited Hermann is as relevant as asking why [Kafka's] Gregor could *really* have turned into a cockroach'.
33 Both are in Pushkin, vol. IV.
34 *The Golden Cockerel* is translated by Fennell, *Pushkin: Selected Verse*, pp. 223–33. On this poem, see Bayley, *Pushkin*, p. 54; and Akhmatova, *O Pushkine*, pp. 39 ff.
35 George Herbert (1593–1632), *The Flower*.

Chapter Twelve, *Ambiguous Relationships*

1 S. L. Abramovich, *Pushkin: Poslednyi god* (Sovetskii pisatel', Moscow, 1991); and V. V. Kunin, *Poslednyi god zhizni Pushkina* (Izdatel'stvo Pravda, Moscow), 1988. In spite of the similarity of their titles, these two books complement each other to a considerable extent.
2 P. E. Shchegolev, *Duel' i smert' Pushkina: issledovaniya i materialy*, 4th edn (Kniga, Moscow, 1987) was first published in 1917 and is now out of date. Anna Akhmatova's 'Gibel' Pushkina' (in her *O Pushkine*, pp. 110 ff.) is far more recent; but although it is brilliantly written, it reflects the passionate nature of its author.
3 E.g. in Simmons, *Pushkin*, p. 388 (on Pushkin's alleged 'visits to brothels') and p. 396 (the author's 'certainty' that Pushkin had 'intimate relations' with Alexandra Goncharova).
4 See Troyat, *Pouchkine*, passim, but a notable example is p. 643: *Le corps de Nathalie et l'âme d'Alexandrine formaient un tout indissociable. Le poète, sans le savoir, aimaient deux femmes à la fois.*' (Both English translations are out of print.)
5 The most recent attempt made in English – Walter Vickery's *Pushkin: Death of a Poet* (Indiana University Press, Bloomington and London, 1968) – was written before the Russian studies referred to in note 1 above. Nor could it take account of Akhmatova's (note 2). It will be evident from what follows that my own account also differs from Vickery's in other respects.
6 Pushkin, vol. X, Pushkin to van Hekkeren, between 17 and 21 November 1836 (no. 651 in Shaw, *Letters*, vol. III). This letter was not sent.
7 A view vigorously maintained by Akhmatova, *O Pushkine*, p. 132.
8 When Charles X was forced to flee the country and was succeeded by the Orléanist Louis-Philippe as King of France.

9 D. F. Fiquelmont, entry of 9 July 1829, cited in Chereisky, *Pushkin i ego okruzhenie,* p. 92. The reason why Hekkeren was a minister, not an ambassador, was simply that in those days ambassadors were rare birds (Britain had only five in the whole world).

10 Abramovich, *Pushkin: Poslednyi god,* p. 214; and Troyat, *Pouchkine,* p. 672.

11 A. V. Troubetskoi, *Ob otnosheniyakh Pushkina k Dantesu,* cited in Shchegolev, *Duel',* p. 400.

12 A significant point, to which Akhmatova (who had lived in Paris before the First World War) was the first Russian writer to pay the attention that it deserves, in her 'Gibel' Pushkina' (note 2).

13 Pushkin, vol. VIII, *Dnevniki.*

14 Chereisky, *Pushkin i ego okruzhenie,* p. 124 suggests a date early in 1834, accepting an account given to A. N. Ammosov in 1863 by Pushkin's schoolmate, Konstantin Danzas.

15 Letters cited by Obodovskaya and Dement'ev, *Natal'ya Nikolaevna Pushkina,* pp. 124–32, 179–80.

16 Pushkin, vol. X, Pushkin to his wife, 18 May 1836 (no. 618 in Shaw, *Letters,* vol. III).

17 Letter written in July 1836, cited in Kunin, *Poslednyi god Pushkina,* pp. 215–16. (For the subsequent reference in this letter to the state of Pushkin's health, see Chapter 14.) Examples of the jokes made at the time about Pushkin's 'harem' are given in Akhmatova, *O Pushkine,* p. 136.

18 The letter is cited in full in Obodovskaya and Dement'ev, *Natal'ya Nikolaevna Pushkina,* pp. 185–6.

19 Ibid., pp. 186 ff.

20 A. P. Arapova, in *Novoe vremya,* 1907, no. 11413, p. 6.

21 Cited in Shchegolev, *Duel' i smert' Pushkina,* p. 284.

22 Akhmatova, *O Pushkine,* p. 173.

23 Pushkin, vol. X, Pushkin to his wife, 4 May 1836 (no. 611 in Shaw, *Letters,* vol. III).

24 Arapova's allegation was made in the article referred to above in note 20 (see also note 3). 'Speculative' – unless *A. S. Pushkin, Tainye zapiski 1836– 1837 godov* is regarded as authentic. Published by the M. I. Co., USA, 1986, in Russian and allegedly translated 'over a number of years' from notes written in French by Pushkin during the last months of his life, this 'secret journal' has since been published in English. Non-Russian speakers with time on their hands can therefore now judge for themselves whether these notes have anything whatever to do with Pushkin, or whether the 'journal' is

merely an example of a genre of writing that was rare in the Soviet period – namely pornography. In any case the introduction to the 'journal' (by Mikhail Armalinsky) includes an account of an alleged meeting in a western embassy in the 1970s which bears no relation to western diplomatic life in Moscow as it was in reality in that decade.

25 Marina Tsvetaeva (1892–1941), in her *Moi Pushkin*, 3rd edn (Sovetskii Pisatel', Moscow, 1981), p. 132.

26 The French text of both letters is cited in Troyat, *Pouchkine*, pp. 677 ff.

27 Obodovskaya and Dement'ev, *Natal'ya Nikolaevna Pushkina*, pp. 172 ff. This attempt at demolition ends with the curious suggestion that, in the letters ascribed to d'Anthès, Idaliya Poletika (see Chapter 13) may have taken a hand.

28 By Troyat.

29 Abramovich, *Pushkin: Poslednyi god*, p. 282.

30 Akhmatova, *O Pushkine*, pp. 132–3, gives a résumé of her preceding 'Gibel'' Pushkina'.

31 Abramovich, *Pushkin: Poslednyi god*, p. 75.

32 Shchegolev, *Duel'*, p. 374.

33 David Cecil, *Melbourne* (Constable, London, 1965), p. 321.

34 The other was the insufferable Lord Brougham, whom the previous Whig Prime Minister, Lord Grey, had – perhaps unwisely – appointed Lord Chancellor.

35 Jasper Ridley, *Lord Palmerston* (Constable, London, 1970), p. 159. Princess Lieven (1785–1857) was Benckendorff's sister.

36 Chereisky, *Pushkin i ego okruzhenie*, pp. 129–30.

37 I am indebted to the Historical Branch of the Library and Records Department of the Foreign and Commonwealth Office for kindly supplying me with a copy of this despatch (from FO 65/234 in the PRO). Shchegolev (*Duel'*, pp. 373–4) obtained a copy from the British Foreign Office archives in 1916, with the help of the Russian Ambassador in London and Lord Lansdowne. Shchegolev also published extracts from other diplomatic reports.

Chapter Thirteen, *A Fighting Withdrawal, 1836*

1 Pushkin, vol. III, 'Na vyzdorovlenie Luculla'.

2 Abramovich, *Pushkin: Poslednyi god*, p. 37.

3 Pushkin, vol. X, Pushkin to (?) A. N. Mordvinov, late January/early February 1836, not sent (no. 591 in Shaw, *Letters*, vol. III).

4 Ibid., Pushkin to Egor Kankrin (Minister of Finance), 6 November 1836 (no. 647 in Shaw, *Letters*, vol. III).

5 Ibid., Pushkin to his wife, 6 May 1836 (no. 612 in Shaw, *Letters*, vol. III).

6 V. G. Belinsky, *Molva*, vol. XII, no. 13, 3 August 1836 : full text in Kunin, *Poslednyi god zhizni Pushkina*, pp. 227–9.

7 The complete list of Pushkin's creditors and what he owed each of them is reproduced in Kunin, *Poslednyi god zhizni Pushkina*, pp. 657–60.

8 Blake, *Disraeli*, p. 424.

9 Abramovich, *Pushkin: Poslednyi god*, p. 18, and for the Pavlishchev correspondence, see Kunin, *Poslednyi god zhizni Pushkina*, pp. 204 ff.

10 Pushkin, vol. X, Pushkin to N. I. Pavlishchev, 13 July 1836 (no. 629 in Shaw, *Letters*, vol. III).

11 Ibid., Pushkin to his wife, 14 and 16 May 1836 (no. 617 in Shaw, *Letters*, vol. III).

12 Ibid., Pushkin to Nashchokin, 27 May 1836 (no. 619 in Shaw, *Letters*, vol. III).

13 Ibid., Pushkin to Sollogub, early February 1836 (no. 594 in Shaw, *Letters*, vol. III).

14 *Vospominaniya Solloguba* was published in *Russkii arkhiv*, 1865 – extracts cited in Abramovich, *Pushkin: Poslednyi god*, pp. 168–70 and in Veresaev, *Pushkin v zhizni*, pp. 424 ff.

15 The story of the permutations suffered by the text of this poem during the first hundred years after it was written is related in Kunin, *Poslednyi god zhizni Pushkina*, pp. 182 ff.

16 Pushkin, vol. III, 'Byla pora'; and Annenkov, *Materialy*, p. 378.

17 Pushkin, vol. X, Pushkin to Sergei L'vovich Pushkin, 20 October 1836 (no. 638 in Shaw, *Letters*, vol. III).

18 Letter from Natalya Pushkina to her brother 10 July 1836, cited in Abramovich, *Pushkin: Poslednyi god*, pp. 269–70.

19 L. N. Pavlishchev, *Konchina Pushkina*, p. 87, cited by Veresaev, *Pushkin v zhizni*, p. 463.

20 Pushkin, vol. X, Pushkin to P. Ya. Chaadaev, 19 October 1836 (no. 637 in Shaw, *Letters*, vol. III).

21 For the Third Rome, see Introduction, note 28.

22 Pushkin, vol. X, pp. 653–4. The breathless syntax of this translation follows that of the French original.

23 Letter cited in Abramovich, *Pushkin: Poslednyi god*, p. 344.

24 Ibid., pp. 365–6.

25 The allusion to Prince Naryshkin, whose wife was Alexander I's mistress, made this letter even more pointed: see Kunin, *Poslednyi god zhizni Pushkina*, pp. 309–10.

26 Abramovich, *Pushkin: Poslednyi god*, pp. 396–7. Earlier Russian studies accepted Arapova's version of this meeting as having taken place not in November 1836, but in January 1837. For an exhaustive analysis, see S. L. Abramovich, *Pushkin v 1836 godu* (Nauka, Leningrad, 1989), pp. 66 ff.

27 Pushkin, vol. X, Pushkin to Benckendorff, 21 November 1836 (no. 652 in Shaw, *Letters*, vol. III). Whether this letter was despatched is a matter of opinion: see Chapter 14.

28 *Ogonek*, 1987, no. 6. For the successive phases of this protracted controversy, see Kunin, *Poslednyi god zhizni Pushkina*, pp. 313 ff. Kunin, pp. 325–7 gives a résumé of the course of events from 4 to 23 November 1836.

29 Pushkin's draft letter to Hekkeren, written between 17 and 21 November 1836, is in his vol. X, as is his letter of 17 November to his second (none other than Count Sollogub), withdrawing his challenge (nos 651 and 649 in Shaw, *Letters*, vol. III). Abramovich, *Pushkin v 1836 godu*, pp. 163 ff. analyses both the events of the weeks preceding Pushkin's meeting with the tsar and the evidence regarding the meeting itself.

30 For Benckendorff's letter to Natalya Pushkina, see Abramovich, *Pushkin: Poslednyi god*, p. 462.

31 See Leonard Schapiro, *Turgenev: his life and times* (Oxford University Press, Oxford), 1978, p. 141.

32 Blok's (1880–1921) remark was made during his last public speech: see his *Sobranie sochinenii*, 8 vols (Khudozhestvennaya literatura, Moscow, Leningrad, 1962), vol. VI, pp. 162–7.

33 This letter to Olga's father is cited in Abramovich, *Pushkin: Poslednyi god*, p. 453.

34 Ibid., p. 457; the quotation is from a letter by Sophia Karamzina.

35 Translated from the full Russian text in Kunin, *Poslednyi god zhizni Pushkina*, pp. 521 ff. Paragraphs have been inserted in my translation, which are not in the original, in the interests of readability. For a full discussion of letters written by Pushkin's friends after his death including this one, see *Pushkin: Issledovaniya i materialy* (Academy of Sciences, Institute of Russian Literature, Nauka, Leningrad, 1989), vol. XII, pp. 146 ff.

Chapter Fourteen, *Duel and Death, 1837*

1 See Introduction.

2 Not much is known about Linev; and the exact dating of this extraordinary picture in St. Petersburg is uncertain. See E. V. Pavlova, *A. S. Pushkin v portretakh*, 2 vols, 2nd edn (Moscow, 1989), pp. 64–7. And there is a detailed discussion in T. G. Aleksandrova, 'Zagadochnyi portret', *Vremennik Pushkinskoi Komissii* (Academy of Sciences, Nauka, Leningrad, 1989), pp. 174 ff.

3 On 23 June 1836: see Abramovich, *Pushkin: Poslednyi god*, p. 251. All unascribed references in the remainder of this chapter are derived from Abramovich, pp. 469 ff.

4 Pushkin, vol. VII, p. 492.

5 Korff's account was published in *Russkaya starina*, vol. 99, 1899, pp. 310–11.

6 Arthur Clough (1819–61), in *The Latest Decalogue*.

7 Pushkin, vol. X, Pushkin to Benckendorff, 21 November 1836 (no. 652 in Shaw, *Letters*, vol. III). Shaw also suggests that Benckendorff was present at Pushkin's audience with the tsar in that month – a view no longer generally accepted by Russian Pushkinists: see note 8 below.

8 See Abramovich, *Pushkin: Poslednyi god*, pp. 406 ff. and p. 563, and Kunin, *Poslednyi god zhizni Pushkina*, p. 327.

9 Pushkin, vol. X, Pushkin to Hekkeren, 25 (26) January 1837 (no. 670 in Shaw, *Letters*, vol. III).

10 Abramovich, *Pushkin v 1836 godu*, pp. 243 ff. analyses all aspects of the questions raised by Vrevskaya's talks with Pushkin and by the subsequent correspondence between her mother and Alexander Turgenev.

11 Magenis served as a paid (as opposed to honorary) attaché at the St. Petersburg Embassy from November 1830 to October 1838. Durham thought highly of his ability. His long career subsequently earned him a knighthood. Unfortunately his private papers contain nothing about his earlier years in Russia. I am indebted to the Foreign and Commonwealth Office Historical Branch for this information.

12 The Russian translation cited in Veresaev, *Pushkin v zhizni*, p. 558 differs in putting Danzas' signature above that of d'Archiac. Pushkin's letter to d'Archiac, 9.30 a.m. on 27 January 1837 (no. 673 in Shaw, *Letters*, vol. III) is in Pushkin, vol. X.

13 Kiernan, *The Duel in European History*, p. 262. The other facts related in this paragraph are also indebted to this work.

14 Pushkin, vol. X, Pushkin to A. O. Ishimova, 27 January 1837 (no. 674 in Shaw, *Letters*, vol. III). The enclosure was a book by Barry Cornwall (Bryan Procter), poet and dramatist.

15 Nepomnyashchy, *Poeziya i sud'ba*, p. 365.

16 These words are an extract from the first verse of Voltaire's *Au roi de Prusse*. For a full discussion, see V. A. Snitanov, 'Proshchenie s tsarem', *Vremennik Pushkinskoi Komissii*, vol. 20 (Academy of Sciences, Nauka, Leningrad, 1986), pp. 36 ff.

17 The correspondence with Paskevich is that quoted in the Introduction, note 2. The Tsar's letter to his brother, dated 3 February 1837, was also first published in *Russkaya starina* (vol. 110, 1902), pp. 225–6.

18 Listed by Shchegolev, *Duel' i smert' Pushkina*, p. 217.

19 Ibid., p. 389.

20 Reproduced in Veresaev, *Pushkin v zhizni*, p. 446.

21 Ibid., pp. 614–15.

22 The crucial final words of the poem *Death of a Poet* have been quoted in the Introduction. For a detailed account of this episode, see Kelly, *Lermontov*, pp. 59 ff.

23 Despatch of 3 April 1837, cited by Shchegolev, *Duel' i smert' Pushkina*, p. 391.

24 Major-General Petr Lanskoy (1799–1877). His career advanced rapidly after his marriage.

25 Akhmatova believed this story, which she mentions twice in her *O Pushkine*. For the evidence, see the notes in *O Pushkine*, pp. 244–5.

26 See the passage from Akhmatova forming the first epigraph to this book.

Epilogue, *Posthumous victory*

1 Cited in Shchegolev, *Duel' i smert' Pushkina*, p. 221.

2 See *The Memoirs of Alexander Herzen*, trans. J. D. Duff, Yale University Press, New Haven, 1923.

3 In 1954 Isaiah Berlin delivered a fascinating series of lectures on this decade. Subsequently broadcast (and published as 'A Marvellous Decade' by *Encounter* in four issues, 1955–56), it is included in his *Russian Thinkers* (see Bibliography) as 'A Remarkable Decade', pp. 114–209.

4 The Russian army had little difficulty in defeating the Hungarians.

5 A. V. Nikitenko, *Diary*, first published in extracts in *Russkaya starina*, February 1850, p. 386. (The modern edition is *Dnevnik v trekh tomach*, ed. I. Ya. Eizenshtok (Khulozhes tvennaya literatura, Leningrad, 1955–6).

6 See Seton-Watson, *The Russian Empire*, pp. 277 ff.

7 For the tsar's conversations with the British ambassador in the early months of 1853, see ibid., pp. 317 ff.

8 Nikitenko, *Diary*, p. 627.

9 'Before him, all Rome used to tremble' (Tosca's words in Verdi's opera) might also have applied, if Nicholas' death had been violent.

10 See Marcus C. Levitt, *Russian Literary Politics and the Pushkin Celebration of 1880* (Cornell University Press, Ithaca and London, 1989), p. 23.

11 Cited in ibid., p. 48; and see note on p. 188.

12 Ibid., pp. 49–50.

13 See ibid., pp. 98–102; and Seton-Watson, *The Russian Empire*, pp. 428–9.

14 Levitt, *The Pushkin Celebration*, pp. 79–80. This paragraph and the next, including the Turgenev quotations, are indebted to Chapters 3 and 4 of Levitt's book.

15 Both the foreword and text of the speech itself are in F. M. Dostoevsky, *Polnoe sobranie sochinenii v trivsati tomakh* (Nauka, Leningrad, 1984), vol. XXVI, pp. 129 ff. which is the source from which the translated passages that follow are derived.

16 Levitt, *The Pushkin Celebration*, p. 155.

17 A. Luppol's introduction to *Pushkin: a collection of articles and essays on the great Russian poet A. S. Pushkin* (Mezhdunarodnaya kniga, Moscow, 1939), p. 24: a comparison of 'the great Pushkin' with 'the great Stalin'.

18 Abram Terts, *Golos iz khora* (Stenvalley Press, London, 1973), p. 155. Kyril Zinovieff (FitzLyon) drew my attention to this passage; and my translation of its Gulag camp slang is indebted to his help. Since my biography was written, an English translation of *Golos iz khora* has been published (by Yale University Press) under the title *Strolls with Pushkin*.

19 See Chapter 13.

20 A. I. Herzen, 'S togo berega', *Sobranie sochinenii v tritsati tomakh* (Academy of Sciences, Moscow, 1955), vol. VI, p. 18.

21 This sentence is not intended to imply that Pushkin's earlier poetry is in any way negligible – simply that from 1823 onwards it becomes outstanding.

22 A. D. P. Briggs, *Alexander Pushkin: Evgenii Onegin* (Cambridge University Press, Cambridge, 1992), p. 113.

23 Lampedusa divided writers into two categories: 'fat' and 'thin'. The latter wrote concisely and allusively whereas the former explained all their nuances and left nothing for the reader to deduce: 'The Last Leopard', *New York Review of Books*, review of David Gilmour's biography (by Gabriele Annan), December 1991.

24 See, for example, Robert Blake and Roger Louis, Preface to *Churchill* (Oxford University Press, Oxford, 1993), p.v.

25 Pushkin, vol. III, *Elegiya*: 'Bezumnykh let ugashee vescl'e'. For a full translation of this poem, see Fennell, *Pushkin: Selected Verse*, pp. 60–9.

Select Bibliography

This bibliography has been compiled in accordance with the fifth paragraph of the 'Note on Sources', p. 249.

Abramovich, S. L., *Pushkin: Poslednyi god* (Sovetskii pisatel', Moscow, 1991).

—— *Pushkin v 1836 godu* (Nauka, Leningrad), 1989.

Aitken, Gillon R. (trans.), *The Complete Prose Tales of Alexander Sergeyevitch Pushkin* (Michael Russell Publishing, Wilton, 1978, first published Barrie and Rockliff, 1966).

Akhmatova, Anna, *O Pushkine: stat'i i zametki* (Sovetskii pisatel', Leningrad, 1977).

Aksakov, S. T., *Semeinaya khronika i vospominaniya: znakomstvo s Del'vigom* (Moscow, 1856).

Annenkov, Pavel, *Aleksandr Sergeevich Pushkin v Aleksandrovskuyu epokhu, 1799–1826 gg.* (St. Petersburg, 1874).

—— *Materialy dlya biografii A. S. Pushkina* (Sovremennik, Moscow, 1984, first published St. Petersburg, 1855).

Archibald, Liliana (trans.), *Peter the Great* (Macmillan, London, 1958) (vol. IV of V. O. Klyuchevsky's works).

Arnold, Matthew, *Essays on Criticism*, second series (Macmillan, London, 1954).

Bayley, John, *Pushkin: a Comparative Commentary* (Cambridge University Press, Cambridge, 1971).

Belinsky, V. G., *Polnoe sobranie sochinenii*, 13 vols (Moscow, 1953–9).

Beloff, Max, *An Historian in the Twentieth Century* (Yale University Press, New Haven, 1992).

Benson, A. C. and Esher, Viscount (eds.), *The Letters of Queen Victoria* (John Murray, London, 1908).

Berlin, Isaiah, *Russian Thinkers*, ed. Henry Hardy and Aileen Kelly (Hogarth Press, London, 1978).

Blagoi, D. D., *Tvorcheskii put' Pushkina, 1813–26* (Academy of Sciences, Moscow/Leningrad, 1950).

Blake, Robert, *Disraeli* (Methuen, London, 1969).

Blake, Robert and Louis, Roger (eds), *Churchill* (Oxford University Press, Oxford, 1993).

Blok, Alexander, *Sobranie sochinenii*, 8 vols (Khudozhestvennaya literatura, Moscow, Leningrad, 1962).

Boyd, Brian, *Vladimir Nabokov: The Russian Years*, 2 vols (Chatto & Windus, London, 1990, 1992).

Briggs, A. D. P., *Alexander Pushkin: A Critical Study* (Croom Helm, London, 1983).

—— *Alexander Pushkin: Evgenii Onegin* (Cambridge University Press, Cambridge, 1992).

Cairns, David, *The Memoirs of Hector Berlioz, 1803–65* (Spear Books [Cardinal], 1990, first published Gollancz, London, 1969).

Cecil, David, *Melbourne* (Constable, London, 1965).

Chereisky, L. A., *Pushkin i ego okruzhenie* (Nauka, Leningrad, 1975).

Cross, S. and Simmons, E. (eds.), *Centennial Essays for Pushkin* (Harvard University Press, Cambridge, Mass., 1937).

Custine, Marquis de, *Lettres de Russie: La Russie en 1839* (Gallimard, Paris, 1975, first published 1843).

Debreczeny, Paul, *The Other Pushkin: A Study of Pushkin's Prose Fiction* (Stanford University Press, Stanford, California, 1983).

Dostoevsky, F. M., *Polnoe sobranie sochinenii*, 13 vols (Nauka, Leningrad, 1984).

Eidel'man, Nathan, *Conspiracy against the Tsar: A Portrait of the Decembrists*, trans. Cynthia Carlile (Progress Publishers, Moscow, 1985). (No copy of the Russian original of this work seems to be available in British libraries.)

—— *Pervyi dekabrist* (Politicheskaya literatura, Moscow, 1991).

—— *Pushkin i dekabristy* (Khudozhestvennaya literatura, Moscow, 1979).

Efros, Abram, *Pushkin portretist* (Goslitizdat, Moscow, 1946).

—— *Risunki poeta* (Academia, Moscow/Leningrad, 1933).

Fennell, John, *Pushkin: Selected Verse* (Bristol Classical Press, 1991, first published by Penguin Books, 1964).

—— (ed.), *Nineteenth-Century Russian Literature: Studies of Ten Russian Writers* (University of California Press, Berkeley and Los Angeles, 1976).

Grene, David, Introduction to Thomas Hobbes' translation of Thucydides' *History of the Peloponnesian War* (University of Chicago Press, Chicago and London, 1989).

Gessen, A., *Zhizn' poeta* (Detskaya literatura, Moscow, 1972).

Gukhovsky, G., *Pushkin i problemy realisticheskogo stilya* (Moscow, 1957).

Herzen, A. I., 'S togo berega', *Sobranie sochinenii v tridsati tomakh* (Academy of Sciences, Moscow, 1955).

—— *The Memoirs of Alexander Herzen,* Parts I and II, trans. J. D. Duff (Yale University Press, New Haven, and Oxford University Press, London, 1923).

Hillier, W. and Bloom, Harold (eds), *From Sensibility to Romanticism* (Oxford University Press, New York, 1965).

Hingley, Ronald, *Russian Writers and Society, 1825–1904* (Weidenfeld & Nicolson, London, 1967).

Hughes, Robert, *Culture of Complaint: The Fraying of America* (Oxford University Press, New York and Oxford, 1993).

Jenkins, Michael, *Arakcheev, Grand Vizier of the Russian Empire* (Faber & Faber, London, 1967, and Dial Press, New York, 1969).

Johnston, Charles (trans.), *Eugene Onegin* (Scolar Press, Yorks, 1977; republished with minor revisions, Penguin Books, Harmondsworth, 1979).

Kelly, Laurence, *Lermontov: Tragedy in the Caucasus* (Robin Clark, London, 1983, first published Constable, London, 1977).

Kern, A. P., *Vospominaniya o Pushkine* (Sovetskaya Rossiya, Moscow, 1988).

Kiernan, V. G., *The Duel in European History: Honour and the Reign of the Aristocracy* (Oxford University Press, Oxford, 1988).

Klyuchevsky, V. O., *Sochineniya,* 5 vols (Sotsial'no-ekonomicheskaya literatura, Moscow, 1958).

Kunin, V. V., *Poslednyi god zhizni Pushkina* (Pravda, Moscow, 1988).

Lermontov, Mikhail, *Sobranie sochinenii,* 4 vols (Khudozhestvennaya literatura, Moscow, 1964).

Lednicki, Walter, 'Mickiewicz's Stay in Russia and His Friendship with Pushkin', in *Adam Mickiewicz in World Literature* (University of California Press, Berkeley and Los Angeles, 1956).

Luppol, I. et al., *Pushkin: A Collection of Essays on the Great Russian Poet A. S. Pushkin* (Mezhdunarodnaya kniga, Moscow, 1939).

Magarshack, David, *Pushkin: A Biography* (Chapman & Hall, London, 1967).

Mickiewicz, Adam, *Sobrannye sochineniya,* 5 vols (Goslitizdat, Moscow, 1945).

Mikhailova, N. I., *Vasilii Pushkin: stikhi, proza, pis'ma* (Sovetskaya Rossiya, Moscow, 1989).

Mirsky, D. S., *Pushkin* (Routledge, London, 1926).

Modzhalevsky, B. L., *Pushkin pod tainym nadzorom* (St. Petersburg, 1922).

Nabokov, Vladimir, *Eugene Onegin*, 4 vols, revised edn (Princeton University Press, Princeton, New Jersey, 1975).

Nepomnyashchy, V., *Poeziya i sud'ba* (Sovetskii pisatel', Moscow, 1983).

Nikitenko, Alexander, *Dnevnik*, 3 vols (Khudozhestvennaya literatura, Leningrad, 1955–6).

Obodovskaya, P. and Dement'ev, M., *Natal'ya Nikolaevna Pushkina po epistolyarnym materialam*, 2nd edn (Sovetskaya Rossiya, Moscow, 1987).

Obolensky, Dimitri (ed.), *The Heritage of Russian Verse* (Indiana University Press, Birmingham, 1976, first published Penguin Books, Harmondsworth, 1962, as *The Penguin Book of Russian Verse*).

Offord, Derek (ed.), *The Golden Age of Russian Literature and Thought: Selected Papers* (Macmillan Press, Basingstoke, 1992).

The Oxford Book of Latin Verse (Oxford University Press, London, 1934, (first published 1912).

The Oxford Book of Russian Verse (Clarendon Press, Oxford, 1st edn, 1924, 2nd edn 1948).

Pavlova, E. V., *A. S. Pushkin v portretakh*, 2nd vols, 2 edn (Moscow, 1989).

Porter, Robert, *Travelling Sketches in Russia and Sweden* (London, 1809).

Praz, Mario, *The Romantic Agony* (Fontana Books, London, 1962, first published Oxford University Press, Oxford, 1933).

Pushchin, I. I., *Zapiski o Pushkine*, ed. and biographical sketch by S. Ya. Shtraich (Moscow, 1925, first published 1859).

Pushkin, Alexander, *Polnoe sobranie sochinenii*, 16 vols (Academy of Sciences edition, Moscow, 1937–59. This was followed in 1962–6 by the 10 vols 'Little Academy' edition, general editor B. V. Tomashevsky. (See the opening paragraph of Notes.)

Ridley, Jasper, *Lord Palmerston* (Constable, London, 1970).

Schapiro, Leonard, *Rationalism and Nationalism in Russian Nineteenth-Century Political Thought* (Yale University Press, New Haven and London, 1967).

—— *Turgenev: His Life and Times* (Oxford University Press, Oxford, 1978).

Seaman, W. and Sewell, J. (eds), *Russian Journal of Lady Londonderry, 1836–7* (John Murray, London, 1973).

Semevsky, V. I., *Krest'yane v tsarstvovanii Imperatritsy Ekateriny II* (St. Petersburg, 1901–3).

Seton-Watson, Hugh, *The Russian Empire, 1801–1917* (Clarendon Press, Oxford, 1967).

Shaw, J. Thomas (trans. and ed.), *The Letters of Alexander Pushkin*, 3 vols (Indiana University Press and University of Pennsylvania Press, Bloomington and Philadelphia, 1963).

Shchegolev, P. E., *Duel' i smert' Pushkina: issledovanie i materialy*, 4th edn (Kniga, Moscow, 1987).

Shil'der, N. K., *Imperator Aleksandr I:ego zhizn' i tsarstvovanie*, 4 vols (Suvorin, St. Petersburg, 1897).

—— *Imperator Nikolai I: ego zhizni tsarstvovanie*, 2 vols (Suvorin, St. Petersburg, 1903).

Simmons, Ernest, *Pushkin* (Oxford University Press, London, 1937).

Terts, Abram (pseudonym of Andrei Sinyavsky), *Golos iz khora* (Stenvalley Press, London, 1973).

—— *Progulki s Pushkinom* (Overseas Publications Interchange (jointly with Collins), London, 1975).

Thompson, E. P., *The Making of the English Working Class* (Penguin Books, Harmondsworth, 1980).

Tolstoy, Lev, *Voina i mir*, 4 vols (Molodaya gvardiya, Moscow, 1978).

Troyat, Henri, *Pouchkine*, 2 vols (Albin Michel, Paris, 1946, reprinted Librarie Académique Perrin, Paris, 1976).

Tsvetaeva, Marina, *Moi Pushkin*, 3rd edn (Sovetskii pisatel', Moscow, 1981).

Tsyavlovsky, M. A., *Letopis' zhizni i tvorchestva A. S. Pushkina, 1799–1826*, 2nd edn (Nauka, Leningrad, 1991).

Tsyavlovskya, T. G., *Risunki Pushkina* (Iskusstvo, Moscow, 1970).

Veresaev, V. V., *Pushkin v zhizni* (Moskovskii rabochii, Moscow, 1986).

Vickery, Walter, *Alexander Pushkin* (Twayne Publishers, Boston, Mass., 1970).

—— *Pushkin: Death of a Poet* (Indiana University Press, Bloomington and London, 1968).

Volkonsky, Marie, *Mémoires de la Princesse Marie Volkonsky* ed. Prince Michel Volkonsky (St. Petersburg, 1904).

Volkov, G. N., *Mir Pushkina* (Moscow, Molodaya gvardia, 1989).

Vremennik Pushkinskoi Komissii. A schlolary journal, regularly published by the Academy of Sciences (Nauka, Leningrad/St. Petersburg), containing valuable articles by Pushkinists.

Vyazemsky, Pavel, *Sobranie sochinenii* (St. Petersburg, 1893).

Vyazemsky, Petr, *Polnoe sobranie sochinenii*, 7 vols (St. Petersburg, 1879).

Webster, C. K., *The Congress of Vienna, 1814–15* (Humphrey Milford, London, 1919).

Wilson, A. N., *Tolstoy* (W. W. Norton, New York and London, 1988).

Wolff, Tatiana, *Pushkin on Literature* (Athlone Press, London and Stanford University Press, Stanford, California, 1986, first published Methuen, 1971).

Woodhouse, C. M., *Capodistria: The Founder of Greek Independence* (Oxford University Press, London, 1930).

Yakushkin, I. D., *Zapiski, stat'i, pis'ma* (Academy of Sciences, USSR, Moscow, 1951).

Index

NOTE: *Works by Pushkin appear directly under title; works by others appear under author's name*